Best Wishes
and Happy Reading!
Chris + Ralph Dull

More Praise for Soviet Laughter, Soviet Tears

With caring, yet candid discernment, they recorded their remarkable experiences in a manner that illumines both the promise and the problems of a radically changing Soviet society. I highly recommend *Soviet Laughter, Soviet Tears* as a book to enjoy and ponder—**Richard L. Deats, Director US-USSR Reconciliations Projects, Fellowship of Reconciliation**

Ralph spent endless hours walking the fields, observing Soviet agricultural practices, and drawing conclusions about why their agricultural system is near collapse . . . an excellent book filled with insights, humor, and personal stories—**Dr. William P. Shaw, President, Crosscurrents International Institute**

. . . a perfectly superb book! [I will] steal shamelessly from it for my Soviet class. The warmth comes through in all your [Christine's] lovely anecdotes, and none of that is diminished by Ralph's solid, hard-hitting reformer's advice. The world needs more books like yours—**Dr. J. Patrick Lewis, Professor of Economics at Otterbein College and economic reviewer for *The Chicago Tribune* and *The San Francisco Chronicle***

They articulate perfectly what I have observed in 30 years of visiting rural Russian villages. The Dulls capture the flavor of Russian life and hopes. . . . a unique observation by people who know the subject well—**John Chrystal, American bank CEO who has met with Gorbachev, Khrushchev, and Brezhnev**

Someone goofed in awarding the 1990 Nobel Peace Prize to Mikhail Gorbachev. The prize should have gone . . . to citizen diplomats like Ralph and Christine Dull—**George DeVault, US Editor, Rodale Press' *Novii Fermer* (New Farmer) magazine**

"I know now that my unity with all people cannot be destroyed by national boundaries and government orders . . ."

—Leo Tolstoy, 1884

SOVIET LAUGHTER, SOVIET TEARS

An American Couple's Six-Month Adventure in a Ukrainian Village

by
Christine and Ralph Dull

Stillmore Press
7000 Stillmore Drive
Englewood, OH 45322

ISBN 0-9628038-6-3

LCCN 90-071574

Although the authors and publisher have made every effort to ensure the accuracy and completeness of information contained in this book, we assume no responsibility for errors, inaccuracies, omissions, or any inconsistency herein. Any slights of people, places or organizations are unintentional.

ATTENTION UNIVERSITIES, COLLEGES, AND PROFESSIONAL ORGANIZATIONS: Quantity discounts are available on bulk purchases of this book for educational purposes or fund raising. Special books or book excerpts can also be created to fit specific needs. For information, please contact our Special Sales Department, Stillmore Press, 7000 Stillmore Drive, Englewood, OH 45322, or call (513) 832-0152.

CONTENTS

  Tillage
  Equipment
  Labor
  The Supervisor System
  Seeding Rates
  Soil Erosion
  Working Wet Fields
  Storage and Handling of Grain
  Silage
  The Straw Habit
  Fertilizer Losses
  Manure Handling
  Abandoned Land
  Crop and Livestock Selection and Management
     • Corn • Wheat • Soybeans • Peas • Peanuts • Sugar Beets
     • Hay and Green Feed • Dairy Cattle • Hogs • Beef

Foreword

At first blush it all seems vaguely incredible: that an American couple—grandparents, for pity's sake—should arrange on their own initiative to go to the Soviet Union to live on a collective farm for half a year. At a point in their lives when most middle-class Americans are arranging time-sharing deals at oceanside condominiums or playing bemusedly with their grandchildren in the back yard, this unusual pair with the misleading last name set off to experience an alien existence. Indeed, I am not aware of any other Americans in over 50 years to live for this duration in a rural area of the USSR. Clearly, this is not an ordinary couple, and their story contains some extraordinary insights for us.

On the most basic level, they offer us an admirable example of complete receptivity to new people, new ideas, new ways. Immersion in the everyday existence of the village of Makov is a living expression of their personal philosophy that neither language, nor history, nor customs represent insurmountable barriers to communication and understanding. That which unites us—our common humanity, the universality of our most fundamental experiences—is far more significant than any conceivable barriers. The great French social scientist Marc Bloch who gave his life for the French anti-fascist resistance urged historians in effect to assume that "nothing human is alien to me." By their lives and by their actions recounted here Ralph and Chris Dull recommend the same approach to American and Soviet citizens alike. It is a message no less necessary now in a period of relative thaw than it was in the deepest winter of the Cold War.

One of the most interesting aspects of this narrative is the nature of the narrators. I think it fair to say that most Americans think of social activists as long-haired, naive, uncritical radicals. What they will encounter on these pages are the experiences and reflections of a farmer and a former grade-school teacher—two people who in many ways could hardly be more mainstream American. Yet as citizens of both the United States and of the world, these individuals show us that in order to act one need not be a

Sovietologist or a linguist. In fact, in the current conditions in the Soviet Union there is a far greater need for people from practical professions, like farmers and other business people, than there is for additional academic specialists. Again, one of the most important contributions of this book is its function as a model and example.

Readers will also find noteworthy the insistent championing of private agriculture. While he suggests numerous means of improving specific aspects of the agricultural economy, involving crop rotation, animal husbandry, tilling methods, and the like, Ralph's general solution is private ownership and management of the farm. As someone who has managed and worked his own farm for forty years, Ralph knows something that the Bolsheviks never learned: that only an individual with a personal stake in the success of the farming venture will invest the effort necessary to make it go. Furthermore, the locus of decision-making must be the farm itself, because only someone with unfiltered, immediate knowledge of the enterprise and of all the economic factors involved is in a position to make the crucial management decision. This is an unremitting defense of free enterprise as practiced at the level of the family farm and of radical economic democracy in which the individual disposes freely of private economic resources. The model farmer just described amounts to nothing more or less than a modern version of the Jeffersonian homestead farmer—the most venerable American archetype—offered as an example for the Soviet Union by a down-to-earth American peace activist. Once again, Americans will be forced to adjust their intellectual antennas.

Finally and perhaps most significantly, the book affords us a fascinating glimpse at one of the least visible sides of Soviet reality: the countryside. While the general contours of Soviet rural life have been known for some time, I know of no existing study which approaches the intimate interior perspective of *Soviet Laughter, Soviet Tears*. The largest section, written by Chris, lays open for us both the pathos and the possibilities of life in the countryside. Ralph's analysis of the problems of Soviet agriculture and his seasoned assessment of both particular and systemic means of transcending these deficiencies are unquestionably novel contributions to our understanding of the Soviet structure of collective farming. His precise exposition of the flaws in their farming practices yields an understanding that no amount of abstract discussion of the drawbacks of the "administrative-command system" can provide. We are indeed fortunate to be able to share the unique perspective of these remarkable people.

There is no denying that there is a certain idealism to this effort, but it is also true that "realists" with their sour factualism never altered anything, and that it is only through the hopeful efforts of idealists that the world is changed. The Soviet Union is presently engaged in a gigantic and dramatic experiment at renewal and humanization, which if successful will represent a genuine socio-political revolution. No revolution, not the American

Revolution nor any other, was ever undertaken by realists. The German philosopher Nietzsche once wrote that when undertaking a new study or examining a question for the first time it is necessary to do so wholeheartedly and uncritically. There will be plenty of time for criticism and qualification later, and in the meantime the enthusiasm of your initial exploration will carry you far into the field and deep into the subject matter. Without this sort of idealistic enthusiasm the Dulls would never have engaged in their project, but it is that very idealism, tempered and reinforced by the insights of these two practical people of the world, which makes this study worthwhile. I urge everyone who would both know the world and change it to take to heart this remarkable book.

Dr. J. Thomas Sanders
Assistant Professor of Russian and Soviet History
United States Naval Academy, Annapolis

Introduction
by Ralph

"World conquest," "Atheist," "Oppression," "Everybody wants out," "Totalitarian," "We'll bury you," are phrases we heard for 44 years. Are they true? We wanted to find out. The two superpower governments were doing poorly at getting along, so we became part of *citizen diplomacy*—that is, ordinary citizens of both countries coming together heart to heart in an effort to break down barriers to understanding, truth, and fearless living.

Our first trip (1983) was eye-opening. We went again in 1985, but our curiosity was still unsatisfied. We asked ourselves, "How can we find out what Soviets' lives are *really* like?" Maybe we could live there for awhile. I was willing to dig ditches if necessary, and Christine was ready to carry water, walk through mud, and chop wood. We realized the impossibility of living exactly as a Soviet family lives, but maybe we could come close.

For three years, we contacted every person and group we could think of in the United States, but no one knew how we could be long-term guests in the USSR. So we decided to try the other side. By this time, Mikhail Gorbachev was in power. Because he wanted to transform the failed Soviet agricultural system, we thought my life-time experience as a farmer might be the key that would let us in. With the help of a resume listing my qualifications and featuring photos of the family farm's pigs and crops, we decided to invite ourselves to live in the Soviet Union.

One January night in 1988 in Leningrad, we met Vladimir Gulich in the apartment of an English-speaking acquaintance. Vladimir lived in Ukraine prior to World War II. After being seriously injured in the war, he acquired an education and was now a professor of agriculture in Leningrad. Gulich was fascinated with Midwest farming and eagerly asked about our farm.

After an evening conversing through an interpreter and converting acres to hectares, bushels to centners, and pounds to kilos, we mentioned we wanted a year-long visit in the USSR. He was excited at the prospect of an American farmer living in his native Ukraine, so he offered to send our resume to a friend, a top official there. The door of opportunity was opening for a dual purpose—friendship and agriculture.

Eight months later, our home phone rang in Ohio. It was Nikolai Pervov, agricultural attache at the Soviet Embassy in Washington, D.C. He verified our interest in living in the USSR and asked us to send him a written proposal for consideration (a typical Soviet procedure, we later learned). He also suggested we host a Soviet farmer on our family farm, to which we instantly responded, "Why not?" The plan was for us to go to the USSR while a Soviet farmer and his wife came to Ohio for a year; the Soviets would spend the winter on a dairy farm and the summer on the Dull farm.

Some weeks later, Mr. Pervov informed us the USSR has only specialists—some grow crops while others raise livestock. So the plans changed. We would now have two Soviets—a crop and a livestock farmer—for six months, while their wives stayed in Ukraine. (By the way, Ukrainians prefer *Ukraine*, not *the Ukraine*, just as we don't call our state *the Ohio*.)

In the meantime, our invitations had suddenly gone from one to three. Would we accept the invitation to Ukraine, to a Volgograd state farm, or to a Moscow co-operative just getting started in farming? We were keeping all options open.

We'd assured Mr. Pervov that no matter where we went, the Ukrainian farmers would be welcome in Ohio. When we said we hadn't decided which invitation to take, he said with quiet assurance, "You will go to Ukraine. The place we have in mind is an exceptionally beautiful area of the Soviet Union." We thought he was wrong about where we would live because our first choice was the Moscow cooperative. But we had a problem. We had expected to go in January, but it was now March and we were still waiting for a formal invitation.

About this time, we discovered Ukraine had an advantage: there was an English teacher—Anatoli (Toli) Kushnir—who could be our interpreter in the village of Makov where we were to live. On March 10, he called at the request of the crop farmer we were to host on our farm, Viktor Palamarchouk. Palamarchouk wanted the ages of my grandchildren so he could bring gifts for them when he came to Ohio in April. Toli's English skills impressed us; we knew we needed help with the language. Christine had taken only two quarters of Russian, and I none.

After hanging up the phone, which awakened us in the middle of the night, we looked at each other and said, "It's time to go to the USSR!" Our friend Bill Shaw, head of Crosscurrents International Institute, had a ski trip scheduled to go there March 20. Even though we don't ski, we picked up the phone, called him in Moscow, and signed on for the trip. At its end, we decided, we would simply accept one of the three invitations and stay. Our former experience with Soviet hospitality gave us confidence something would work out.

When we arrived in Moscow, we told the co-op officials they must produce the written invitation by the time our three-week visa expired or we would go to Ukraine. Nearly three weeks later, our tour group visited Kiev, capital of Ukraine. Since we still had no co-op invitation, we told officials at Ukraine Gosagroprom (Department of Agriculture) we were accepting their offer. We said we would pick up our six suitcases in Moscow, return to Kiev in three days, and continue on to the village.

We found out later that as soon as we left the office, a Kiev official traveled to Makov to make arrangements for our arrival. Whirlwind activity began on our house there. When we moved in four days later, we stepped in wet paint on the doorsill.

We lived in Makov from April 7 to September 25, 1989. At approximately the same time (March 30 to October 17), Palamarchouk and Nikolai (Nik) Zubyets worked, respectively, on the Dull farm and the Harms farm in Ohio. Palamarchouk was from the same farm (Ukraina) and village (Makov) where Christine and I were hosted. Nik was from the mountainous Transcarpathian Region near Czechoslovakia.

From left: Nikolai Zubyets, Viktor Palamarchouk, Christine and Ralph Dull in front of the Dull's house in Ohio.

Experiencing Soviet life in the boondocks was a step beyond reading and hearing about it. I'd been accustomed to hard, physical labor all my life, but there were three reasons why six months in Ukraine would not be just working on the farm. First, both Mr. Pervov and Moscow Gosagroprom officials requested we be available for meetings around the country to respond to questions about American life and agriculture and to analyze

Soviet farming. Second, there was a surplus of workers on the collective farm at Makov. And third, the previous November, I'd had back surgery, so heavy work may have been difficult at Makov. However, had we stayed in Ohio, I would have planted corn as usual.

Ukraina collective farm was prosperous, but because we had the advantage of a car, we also traveled frequently to poorer farms for observation and informal conversations. Our desire was to get to know people and exchange ideas, and certainly that became a reality as we discussed every subject imaginable with anyone who was interested. We tried to see everything, resulting in some officials considering us much too nosy.

We were convinced the grassroots level was the place to learn about failures in the economy—agriculture in particular. This way, perhaps we could be a part of the impending revolutionary changes for the better. Our mission became one of learning and of planting seeds in minds rather than fields. We wanted to be available but not pushy. The Chairman of the collective farm became supportive of this routine.

Curiosity about Americans was evident at our meetings with groups of Soviets. The desire for a more Western way of life was in the air—yet they wished to avoid our problems while still preserving their basic benefits for everyone. The greatest crowd response came after comments about farmers having a choice when buying and selling. Just thinking about being free to produce what crop and how much caused great excitement. Though the capability of people to help themselves is the same in any country, circumstances have made life hard for most Soviets.

Although both the US and USSR are considered superpowers, the Soviet Union is an undeveloped nation materially, except for their subways and space and military programs. It's a land of striking contrasts—from the primitive to the sophisticated. This is illustrated by a Soviet cartoon—a sleek spacecraft slowly being rolled to the launch pad on rickety wooden wagons pulled through the mud by horses.

Soviets are now learning to participate in democratic political and economic decisions. It is torturous for those accustomed to giving commands and equally difficult for the multitudes who have relied upon being commanded.

There are questions in the legislative hopper such as, "Will the government continue to subsidize the consumers' food supply?" and "When will there be private land ownership?" And there are other questions no one can confidently answer as yet: "Can Gorbachev stay long enough for economic and nationalities problems to recede?" or "Is there anyone to replace him who can solve the problems more quickly?" The party secretary of our collective farm asked, "How many years will it be until the USSR can stop importing grain?" We answered with another question, "How many years until you have independent farmers?" We laughed, but he didn't.

In any case, we're optimistic: glasnost and democratization will push perestroika (restructuring) forward, the economic system will start to make some sense, individuals will learn to take more responsibility, management decisions will be made by independent people, and work will be more fun.

We've tried to do a critical analysis of the system without blaming people, even officials, who, in a sense, are victims of the system as well. Many occurrences we wouldn't have believed if we hadn't seen them. Just because we come from a nation where a surplus of almost everything is a problem and went to a country where a shortage of most things is a problem doesn't give us license to look down on the Soviets. We can no more take credit for our economy or choose our parents or birthplace than they can.

Our American friends may ask why we want to increase crop production in the USSR, thus decreasing US exports. Americans, of course, want to export more grain. But should we wish a crop failure for *anyone* in the world? Can we imagine our lack of contentment if we in the US depended on other countries for a fourth of our food?

We feel perestroika must succeed and production must improve or there could be a violent reaction by Soviet consumers. This could precipitate a reversal in the progress of human rights, to say the least. It's best for us all when the Soviet people are happy, well-fed, and an integral part of the world economy. It's best for as many nations as possible to be self-sufficient. We want good agricultural practices everywhere, regardless of a country's ideology. The US Peace Corps is an example of that philosophy. We are citizens of the world, and we don't want any part of it to hurt.

This sojourn looked like a daring adventure to some of our friends, but for us it was part of a natural progression. We went with the hope we wouldn't be too much bother to anyone and that the benefits in human relations and agriculture would outweigh the inconvenience to the Soviets. In the long run, we think Nik and Viktor's visit to America will be of more aid to the USSR than our stay in Makov. Still, we have made friendships which endure, and we hope the book we wrote for Soviets and now this one will be beneficial for Americans and Soviets alike.

Our intention is for this book to give pleasure to the reader as we describe our experiences. We reveal how Soviets far from Moscow live and think. While we were there, the old system and the new freedoms were locked in conflict. It was fascinating to watch the successes and failures of both. We learned by asking questions, listening to answers, watching, and absorbing the atmosphere. It was a time of high discovery, and we hope your understanding will grow as you watch how ours evolved. After the stage is set the tempo picks up.

The major part of this book, Part I, is taken from Christine's journal, with a few of my observations about Soviet life woven in from time to time. Another chapter covers the letters we received from Soviets while we were in Makov. Part II addresses the Soviets' reaction to us or to life in America.

This section features Toli's commentary on our stay in Makov and contains Marcella Harms' and Sue Dull's chapters about the experiences of Nik and Viktor in Ohio. It also includes an update on the people we came to know during our stay on the collective farm. Part III, the remainder of the book, is devoted to Soviet agriculture, which may or may not be of interest to urbanites.

Cast of Characters

PRINCIPAL CHARACTERS

RALPH & CHRISTINE DULL - American couple in the village of Makov, Ukraine, USSR, for six months.

VIKTOR PALAMARCHOUK -
VALENTINA - Wife
TATIANA - Daughter

Soviet farmer from Makov, Ukraine, on the Dull farm, Ohio, for seven months.

NIKOLAI ZUBYETS - Soviet farmer from Ukraine on Dirk Harms farm, Ohio for seven months.

TOLI - ANATOLI KUSHNIR -
TANYA - Wife
VOVA & YURA - Sons
ANNA - Tanya's mother
NINA - Anna's sister-in-law
LUSA - Tanya's sister, living in Kiev
VALERI - Lusa's husband
VASILY - Anna's brother, living in a distant Ukrainian village

Makov English teacher and interpreter for the Dulls.

THE CHAIRMAN - Vitaly Stengach, chairman of Ukraina collective farm, Makov, Ukraine.

BUDDHA -	Anatoli Dovgal, Director of International Relations, Khmelnitski Department of Agriculture (Gosagroprom).

THE GREENHOUSE GANG -
   STEPAN - Later visited Dulls   Ralph and Christine's Makov neigh-
             in Ohio.   bors.
   NIKOLAI
   SASHA PROFESSOR
   OLEG
   SASHA SPORTSMAN

MIKE & SUE DULL -	Ralph's second son and his wife, close friends to Palamarchouk.

DIRK & MARCELLA HARMS - Nikolai Zubyet's Ohio hosts.
   DAVID - Son
   SHARI - Son's fiance

BECKY & JIM OSSWALD -	Ralph's daughter and her husband, Palamarchouk's Ohio hosts.

OTHER RECURRING CHARACTERS
(IN ORDER OF APPEARANCE)

BILL SHAW -	President of Crosscurrents International Institute, Dayton, Ohio.
VALENTIN OOZHIN -	Interpreter attached to Kiev Department of Agriculture (Gosagroprom).
JOHANNA -	Zoo-keeper and the Chairman's "watchdog" at Stupentsi.
VALAROVSKY -	Head of District Gosagroprom.
BOB MEYERSON -	Ralph and Christine's American friend who works for the *Moscow News*.
NIKOLAI VASILIOVICH -	Makov taxi-van driver.
SAVKOV -	Ukraina collective farm agronomist and a People's Deputy of the USSR.
ALLA & NATASHA -	Students tutored in English after school by Toli, went sight-seeing with the Dulls.

LUDMILA & NIKOLAI - Couple appointed by the Chairman to deliver food to the Dulls for two months.

VANYA & TANYA - Friends of Toli and Tanya.

NIKOLAI & NELYA - Neighbors of Toli and Tanya.

SASHA & OLA - Friends of Toli and Tanya.

KOSTYA - Toli's friend, English teacher at the military school in Kamenets-Poldolski.

SOLODKY - Kiev Gosagroprom's Director of International Relations.

MISHA ALEXEYEV - *News From Ukraine* journalist from Kiev. He twice interviewed the Dulls, once at Stupentsi. He later came to the US.

VIKTOR PARTY SECRETARY - Young party secretary of Ukraina collective farm, Makov.

ANDREI & SERGEI - Students of English at Pedagogical Institute at Kamenets-Podolski. Andrei was Komsomol leader there.

VOLODYA - Jewish student of English at Pedagogical Institute.

ROZA & VIKTOR - Jewish couple who live in Kamenets-Podolski. Roza teaches English at the Pedagogical Institute, and Viktor is Director of the Shatava area school in Makov.

TAMARA - Young Kamenets-Podolski hairdresser who cut Chris' hair.

VAL & IGOR - Independent eleventh-graders in Makov.

WENDY SLOANE - American *Time* reporter who interviewed the Dulls in Makov.

SASHA BEKKER -   *Moscow News* reporter who interviewed the Dulls with Wendy.

ZHENYA -   Gentle, artistic believer called "Little God" by Makov people.

EDA -   Elderly Jewish woman, mother of Edward, who stayed at guest lodge at Stupentsi and hosted the Dulls in Chernovtsi.

SERGEI & MARINA -   Young Moscow couple who visited the Dulls in Makov and later came to Ohio.

RAISA -   Khmelnitski teacher who taught Russian in Modesto, CA, for several months.

VLADIMIR -   Director of Vladimir Co-operative, Moscow. Visited the Dulls in Makov and later in Ohio.

IVAN FROM YALTA -   Visited the Dulls at Stupentsi and later sent them a sad letter.

VIKTOR LESIK -   Brave newspaper reporter from Dunaevsti.

VOLODYA CHERNOV -   Consultant to Volgograd Journalists Union and a friend of Ralph and Chris.

Part I

*The Americans:
A Ukrainian Odyssey*

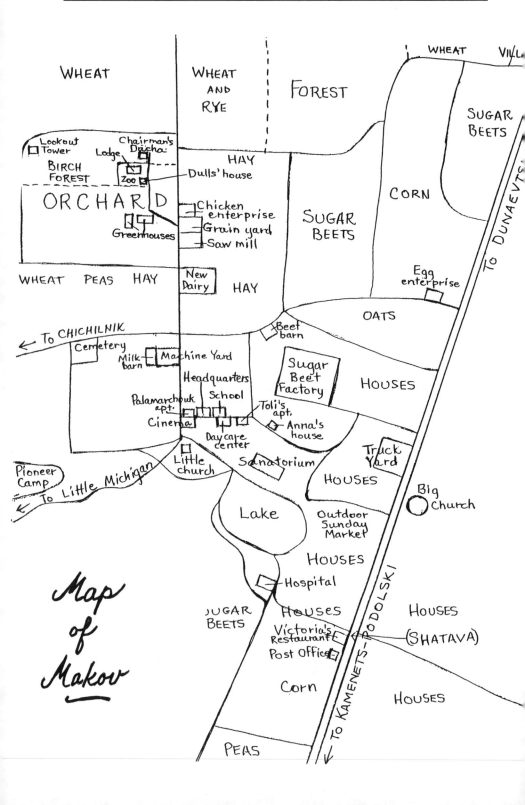

CHAPTER 1

Christine's Journal Excerpts

FIRST WEEK IN THE VILLAGE

April 7: What a long day! A little before midnight, we rode into Makov—the village where we'll live for the next six months.

At nine this morning, our train from Moscow rolled into Kiev and stopped with a familiar jerk. A minute later, two smiling young men opened our compartment door and handed me bouquets of carnations. (I love this European custom of giving flowers!) They excitedly introduced themselves as Anatoli Kushnir, our interpreter, and Valentin Oozhin, who also speaks English and was representing Ukraine Gosagroprom, the U.S.S.R. Department of Agriculture.

We felt at home with both men, who are in their mid-thirties and kind, intelligent, and friendly. While Valentin took care of our paperwork, Anatoli took us to a hotel where we had two meals and talked constantly until 5 P.M., when Valentin returned with our visas, extended to October 17. As the three of us climbed into the van with its waiting driver, Valentin told us we could contact him should any problem arise.

During our seven-hour drive west, Anatoli and I continued to converse, while Ralph, a contemplative person, quietly gazed at the passing landscape—the breadbasket of the USSR. We'd envisioned Ukraine as flat, so it surprised us to see rolling terrain—a multi-colored quilt of fields in spring time. The standard of living looked better than we had viewed from the train windows in other parts of this vast country, but still, the living conditions would remind older Americans of the 1930s. We stopped once for a herd of cattle clogging the highway. They were moved away by cowboys on horses.

As we drove through Makov, we could see by the light of the street lamps it was even more beautiful than its black and white photograph proudly displayed on the wall at the Gosagroprom office in Kiev. There were rows of well-kept, two-story homes, each enclosed by a picket fence or stone wall. We passed the "center," consisting of several attractive large buildings. Nearby were playground equipment and five miniature cottages, each a different shape, with colorful pictures of people and animals painted on them. "Children at the day care center play in them," Anatoli told us.

At the far edge of Makov, we reached our destination. Our van turned off the smooth dirt road onto a long lane that passed through an orchard and stopped at a gate. The gate was hastily unlocked, allowing us to ride into a lighted courtyard.

An old man with strong breath motioned us to follow him into what looked like a guest lodge, where, without saying a word, he showed us around. In the lodge are three upstairs bedrooms, two single beds in each; a vast living-dining room; a sauna next to a jacuzzi-size swimming pool; and a small bathroom and kitchen.

A midnight snack was neatly laid out in the largest bedroom—lots of heavily buttered bread with caviar or sausage slices on top, and fixings for tea, including a thermos of hot water. A vase of lavender wildflowers and lacy pillow covers graced the room. It was all very thoughtful and lovely, but our hearts fell at the large size of the building. As the men lugged our six heavy suitcases into this resort-like house, Ralph asked Anatoli if he could find a small flat in the village we could move to.

We rejected the large bedroom for a smaller one and moved the beds together for sleeping. Well, here we are, just we two! We're actually going to live for six months in this mysterious country—the fruition of a notion that hit us three years ago. And so to sleep.

April 8: We slept fitfully last night because we kept hearing ear-splitting shrieks from birds of some kind. What a surprise we got when we opened the draperies this morning! There were 14 peacocks right outside our upstairs windows, roosting in the pine trees. Then we remembered Toli (Anatoli) saying something about our being in a zoo.

We walked around the zoo first thing. It has the following animals:

    2   bears
   15   peacocks and peahens
  100   parakeets
    1   ostrich
    5   swans—2 of them trumpeters
   10   pheasants—2 of them Royal Pheasants from China
   30   spotted deer
    6   wart hogs—a family with 4 striped babies
   20   roosters
  100   hens
    1   doleful-sounding dog, chained to his house

Face to face with the Russian Bear

"And now two Americans!" said Ralph. Feeding the animals was Johanna, a babushka (grandmother) in colorful dress and flowered headscarf. Her quick smile flashed a row of gold teeth as we joined her on her peaceful rounds.

Toli arrived and told us the Chairman of the collective farm, Vitaly Stengach, was on his way to see us. Indeed he was! He came in and bounded right on upstairs with roses for me, accompanied by Mr. Valarovsky of District Gosagroprom. Luckily, I was dressed.

We all went for a late breakfast to Victoria's Restaurant. We were served a large assortment of good food, all the while being urged to eat more by the large, red-haired, gold-toothed proprietress. (Dyed red hair is popular in the USSR, and gold teeth indicate affluence.) The heavy-boned Chairman smiled a lot, but his eyes were vigilant. He's 67 but looks younger and is very energetic. He had originally worked in a KGB office, then at the local sugar factory, and later he was tapped for the powerful job of collective farm chairman.

Near our lodge is a smaller two-story house, where we noticed several people busily going in and out all day. Just as we began to unpack our suitcases, we were told to move to that house, as it hadn't been quite ready when we arrived. We were relieved we didn't have to live in the lodge—two people echoing in all that space.

Our new house, which we were told was once a day care center, had been repaired and newly furnished with us in mind. There's an unheated entrance hall, where people exchange their shoes for slippers—a nice custom. Big, blond Volodya was in charge of renovating the house, and as we walked through, exclaiming about everything, he beamed. The Chairman was with us, getting his first look also. Volodya was clearly more interested in the Chairman's opinion than ours.

Downstairs, we have a living room with a color television, a shortwave radio, art books, a floor lamp, and an attractive couch and chair. The couch, however, is badly designed; my feet don't touch the floor. There's a brand-new kitchen with a four-burner, apartment-size stove; a sink; a five-foot-tall refrigerator with a small freezer compartment; a dozen porcelain or stainless steel pans, utensils, and even a big Lazy Susan in the finished wood cupboard. A novel convenience (standard, I think, in the Soviet Union) is the cupboard above the sink: it's virtually a big dish drainer. The dishes are washed and rinsed in the sink and then set in this open-bottomed cupboard to drain into the sink. There, they are stored with the door closed. Pretty neat!

As modern as the kitchen is by Soviet standards, however, it would be crude in American suburbia. Water pipes, though painted, are exposed. Our two-section bathroom has a toilet and a sink on one side, and a bathtub, a shower, and another sink on the other. There's a tiny eating room off the kitchen, with a cut glass, footed, fruit dish on the little table, and a well-stocked china cupboard.

Upstairs, there's one bedroom with a king-sized bed (two singles together with one headboard), an upstairs (!) dining room, and a room containing a desk and a bookcase. Carpets and white, lacy curtains are everywhere, and the bedspread and all the draperies are made of a golden, silky material. The plaster walls display colored airbrushed patterns, a different one in each room. We also have two phones—one for long distance and one for local calls. Our home and its grounds, which include the lodge, the zoo, a pond, a small birch forest, a commercial orchard, and two greenhouses, is called Stupentsi (STOO-pen-tsi). All this is much more than we expected.

We appreciate the effort made to give us comfortable quarters, but we'd wanted to live like the people—and closer to them. The orchard is between us and Makov, so we're somewhat isolated. As a child, Russian fairy tales enchanted me, and I romanticized about the little blue cottages that still predominate in Soviet villages, including this one. We had hoped to live in one of them. Ralph and I are no strangers to outhouses. When he was young, his family had one, and my family used one every summer in the woods near our vacation cabin. We wouldn't have minded living under those conditions now—as most of the world does.

April 9: This afternoon, Valentina Palamarchouk, Viktor's wife, arrived at Stupentsi bringing long-stemmed roses and a big box of chocolates. We liked her immediately. While she was here, we phoned Ralph's daughter, Becky, in the States, where Palamarchouk is staying. (Everyone here, even his wife, calls him Palamarchouk.) He was at home! Valentina, flushed with excitement and happy tears, talked with him, and her devotion touched Toli. Ralph and I had been disappointed we didn't get to meet Palamarchouk and Nik before we left. Their American visas were late, so the men didn't arrive when expected. We'll try to get back to the States in October before they leave.

All's well in Ohio, except Palamarchouk is having some difficulty communicating. Toli tutored him in English, but many nights, Palamarchouk threw down the book and exclaimed, "How do I know I will really go to America? Let's relax." We realize how lucky we are to have Toli! It would be a fluke to find a teacher of Russian in an American village, but in Makov, there are *two* English teachers. Our beloved country is sadly behind most others in foreign language study—our loss because knowledge of other languages and cultures enriches us.

After the phone call, we boarded Valentina's little red car, and she bounced us down a rough car path into a picturesque valley right outside Makov. We saw a meandering stream, children in their brown uniforms and red neckerchiefs walking home from school, and nanny goats grazing, their kids frisking around them (only the mothers need be tied). Stooped babushkas in flowered headscarves and black, crushed-velvet coats, sat alone or talked in twos on benches in front of their cottages, passing the time. Rural people don't have houses and barns out in the fields, as our farmers do. They live in villages, tucked into the hilliest areas, leaving flatter ground for fields.

Towards evening, Ralph and I took a long walk in the birch woods behind our house. The light green lace of leaves is just appearing, but the ground is a thick carpet of violets and yellow, white, and pink flowers unknown to us as spring comes to Ukraine.

We saw frogs, ducks, and swans on the pond and were fascinated by the tandem moving and honking of the trumpeter swans. We couldn't figure out which was the leader. As if singing a duet, they begin together on some invisible cue, stretch their heads skyward, flap their wings, and trumpet forth. Their uproariousness rivals the peacocks. The sight of a human being seems to set them off, so they'd make great watchdogs.

When we came across a wooden observation tower at the edge of the woods, we joked it was a KGB lookout. From its windows we viewed (oh, so beautiful!) deep green forests; long, golden strawstacks like huge loaves of bread; and an ever-unfolding, rolling expanse of fields—yellow, green, and brown—unspoiled by buildings or billboards. A slender, white, ribbon road sliced through the scene and disappeared into the far horizon.

By this time, the peacocks aren't disturbing our sleep. Goodnight!

April 10: Today, we ate again at Victoria's. We're now insisting on two meals a day instead of three. It's just too much food! For example, breakfast might be smoked salmon, pork, sausage slices, fresh and pickled tomatoes, sliced cucumbers, cottage cheese curds with sour cream over the top, creamed hard-boiled eggs, and my favorite: cherry pelmeni (sweetened cherries inside ravioli-shaped dough) topped with sour cream. People don't eat like this every day, of course. These meals—the best and most they can provide—exemplify the hospitality for which Soviets are renowned. Talk about cholesterol!

On our way home from Victoria's, we stopped to look inside a little church which is now a picture gallery. There were several people gathered on the corner. A small group approached us, just as if they'd been waiting for us. An old man acted as spokesperson, and he confidently asked us to help them get permission to open up the church. Toli advised that, in our position, we should not get involved, even though we wanted to help. He told us later there was a rumor we'd come to open the church.

Most of the day was spent putting away our things. We brought enough for a year, in case we stay that long. One suitcase contained summer clothes; another, clothes for winter. A third was full of small gifts: cosmetics, shaving equipment, t-shirts and sweatshirts with English writing, gym shoes, pantyhose, little toys, blank audio cassettes, music cassettes, a couple of video cassettes, paperback books, solar calculators, artist's supplies, good ballpoint pens, kitchen towels, pot-scrubbers, instant coffee, second-hand jeans and jackets from my sons, silk scarves, lingerie, etc. One suitcase held a shortwave radio (unnecessary), a tape recorder with extra batteries, an inflatable double bed, an iron, and boots for mud. A fifth had supplies hard to get in the USSR: toilet paper, soap, toothpaste, and laundry powder. Most of the laundry powder was for an American friend living in Moscow, Bob Meyerson, who works for the *Moscow News*. The sixth suitcase held extra coats, shoes, a large outdoor thermometer with both Fahrenheit and Celsius on it, a few kitchen supplies, towels, and miscellaneous items.

Our three small carry-ons were full of writing materials and books, including my Russian language texts and tapes. Toli said the number of our suitcases was the talk of the village.

In the afternoon, the Chairman came, accompanied by his pleasant daughter and teenage granddaughter who wanted to see the house. He asked that Ralph apply to develop a plot of land. We were shocked! We told him Ralph had never been asked to take over land and was not prepared to do so. We're not sure where this idea came from, but it would be ridiculous to drag American machinery, seeds, and fertilizer across the ocean, which is what the Chairman had in mind. I would think the highest officials, with their chain of command, would have gotten word down to the Chairman about what they wanted Ralph to do—discuss agriculture with anyone interested.

April 11: Our meals today were at a different place—the canteen. It's in an impressive workshop building at the farm's largest machine yard where both Viktor and Valentina Palamarchouk work. His job is chief engineer for machinery on the farm, and she's in charge of the parts department.

There are four machine yards on this collective farm. Rather than dividing the available money up evenly, this yard was given a fancy building, with lounging rooms for the workers, offices for supervisors, and the canteen. The shop part is large enough to repair eight tractors at once. No hand-tools are in the shop; they're locked up in a small room to prevent their walking away. Meetings are held in the auditorium, training is done in its class-rooms, and the whole facility is shown to visitors. Between the modern shop and the village street is an acre of well-paved yard (except for strips of flowers) where equipment is stored under several open shelters—eight grain planters, six combines, and more. It was out of character, however, that behind the building the outdoor area for caterpillar tractors and welding machinery was unpaved. This low area is a mud hole after heavy rains.

After dinner, Ralph, Toli, and I walked into the machine yard's indoor repair area and began talking and showing the 60 photos of Ohio we brought. These included shots of our families, Ralph's pigs and crops, our house, and the local supermarket. Only two workers were there when we began, but about twenty more soon appeared. The men looked long (and longingly) at the pictures of the fruit and pork departments of our supermarket; Ralph's no-tillage planting photo, showing little green wheat plants coming up in between last years' cornstalk stubble (no-till means the soil is never tilled during the year); a 37-year-old tractor that still works; and the photo of 4 men, Ralph's 3 sons and his son-in-law, who are running the entire Ohio farm. At the Ukraina collective farm's rate, there should be 140 people on the Dull farm, 20 of them supervisors. The 140 would include bookkeepers, truck drivers, repairmen, grain and feed handlers, hog workers, an economist, and others. At first, Ralph didn't want to show the supermarket photos, but Toli said, "People need to know what's possible." After looking at the pictures, the workers proudly led us to see their new combine.

Another farm driver, Nikolai Vasiliovich, a congenial yet quiet man, drives us around in a van. I try to speak a few words of Russian to him, and I think he enjoys that, as do I. Toli told me our driver likes that I call him by both his first and middle names, which indicates respect, because most people just call him "Grandpa." I didn't know the significance; I just lucked out.

It's the custom here for everyone's middle name (patronymic) to be the name of his or her father, with "ovich" or "evich" added for boys and "ovna" or "evna" for girls. "Stevenson" or "Johnson" could be patronymics for us. Also, we've learned that titles, such as Dr. or Mrs., are not used here because they smack of pre-revolutionary inequality. Instead, people say formally, "Comrade So-and-so" or, more often, the first name with the patronymic; thus, Toli's students and fellow teachers call him "Anatoli Arkadyevich," his father's name being Arkady.

Ralph showing photos of Ohio to workers in Makov machine
yard.

Most people also have pet names. As Americans tend to add "y" or "ie"
to names for an intimate touch (Nellie), Soviets often add "ya" (Nelya).
Toli's wife, Tanya, calls him "Tolik"; his friends call him "Tolya"; and only
Ralph and I call him "Toli." "Tanya" is actually an affectionate name for
the birth name, Tatiana. Then there are other nicknames. For example,
Mikhail Gorbachev is probably "Misha" to his friends, "Sasha" is the pet
name for both Alexander and Alexandra, and "Volodya" and "Vova" are
nicknames for Vladimir.

This afternoon, the Chairman visited us again, this time accompanied by
Ukraina's chief agronomist, Vladimir Savkov; Valarovsky of the District;
and an official from the Regional Gosagroprom. (We've learned a district
is about five-eighths the size of one of our counties, and a region might
have two dozen districts in it. There are 25 regions in Ukraine.) The men
said nothing about Ralph's taking a plot of land. Instead, he's to be "in
charge of corn planting." But that doesn't seem feasible either. Obviously,
the word still hasn't reached these men about why Ralph is here.

"You may go to Stavropol and Krasnodar at the end of May," the
Chairman announced. (That unreliable Moscow cooperative has promised—again—to get an invitation to us to visit Krasnodar so Ralph can see
if he would like to be a consultant there in 1990.)

When we go to Krasnodar, we also want to travel to the Stavropol
Region, Gorbachev's birthplace, to see if the American grain bins the local
authorities ordered have arrived. It's frustrating we can't just jump in a car
and go. Soviets, however, have always traveled throughout their country,

except for designated military areas. Internal passports still exist, though, for identification.

"The rest of this week is to be a cultural program, and Anatoli is to have a free hand," said the Chairman. "And Mr. Dull, you are to have the use of a car."

Of course, when we leave, the collective farm will have the car and our furnished house. Toli asked us later if Americans might want to rent the house as a vacation spot. We think it's unlikely, although as an off-the-beaten-path place for someone like a writer to have uninterrupted time and space in a beautiful, natural setting, it would be perfect.

This village has dozens of new individual houses going up, a few of them three stories high. They're built of rough brick and stone, then covered with colorful ceramic tiles or gray stucco with little, white curlicues artfully etched into or applied on the surface. They are fancier on the outside than our houses in the States. At least half the village, however, is made up of pastel stucco cottages. Most families have a lilac bush and many well-tended flowers in addition to their half-acre of vegetables and fruits out back.

We thought Makov might be the richest rural village in the USSR, but Toli says there are some that are wealthier. Makov and four other villages are supported by this prosperous collective farm, Ukraina, yet about 900 people in Makov don't work for the farm. They go by factory buses to factories a half hour away in the neighboring city of 100,000, Kamenets-Podolski. There they work fewer hours and make more money. It's a bone of contention that they benefit from the amenities of the village, which come from the collective farm's profits, but don't contribute labor or money.

April 12: Today was the first day of our cultural program. Toli arranged a trip to Kamenets-Podolski and its historic Old Town where several ancient cultures crossed paths. Two of his best English students, Alla and Natasha, who get extra tutoring from Toli after school, accompanied us for sightseeing. We walked on the fortress and looked into the door of a cathedral. Storage! It reminded me of the time in Leningrad when we walked expectantly into an intricately painted, turquoise and white Russian Orthodox church and were shocked to see the entire inside painted white, including the stained-glass windows. Communist slogans were slathered on the walls above cases of modern technological displays and busts of Lenin. Actually, there was one image in stained glass—Lenin's face! To us, this was joltingly incongruous!

Alla hopes to join the Communist Party someday because both of her beloved parents are members. Her mother draws maps, and her artistry was apparent in the long, hand-knitted, white sweater that Alla was wearing, complete with a knitted-in red hammer and sickle. Alla is pretty, bright, and charming; blond Natasha is shy and sweet. In general, young people here are more slender and firm than their American counterparts, perhaps because they walk so much.

Chris, Alla, Toli, and Natasha. Kamenets-Podolski fortress in background.

Around noon, we stopped for ice cream and coffee at a small restaurant nestled into a hillside near the fortress. Yummy!

By this time, we have our own food, and I am cooking. A pleasant couple, Ludmila and Nikolai, deliver what I order. My first food delivery included:

2   unwrapped loaves of dark bread
1   big piece of good lean pork
20 pounds of small potatoes (Ralph eats potatoes like apples, raw and unpeeled)
    carrots
    beets
    a large, shapeless hunk of butter
    a bottle of cooking oil
    catsup in a can
    bottles of apple-and-birch juice
    a large jar of pickles
2   large jars of cherry compote—sweetened, home-canned cherries in their own juices
2   liters of kefir—like saltless buttermilk
6   packages of cookies—not very sweet or rich
6   packages of crackers—very tasteless

    cucumbers
    fresh dill
    white sugar—coarser than ours
    white flour—must be sifted for impurities
    salt
2   dozen eggs
    milk—straight from the ccw
    cottage cheese—dry curds, to which I add sour cream
    sour cream—thinner than ours but tasty
    vinegar (I like to say it in Russian—"ooksooce")
    navy beans
    white, short-grained rice
    macaroni

It's good basic food, and Nikolai threw in a case of Fanta soda.

Volodya brought us some things, too—a small wringer washing machine and a little vacuum cleaner. Then he put up an outdoor clothesline for me. He's "on call" for those sorts of things. We feel as if we have servants—driver, translator, food people, houseman—and we're not used to that. At least I do our cooking, cleaning and laundry.

Every night, Ralph and I go out to watch the peacocks, who begin their ritual parade at dusk, shrieking and edging slowly toward the guest lodge. Then they walk up the back hand rail of the building, fly to the lower roof, then fly to the higher roof. There they pace around, looking up at the pines, as if to gather courage for that last flight. Finally, about dark, they fly to the tall pines. The most beautiful, whom we call Longtail, gives an extended cackle as he struggles to reach the pine. In the morning, they glide one by one across the courtyard to the ground.

I'm gradually writing the first of six articles for the *Dayton Daily News*. It will be about why we are here and the changes we've seen in Soviet life since 1983. Ralph will write two: one describing the village and one about Soviet agriculture. The others will be on the church and spirituality, our daily routine, and finally, a summary of our six months here. Also, I'm beginning the first of six "Newsletters," which will contain more intimate information, inappropriate for the newspaper. A friend in America will make copies and send them to 150 people interested in hearing from us.

April 13: Horrors! My teeth have turned black! Well gray anyway! Yesterday, a week late, Johanna told me not to drink the water in the house but to carry cooking water from the nearby, old-fashioned well. Now I know what that big bucket in the kitchen is for!

To get water, I take the bucket out to a well covered by a decorated cubicle the size of a person. Inside is a winch and a bucket with a hole and a flapper on the bottom. When I drop that bucket in the well, water flows in through the hole, and as I crank it up, the flapper retains the water. Then

I pour the water into my bucket, which is sitting on the ground beside the cubicle.

This morning, Toli came with a reporter from a regional newspaper to interview us. As soon as he left, we spent over six hours with a journalist and a photographer from TASS. They told us the information would be put out around the world. Ralph has had extensive experience with the media—especially when he was a candidate for the US Congress—and it serves him well. The reporter, whom we liked, told us journalists have led the way in perestroika. One thing they do, he said, is ferret out and expose those who say they support Gorbachev but really don't. "Things are in one big knot in this country, and it's extremely hard to untie," he said.

In the past, poets were the foremost heroes. With their cryptic criticism, they inspired solidarity. But now that glasnost has arrived, journalists have taken up the mantle, speaking out directly. Glasnost is more than freedom of speech; it means "speaking forth"—actually using that freedom. But there's another part to glasnost: access to information. That has improved greatly but is still less than perfect.

I gave the men peanut butter and jam sandwiches to see their reactions to peanut butter, which is virtually unknown here. They liked it. Peanut butter could be a valuable addition in this country since there's a shortage of high-quality protein.

Every day, little red ants come into the kitchen. I step on them during the day, and now they have the good sense to come only at night.

April 14: As we were dressing this morning, a big, blustery RadioKiev interviewer walked into our house unannounced. The Chairman arrived shortly afterwards. These two knew each other and laughed and talked together, calling each other "Brother." It amused me the Chairman's interview was much longer than ours, but he did say he knew Ralph was a real farmer because his hands showed hard work.

Later Ralph took a walk to the fields while I did the laundry in the bathtub. It's easier than using the washing machine because the heavy crank wringer on top is hard to handle. Also, I have to fill the machine by carrying buckets of water. Our hot and cold running water is rusty and leaves black splotches—like those on my teeth, so I'll have to wash our white things in water from the well and heat it on the stove, as my grandmother did.

In the middle of the afternoon, Toli came to go with us to his flat for what he said would be a small supper, followed by his school's folk dance concert. Small supper, indeed! There were several courses: first, salads, including meat and fish salads; next, soup and bread; then the main course of two meats, potatoes, and cooked vegetables; and finally dessert: cakes, chocolates, and tea. Toli's pretty, voluptuous wife, Tanya, and her mother, Anna, are superb cooks! Two-year-old "terrorist" Yura took to Grandpa

Ralph, who has 11 grandchildren. Handsome Vova, 10, spent most of his time outside with playmates—human and canine.

Everything was wonderful, including the concert. Toli danced and sang, along with other teachers and students from his school. The performance was quite good, and the rich costumes were authentically Ukrainian. I especially like the women's headdresses of colorful roses and long, silken ribbons. Teachers are required to participate, but Toli considers it a waste of time. Schools compete in the District, and the best one goes on to the Region. In this way, traditions are continued.

The audience, however, seemed more interested in us than the performance. As we entered and left the auditorium, every eye was on us. When we returned their gazes, people continued to stare. "Virtually no one in Makov has ever seen an American," Toli had told us.

On our other five trips to the USSR, Soviets seldom approached us (unless they wanted to trade money or buy something). But we learned if we approached them, they would be warm and open. So at the concert, we said, "Dobre dane" ("Good day" in Ukrainian), and people smiled and spoke. It was good to see Natasha there—someone we knew. Also, we met the second-grade teacher, Toli's dance partner. I told her I had been a second-grade teacher, too.

After Toli changed out of his costume, we returned to his apartment for tea and conversation. By that time, more people had gathered: Anna's sister-in-law, Nina; plus young couples Vanya and Tanya and Nikolai and Nelya. Vanya said he liked the business-like attitude of Americans, a compliment we've heard before.

We shared how people in our respective countries viewed each other before the Gorbachev Era. We were astounded to discover, unlike the attitude in the US, Soviets have always liked Americans or at least not disliked us. The old people remember good experiences as allies during World War II as well as the US giving them food afterwards. The young people like our rock music and clothes. Soviets have always made a distinction between our people and our government while many Americans lump everything Soviet together. We were also surprised the Soviets have changed their minds about Reagan. On our earliest trips, they expressed dislike for him, but since he came here and signed the INF Treaty, most people now like him. They don't like Jimmy Carter, however, because of the 1980 Olympic boycott and grain embargo. We told them that wasn't the real Jimmy Carter. "Jimmy's his real self now: *Time* calls him America's best ex-president."

Actually, we've always found the infamous mirror image alive and well in both countries. Both sides have feared each other and were convinced the other side was out to conquer the world. Each was just as sure their country would never be the one to start a war. Each knew they were the ones who really wanted peace and felt their arms buildup had to continue due to the other's massive arms propagation.

In both countries, propaganda during the long cold war exaggerated the negative while never mentioning the good. As I grew up, it was in the air I breathed that all Soviets were communists (only six percent are). They were portrayed in our movies as ruthless, lying, godless psychopaths, single-minded in their primary goal of "taking over the world." Somehow the KGB was everywhere, and every Soviet was tracked by his own personal agent who knew his every act and word.

I went through the era of the "duck and cover" preparation for a nuclear attack, and at the height of the cold war, it was even unwise to wear bright red clothes. From somewhere, I had the vague idea that any Soviet who dared express a critical word was turned in by his children or whisked off the street into a black limousine and sent to a Siberian labor camp or psychiatric hospital. All Soviets were miserably unhappy slaves, I thought. Stalin's reign was heinous, but many Americans are unaware human rights for Soviets have continually improved since he died.

On the other hand, the US has been portrayed in the USSR as a country of homeless, unemployed, drug-crazed people, ruled by fat, bigoted, self-serving tycoons surrounded by full moneybags. Neither picture is the whole truth. But it is necessary to dehumanize people to make them enemies. For example, we weren't fighting *people* in Vietnam; to Americans, they were "gooks."

After a good discussion at Toli's, most of us ended up strolling down the middle of Makov's main street toward Stupentsi. When we began to examine a rolled-up hedgehog, the streetlights went out. (What a powerful hedgehog!) Only the major streets of Makov have street lights, and these automatically turn off at midnight. We continued on to Valentina's, squeezed into her car, and rode the rest of the way home. There, everyone oohed and ahhed their way through the house, declining to look into the bathroom because that's bad luck. A wonderful evening!

We've been here one week now and feel right at home.

CHAPTER 2

Makov and the Ukraina Collective Farm
by Ralph

The Ukraina collective farm surrounding Makov is 265 miles southwest of Kiev. Its uneven borders contain 17,000 acres (26 square miles) of irregular-shaped fields, medium-sized forests, five villages, and a few dirt roads slanting through the farm. A blacktopped highway cuts through the south side on its way from Kamenets-Podolski (population 100,000) 30 minutes to the west. It travels on to Dunaevtsi (population 25,000), twenty minutes to the east; to Khmelnitski (260,000), another one and one-half hours away; and on to Kiev (2.5 million), six hours farther east.

Shatava, formerly a separate village and now part of Makov, is located on that two-lane, winding highway. Houses and stores in Shatava crowd both sides of the blacktop, which is burdened by a steady flow of trucks, buses, tractors, and a few cars passing through. Also along the busy thoroughfare are a machine yard, a truck yard, a Russian Orthodox church with a huge onion-dome, a post office, and cattle barns.

Usually, there are people standing along the highway, waiting to catch a bus or hitch a ride with anyone going to the next town. It's not uncommon to see a woman in fancy dress climb into the cab of a cattle truck or into a motorcycle sidecar for a ride. We seldom go anywhere without picking up someone and then experiencing his or her excitement at meeting Americans.

Heading north from the highway through the Shatava part of Makov to the lake, we can see the other end of Makov on higher ground. Hitchhikers are in the back seat of our car, as usual. We drive halfway around the lake, past an old water-driven mill, and up the hill to the center of Makov. When we enter the central part from any direction, we drive under a horizontal five-inch pipe placed seven feet above the street. This pipe keeps trucks and farm equipment out of the housing and headquarters district and makes visitors duck their heads when their cars go under it.

In the center of Makov is a wide, smooth, straight street bordered by multi-colored flowers. Public buildings, such as the school; Headquarters, which houses party and farm offices; the new and old Houses of Culture; and the day care center with its Disney-like play houses are all set back from the road.

Near one end of the short street is a three-story, 18-apartment structure where Toli's family lives, and along the other end of the street is a similar apartment building where the Palamarchouks live. Soon the Palamarchouks will move to the big, new house Viktor is building overlooking a wooded valley leading to the lake.

The crop land is 12,500 acres and, with little exception, very fertile. Half is relatively flat and the rest rolling enough to cry for better soil conservation management. So far, the topsoil is still deep.

Included within the boundaries but not controlled by the collective farm are five enterprises managed by the state: the sugar beet factory, a beef-feeding facility for 1,000 cattle, a chick-growing facility, an egg-producing plant, and a sanitorium for workers who come from as far as Moscow for rest and healing. The collective farm has 1254 working members (including 150 supervisors) who have 2 official meetings a year, and a local soviet (council), which meets quarterly.

The biggest contributor to the farm's prosperity are the 7,000 Holstein cattle raised and sold for beef. The calves are acquired from dairy collectives and fed corn silage and legume silage during the winter and fresh-chopped forage in summer. Plenty of straw and a small amount of grain are fed to the animals year round. In contrast, American farmers feed no straw but large quantities of grain.

One family rents a feed lot for 700 cattle, but it is tightly controlled by the collective farm. A group of 5 men in their 30s are renting a 185-acre orchard with two greenhouses. Field crops on the farm include 3,700 acres of corn (60 percent for silage), 2,250 acres of wheat, 2,100 acres of sugar beets, 800 acres of peas, and 2,200 acres of forage crops. There are also many acres of vegetables, beans for feed, vetch, rye, barley, and oats.

Ukraina farm, which actually started in 1924, five years before forced collectivization, has a chairman, an agronomist, an economist, and a party secretary. There are four divisions of cropland, each having a brigadier to organize the peasant workers, a machine yard, a grain yard, and a village.

During the collectivization period 60 years ago, collective farms were typically 2,500 acres around one village. Since then, they've merged to become large collectives. Often a failing collective has become a state farm or joined a more successful collective farm, so now there are about 22,000 state and 22,000 collective farms in the USSR. Also, millions of acres have been abandoned altogether. Bigger is not necessarily better, and medium-sized farms may develop in the future to allow more personal care and, thus, more efficiency.

Individual farming in the old communal structures was rebounding well from the trough of civil war at the time of Lenin's death in 1924. Typically, though, for this century, when the sickle was too successful, the hammer came down on it. Prosperous farmers were eliminated by Stalin. One of Toli's theories is that Stalin was mediocre and wanted to be surrounded by mediocre people. Thus, he eliminated the most capable politicians, military officers, and intelligentsia, and apparently didn't mind thwarting the most productive farmers either. Many were killed or herded to Siberia. One reason Hitler viewed Russia as easy game was Stalin had already killed thousands of his best military officers, even close friends.

One hundred fifty houses are under construction in the villages of Ukraina farm. Also a new House of Culture and a two-million-ruble dairy facility are nearing completion. The culture center was started 13 years ago. It takes two to five years to build a house, explaining why so many houses are in process at once. Also, supplies are hard to get. Toli has had two truckloads of rock at his new house site for a year now. Nothing else has happened.

There are two Russian Orthodox churches in Makov. The larger "working" one is located along the highway in the Shatava part of Makov. When we see the crippled and elderly living near the closed church in northern Makov, we understand why they want to worship there instead of walking the extra two miles to the Shatava church. The route is down a long hill, around the lake, and up another long hill to the church. There people stand for five hours before retracing the route home.

Lush gardens of potatoes, beets, and corn are everywhere, and even people who walk bent over have gardens. Apartment dwellers have gardens in fields at the edge of the village and maybe a tiny strawberry patch next to the street where they live.

Only eight percent of the families have a cow, but it seems like more when you see the cows coming through the village in the evening and nudging open the gates to their masters' houses. They are commonly pastured along the sides of roads and streets, watched by children or the elderly.

Milk production is small because the cows don't get grain. Families glean the hay fields, or the Chairman gives them access to standing clover in the corner of a large field. The latter is cut with a sickle and hauled home in a horse-drawn wagon, piled on a motorcycle sidecar, put into burlap and slung over a shoulder, or tied behind the seat of a bicycle. Once the green hay is home, the family hangs it on the fence in front of the house or up on the roof to dry before storing the cured hay in the attic of the barn, just a few feet from the house. Some store hay in their house attics, too.

After the family harvests the garden and puts the fresh produce and home-canned fruits into their root cellar, they are ready for winter. In many ways, rural Soviets are better situated than their Moscow friends who don't have gardens or animals.

The family pigs are confined in the little barns, but multitudes of chickens, ducks, and geese are everywhere, including the streets. They scatter as cars and motorcycles threaten their lives. There's no penalty to a driver who hits a chicken, but if he doesn't miss a duck or goose, he pays damages. I suppose the reasoning is chickens are so unpredictable and quick a driver can't always avoid them.

Some livestock need grain to eat, especially the pigs. Where to get it? Anywhere possible. The half-acre gardens aren't large enough to feed both animals and people. You and I assume people would simply go to the grain yard and buy feed. Not so. The grain there has been procured by the state. Or if the grain yard manager has "managed" to have a surplus (through "careful" bookkeeping), he charges a ridiculous price and acquires a new car or new house. Once when Anna ran out of feed for her two pigs, she sent Toli and me to buy bread to feed them. A little animal feed is grown in the gardens, and some is stolen from the collective farm's large corn fields just prior to harvest time.

Stealing is common in the apple orchard, too. This isn't considered a serious crime against the collective farm. But what about the future when the fields and orchards are privately owned or rented, and the crops belong to individuals? Stealing from the collective or state is one thing, but stealing from individuals is something else. I raised this question with Ukraina specialists, and they chuckled. The orchard renters put up gates at the end of the lanes and have a dog, but it will take more than that to break old habits, especially at night.

The vacation facilities at the edge of the orchard where we stay are used for guests but are not available to local people. Stupentsi was developed many years ago for party members. In 1983, Andropov closed down such places across the country to reduce special privileges. But now we notice Kiev party people vacationing there, and the Chairman visits his dacha, or vacation home, across the pond from our house almost daily. A toot of the Chairman's horn brings Johanna running to open the gate so he can drive through the zoo, past our house, and on to his cabin.

When we first arrived, the farm officials were more uncomfortable than we were because they weren't sure what to do with us. There had been a rumor we were going to take over management of 2,000 acres for a demonstration of American methods and technology. This was highly unlikely, if only for two reasons: first, we didn't know for sure we were even coming to this part of the country until four days before we arrived, and second, a major factor on our Ohio farm is the no-tillage method of growing crops. By this time the Ukraine fields had been plowed and tilled many times, starting the year before.

The Chairman thinks I'm a loafer, and I feel like one as far as physical labor is concerned. But many afternoons, as I sit at my desk "slaving away" writing the agriculture book for Soviets, I hear a toot, and glance out the window to see the Chairman motor by to his cabin. Then I can't help but think, "And he calls *me* a loafer!" Perhaps he's going to the cabin to write a book for Americans to read. Toli said that before the Chairman's first wife died, he was an excellent and progressive chairman. And he's still a strong administrator at age 67. As far as party privileges for top officials are concerned, however, some weeds are hard to kill.

Whether this Ukraine farm will be managed and worked by independent farmers in the future remains doubtful. Many workers think they would like that, but how many are willing and able to try? How much encouragement will they receive from farm officials? And how many roadblocks will there be? We know there are some workers and farm brigadiers (those next in command under the chief agronomist) who want desperately to farm for themselves. Ukraina's a good farm, but, like the Dull farm, it could be better. Renting or owning would drastically reduce costs and losses of products because individuals would suffer the consequences. As Soviet farms go, Ukraina is well organized, gets things done on time, and has good yields overall, though some areas are weak.

Great pride is taken in the appearance of the farm, and scores of women are standing by to rescue fields from weeds or to turn windrows (cut crops gathered in a row and left to dry) after a rain. The Chairman boasts anyone can see where the next collective begins because of the weed contrast. Also, the corn on Ukraina has sufficient nitrogen (and thus is healthy and a deep green) while corn on other farms does not, often because some chairmen can't manage to get it.

Ukraina collective farm receives many visitors, especially foreign guests, so it has a reputation to protect. Many years ago, Ukraina received the Order of Lenin award, and Chairman Stengach was honored as a Hero of Socialist Labor. I'm sure the purpose of awards is to stimulate production and excellence, but there is also a dark side to this kind of competition. Actually, only a few are in the running because if an award is out of reach, why bother to try? The fact is, if prosperous farms would share their supplies with poor farms, there would be more total production.

Even in Ukraine, no more than ten percent of the farms can be classified as prosperous. This isn't due to any lack of total national resources but to the centralized bureaucratic system. The huge Russian Republic is even less prosperous. Yet the Politburo boss in charge of agriculture, Yegor Ligachev, wants only to tinker with the collective system which hasn't worked for 60 years. Most Soviets think the trial period has been long enough. It's time to try self-motivation rather than continuing an attempt to pour motivation down from the top via central planners and bureaucrats.

Ukraina is a beautiful spot, and we thank the people for letting us be their guests. Although it seems rude to write unfavorably about a country and village where 99 percent of the people are such gracious hosts, writing for the public requires honesty. The book we wrote for Soviets also includes a critical analysis of their country—as well as praise for its people.

CHAPTER 3

Christine's Journal Excerpts

APRIL CONTINUED

April 16: This afternoon, Valentina came to take us to dinner at her flat, which was packed with guests. Toli was there, of course, to facilitate conversation, as well as Valentina's mother, who lives with the Palamarchouks. This is a common arrangement for Soviets. It's considered particularly cruel not to keep a dependent parent in one's home.

Thirteen-year-old Tatiana helped her mother (and giggled every time I smiled at her), but Valentina was still busy cooking and had little time to talk. One reason food is served in courses here must be that most people have only two burners on their stoves. This limits the number of hot dishes they can serve at a time. Toli says the many courses are tradition. One guest, a communist, was interested in our Easter celebration. After dinner he gave us roses and a fancy box with a Ukrainian girl painted on its metal front. "She's a symbol of purity," he said.

April 17: Today was supposed to be Ralph's first "work" day, but all that happened was he was driven past the fields for an hour by Vladimir Savkov, Ukraina's chief agronomist, and then dropped off at home.

Later, when Ralph and I walked to the fields, we were told one corn field had been tilled nine times already and would have five more tillages before the year ended. What a waste of time, machinery, fuel—and compaction of the soil! Because the authorities like to see clean fields, some tillage is done only to impress higher-ups.

If farms fall out of favor for any reason, their officials are indirectly punished by being told, perhaps, that there's no fuel or nitrogen for their farms. I wonder how future renters will get what they need when they need it since most authorities are against renting.

Toli says there are 18 million bureaucrats in this country, and we know they are one of the biggest problems. Gorbachev and the progressives on the top and the people on the bottom want change. Would that the bureaucrats in the middle realized perestroika could make life better for them, too, in the long run!

It's slow here for us, and Ralph misses physical work. This farm is clean and neat, so there's not even anything for him to clean up. During March last year he worked on a farm in Georgia, USA, planting corn and clearing debris.

I'm reviewing my Russian. Two quarters isn't much, but it helps. We have to go through the Dunaevtsi switchboard to call long distance, and I've had trouble with the operators screaming at me when I don't understand. Toli called them and asked them to please not yell and to be helpful to the Americans, so now they're pleasant. Sometimes I hear good-natured little chuckles when I butcher the language.

April 20: Our first speaking engagement! We met with teachers at the Pioneer Palace in Dunaevtsi, the seat of our district. Toli, who grew up on a farm, now knows all about Ralph's farm, so he introduced us to the audience and then did a farm lecture by himself. It saved time. Although they were teachers, they were fascinated with farming, getting out their pencils and papers and taking notes. They were also very interested in America.

One teacher asked me, "What do you like about the USSR?"

"We love the kindness and generosity of the people and the fine treatment they give their children."

One of the teachers remarked dryly, "Perhaps you have been misinformed about the children."

In conclusion, Maria, the smiling, hospitable director, gave us tulips and a long Ukrainian bread cloth with *peacocks* on it. How appropriate!

Afterwards, I asked Toli what the woman meant about the children, and he said there had been news articles revealing mistreatment at some day care centers. Also, there are not enough day care centers, and many are not near the workplace.

I told him one of our Intourist guides told us the best food goes to day care centers. He laughed and said, "The food hierarchy goes like this: The best food goes to the houses of the higher-ups; then to the profiteers, who will sell it for much money and give good bribes; next, to the restaurants; then, to distributors; and finally, to the day care centers."

April 23: Today, I took a long walk by myself in the miles-long forest across a field from Stupentsi. It looks as if someone grooms it, yet it still looks natural. There were neat piles of trimmed sapling trunks lying around. I wonder who cuts these and who uses them? Can anyone come in and take them? Because of the grooming, the forests have no tall underbrush, so one can picnic comfortably anywhere.

Ralph is writing "Considerations for Land Renters" and a list of requests for what we would like to do while we're here.

Toli brings us the fascinating *Moscow News* every week. Many people consider it the country's best newspaper though it's hard to get. Toli subscribes to the English edition for his students. Since 1983, Ralph and I have seen it change from a pap-filled, censored paper for foreigners to an outrageously open one. It was beginning to change when Ralph and our American friend in Moscow, Bob Meyerson, wrote an article for it in 1986 about the Fellowship of Reconciliation's youth trip we helped lead. One day in 1987, Ralph was amazed to receive a check in Ohio for $19.51 from a New York bank, payment for his part of the writing. It was completely unexpected. The bank had received hard currency from the *Moscow News*, then wrote a check for dollars.

Nearly every day, Ralph and I walk for an hour or two. In addition, he does extra walking while observing in the fields. Today, someone asked him to plant corn.

When we walk in the village, I try to speak Russian, because only Toli, the other English teacher, and Natasha are able to say more than "Stand up," "Go to the blackboard," and "Sit down" in English. (Alla lives in another village.) Everyone here speaks Ukrainian in their daily lives, but they understand Russian, so when I say, "Pozhalooista, govoreetya po-rooski" (Please, speak Russian), they do.

For most western Ukrainians, it's a matter of principle not to speak Russian. But in Kiev and the eastern part, Russian is the daily language.

April 25: Valentina gave us tulips from her yard and took us through the parts department of the machine yard. Her tiny office has an electric space heater. It surprised me shelves of blankets and boots were part of the supplies to be handed out to workers.

Each day, we talk with Toli about a new subject. For example, today I asked him his opinion of Pamyat, a group of Moscovites who claim they support the restoration of old Russian ways but are really lashing out against Jews. We consider it a dangerous organization, much like our Ku Klux Klan. A Russian Jew once told me she had heard to become a member of Pamyat, one has to supply the names and addresses of four Jewish families, in preparation for future pogroms (organized massacres and looting of innocent people). "It's a chauvinistic Russian organization which does indeed put blame on Jews for all problems," said Toli. "The group is noisy but not large."

"Some psychologists say," I responded, "those who hate categories of people are those who feel no worth or hope themselves. So to feel worthwhile they believe some people are inferior. A group can also become a target for rage in general. It's my guess the hatred of some Soviet ethnic groups for each other may be partly due to bad economic conditions."

I told Toli we once talked about Pamyat with Vladimir Pozner, a famous Soviet journalist, whose father was Jewish. Pozner said, "It's a serious problem, but as the state doesn't want to censor groups anymore, perhaps people will recognize it for what it is." I hope so, but Oprah Winfrey once had some neo-Nazi skinheads on her show, assuming, of course, people would feel revulsion. Instead, it drew troubled people to these groups. Now she says she'll never have anyone with reprehensible ideas on her show again.

Ralph and I haven't met Pamyat members, but we've met a few Stalinists. This group strikes me as being as bad or worse, considering Stalin was pathologically paranoid and killed many millions of enemies and friends alike. I think Stalinists must be basking in Stalin's former *image*—a strong, benevolent, caring leader—and are closing their eyes to his actions.

More is still coming out about him. Roy Medvedev, Soviet historian and now a member of the Supreme Soviet, wrote in *Let History Judge* that Stalin lavished kindness on his friends while simultaneously planning their torture and murder. Once he brought in the best medical care for a friend, and as soon as the man was well, had him tortured and executed. During the time that Molotov, Soviet Foreign Minister, and Poskrebyshev, Stalin's personal secretary, served him, he sent their wives to Siberia. One New Year's Eve, Stalin rolled pieces of paper into little tubes and put them around the fingers of Poskrebyshev. Then the fiend lit them instead of New Year's candles. Poskrebyshev writhed in pain but did not dare take them off.

Years ago, Toli made initiatives to join the party, but he received no answer. Now he's glad. I'm sure he wasn't considered obedient enough.

Toli said a person can now be promoted without being a party member. The chief economist on this farm, for example, doesn't belong to the party. Socially, it doesn't seem to matter if a person is a party member or not; everyone mixes. The ruling officials, however, are a class unto themselves.

Right before we came to Makov, the USSR had its first ever multi-candidate election. Toli campaigned for a 28-year-old man who ran against an established official for the Congress of People's Deputies. At one meeting, Toli spoke out and said, "This young man knows the life of the people because he lives that life, while the incumbent knows it only from his personal car and from his window."

Toli told us, "Those in charge, all over the country, wanted to continue their practice of having just one candidate on each ballot so they could remain in control. But they were afraid of pressure by the people, so in many areas two or more candidates were on the ballot."

In all former elections, there has been only one name on the ballot; a person could either put the ballot "as is" in the box or cross out the name first. Occasionally, a candidate would not receive a majority, and another election had to be held. But until now, this had been the extent of people's ability to influence who got into office.

"Our young man won," exclaimed Toli. "However, some others, like Ivan Dratch, popular Ukrainian poet and leader and a member of Rukh, were not so lucky. He was a victim of the old system in its death throes and was kept off the ballot. Makov officials contributed to this unjust procedure. Several people from Makov, who were told how to vote ahead of time, went to Kamenets-Podolski as nominators: the party secretary, the chairman of the local soviet [council], the chief doctor [head of Makov's sanatorium], and the wife of the head of the sugar factory."

"Rukh," continued Toli, "is the Ukrainian People's Movement for Perestroika. It consists mostly of writers, poets, and intellectuals, and its numbers are growing. They've banded together for protection because it's safer to be part of a group when you speak out critically."

In fact, to insure People's Deputies total freedom of expression, a special statute was passed making them immune to arrest and prosecution, except with the approval of the Supreme Soviet (the primary legislative body, elected by the Congress of People's Deputies). Rukh doesn't seem to be a hot-headed secessionist movement. However, if any republic can make it on its own, it would be Ukraine, with its hard-working people; rich, black soil; coal; and industry. Rukh puts pressure on those party members who make policy, and it will undoubtedly figure prominently in Ukraine's future.

When everything's settled, the USSR may be more democratic than America is, for at least two reasons. First, it is impossible to elect an official without a majority of the popular vote. In the United States, the majority has failed to decide our president twice, once in 1824 and again in 1876, due to our Electoral College system. Second, democracy really means the involvement of as many people as possible in the voting and policy-making of the country, and we are surely lax: only half of us even vote in presidential elections.

In Moscow, we see people standing outside the *Moscow News* offices avidly reading wall newspapers and discussing them. May their caring continue when life becomes easier! Europeans in general are more interested than Americans in the affairs of their countries; we are seen as a non-reflective people, broad but not deep.

Soviets often tell humorous stories which they always call anecdotes. They're a good barometer of what's going on in society, and they help defuse rage. Like parables, they present pungent truth, thinly disguised. Under glasnost, people can be more open these days. Toli told us this one today, though it's more of a joke than an anecdote:

    Q. "When Brezhnev was General Secretary, why did people need windshield wipers on their TVs?"

    A. "Because when he spoke on TV, people watching him would shout, 'Liar!' and spit at him."

The Brezhnev Era is called the "Stagnation Period" because of the boasting and corruption among the authorities while the country deteriorated. Some Soviets tell us the Reagan period was America's Period of Stagnation.

Toli went back to teaching today because no one will give permission for him to be away from work. The Chairman promised to take care of it but didn't. So Toli asked for help from the school authorities on local and district levels. They, too, turned him down. Now he has three jobs, the third being his tutoring. When we need him for meetings, he'll take time off from teaching, and he'll also come to us each day after school for awhile. I think he pays the other English teacher to include his classes with hers during his absences. He stays up late every night doing serious reading—his life's blood. One reason he's able to handle it all is Tanya. She doesn't work outside the home and doesn't pressure him to do housework, though she has her hands full with two-year-old Yura. Some Soviet men are more open to helping with household chores than they were in the past—much like their American counterparts.

April 27: Johanna works for eight hours each day at Stupentsi, riding her bicycle to and from work. She has a staff of four, and though someone is here 24 hours a day, we feel isolated from them because their quarters are behind the tall fence surrounding our house.

Other than these folk, our only close neighbors are a group of five young men who rent Stupentsi's orchard and two greenhouses, just down the lane from our house. They work hard, and lately we've been watching them battle the wind. First, they cover a greenhouse with plastic, then the wind tears it, then they patch it, and the cycle continues. It looks as if they're determined to win. We decided it was time we got to know these neighbors, so on our walk today, we stopped and showed them our photos.

Our meals are beginning to develop a pattern. For breakfast, we have either cooked oatmeal and raisins with milk—Soviets think oats are for horses, so they seldom eat them—or pancakes with jam on top. Ralph occasionally makes his specialty, poached eggs with salt, butter, and bits of toast. We use butter sparingly, like good Americans who are watching their cholesterol. Sometimes we have kefir (buttermilk) for breakfast, too, but we don't eat the fatty sausages that are popular here.

For lunch, we usually have a thick soup of some kind: bean, vegetable, potato soup, or borshch (vegetable-beef soup with beets added); wonderful, crusty Ukrainian bread; tomato and cucumber salad; and fruit for dessert. I especially like green borshch, which Tanya taught me to make—potato soup with diced, hard-boiled eggs and fresh sorrel added at the last minute. It's served steaming hot, with a dollop of sour cream in the middle of each bowl.

Dinner is usually a little meat or fish with potatoes or rice; or tomato sauce with herbs on top of macaroni, more vegetables, and fruit or baked custard for dessert.

I brought cinnamon with me—a nice touch for many dishes. One innovation for me is abundant use of fresh dill, parsley, and sorrel (an herb plant somewhat like spinach), though I miss the fine selection of dried herbs back home. In Ohio we eat a lot of chicken and turkey, but the chicken I tried to cook here was tough and skinny. It looked like one of those silly, rubber chickens people use for jokes. Sometimes I bake a cake, as I did today, and I've learned to make a mean cottage cheese pie.

I brought one cookbook with me, *The More With Less Cookbook*, and it serves me well. We drink well water with our meals, and we snack on English walnuts—after we shell them. Actually, I like the absence of junk food or prepackaged food here. It's a good, earthy feeling to prepare all our food from scratch. And I do mean scratch! For example, I must pull the stem from every raisin we eat.

The Chairman visited us today and invited us to Easter dinner at his house. When he comes, he always says, "Hi!" with great vigor and shakes hands with us, but he won't shake hands across a threshold. It's bad luck. All our encounters with the Chairman have been cordial. He's famous for his hospitality and has been good to us.

He told us we would each receive 15 rubles a day. This, he explained, is the official USSR rate of payment to guests from the US (though it's twice as much as we need or would have asked for). Each country's rate is different, though we don't know who decides that. Deducted from the first month's pack of rubles (we've seen no checks in this country) will be the cost of our hotel room and meals in Kiev on April 7, meals at Victoria's and the machine yard canteen, food delivered to our house by Nikolai, and telephone bills. Sugar is rationed and is purchased from the collective farm and recorded at Headquarters. Toli will pick up the rubles at Headquarters for us each month. When we depart in October, we'll leave some with him to pay for phone bills arriving late.

April 29: Today is Russian Orthodox Easter Eve. When Nikolai came with our food delivery, he brought us special *Paskha* bread and five of those famous, intricately-painted Ukrainian eggs. It humbled me when I remembered later there are five people in his family—he must have given us his family's Easter eggs! Toli surprised us in the evening with an offering of two dozen perfect, cheese-stuffed rolls that Anna had made, and with him came Valentina carrying her still-warm Paskha bread.

At 11:15 P.M., the four of us went by car to an all-night Easter Eve service at the church. We passed many people walking, carrying baskets of Easter bread and eggs to be blessed by the priest at 4:30 A.M. Hundreds of people filled the church and the church yard. The priest and his assistants were intoning the rich, mostly minor-mode harmonies of Russian Orthodox music, and the choir replied in kind. The human voice is the only instrument allowed in the Russian Orthodox service, and there are no pews because they believe it is disrespectful to sit before God. So the people stand, though there's quite a bit of movement around the church as the believers go about their personal mystical rituals. In their church service, they're less conforming than we are, though tonight they stepped up, one by one, to kiss a special icon.

Mostly old women made up the congregation, but there was also a good-sized cross-section of Makov's population. The USSR has a whole generation of women without men, due to the Great Patriotic War (WW II). We've heard that of the men born in 1923, only three percent were alive after the war. In 1983 when we were in the Seventh-Day Adventist Church in Moscow, a man said that 29 of the 31 students in his class had lost their fathers in the war.

Tonight, I watched a stern-looking babushka shepherding her fresh-faced 10-year-old grandson. She directed him to take a candle to an icon, light it, and put it in the candlestand, then do the same to another icon. A little girl sitting in the choir loft with her mother often peeked through the curtains to see what was happening—as children do the world over.

The walls were covered with icons and artificial flowers. There were candlestands everywhere, a booth selling candles, fresh flowers on the altar, and poles with banners on them.

Shortly before midnight, a heavy chandelier of candles hanging high overhead was lowered by rope-and-pulley, and its candles were extinguished. Then, at midnight, the candles were re-lit, and the priest emerged from the inner sanctum to announce triumphantly, "Christ is risen!" At the same time, neon words across the top of the sanctuary lit up to proclaim it as well.

"He is risen indeed!" answered the people. Immediately, they began moving en masse toward the door and out into the dimly-lit churchyard. Out came the banner carriers, then the priest under a canopy, then the choir in full voice. Last came the people who fell into line, walking slowly around the church three times, past the rows of baskets on the lawn, while bells clanged loudly at frequent intervals. Stalin had silenced the church bells. Then in 1987, Gorbachev permitted the bells to ring again, acknowledging that the churches had endured terrible persecution at the hands of the government.

Afterwards, we filled the church again, and worship continued. By now it was 1:30 A.M. and I was nursing a migraine headache. In the press of the crowd, I began to feel faint, so we went outside.

The four of us sat talking in Valentina's car. "Interest in the church has been growing for about 15 years," Toli began, kicking in his natural teaching talent. "During the USSR's early years, many people were fanatical believers in Soviet power, but later, more and more people realized their leaders' actions didn't correspond to Lenin's ideas, so they stopped believing and looked elsewhere.

"The church, however," he continued, "is still mistrusted by many people. It was wealthy in pre-revolutionary times and has continued to be so under Soviet rule. Big sums of money go through the hands of priests. It may be difficult for them to keep empty sleeves. Many people believe in God but not in priests."

"But I wish we could have the religious education that has been denied us all these years," Valentina said wistfully.

"There may be a contradiction between church teachings and the needs of society," said Toli. "Church people are told to just wait for God to act and not change anything themselves."

"That's true in some churches," I said, "but we know that Soviet churches have been prohibited from doing any social service projects because the government prides itself on taking care of the economic needs of its people. Now, under Gorbachev, many churches are doing works of mercy and charity openly. We know of a soup kitchen in Leningrad, sponsored by the Russian Orthodox Church, and of Baptists who work with the mentally ill in Moscow."

"Every year, some of us teachers must go to the church on Christmas and Easter Eves to monitor the young people," Toli said. "We're there to prevent students from going inside or making a disturbance outside."

"What?" I exclaimed. "Do you mean teachers can tell a family whether or not their children may attend church?"

"If kids are there with their parents, we haven't interfered, but older students, Komsomol members, were not supposed to enter a church. However, since perestroika, we are here only to stop disturbances by kids."

This must be part of the anti-religious work teachers were supposed to do. It looks as if the church and the school have been in the same arena here—that of influencing belief systems. Indeed, tonight Toli spoke to a group of young men standing on the church steps, and they left. They'd been drinking, he said, so he told them to either go in or leave.

Toli continued, "When I was a student at the Kiev Language Institute, we were told not to enter a church or we would be kicked out of the Institute. That wasn't state policy but only the decision of an individual. I'm sure it's different now."

As the four of us left the churchyard at 2:45 A.M., people carrying baskets to be blessed continued to stream up the village roads to the highest hill in Makov. At its pinnacle, the onion-domed church gazed benevolently down on the village.

April 30 (Easter): At noon today, we were pleased to see another sign of change: believers were being congratulated on national television on the occasion of Easter.

At 1:30 P.M., Nikolai Vasiliovich arrived in the van with Toli and Tanya to take us to the Chairman's home, a large tiled house (though not the most impressive in the village) with a lush flower garden covering the entire front yard. The garden is the Chairman's pride and joy. It's augmented with soil from his home village up north, soil so rich he said it would be good fertilizer for Ukraina farm.

He videotaped us in his garden with his Japanese camcorder. After we went inside, he popped the cassette into his Japanese VCR and showed it to us. He's often asked where he got the camcorder, and he asked Ralph if he could tell people that Ralph gave it to him. Ralph refused.

Chairman Stengach's wife, Lydia, wore a pleasant expression but said little. She has a summer kitchen, a building separate from the house, where she prepared the fine Easter dinner. Ukrainian Easter eggs decorated the table. Lydia is the Chairman's fourth wife and has no children. He has only one child (by his first wife), his daughter—a lung physician married to a neurosurgeon—and two granddaughters. They and two other couples rounded out the crowd. As at Valentina's dinner, these folk were also interested in our Easter festivities.

There's always champagne at guest dinners here. We don't drink, but we make it clear we don't mind if others do. Eloquent toasts are made, but ours aren't very good because we're not used to toasting.

We gave the Chairman a pin of crossed American and Soviet flags, exactly like the ones Reagan and Gorbachev wore when they signed the INF Treaty. He gave Ralph a pin with Gorbachev's picture on it. I was delighted because I hadn't seen such a pin, and we're strong Gorbachev supporters. It's unusual to see a picture of him here, except as part of the folder of Politburo members for sale in any bookstore. It's his choice not to have his image displayed.

After we returned home late this afternoon, we happened to see the greenhouse renters and their families who were having a picnic in the orchard. They invited us to join them, which we gladly did, adding American instant coffee to the meal. We relished the simple food and the honest, down-to-earth company.

CHAPTER 4

Christine's Journal Excerpts

MAY

May 1: This morning we watched the May Day parade at Red Square on TV. Colorfully dressed people marched, singing and dancing, past Lenin's tomb, where the highest officials stood. We're glad Gorbachev has changed the parade from a show of military power to a celebration of people and the holiday. In the past, whenever news of the USSR was on American TV, a movie clip of missiles and tanks moving across Red Square was always included, as if such parades happened every day. This image instilled fear and reinforced the idea the USSR was a war-mongering country. Actually, armaments were usually paraded in Moscow four times a year: February 23—Military Day, May Day—which honors labor, May 9—Victory Day, the celebration of the end of WWII, and November 7—the commemoration of the Revolution ending the czarist era. Now Gorbachev has omitted armaments from the May Day parade.

In the afternoon, Toli and his kindly brother-in-law, Valeri, surprised us by arriving to take us to Toli's for dinner. Anna didn't want us to be alone on a holiday. The crowd of 13 in Toli's one, all-purpose room included Toli and Tanya, Valeri and Lusa (Tanya's sister) from Kiev, Anna and her sister-in-law Nina, Sasha and Ola (neighbors), Anna's brother Vasily (who was visiting from a distant village), and Anna's four little grandsons, two by each daughter.

Vasily showed great enthusiasm for discussing US agriculture, saying he'd love to rent some land for himself, even though he's 65. It thrilled him to think of being an independent farmer!

I think Toli and his family have adopted us.

May 2: On this second day of the annual holiday, Ralph and I took a romantic walk in the large forest; a highlight was encountering a pair of deer who came close and fearlessly began to graze.

After we returned home, we went to a picnic in the village park with Toli's household and four other young families. In addition to our photographs, which we take everywhere we go, we now include a *National Geographic* magazine with a feature article and pictures about Ukraine and Chernobyl, and a special *Time* issue on the Soviet Union. The men exulted in *Time's* car advertisements. Wouldn't they be amazed to see the vast lots of shiny cars all over America just waiting for people to buy them? To get a car here, people wait up to 10 years, must have all the money up front, and usually need connections. The women, however, asked about Ralph's farm, especially about pig raising. Who said men are more practical?

It was a lively group, but at one point Ralph noticed a quiet scene that would have made a great photograph: two of the little daughters were curled up under a big tree by the lake, pouring over the *National Geographic*. I wonder what perestroika will bring these little ones. How different will their lives be from their mothers'?

As there have been visitors to our zoo today—the first ones we've seen—the nervous peacocks spent the day off the ground. They walked the roofs of the cages and sat in the tree the bears climb. Tonight, as they flew from the bear tree to their regular perch in the tall pines, one flew too far, missing the pines, and became entangled in a thick, deciduous tree. He fell out, looking embarrassed, but tried again with success.

May 3: Today Toli and two other men arrived with our car, a four-wheel-drive Niva. A new Niva had gone to the Chairman, his Niva went to Savkov, and Savkov's Niva came to us. After taking Toli back to school, we went for a drive. We ended up in a remote village and stopped to photograph its working wooden Russian Orthodox church, painted a vivid turquoise.

"Villages are as numerous as mushrooms in the USSR," a Russian friend of ours once said. As for the reason churches are often painted such bright, even garish, colors, I was told it represents affirmation of life.

There's been much more rain this year than normal, and the same thing is occurring in Ohio after last year's drought. Some of the village roads are nearly impassable, making the Niva most welcome. Paved roads are rare in rural USSR, but Makov has two of them. One is in front of Headquarters, an impressive two-story building, which is usually bustling, thanks to the party and farm offices it houses. Even the road to Stupentsi remains unpaved (though Stupentsi is, it's dawning on us, a Communist Party "party" area). The farm's road graders keep it level and in great shape—for a dirt road. In one part of our village, we've seen foot-deep ruts in the soft mud. Even our four-wheel-drive might find these difficult.

Later, we took Toli with us to the Kamenets-Podolski post office and to meet his friend and contemporary, Kostya. He teaches English in a military school there. Kostya is tall and lean, and his extraordinary politeness is relieved by a terrific sense of humor. Both he and Toli speak with a British accent because British English, not American, is taught in the USSR. As we sat in the Niva along a narrow city street, Kostya expressed delight in being able to talk with native English speakers and showed interest in spending more time with us. Toli thought that might be impossible because of his military connections, though Kostya is anything but a militarist.

After that, we stopped at a dental clinic to see about my gray teeth. Toli calls it the "House of Terrors," so I let fear get the better of me when a woman dentist attempted to polish the black off. Though she was gentle, I was worried some enamel might be removed and called out frantically, "Stop! Stop!" When Ralph insisted, she did. While we were there, however, the dentists admired the workmanship on the many gold fillings in my back teeth. Then Ralph climbed into the chair to show them his front bridgework (necessary because of a basketball teammate's elbow). They were impressed. Soviet dentists are handicapped by a lack of basic supplies, such as drill bits and filling materials.

Everything's so peaceful here in our birch woods—few traffic sounds, just bird calls, woodpecker tappings, frog "ribbits," and an occasional horse-drawn wagon's clop-clop, rattle-rattle blending with the zoo sounds. I'll probably never live in a more beautiful natural setting. It's so much more satisfying than a city's asphalt, glass, and concrete.

The view, however, is restrictive. Our house is surrounded by an eight-foot-high, bright-green board fence (probably so no one could witness the frolicking when party "parties" were being held). We always have to run upstairs when we hear a noise outside to see what it is.

We leave the double gate at the end of our driveway wide open to indicate our accessibility. For a long time Johanna and others who work at Stupentsi kept closing it, but we wired it open, and finally, the caretakers gave up.

Since the phone and TV don't take much of our time, I'm working out some childhood trauma. I spend time each day reading spiritual books, among them *Peace Pilgrim* and *A Course in Miracles*.

Another little project, which is taking many hours, is the copying of a small devotional booklet I picked up at the airport chapel in Brussels, Belgium. I'm using carbon paper and a heavy hand to make three copies of these thirty pages' worth of Bible verses in Russian. I want to give them to Anna, Nina, and Valentina—just in case they don't have anything like it. It makes me appreciate the access to copy machines we have in the States. Here, they are few and far-between, even in Moscow. Makov has no copy machine, and we know of only one typewriter. In our Ohio home we use our copier almost daily.

Tonight a friend from Dayton called us from Kiev. She's leading a group of 17 people on a Crosscurrents International Institute tour, and we're to meet them there. But it's sooner than we anticipated.

May 4: "Ohhhh! What a day!" (As my son John says comically). At 8:30 A.M., two young men from *Izvestia* arrived—a journalist from Kiev and a photographer from Leningrad. The journalist thinks land should be owned, not rented, and he says it's already being done in Estonia.

We spent the entire day together. United Press International has ordered seventy photos of us, and we had to pose two hundred times in different places around the village—at the school, church, outside the day care center, with elderly villagers, in the field, etc.

It was chafing for Ralph, who hates to pose for pictures. Easier for him, but more difficult for me, is being interviewed. He thinks well on his feet, while I prefer to write or prepare ahead. He was quite at home with the five-hour interview this morning. Ralph feels comfortable with reporters because during his whole life, he says, they've always been fair with him.

Also, we had our first really frustrating experience with bureaucracy. We wanted to drive our car to Kiev to see the tour group people, some of whom we know, and to pick up what was brought to us from Dayton, including a birthday gift for 14-year-old Tatiana Palamarchouk from her papa. A man we had never met, Anatoli Dovgal, who's in charge of International Relations for Regional Gosagroprom, was in Makov today. (Perhaps he came to check on the *Izvestia* reporters). We asked him about our trip to Kiev. We'd been trying to get permission for two weeks, with no response. Now we were down to the last day.

He and Toli were riding in the back seat of our Niva when he stated, "You have to make out a day-by-day program for the whole time you're here and submit it."

"That would be very difficult," I said, "as we don't know how things will develop."

"Okay then," he countered. "Let's have a one-week, day-by-day plan and a summer plan with the big events on it. Also, you know you're not to drive your car outside the Region."

"A few years ago," said Ralph, "a friend of ours and his wife rented a car in Moscow and drove by themselves all the way to a southern Republic."

"Well, if you take your car," said Dovgal, "you'll have to have a driver."

"What about our borrowing Valentina's car?" I asked.

"Probably the car's in Viktor's name," he responded. "You would have to get his permission, and he's in Ohio. So Valentina would have to go along to drive."

And so it went. I saw the back of Ralph's neck getting pink, and I knew that he was angry—a rare occurrence—but he didn't show it otherwise. After awhile, I decided to change my attitude toward this Anatoli. I began to see him as a man required to carry out orders, who might be as uncomfortable with these restrictions as we were. Of course, that subtly changed *my* behavior.

I decided to call Valentin Oozhin in Kiev to see if he could help us. He said, "I'll call Headquarters and try to talk to Dovgal, but my hands are tied because only my boss, Solodky, has the authority to give you permission." Solodky is Ukraine Gosagroprom's Director of International Relations.

(Incidentally, I find it amusing that Oozhin means "supper" and Solodky means "sweet" in Russian. Are people required to have food names to work at the Department of Agriculture?)

Actually, we were surprised when we met with Solodky in Kiev in early April. We discovered, although he is attractive and personable, that he seems to know little about agriculture. In fact, we think the crazy notion of Ralph's farming land here may have come from Solodky, simply because he had no idea of what else to do with us.

Finally, about 8 P.M., after the Chairman signed a paper saying he had no objection to our going to Kiev, and following two hours of mysterious actions by Dovgal, it was decided. We were to go in a farm van, with Nikolai Vasiliovich driving and Toli accompanying us. What a lot of unnecessary ado! Oh, well. At least we're going!

May 5: At 7 A.M., we stood at our gate with our little suitcase, enjoying the blossoming orchard and the hens cackling across the driveway. At eight, the van arrived with driver Nikolai Vasiliovich, Toli, and Tanya. First, we had to go two places in Khmelnitski to get papers signed. Farther on, a railroad track was being repaired, and that required a 45-minute wait.

Then, just before five o'clock, the van began to make a terrible noise, so we pulled over to the side of the road. Ralph and Nikolai looked under it and saw that a drive-shaft bearing had frozen up. Providentially, we saw a truck yard about a five-minute walk away!

Nikolai took off his pants, right in front of us, revealing striped boxer shorts. He put on his coveralls and a different hat and took off the bearing while Toli and Ralph walked to the truck yard to keep someone there after closing time. As luck would have it, they had a bearing, which they *gave* us (as they are not allowed to sell anything). Nikolai worked another couple of hours while Tanya and I had fun sitting in the van teaching each other English and Russian. She said, "We are good together," which pleased me very much. Most car owners carry tools along and know how to fix their cars anywhere. Periodically there are car ramps beside the road for drivers to change oil or make repairs.

We arrived at the hotel in Kiev about 10:30—eight hours later than expected—found our friend, and talked until after midnight. Toli and Tanya stayed with her sister, Lusa, and husband, Valeri, but Nikolai preferred to sleep in the van, though he had a hotel room. His room cost ten rubles, but ours—the same size—cost fifty because we are foreign tourists.

May 6: We met this morning with Solodky at the large Gosagroprom building in downtown Kiev. Mild-mannered Valentin Oozhin struggled with the translation, but after an hour, Toli arrived, and the atmosphere changed dramatically. He spoke with authority about problems we were having: the lack of meetings, isolation, use of the car only in the Region, etc. He also talked about the possibility of my youngest son, 19-year-old Joel, coming to Makov for awhile this summer, and our going to Krasnodar.

After Toli finished speaking, Solodky smiled at me and said, "Well, we've met the other member of your family now! I'll try to help you with your problems at Makov and your desire to go to Krasnodar *if* you can get me in touch with someone there who will take responsibility for you. But I can do nothing to help your son get to Makov. Frankly, it's something new, and there's no procedure for it."

Over the years, initiative has been punished rather than rewarded, so few will risk making a change. We're learning everything we do must be done officially and with permission, and someone at our destination must take responsibility for us. We think Ukraine may be more finicky about this than the Russian Republic. There's a Soviet saying that fits here: "Without a paper, I am an insect. With a paper, I am a man."

The suitcases of the Ohio group were laden with treasures for us—a movie about soil conservation, mail, five pounds of sweet corn seed, bug spray for our ants, farm magazines, and Viktor's birthday gift to his daughter—a walkman. Sue, Ralph's daughter-in-law, had gathered these for us. She also sent along two long letters she'd written about what was happening on Ralph's farm. These were most welcome, especially to Ralph, as his farm is so important to him. It sounds as if Palamarchouk, Nik, and Ralph's family are all getting along well together.

At first, when we discovered that Nik (the son of a higher-up in the Ukraine Gosagroprom) had been sent to America to "learn more language," we were worried he wouldn't work out. However, Sue said he's doing very well. He's industrious, always smiling, and friendly.

A couple of places in Sue's letters brought tears to our eyes—descriptions of warm, loving interchanges between the Ukrainian farmers and Ohioans. Often an American would remark, "Wow! I've never met a Soviet before!" and then, "Welcome!"

In the evening, Ralph and I joined the Dayton group in their "home visits" around Kiev. Nikolai Vasiliovich took our group in the Makov van to the apartment of a young man in his early twenties and his mother. He teaches English to pre-teens "independently" (meaning he is paid not by the state, as is usual, but by the children's parents). Several of his students were there, and we had fun playing English language games with them. He said he'd taught for a co-op, but they took so much of his income he decided to go out on his own.

While we were playing the games, his mother set up a fancy table for us, loaded with food and drink. Later, she gave us beautiful napkins her grandmother had embroidered. When we departed, I left mine behind. To refuse a gift is insulting to the host, but I simply couldn't take a family heirloom.

"I want to get married," said our host, "but I just don't have the money. My mother and I have only enough money for two to live."

He continued to talk, and his criticism of the party led me to think he was not a member. I was surprised when both he and his mother proudly claimed membership. I was under the impression all party members had larger apartments, special stores, hospitals, resorts, and other privileges. It must be only the upper echelons of the apparatus who get these luxuries. I also thought members were not critical of the party, but obviously some are. I'm glad to have my misconceptions corrected.

May 7: Before we said goodbye to our Dayton friends, we had a good interview with Misha Alexeyev of *News From Ukraine*, an English-language newspaper sold mostly in Canada and the States. Misha is 26, handsome, and exuberant. His English is so perfect he has passed for a Britisher. He was in the States recently as a translator for the Kiev Soccer Team.

It felt good to get back to our house in Makov. Now that I have the ant poison, I really don't want to use it, but the ants are marching into my kitchen cupboards during the daytime again. I informed them they had better just come at night from now on or I will have to use the poison!

Today, my third son, Neil, 22, graduates from Miami University in Ohio. I really hate to miss it!

May 8: A man from the newspaper *Silski Visti* (Ukrainian Agriculture), with a circulation of two million, interviewed Ralph for four hours today, intending to print a long article. Ralph considered it his best interview to date because the reporter knew so much about farming. We were pleased Anatoli Dovgal sat with us, too, taking notes. Savkov and Valarovsky of the District were also here, and we invited them in, but they preferred to stand outside for a couple of hours, waiting to talk to the journalist after he finished with Ralph. All these officials have drivers, so these men were also waiting outside our gate in their cars. It seems that Savkov has been trying to avoid Ralph. I wonder what's bothering him?

May 9: Today is Victory Day. Toli, Ralph, and I went to Chechelnik, the next largest of Ukraina's five villages, to attend the dedication of their new memorial to the dead of WWII. It was a gilded statue of a soldier, head lowered, standing on a concrete platform about ten steps higher than the street where we stood. As the rain fell gently, a war veteran and Viktor, Ukraina's meek party secretary, each read their part of the ceremony, followed by the contrasting style of Chairman Stengach, who needs no notes.

A man was busy using the Chairman's camcorder, including taking closeups of us as we stood near the back. Children in rainbow-colored clothes held portraits of dead Chechelnik soldiers and sang forcefully from their formation on the steps. (Child soloists are trained to be heard 100 yards away.) A four-foot wreath was then placed at the foot of the statue.

It seems strange to us new monuments are still being dedicated so many years after the war—though we know people were deeply affected and with good reason. Few Americans are taught Soviets lost one-tenth of their population—twenty million people, forty times as many as we did—and sustained great devastation to their industry, land, and housing. After the war, many people lived in tents and starved. Post-war life for Soviets was far different from life in post-war America.

There's a priority of values ingrained in Soviet culture we dare not judge. This different value system was apparent in the monumental efforts after World War II, especially during the first decade. Americans can't comprehend why, for instance, Russians at Stalingrad (now Volgograd) would rob the overwhelming reconstruction effort of manpower and resources to build a 200-foot-tall steel monument. There stands a woman brandishing a sword the weight of a boxcar beckoning her people to defend the motherland from invaders.

Monument-building all over the country took priority over house-building, industry, and food production. Stalingrad was 99 percent destroyed when the Soviets turned Hitler's army around in 1942. Only three trees in the entire city were green the next year. Millions of the strong lay in graves. The people suffered enormously—more than we as Americans can even imagine. But we think it's time for them to move on. They should remember the horrors but stop blaming problems on the war.

In the evening, Toli's family and Kostya and his wife from Kamenets-Podolski surprised us by bringing food for supper. I added more food and soft drinks. Another fruit of perestroika is that Kostya can have contact with foreigners. In the past, this was strictly forbidden for those with military connections. We used the dining room table upstairs for the first time, and Kostya helped me carry dishes. His wife, whom he calls "The Colonel," enjoyed sitting. We've heard there's a lot of male chauvinism in the USSR, but as everywhere, it depends on the man. Toli sometimes cleans his family's apartment, for example, and helps in the garden.

We notice Soviet people serve each other at the table, and some reach for what they want without asking. We showed them "family-style" passing of food, with each taking his or her own food, and most of them said, "This makes sense because I'm the one who knows how much I want." Toli, however, prefers to have Tanya put everything on his plate. Ralph and I try to remember that if something isn't done in our particular way, that doesn't make it wrong, just different. After all, one could argue the Soviet way of reaching for what he wants is better because it inconveniences no one.

Late in the evening, we all piled into the Niva and delivered both families to their homes. We've discovered Soviets walk guests to their car or home instead of waving goodbye at the door as Americans do. Several times on our trips people have taken us from their apartment across the city on the bus or subway and dropped us at our hotel door. Tonight, we appreciated these folk coming to be with us on the holiday. Many Americans would also do this, but, in general, Soviets have a stronger sense of being involved with each other—a connective, collective, protective feeling.

May 10: The Chairman paid us a visit to tell us we can go anywhere in the Region and do whatever we want, and he'll take full responsibility. Maybe we've passed a test of some kind and he feels he can trust us, or maybe he's just feeling expansive. In any case, we're glad, although we've never felt restricted—in the *Region*, that is.

In the afternoon, Viktor Party Secretary spent a couple of hours getting to know us, looking at farm magazines, pictures, etc. He's a mild, smiling young man who used to be a teacher before he was chosen to be party secretary. This post is the most powerful one in the cities or farms, though the Chairman is definitely the main man in Makov. We had met Viktor earlier and, not knowing his last name, decided to call him "Viktor Party Secretary." (We've dubbed Anatoli Dovgal "Buddha" because he's round, gentle, and rather looks like a Buddha. We're not sure if he'd like the nickname, so we've kept it to ourselves.)

Viktor Party Secretary got his prestigious post when he married a relative of the Chairman, and he's now a go-fer for Stengach. He knows little about farming and so isn't respected by those who do. A cruel joke was played on him once: The peas didn't come up one year, and when he asked why, the farmers said it was because they were planted upside-down. He believed this and scolded them, telling them never to do it again. Of course, this made him a laughing-stock.

May 11: Toli was able to engage the village film projectionist so we could preview our 25-minute soil conservation film. There's no theater in Makov, so I thought the projectionist wouldn't have a full-time job. However, Toli says he does, as the House of Culture, the sanatorium, and the sugar factory regularly show movies. Our film was originally requested by the World Family Clubs. Its president told us in Moscow right before we came to Makov that they would fly Ralph to speak at various cities throughout the USSR, but we haven't heard from them. Perhaps the film can be used to some advantage at other speaking engagements. We tape-recorded the English narrative so Toli can write the Russian translation on paper.

Later, we stopped at the house of Ludmila and Nikolai, who are always so cordial to us. They greeted us warmly, and Nikolai's smile of delight wriggled his whole body. I use my Russian more with him than with anyone else because we discuss my food order. The dear man is one of those persons, like many all over the world, who speaks *louder* but just as quickly when asked, "Please, speak more slowly." (I'm not deaf, just dumb.)

Nikolai tried to make us feel at home by showing us an American movie on their Panasonic VCR. It was a crazy story about a man who'd forgotten to put out his garbage and was running after the truck, waving a full trash bag. Instead of stopping, the garbage men downed him with their machine guns. We didn't watch long enough to find out why. After five minutes, we asked Nikolai to turn it off. It gave us reverse culture shock.

One thing we enjoy about the Soviet Union is the lack of television violence. Children's cartoons have gentle, human plots and sometimes beautiful art work. One cartoon I remember showed a little bear happily running through the forest, but when he saw his inquisitive reflection in the pond, it scared him. He asked the wise owl what to do and was told to make friends with his enemy. So he went back and smiled into the pond, and, of course, his reflection smiled back. Happy ending!

Nikolai proudly showed their house of six large rooms. Their curtains and bedspreads are the same golden, silky material as ours.

I wondered how this family could have a Japanese VCR and American videos. Ludmila has a tiny salary as head of the machine yard canteen, and Nikolai works for her. Toli told us later Ludmila and Nikolai are part of the Chairman's entourage, people who serve him for favors. They're members of the local nomenklatura, party people appointed by ruling officials. (These ruling officials are called the apparatus and are part of the huge nomenklatura.) The nomenklatura receive bureaucratic jobs, and if they botch their work, aren't fired but are moved to another bureaucratic job.

For example, Gorbachev created Gosagroprom four years ago to consolidate farm programs. It soon became so bureaucratic it was supposedly abolished—nationwide—about the time we arrived in Makov. Yet most of the people still work in the same building, and even the name's the same.

One time I heard an American socialist say on the radio that the system in the Soviet Union is simply another form of class society. And so it is. The apparatus/nomenklatura is the privileged ruling class. They even try to marry within their ranks. I think that's why the Chairman called the blustery RadioKiev man, "Brother." Most of them are the real enemies of perestroika. They selfishly want to keep the status quo.

The local apparatus—the Chairman—has kingly powers in the village and farm. He decides who gets which job, who gets a car, who gets a larger apartment, who gets a plot of land for a home, and even who gets bricks to build one. Thus, many people ingratiate themselves with the Chairman.

Toli says there are basically four categories of people in the village: the high officials and their entourage; those trying to court the officials for future favors; the thinking people of integrity like Toli and the Greenhouse Gang; and the common laborers who work hard and live as best they can.

Toli has one of the highest salaries in the village, but he and his family have only a one-room apartment (though, in addition, they have a small kitchen, hall, and bathroom with cold, running water). Toli has asked the Chairman twice for a bigger apartment, and the answer both times was, "Impossible!" In one case, a larger apartment went to a smaller family a week later. The national rule of allowing a certain number of square meters of living space per person is obviously disregarded in this village. According to Toli, the cruelest part of the system is that one cannot rely on oneself.

Toli said the Chairman originally wanted to hire the other English teacher to be our translator. However, her poorer English might have been embarrassing for the farm when the media descended on us. So he reluctantly hired Toli at the last minute.

Salaries are discussed freely, and the average on this farm is 160 rubles a month. The average nationwide is 250 rubles. Forty million Soviets (out of a population of 290 million) live under poverty level—75 rubles. Many of them are pensioners, Central Asians, and students of higher education. "Decency level" (when one doesn't have to watch every kopek) is 280 rubles. Toli's salary is 300 rubles.

The stated number of rooms in an apartment (the home of all city-dwellers and five percent of Makov's inhabitants) never includes kitchen, halls, and bathrooms. The bathroom, by the way, is nearly always divided into two tiny rooms—one for a sink and a bathtub, which may have a flexible shower attachment—and one for the toilet.

Probably the reason these rooms are not officially included is many Soviets still share those facilities with other families in crowded apartments. It's reported only 15 percent of people live that way now, fewer than ever before. Almost no *houses* have running water or inside toilets, so in Makov, there's a public building where people take showers. Journalist Misha Alexeyev had wondered aloud which was better: the thousand of homeless in the US or the generally poor living conditions in the USSR.

May 12: Every two or three mornings we're greeted by a tiny toad or a salamander in our bathroom. We gently put it outside in the flowers. The ants took my advice the very next day, disappeared from the kitchen, and haven't been back, so I don't have to use the poison.

We went to Kamenets-Podolski to speak to English language students at the Pedagogical Institute where students are training to be teachers. Roza, who teaches there, and her husband, Viktor, the director of the school in the Shatava part of Makov, came early one morning last week to ask us to speak, catching me in my bathrobe.

As we entered, we saw a hundred or more smiling, expectant faces. They asked many questions, and then a small group sang the Beatles' "Let It Be" (one of my favorite songs). I responded by singing in Russian and English the chorus of "May There Always Be Sunshine," that famous Soviet children's song all American citizen diplomats have heard. They gave us gifts, and pretty girls in lavish Ukrainian costumes sang folk songs and served us pelmeni stuffed with meat.

Toli, Christine, and Ralph speaking at language institute in Kamenets-Podolski.

Many people stayed afterwards for additional discussion, and Janna, one of the teachers, enthusiastically approached me to say how happy she was to speak to Americans. But when I suggested our getting together for more conversation, her mood changed to one of fear, and she made a quick getaway. The fear is left over, I'm sure, from the years when having contact with foreigners could be punished. It's difficult for people to go from doing *what is permitted* to doing *what isn't prohibited*, an important step in perestroika.

The young people are bolder. Two boys, Andrei and Sergei, told Ralph they want to visit us in Makov, and several students gave us their names and addresses for American pen pals. Andrei is the busy, bustling Komsomol leader of this institute's language department, and he asked many questions during the meeting. I remembered him from among the questioners because of his radiant smile and bright eyes.

Volodya, a genteel, half-Jewish young man talked to me about his great love for music. When I asked him who he liked, he mentioned the Beatles—most Soviets adore them—Michael Jackson, and Jethro Tull. He also took me aside to ask if his five-year Institute degree would be recognized were he to emigrate to America. I thought not.

This evening, we spent two hours watching Vladimir Pozner interview Valentin Berezhkov on television. It was especially interesting to us because we've met both men. We spent ten days with Berezhkov, an unassuming, white-haired yoga practitioner, on a Crosscurrents International Institute Volga River Cruise in 1988. He was picked at age 22 to be Stalin's interpreter and was with him at Yalta and the Potsdam Conference with Roosevelt and Churchill. He also went with Molotov to Berlin to meet with Hitler, and he remembers all that was said. Toli interpreted the program for us.

Valentin Berezhkov, Stalin's interpreter (white hair). Gray-haired man, as a boy, heard Lenin speak.

Ralph has read Berezhkov's book, *History in the Making*. There he gives his personal impressions about WWII. For example, he tells how unimpressed he was when he saw Hitler in person. The book came out in 1978, and in it, Berezhkov never faulted the Soviet Union, though he accuses the Allies, especially Britain, of bad motives.

It's amazing the wheeling and dealing all parties did in that war. For instance, it is widely believed one reason the British appeased Hitler early on and later delayed the Western front was their hope Hitler would beat up the Soviets awhile. Berezhkov said the Big Three (Stalin, Roosevelt, and Churchill) considered their union temporary and forced, though a great front was put on to suggest otherwise.

Earlier, when Hitler was initiating the German/Soviet pact—the one in which he gave the Baltics to Stalin—the two felt a special kinship with each other, although I think they never met personally. When Hitler killed his best friend, Roehm, Stalin called Hitler a "bright boy" who knew how to deal with his political enemies. Berezhkov said, "Hitler and Stalin felt they could read each other's thoughts."

But Stalin didn't read Hitler's. He never thought the Germans would break their pact and invade the Soviet Union, even after the Soviet ambassador to Germany and many others warned him they would. But it happened, and Stalin went into stunned seclusion for days. When he emerged, Berezhkov saw for the first time not a giant but a man, a fallible, small, thin, and ill-looking man with a gray face and one arm shorter than the other.

On the program, Berezhkov spoke of things he was compelled to be silent about before. He told of Stalin's weaknesses and lapses, but said, at that time, he was in awe of Stalin. "Stalinists should be treated carefully because they really believe. I did," he said.

In Berezhkov's opinion, Stalin's most horrible crime was convincing people the way of life he created represented true socialism. "We lived like half-slaves in such a big country, and we thought it was normal," he said.

"Now, when I know of all his crimes against people, I wonder how I was able to survive. One time, I was interpreting during dinner and bit off a piece of sausage, creating a situation in which I could neither swallow nor speak, and Stalin became angry. His mass-murdering henchman, Beria, was there, but the moment passed. Others were killed for lesser crimes.

"Stalin continued his policy of terror after the war," he said, "because the Soviet soldiers who went into Germany saw that the Germans had hams in their basements and lived well, even though they were losing the war. We'd been told our way of life was the best in the world, other than the 'money-bags' who ruled America, so Stalin had to put a stop to the questions."

The last time we were with Pozner was in January, 1988. While we were in Tallinn with a group from Fellowship of Reconciliation, I found myself on an elevator in our hotel with one other passenger—Vladimir Pozner. I said, "Hi!" and he responded in kind. Then I said, "I hugged you once."

"When and where?" he asked.

"In the House of Friendship in Moscow in 1985," I answered. The elevator went up and down, up and down, as we talked. Finally, I said, "I'm here with a group. Would you be so kind as to speak to us? It would be a highlight of our trip."

He laughed and said, "It's kind of short notice, isn't it?"

But he met with us—actually wishing his schedule permitted him more time—and he spoke thoughtfully about the changes in the Soviet Union. He said, "You may not see me so much anymore [on American TV] because I'm now dedicated to working on the changes in my own country. I want very much for perestroika to succeed, but we may not make it, and this is our last chance."

Vladimir Pozner and Christine in 1985. Dr. Kenneth Brown
enjoying the activity.

He also talked about the value of people-to-people contact. "In 1980, no
one would have given you two cents for the citizen diplomat movement,"
he said, "but it has been extremely valuable and has had great effect on both
our countries."

Later, Ralph and I went to see him in his hotel room, told him of our
desire to live in the USSR, and gave him Ralph's resume. "Do you mean
you'd let our farmers pick your brains?" he asked. Ralph assented. "Well,"
he said, taking the resume, "I think maybe I can help you." We didn't hear
from him again; we realize how extremely busy he must always be. But we
were delighted our first resume went to Vladimir Pozner.

Ralph and I agree with him on the value of citizen diplomacy. On all our
visits to the USSR, we and others ignored some of the Intourist tours and
instead went to the streets, subways, and churches to meet people. In the
big cities, many people speak English, so language was usually not a
problem.

To continue our work as citizen diplomats after returning home, we gave
programs about what we had experienced in the USSR. We've witnessed
wonderful changes in the attitudes of Americans who expected to see
desperately unhappy Soviets (or people with horns on their heads!). Instead
they saw our slides of people we'd seen—babies, smiling teenagers in jeans
and gym shoes, well-educated young marrieds, and generous babushkas.

One common American misconception is that Soviets don't smile. They
smile as much as we do, but not on the street, where visiting Americans are

most likely to see them. There, they wait in line, and historically have been careful not to be too conspicuous or friendly to strangers.

At one of our programs, in a Methodist country church in Ohio, two seminary students doing a paper on reactions to our program had the audience fill out questionnaires. Here are some of the comments, typical of what we've often heard:

"We are really a lot alike in many respects."

"It was very interesting to learn more about the Russians and how they live. It's so great to feel we may be able to communicate and live in peace."

"I never understood much about how the Soviets lived. You never hear about the people; it's always the government in the news."

"I was happy to learn that the people are warm. I had pictured them as cold and distant."

"I was surprised to learn that only six percent are Communists."

"We thought that everyone there was an atheist. We didn't know that the church has as much freedom as it does."

"I didn't realize how much they suffered during WWII and therefore want peace so much."

"It humbles me to realize that Soviets actually like us, when we have disliked them all these years."

May 13: Every day I write to someone—friends in the US and the USSR. The first letter we received, other than those brought to us in Kiev, was from a friend in Tallinn, Estonia. Now we're beginning to get letters from Soviets who've read about us in the media.

This evening, as we were taking a ride to inspect the farm, we saw three large animals loping across a field. At first we thought they were foxes, but as we came closer, we could see they were jackrabbits—the first we've seen here.

On a lonely road we picked up a babushka who talked continuously. After awhile, I kept hearing the word "toot" interspersed in her stream of chatter, and I told Ralph I'd have to look up that word in the dictionary when we got home. I knew she wanted to go to the Shatava part of Makov, but she didn't indicate a stopping place. She just kept talking. Finally, when we drove through Shatava and started toward Kamenets-Podolski, her cheerful expression changed to one of alarm. Then she indicated she wanted out! After kissing our hands, she began walking back towards town. We had a good laugh when we discovered "toot" means "right here!" I'd learned "zdes" for "here."

After midnight, the phone rang. It was my oldest son, Ted, calling to wish me Happy Mother's Day. What a treat! It's hard getting telephone calls to and from the States in this country village. When it happens, the line is often so bad, one must scream into the mouthpiece. I've designated Ted to be official caller for my family and any friends who want to get quick messages to us—Ted's persistent and knows some Russian.

May 15: As a former teacher, I've been itching to get into the village school. It seems strange we've not been invited to see places in the village, nor has there been an official gathering for us to meet the people. After being here over a month and not being invited to visit the school, I decided to take the initiative and asked Toli if we could visit his class. He replied, "Of course!"

So today we watched him demonstrate a lesson, and then he had us and the children ask each other questions in English. He creates a relaxed but professional atmosphere, and it's obvious the students like him.

Every child in this village is required to take English from fourth grade through high school; and nationwide, 60 percent of students choose to study English. Children here learn to read in Ukrainian; then, in the second grade, they begin to study Russian. When they graduate at seventeen, they have mastered Ukrainian and Russian and have a smattering of English.

When we met Olga, the other English teacher, I said I'd expected more regimentation in the school. She laughed, saying, "Oh, no, it's impossible! They're children!" To me, the atmosphere seemed very familiar, with children chatting in the halls while they hurried to class and teachers gathering in the lounge for a break.

The teachers' meeting room and every classroom and hall were nicely decorated with flowers, plants, and natural objects. Many of the plants, for example, were placed on stumps instead of tables. A large indoor garden with cacti and other plants was on the floor near the front door.

This Soviet regard for natural beauty doesn't mean the USSR doesn't have a terrible pollution problem. It does. But the people recognize the personal worth of frequent contact with nature. I've been gratified to see here, for example, that many television interviews are deliberately done out-of-doors, even when the story has nothing to do with nature.

The *Izvestia* article about Ralph came out today. I thought it was rather sensationalized. There was a long quote from the Chairman, saying he was disappointed Ralph didn't come with his machines, seeds, and fertilizers to take a plot of land and show what he could do. The story emphasized what the Chairman had done for us and ended with the question, "What does this American farmer have to teach us?"

Wouldn't the available space have been better used *answering* that question, especially since Ralph spent five hours detailing his suggestions for Soviet agriculture? Perhaps the journalist needed to please conservative superiors. On the other hand, maybe it was a positive question, and something got lost in the translation. *Izvestia* is much more open now, but old habits die hard. What a tug-of-war is going on in this country!

The country's two main newspapers are *Izvestia*, the newspaper of the government, and *Pravda*, the party's paper. Each has a circulation of 10 million. Izvestia means "news" and pravda means "truth." There's an old saying here: "There is no news in *Izvestia* and no truth in *Pravda*." That has changed greatly in both papers, but *Izvestia* outstrips *Pravda* in forthrightness. Still, glasnost hasn't allowed absolute freedom of speech yet.

Here's an appropriate Soviet anecdote:

> There was once a king who decreed that 2+2=6, and all his subjects echoed that. When he died, the next king changed the decree to read 2+2=5, and the people declared this to be the truth. But a young scientist working in his lab one day discovered that 2+2 really equals 4. At that very moment, two men dressed in black overcoats and hats appeared in his lab and announced, "You may not tell anyone that 2+2=4."
>
> "Why not?" asked the young scientist. "It's the truth."
>
> "Would you rather that 2+2 equaled 6 again?" was the ominous response.

(Do Moscow and Washington sometimes tell us 2+2=5?)

Another interesting happening today was Ralph's meeting with Ukraina's young economist. This tall, lean young man with thick glasses and enormous hands, came to our house and had a four-hour session with Ralph. He wanted to know all kinds of figures about Ralph's Ohio hogs. He'll come again for a session on crops sometime.

Afterwards, instead of taking Toli home, we took him to Anna's house, where he does his tutoring in its quietness. Anna and Nina each have a flat in a four-apartment, 100-year-old house painted that shade of sky blue I love. The inside of Anna's flat is the same blue, and everything, including her floor-to-ceiling stuccoed stove for heating and cooking, is scrubbed clean. The stove has a little door in the side for fuel (wood or coal) and a niche with two places to put pans for cooking. She has two rooms, plus a tiny kitchen and bathroom. The latter is for taking sponge baths because there's no running water or a toilet in the house. Correction! She does have running water. It works like this: There's a little tank above the sink which she fills from the top with buckets of water from an outside well. When she turns on its faucet, that's her running water.

Her furnishings are pretty, from the oriental rugs on the wall (even the poorest families seem to have these), to the highly lacquered wardrobe, to her nine-by-twelve-inch silvery icon. In a prominent position on a shelf are the peace prayer card and the tiny creche I had given her. She pulled out a worn, 1903 New Testament and a prayer book, dated 1970, and asked Toli to translate one of the prayers for us. He refused, saying, "The language is archaic."

Her chickens and pigs are kept in a shed out back, and her half-acre garden and outhouse are behind the shed. I spotted her root cellar, a grassy mound with a wooden door on one side, and descended a short flight of stairs into the cool underground. There I saw root crops—potatoes, carrots, beets, and onions—and neat shelves of home-canned fruit and juices. This is probably the same life lived by Ukrainian and Russian villagers for hundreds of years, except now nearly everyone is educated and has electricity and a television.

Anna's eyes are that brilliant Ukrainian blue that always dazzles me, and she's very energetic. She has been a widow for many years and worked hard to raise Tanya and Lusa, even giving Lusa room and board money during her years at an institute. Tanya was just 17 when she married 24-year-old Toli, though she went to business school afterwards.

Anna's now 60 and retired, but she helps with her grandchildren. Ten-year-old Vova often sleeps at his grandmother's to ease cramped quarters at home. And the help goes the other way, too, with Toli and Tanya giving a hand to Anna when she needs it. It's a typical babushka/family relationship. Nina's 65 and alone, being a widow with no children, but she's also part of the family. Her brother was Anna's husband, and the two babushkas are quite close.

Toli once told us a sad tale about Anna and her husband. They married when they were in their early 20s, but he was an alcoholic. They bickered, and sometimes he beat her. So Anna, with her two little girls, left him. One night he got drunk, came to her house, and stabbed her repeatedly in the chest. She survived only because a caring doctor stopped the blood with his fingers and then performed surgery. When her husband sobered up and realized what he had done, he went to the place he was born and hanged himself. She has been alone ever since.

After we left Anna's, we jounced along narrow, winding lanes through the poorer sections of Makov where all the houses are stucco cottages like Anna's without any plumbing. The yards were neat with stacks of wood by the houses and manure piles beside nearby animal sheds. Full clotheslines were often visible.

In many ways, the Soviet Union is like a developing country—certainly when it comes to toilets or the lack of them. Public toilets in this country are filthy and can be primitive. We prefer to use the forest if we're not home.

May 17: We visited the school again today and observed three classes—the second and eleventh grades and a music class. We enjoyed them all but saw they are indeed more regimented than American classrooms. In their uniforms, the children stand next to their chairs to recite. In Ukraine, girls wear brown dresses, with black aprons for everyday and white aprons for special occasions, and boys wear white shirts with brown pants and jacket. Of course, as in our parochial schools, they wear their own colorful sweaters and socks.

We watched the cheerful music teacher directing a variety of activities with the first grade: singing, moving to music, marching, reading music, and clapping different rhythms. He has no piano, so he uses an accordion.

The second grade teacher demonstrated a math lesson, sometimes tapping impatiently on her desk with a baton to hurry the children along, or moving around the room to see how the written work was going. In between lessons, a little boy led his class in exercises to music.

In the eleventh grade, the final year of high school, the standing recitations were long, and of course we didn't understand them, though the teacher had Natasha sit by us to interpret. These students are preparing for their three weeks' of exams in June which they must pass to graduate on June 17. Ralph gave a five-dollar solar calculator to this teacher, which she later flashed around to her gaping colleagues. He didn't realize it was inappropriate; its value in Makov is 20 times more than in the States.

When we talked with the teachers in the lounge, they asked us to come back Monday at 5 P.M. for an official meeting. The eleventh graders invited us to their Last Bell ceremony on May 25, too. As we were leaving, we saw the geography teacher showing children a live, half-grown owl she had found, just as an American teacher might do.

We saw no school buses, and Toli said some children must walk as far as seven miles (one way) to school. I could hardly believe it, but I've read Gorbachev had to walk 12 (!) to get to school. He showed such promise the people in his village pooled their money to buy him good shoes for the road. One can easily see why the pace of life is much slower here in the countryside, with only one out of every 40 families owning a car. Toli has none, nor do any of the teachers.

One room in the school is devoted to Lenin, with pictures of his life on the walls. Children are taught to revere him and his words. One young person told us she didn't know he was dead until she was ten years old, and she was terribly disappointed to find this faithful friend was not someone she could count on in person. Toli says some ideology is taught in the last year of school, but because many of the rural boys quit at the end of eighth grade, they learn little of it. Most ideology is taught on the university level.

Soviet schools remind me of our church-related schools because a belief system is taught along with academic subjects. The critical difference—besides content, of course—is that the ideas taught here are the choice of the state and not of the family.

From ages seven to ten, nearly all children belong to a national organization called the Octobrists. October is the month on the pre-revolutionary calendar when the 1917 revolution occurred; it's November on the present calendar. The Octobrists are like coed cub scouts. They learn what Lenin was like as a child ("helpful," "studious," etc.) and take part in small service projects.

Then, at age ten, children become Pioneers, roughly like Girl and Boy Scouts, again coed. They're the ones who wear the familiar red neck scarves. All children except those from defiant religious families are Pioneers.

One day, on our way to Kamenets-Podolski, we saw about a hundred children standing around a large pile of wood in a field. Naturally, our curiosity pushed us out of the car to join them. A ceremony was in progress, with a female leader putting red scarves around the necks of fledgling Pioneers. Then the children lit the fire, and the flames leaped high. I asked Toli later what the fire meant, and he said, "It's just a campfire for celebration."

After Pioneers comes the Komsomol (the Young Communist League) which nearly all young people join at 14. It's from these ranks that the best are chosen between ages 18 and 28 to join the Communist Party. They must show promise of being hard-working, obedient communists with flawless records. In the past, if a person was asked to join the party, he had better not refuse. If he did, he would never get a promotion, for instance. Who can blame people for being party members? Now, however, many who are asked to join, decline. And many are turning in their party cards.

This afternoon, Toli, Buddha, and Ralph discussed developing a joint venture to test soybeans in the Region. However joint ventures are difficult because the ruble is still non-convertible. Rubles cannot purchase anything outside the USSR, nor can they be converted to dollars or other hard currency. This must change, of course, but it will cause high inflation and more hardship for the Soviet people. In the meantime, Western companies barter. Italian, West German, and South Korean companies are swarming over the USSR, getting their feet in the door for future business. Our cautious country may be left behind.

After Buddha left, Toli told us it was only Buddha's insistence 12 days ago that got us to Kiev. Even the powerful Chairman had been unwilling to take responsibility. Good old Buddha! Even before we knew this, we'd become very fond of him.

Afterwards, we had a special evening with our neighbors and friends, whom we've affectionately dubbed the Greenhouse Gang. Sasha Sportsman—we call him that to differentiate him from the other Sasha, Sasha Professor—invited us over about dusk to eat roasted potatoes. I brought cottage cheese pie, and we sat around the campfire with Sasha Sportsman, Oleg, Stepan, and Nikolai and his wife. Of the five renters, only Sasha Professor was missing.

After the campfire burned down to coals, Sportsman tossed in some of his Romanian grandmother's tasty potatoes and raked the glowing embers over them. Fifteen minutes later, he fished out a potato with a stick and pressed a matchstick into it to feel if it was done. We tried not to burn our fingers as we gingerly picked the skin off our potatoes and ate them. To communicate, we used my little Russian, Oleg's little English, a dictionary, lots of well-placed gestures, humor, and good will. It was very satisfying. They invited us to go with them to a place called "Little Michigan" on Sunday.

Earlier today, four women came to plant and hoe flowers in our yard. They care for the village's public flowers, and do they work fast! I like our yard. Part of it's jungle-like, with large plants above my head. The village has cows and goats to keep the grass down; no lawn mowers are needed in Soviet villages.

I took some chocolates outside for the women, and we talked. The brigadier (supervisor) said she thought the USSR wasn't much good. She has her own greenhouse where she raises flowers to sell, and until two years ago, she was restricted by the government to 32 square meters. She said life is hard for women in the USSR. Amen! Toli told us later she'd indeed been restricted by the state, but the Chairman allowed her to use her whole area, telling the authorities she was raising flowers for the collective farm. Of course, he got some kind of pay-off. That's the way things work.

We're gradually learning about the shadow economy. The biggest shock we've had during this stay is how pervasive it is in the lives of the people. "People must participate in the shadow economy to live," Toli told us, "and that's extremely painful for honest people." When I learn more, I'll write about it.

May 18: A big day! And very good it was! After we checked out the fields, we dressed up and drove Toli to the Kamenets-Podolski Agricultural Institute where he interpreted for us at a meeting. He always says he's the only Soviet with two American chauffeurs. We were ushered into a large auditorium filled with more than 1,000 people. As we walked the long aisle to sit in front, the audience waited expectantly on the edges of their chairs.

Ralph's movie on soil conservation was first on the program, with the sound turned low and Toli reading his translation in Russian. Then Ralph took the podium and gave a warm five-minute greeting. When it was my turn, I began to say in Russian I was very glad to be here, but warm, spontaneous applause stopped me in mid-sentence. I felt like John F. Kennedy must have when he spoke in German at the Berlin Wall, and the Germans cheered. It felt great! Anyone with a self-worth problem should spend a little time in the USSR.

Written questions began to come in then, and Ralph answered them. Most questions were about US agriculture and how Americans live. When they asked what we liked and didn't like about Ukraine, Ralph handed me the mike. "We think this part of Ukraine is one of the most beautiful spots on earth," I said, "and we love the people very much. But we wish two things for you—that you could be freer to make your own decisions and that you could have more things to buy and an easier way to get them." More applause.

After two hours, the meeting ended, and we went to a spacious office for coffee and conversation. The woman who served us gave me two large cloth napkins she had made and embroidered. I was touched. Last of all, there was picture-taking.

We went immediately from there to the Kamenets apartment of Roza and Viktor for dinner and good conversation. Viktor is director of the Shatava area school that graduates students after they complete ninth grade; many will go to a trade school. He and Toli respect and enjoy one another, and they spent much time on the porch smoking, talking, and laughing. During these times, Ralph and I talked with Roza, the English teacher at the Pedagogical Institute. She is tiny and charming, with naturally curly, red hair. She and Viktor are both Jewish.

When I questioned Viktor about Gorbachev, he said, "I'm skeptical of him because he rose through the ranks under Brezhnev. He's good internationally, but he's done nothing at home."

I think Brezhnev had little to do with Gorbachev's rise to the top, but Andropov, for whom few have a bad word, had a great deal to do with it. Gorby became Andropov's protege after the two met on a train platform. Andropov liked him, and they began a long, close association, often vacationing together with their wives in Gorby's home region of Stavropol.

Ralph and I dislike hearing people say, as so many of them do, "In four years, nothing has happened," and "There is no food." Both are overstatements. We've seen tremendous changes since our first trip in 1983: walking through customs without our bags being opened, joking with formerly intimidating KGB officers, hearing Gorbachev criticized to his face on TV, knowing hundreds of churches are being reopened or built, seeing grassroots groups springing up all over the country, and observing the media discussing problems like rising crime, drugs, poverty-stricken pensioners, abandoned children, mafia activity, environmental neglect, AIDS, and the ineptness of the Communist Party.

"One of the main problems," said Viktor, "is that simply change is hard, even for those like myself who want it." He also remarked, "The CIA was very clever to send you, for if all Americans are like you, then I'm in favor of good relations between our countries."

Upon returning to Makov about 9 P.M., we went with Toli to his friend Vanya's birthday party at Victoria's restaurant. Five couples and Tanya were already there, eating, drinking, and dancing, and other small groups were there, too. Vanya had a birthday cake and blew out the candles. Where did that custom originate? Ralph danced for the first time in his life and did very well, and this babushka forgot her inhibitions and cut loose in the fast ones. Memorable day. Full of surprises.

May 20: I needed a haircut, so Roza arranged for me to have one in Kamenets. The young hairdresser, Tamara, breezed in, talking a mile a minute. I became slightly apprehensive about how my hair would turn out. I noticed she was cutting it awfully short, exposing my ears completely. I watched nervously as she blow-dried it into a high, glamorous style too fancy for me. But it was a superb cut, and, ultimately, I was quite happy with her work. And I should have known Roza wouldn't let me pay. Ralph was relieved a few days later when my hair settled down to normal. Wearing sunglasses and being a woman driver already make me too noticeable here.

We visited the outdoor market in Kamenets and bought a cabbage, potatoes, strawberries, and calla lilies from the babushkas who grew them—a bit of private enterprise.

When I say "private enterprise," I always remember the tongue-lashing Ralph and I sustained at the home of some *nouveau riche* people in Dayton. They had asked us to do our slide show, which we always give gratis. First, one of the men accidentally knocked over our screen, resulting in a foot-long rip. He didn't so much as apologize, let alone make a replacement offer. I had narrated half the slide show and was showing a market in Moscow with the comment, "Here's a little free enterprise," when suddenly one of the group erupted.

He began a five-minute tirade, "There is *no* free enterprise in the Soviet Union!" Then he said we were dupes of the communists, we were hurting our country, etc. On and on ranted the man, a state legislator. When we thought he had finished, Ralph tried to speak. The man thrust his finger at him, demanding, "You be quiet! I'm not finished yet!" I wonder if he does that on the floor of the Ohio House of Representatives.

When he finally finished, Ralph quietly asked, "How do you envision the relationship of our two countries fifty years from now?" (In other words, is improvement in relations never to be allowed? What is *your* solution?)

The state representative replied, "That's not a fair question!" Then the whole group took turns berating us. Only one man, who had been to China and had a broader view, understood what we were about. The rest were blind with arrogance and anti-communist fervor. Of course, there has been much to be anti-communist about, but many of us are more hysterical than rational.

One woman said, "There will always be wars. That's the way God wants it because that's what happened in the Bible." I could hardly believe my ears! These were wealthy, educated people.

We finished the slide show and had refreshments, but before we left, I asked our hostess why she'd invited us, knowing we'd be treated like this. "Oh," she said. "We like controversy."

An older couple, who'd gone with us on our first trip to the USSR, had accompanied us. The man was nearly deaf. As we shakily made our way out, he asked cheerily, "Well, how'd it go tonight?" Then *we* erupted—with laughter!

About noon today, a television crew of two—reporter Svetlana and photographer Vasily—from Kiev TV, sauntered in. Vasily is the father of Andrei, the Komsomol leader from the Kamenets Pedagogical Institute. He handed me a letter from his son. Andrei had written, "Your simple and polite manners made us closer. It seemed that we were acquainted for many years . . . . I think if every man of us can have such manners of behavior, we will be able to break all the borders in people's relations. If this was the policy in the world, all people would live in mutual understanding and human love." I'll answer him right away.

Svetlana and Vasily, along with Toli, the Chairman, the First Party Secretary of the District, and the head of the District Soviet took us to a rented beef farm. Actually, I think those two extra officials came to see pretty TV star Svetlana.

Ralph, standing by the cattle, was immediately asked to give his impressions for the camera. He did very well, considering we'd just arrived there. The beef-feeding enterprise is run by a family of four—mother, father, a son and his wife. Conditions looked good, with the cattle outside and straw on the ground for a dry place to lie down. We'd been appalled when we saw the beef barns at Ukraina. The cattle were tied with neck chains and lived in stalls without bedding. One barn of small calves was especially hot and messy.

Following this, we went en masse to a sugar beet field where 25 women hoed weeds. Svetlana asked Ralph what he'd do differently. "I've never had experience with sugar beets," he responded, "but I question the use of the women hoers. I know what difficult work it is because I did plenty of hoeing when I was a youngster."

The Chairman then stated his position to Svetlana. "I have to be concerned not only with profit but with employing everyone. We don't have mechanization to take care of weeds in the sugar beets. I'd like to have the freedom to make my own decisions, like Mr. Dull has in the US."

The hoers gathered around with interest, and Ralph shook hands with each of them, and I kissed them. The District Party Secretary asked Ralph, "Don't *you* kiss women?"

In response, Ralph drew me to him, kissed me on the lips, and said, "Yes!"

When we returned to Stupentsi, the Chairman asked if I could give some supper to Svetlana and Vasily. I gladly did, though I was surprised they were not being taken to Victoria's Restaurant by one of the officials who had accompanied us all afternoon. Toli stayed to interpret.

I've read Soviet women don't have the self-conscious obsession about needing to improve their looks and life-style that many American women do. Perhaps it's because Soviet women are so burdened with work. Svetlana's solid self-confidence seems to confirm this. I was fascinated by her, and felt I could learn from her how to happily use what I have instead of worrying about what I lack.

During supper, we were talking about the prejudices many Americans have had against Soviets, and Ukrainian Svetlana said passionately, "Soviets are the most hard-working, kind, generous, sincere, patient people in the world, and they have very little evil in them!"

Well, I wouldn't go so far as to say "the most" because we have found people to have the same human nature everywhere. But her assessment is surely more true than the evil image we've been taught.

In the Dayton area, there are two programs offered to the public by people from Wright-Patterson Air Force Base. I'm sure they're not official, but the people who present them are in the military. The program I saw was a conversation between two people, one representing the Soviet military and the other representing the American military. The "Soviet" officer was arrogant and obnoxious, but the American officer was a pretty, mild, conciliatory young woman. I asked the man representing the Soviet officer if he'd ever met a Soviet person, and he said he hadn't. But he'd probably seen plenty of them in American movies!

The other presentation, according to what I've been told, involves an officer whose expressed goal is to show that the Russian personality is different from others in the world: inhumanly cruel and ruthless. He goes through centuries of their history, showing all the evil they've done.

Horrible things certainly did happen there, but we have some embarrassing history of our own: our treatment of Native Americans and our breaking of virtually every treaty we made with them, for example. Or how about the kidnapping of Africans and their voyage in ships where they lay like spoons in an 8-inch-high space? Half died en route. Later, families were torn apart at slave sales, and many blacks were treated worse than animals. We know US history, but we overlook the ugly episodes. Christianity also has some terrible annals. And what if we judged all Germans on the basis of Hitler? Besides, Stalin was Georgian, Kate the Great was German, and the czars, including Ivan the Terrible, had some Scandinavian blood. Where does that leave the Russian personality question? Every culture has cruelty in its history.

Late this evening, we turned on the television and caught a Diana Ross concert. Whenever there's English being spoken or sung, our ears perk up. We enjoy seeing groups from the US who are visiting the USSR. They're often featured on the morning TV program *120 Minutes*, which is like American early morning programs.

May 21: After Svetlana and Vasily filmed their last interview this morning, the Greenhouse Gang and their families took us to their favorite spot, an exquisite blue gem of a lake in a forest setting, which they call "Little Michigan." Sasha Sportsman gave me a ride in his canoe and picked a large, yellow flower for me on the far bank. Meanwhile, Nikolai and Stepan barbecued chicken, and the wives set a table with food.

At one point, when Ralph was playing badminton with Sasha Sportsman, Nikolai's dog Alma got under Ralph's feet. Both he and Alma went rolling! It was hilarious, especially as neither was hurt.

We thoroughly enjoyed the day. They wouldn't let us carry a thing, and one of Nikolai's little sons gathered wild flowers for me. Our relationship with these men and their families transcends boundaries; it's a kind of mystical oneness, a true heart-to-heartness.

This evening, we went to the House of Culture to see the American movie, *Romancing the Stone*. While a small crowd of us were waiting for it to start, the tallest student in the eleventh grade came over and said politely in English, "Good morning!" We teased him because it was evening, but we were pleased he approached us.

We left halfway through the movie, having seen it before. Just as we came out, a wedding procession was passing by. Whenever we hear a band blaring from one of the two restaurants or someone's yard, we know a three-day wedding ceremony is in progress. It was a new experience to see the procession moving slowly down the street. People were waving green branches as they danced around the smiling bride and groom. Sometimes parents put up a 30-by-60-foot tent at their home for the days of dancing, eating, and drinking with friends and relatives. Ritual tricks are played by friends of the couple during these days, including one in which the young men try to steal the bride from her husband.

As we watched the procession, a woman we'd never seen before handed us her bag of wedding sweets. These kindnesses by people, knowing they'll not receive anything from us in return, continue to amaze us.

May 22: We're always looking for new territory to explore, and today we came upon a cemetery that included a shrine with a large statue of Mary. A picture of the Last Supper stood at its base. This would indicate Catholicism rather than Russian Orthodox Christianity because the latter does not allow statues. Statues are considered "graven images" forbidden by the Ten Commandments. The Ukrainian Catholic Church has been illegal here since early Soviet history, and their church buildings were taken over by Russian Orthodox. Now there are rumblings the church will be legalized again.

Nearly every grave has a cross of some kind, but a few have secular monuments with bas-reliefs of the face of the deceased. People are buried in a row in the order of death rather than in family plots, so the cemetery continually enlarges. We noticed few lived beyond age 60. Toli told us later that poor health in adult years could be due to terrible times during the war or famines during childhood. People who die as young people usually drown in the lake when intoxicated or are killed in traffic accidents, Toli said. It felt strange to see fresh graves of Makov residents who had died since we arrived.

One day on the main road to Khmelnitski, Ralph was stopped in a long line of traffic. A funeral procession came up the highway. It was led by a few marchers with wreaths, followed by a flatbed truck with the casket and more flowers, and then came about a hundred more marchers. Behind them, a mile of trucks, buses, and cars crept along. Ralph didn't know how far the people had walked. They were about to turn left into a cemetery along the highway, detaining hundreds of respectful motorists in both directions.

Another event today was that our sweet corn seed was checked and okayed at the Regional headquarters. We divided it into 25 packets of 200 seeds each for Toli to distribute to people for their gardens. We gave an extra large measure to the Greenhouse Gang.

By this time, however, most gardens are fully planted, so sweet corn seed will probably be planted in with potatoes and beets—not good practice as corn grows slowly and shouldn't have competition. Toli had his students copy our short set of instructions for planting and cooking on each package: "Boil only five minutes and eat with salt and butter," we advised. Makov people eat corn on the cob, but it's just immature field corn boiled for at least an hour. We think they'll love this!

A letter from my lively 86-year-old father came today. It was especially welcome because of his good news. He's doing well, and so's my mother, considering her condition (Alzheimer's Disease). She lives in a special hospital unit in a retirement home. It's one of life's wonderful twists that Daddy visits Mother despite their divorce forty-five years ago. One of the few things they shared was a deep love of music, so he plays classical music tapes for her. Sometimes he sings too, which she loves. They even cuddle together. He's her best medicine!

Today, I made a cassette tape of myself singing eight American children's songs for the music teacher. Then I wrote out the words in English so Toli can teach the words to the children.

At our meeting with the teachers at Toli's school, they showed great interest in everything, including farming, and they were so impressed with Ralph's comments they wanted to make him chairman of the collective farm! Towards the end, when I asked what they taught about the US, the history, geography, and literature teachers were ready for me. Each rose and recited as their students had, ending up with the statement that only positive things about the US are taught. Maybe *now*.

A final question I had was, "How many of you support Gorbachev?"

The music teacher answered, "All of us."

"But we supported Brezhnev, too!" the physical education teacher added. Everyone laughed. They're getting sick of supporting their leaders and finding out later what jerks they were. That's a handicap Gorbachev has. Because of glasnost, however, we think there will be no surprises after he dies.

It was a great meeting! I gave the music teacher the cassette tape and words, and he gave me a music book containing the complete Russian words to the song, "May There Always Be Sunshine."

May 24: Toli, Ralph, and I went to Dunaevtsi this morning and visited a bookstore. What a difference from our bookstores at home! Those in America are virtual fairylands for readers. Soviet stores have mostly tiresome ideological or scientific tomes. (There's a great emphasis on science here; even the ideology is supposed to be scientific.) We've often seen crowds on city sidewalks surrounding a table of books. People look them over ravenously. Yet these offerings pale beside the variety and quality in American bookstores. Whenever there are really good books here, they're snapped up quickly. We did get a good map of the USSR today, however, and Soviet children's books can be nice. American musicians should get an armload of printed music here because it's dirt-cheap. But good books? Slim pickings. Good books and good food are seldom found in stores.

I became sick, so we tried to find a toilet for me. I couldn't get near the public outhouse because of the filth, so Toli asked for a toilet at an official building. The woman there said, "We have one, but it's not in good condition, so I don't want her using it because she might take a picture of it and publish it in the US."

"She doesn't have her camera with her," Toli said.

"Maybe she has a camera in her pen!" she retorted. Toli was both outraged and amused, but she was adamant.

We tried the library, which had no toilet, and then we thought of the Pioneer Palace where we had our first speaking engagement. There, Maria graciously showed me to the row of toilets. Though they were only flushable holes in the tiled floor, they were clean, and I was grateful.

Late this afternoon, we had another meeting at Toli's school, this time with eleventh graders. About two-thirds of the young people came, and they'd laid out some Fanta sodas and candies for us. The boys, particularly Val, dominated the conversation.

One of them wanted to know what we thought about Soviet TV. (He didn't like it.) Actually, we enjoy it, with its PBS-like educational, cultural, and news programs. I like being able to turn on the TV and see Swan Lake or Uzbek dances, but Soviets want more. That's one of the reasons people here read so much.

But Soviet TV is changing. We've seen a few bare breasts and a semi-violent Mafia series from Italy on it, so more people are deserting their books in favor of TV. There are also interesting current events and opinion programs now, too, on a variety of subjects, programs definitely more mature than most US sitcoms. People here find opinion programs fascinating.

When I asked the young people in what ways they wanted to be like Americans, Val answered, "All!" He's an example of a current prevalent attitude in the USSR: the idealization of everything American. It's been a revelation for them to learn a majority of Americans live in unprecedented comfort, not just the top capitalists. In fact, in Uzbekistan in March, when a group of kids discovered we were Americans, they gathered around us and chanted, "We know the truth about America now!" They liked that truth, and they wanted some of it for their own lives.

Naturally, we hope Soviets can have our country's advantages without acquiring our problems. This, in fact, is a goal of progressive Soviet officials. They want a freer market and other individual freedoms, but they also want to retain the socialist benefits of free medical care, free education on all levels, and inexpensive housing. Most Soviets who visit America are appalled a country as rich as ours has such a large underclass, with one-fifth of our children living in poverty. It seems heartless to them.

Val asked us what we thought was the most important thing in life. I said, "Love." His choice was Justice, which shows he's aware of the many injustices around him. He also thinks Ukraine is probably the most corrupt of the republics and the national authorities won't challenge the officials here because Ukraine is essential to the Soviet Union.

Toli said admiringly that Val, who plans to go to the Agricultural Institute in Kamenets, has always been independent. Independence in children can be disruptive in American schoolrooms, so just imagine its undesirable image in a culture of conformity and obedience.

Two of the girls were wearing good-looking, American-type jeans they said came from Turkey. Other than high school girls, we've seen no village women wear slacks of any kind. Gardening, fieldwork—everything is done in skirts. In the cities, it's different, but still, skirts predominate. It's the same with headscarves. Every woman over 40 in the village seems to wear one, but they are rarely seen in cities. They are on their way out, Ralph thinks.

Val also wanted to know if our teenagers read books. I answered that some do but more watch television. His next question was, "How many of our films and books have you seen?" I'm ashamed we are exposed to so few of their great writers. Many of our authors are a regular part of their school curriculum—Twain, Hemingway, Steinbeck, London, Faulkner, and others. Outside of school, some of our other books are popular, such as Bel Kaufman's *Up the Down Staircase*, Dale Carnegie's *How to Win Friends and Influence People* and Kurt Vonnegut's novels.

They've seen *Tootsie* and many of our films, but I can hardly remember seeing an authentic Soviet-made film other than the sexy *Little Vera*, which has played in the States in the Gorbachev Era. Beyond their marvelous music and the ballet, we aren't exposed to much Soviet art in any form. It's ironic Americans may read anything but most don't, and Soviets' reading has been censored, but many read whatever they can. One person told us a good book in the USSR has 33 readers. Consequently, they really know more about us than we do about them.

So, when I mentioned I had read some Tolstoy and Dostoyevsky, Val said, "Is that all?" I added Solzhenitsyn, Pasternak, and Nabokov. "We don't have those authors here," he said.

They talked about their exams. Two hundred questions have been prepared, and each student draws three and answers them orally. There would surely be no way to cheat on those tests!

They wanted to know what we like to eat and when we get up and go to bed, questions that earthlings might ask a creature from another planet. What a great chasm we've had between us!

The young people didn't want to stop talking, but after three hours, Toli was tired, so we invited them to visit us at Stupentsi some evening.

May 25: At noon, we went to observe the school's Last Bell ceremony on the soccer field behind the school. The weather cooperated perfectly. The lines of schoolchildren, each holding a bouquet, made three sides of a large square, leaving an open side for a podium with microphone and the center area for dance performances. Val and Igor gave their flowers and graduation pins to Ralph and me, and I walked down the row of eleventh graders giving each one a button with "Peace" in English and Russian. Someone asked me to speak, so I did, and then two dozen children gave us their roses and peonies.

While Ralph was taking a picture of Tatiana Palamarchouk holding her flowers, I sat on the bleachers under the trees. Suddenly, I felt a pebble hit my arm. I turned to see two-year-old Yura the Terrorist looking at me. It was his special way of letting me know he was in the vicinity!

Afterwards, the eleventh grade class wanted a photo with us. When it was time to snap the picture, their expressions changed abruptly from carefree smiles to affected sternness. Seriousness, I think, is a prized communist quality denoting discipline and purpose. The glory boards in each town and village, billboards featuring outstanding citizens with grim expressions, look like rogues' galleries to us.

The big jolly photographer said he was in town to make a newsreel of us. He asked if we were going to write a book about our experiences, saying it would do well in this country.

After lunch, we drove through a poor farm and its village, returning just in time to get to the school prom the tenth grade sponsors in honor of the eleventh. Sound familiar? The school gym was decorated with balloons, crepe paper, and evergreen branches. Tables were set with cakes, sweet cherries, chocolate candies, and cokes. We joined the teachers who led the line of eleventh grade students into the gym through a tunnel of balloons. The tenth graders and parents, seated in the small gym, were there to heartily applaud.

Children have the same teacher for the first three grades, so the teacher who had the graduates-to-be took the microphone and told endearing stories about them from those early times. She also gave them each a booklet of pictures from those years.

Then the teacher who has been "responsible" for them for so many years spoke. She and they had become close, and she tearfully quoted some poetry to them at the end of her speech. In the Soviet Union, each grade has one teacher who's responsible for the moral and intellectual development of children from the fourth grade until a year after graduation. When a student does something wrong outside school, the teacher is contacted, not the parents—though the parents usually become involved at the request of the teacher. The class Toli's responsible for are now eighth-graders. Half the time he spends on school duties involves seeing to the study and moral habits of these students, though he is paid only 30 rubles a month for that.

The school director then spoke, wishing the graduates success, "especially as the USSR is changing," he said. He stressed how unusual it was for Americans to be at their event, a sign that Soviet-American friendship is deepening.

Next in the ceremony, each graduate-to-be took the mike. A tenth grader asked him or her one question, such as "What do you want to do in life?" or "If you had these eleven years to do over again, how would you do them?" or "What teacher do you most want to be like and why?" This latter question was nearly always answered "Anatoli Arkadyevich." Toli said last year in a contest for favorite teacher he got nearly every vote. It was so overwhelming, the school director discontinued the contest.

After each student answered his or her question, that student's favorite song—usually a rock tune—was played. Everyone danced. Students danced with each other, with teachers, with us, girls with girls, two together or as a group, and all kinds of steps were used. Not all aspects of Soviet society are caught up in cookie-cutter conformity!

As we were leaving, a bit earlier than others, the students asked how we liked their prom and school. I said, "We like them very much and feel completely at home with you!" They were delighted and called out, "Spaseeba!" (thank you).

Ukraine has three TV channels, two from Moscow and one from Kiev. When got home, we turned to the Kiev channel and saw ourselves being interviewed by Svetlana. They even showed some close-up shots of our Ohio photos—pictures of Ralph's farm, my kitchen, and our supermarket.

May 27: This morning, I took Tanya and Yura to the clinic in Dunaevtsi. Our first stop was the children's doctor, who was female, as are most Soviet physicians. Three nurses were with her. One of the nurses was fastening people's records together with paste, because she had no stapler. Another one—quite young—had fingernails with silver polish. But she was cracking her knuckles the way my sons used to do in adolescence.

After Tanya reported Yura's symptoms, we were sent upstairs to the ear, nose, and throat doctor. People stood outside his room holding their sick children. The crowd seemed to have no order, but everyone remembered who was next. It made me angry to see that people burdened with sick children couldn't (or didn't) sit down to wait. Chairs remained unused. Very often in the Soviet Union, the most difficult way to do something is the method employed. Tradition reigns, and innovation is punished. It would be so easy to use our system of writing one's name on a list and being called in that order.

I've seldom noticed anyone cutting into line here. In fact, people's places are often held by strangers while they do something else. Another common practice is for a person to go to one line and buy bread or grapes or ice cream cones for a whole group, while someone else stands in another line for the group. Body contact is common where there is no line, just gentle mass pressure.

When I went with Tanya and Yura into the doctor's room, I thought I'd stepped into a Norman Rockwell painting. In a clean, old-fashioned office sat a pretty nurse and a bespectacled male doctor, both in white. The doctor wore one of those mirror headbands. After looking into Yura's facial orifices, the doctor said he saw a slight ear infection.

When Tanya went to the pharmacy to get Yura's medicine, they were out of it, so she must try to get it in Makov. Toli says, "Proper medicine is in great deficit, and sometimes people pay up to one-hundred-fold for it."

On the way home, we stopped at one of three clothing stores in Makov, and I got another lesson in the way the shadow economy works. Tanya went into a storage room with the proprietress, came out with a bra, paid for it at the counter, and took it home. Why was it hidden? Toli told us that deficit or imported goods are kept "under the counter" so they can sell for extra money. I'm not sure if Tanya gave the woman something extra in the back room or if the hiked-up price was paid at the counter.

The Congress of People's Deputies is meeting now in Moscow, and people are glued to their TVs and radios. Everyone has high hopes great changes will be made. Savkov, our agronomist, is there, having had the honor of being elected a Deputy by the National Collective Farm Union. Most of the People's Deputies are party members, but many are new-breed communists on the scene.

Popular Boris Yeltsin was not elected to the Supreme Soviet today, which means there were covert movements to stop him. One young man put himself up to oppose Gorbachev, just for the sake of having more than one candidate. I asked Toli if Gorbachev is afraid of Yeltsin. He said, "Gorbachev is not, but some of his men are."

Just now, the TV is on, and I see Sakharov, who's always trying to speak, standing up to Gorbachev. Sakharov is saying to Gorbachev, "I'm not finished!" So Gorby is giving him the floor. Sakharov is saying, "There have recently been some laws that weren't democratic enough."

People are getting up and saying whatever they think; they're very open. One man says, "Five years ago, I would have been in the Far East [Siberia] tomorrow."

Another, from Moldavia, is speaking against the apparatus. He says, "When a farmer goes to his chairman or supervisor for something, he's asked, 'For whom did you vote?' We have to take care of our voters. Many of our people were elected by organizations, but we who were elected by the people are here with wounds."

The next speaker is touting scientific and technological development as what the country needs most.

Now, a man is speaking on education. "We spend only 5.6 percent of our budget on education. We need computers in our schools. Teachers' salaries are lower than the average for the country. Don't forget about teachers."

Next, a speaker from Central Asia is saying, "Our republic is rich, but our people are poor because our raw materials are taken away by Moscow."

Now the head of the Soviet Children's Fund is speaking, a good man, Toli says. "Children are never to blame. It's the adults. I'm against our tradition of displaying children giving flowers to our leaders, as if they were all well-bred and prosperous. It's only a line that all children are like that. After staying at our orphan houses, I found that 300 children and teens were killed, and 2,000 committed suicide. We should have a special law on the rights of children. I propose a report for Congress about children in the USSR."

Now we have a famous writer who has lots of complaints. He wants agriculture to be different and soviets (councils), not the party, to be the real masters of the territory. He asks why only a few people should act for the whole country. "There are 18 million supervisors in our country, and 40 billion rubles are spent on them each year. It's wrong. Also, all our agreements with other countries should be published openly."

Here's the first woman speaker. She's saying, "We women are for equal rights but not for hard work [physical labor]. A woman should be engaged in bringing up children."

Next, we have Yuri Chernichenko, a fiery, popular writer who's a specialist in agriculture. "For 25 years, we have been importing grain. People will never be fed by centrally-commanded agriculture. We have 200 million hectares of black earth. We're behind in agriculture for political reasons. In comparison with the US, we have five times more tractors and ten times more combines than they have, but we produce half as much. We produce three times as many shoes as the US, but we still need shoes. The man counting our votes is a specialist in computers, but he must use an abacus." That's tellin' 'em, Yuri! Gorby is making notes; the agricultural problem is dear to his heart.

Grievances continue to be brought before the Congress. The handicapped, the small ethnic groups, the veterans of war and labor who say their pensions are too low—all take their turns to speak. A man from one of the Baltics brings up the non-attack agreement between Hitler and Stalin in 1939. He wants to know if there were any secret articles in the pact. Gorby says there were not.

Now, controversial Gdlyan, who's been fighting the mafia for six years, is speaking. "What's controversial about him?" I asked Toli.

"He's a hero to the people because he brought to justice some dishonest high officials in Uzbekistan, but his methods may have been unlawful. Also, the Uzbeks are now complaining there's racism involved in their being singled out of all the republics that are corrupt."

Gorby keeps trying to adjourn, but they won't let him. Toli says, "This is better than any movie!"

Later, I was stunned when a woman Deputy was shown on the TV, and Toli remarked "Ha! She thinks she's a Deputy!"

"What do you mean by that?" I asked hotly.

"Women aren't reasonable like men are," he said. "They can't think, and they're only interested in trifles."

I was infuriated and said, "When women are put into the position of servants, they *have* to be interested in trifles, and then they're criticized for it! But they're also interested in deeper things and can contribute just as much as men can!"

Toli just laughed and said, "I'm afraid I get a perverse pleasure out of teasing women, especially you and my sister!"

"Do you tease Tanya?" I asked.

"Ah!" he replied. "That's too dangerous! Besides," he continued, "as late as the thirteenth or fourteenth century, the Catholic Church disputed whether or not a woman is a human being."

By this time, my feathers were extremely ruffled. I resented the inference that I can't think, and I'm sure Ralph wouldn't like being told he can't feel.

Toli explained: "Men and women are different. Women intuit and men reason, and they need each other. I'm not sure reason is superior to intuition. In fact, I think the opposite is true."

My feathers settled down slightly, but I told him, "We think anyone can use both sides of his or her brain [although we now know it's more complicated than that] to intuit or to reason—whichever the situation calls for. But our friend, the head of the counseling department at the University of Dayton, says studies show women are somewhat better at using both sides of their brain than men are."

Toli responded, "I think it's against nature for people to use both sides of their brains. Men and women are just different."

We've found much male chauvinism in this culture, and we've heard a couple of ugly sayings about women:

1. "The hair is long; the intellect is short."
2. "If you want to know what to do, ask your wife's advice and then do the opposite." Nasty!

Women here not only have to endure such disrespectful slurs, but tradition dictates their taking on the burden of family and even society. Whenever anything goes wrong in the fields, for example, a couple truckloads of women are ordered up to take care of it.

Soviet women certainly have the worst jobs. They lay the railroad ties the country over, do the hand labor in the fields, and on Ukraina mix and carry cement for construction. One day we found them on the road spreading asphalt with shovels while men drove the machines. Most of the supervisors are men, though there'll be a token woman at some places.

Women here have equal rights on paper, but they're tired of doing the menial jobs. Their salaries *are* equal for the same kind of work men do, but some professions are traditionally women's, such as medicine, and they pay small salaries. There are no restrictions on women going into any profession, however.

Because of the system, many men are resigned to certain aspects of their lives, and it's even more true of women because of sexist restrictions. (But ah, in many souls the passion for freedom has always burned!) In the past, the party supposedly gave women equal rights and met all economic needs (not wants). Thus, until perestroika, people weren't allowed to organize for better conditions. Most women, however, are too busy to lobby. We do know of a Kiev mothers' demonstration for more pre-schools. It worked, too! Women will eventually be full contributors.

But now, their days don't end at sundown. It's their role to do the domestic chores, estimated at 6 hours daily, besides their 41-hour-a-week job. Much time is spent standing in line or, for Moscovites, crisscrossing the city to find stores with food or crates of produce on the street and *then* standing in line. There seems to be (barely) enough actual food, but diets are unbalanced. And there's anger at having to spend so much time getting so little. Soviet women are geniuses at putting together meals with such a limited selection.

Here are two food anecdotes:

1. A woman entered a store and asked, "You don't have any meat, do you?"

   "This is a fish store," answered the proprietor. "You know the meat store across the street? That's where they don't have any meat."

2. Three men, a Britisher, a Frenchman, and a Soviet, were talking about how pigs are killed in their countries. The man from Britain said, "I think they shoot them in my country, for I've seen bullet holes in their heads."

   "No holes in our pigs' heads," said the Frenchman. "I think they must gas our pigs."

   "In our country, they must dynamite them," said the Soviet, "because all we ever see are ears and hooves."

Young Soviet women console themselves by dressing well when they have the chance and using "make-ups" (as they call cosmetics). Spike heels, which I gave up at 25, are popular. Most women have long hair, often permanented; but the beauties who announce the shows coming up on TV all have chic, short hairstyles. Women's legs remain unshaven, as is usual in Europe. Once Anna felt my cleanly-shaved leg and nodded approvingly. Here, men have trouble finding shaving equipment, but somehow they manage. As for sanitary napkins, they're practically non-existent; women use big wads of cotton. And birth control? Forget it!

Women who have babies get a paid leave of two months before the baby is born and three months afterwards. If the birth is complicated, they get 78 days. (There's usually no anesthetic, by the way.) Then, if they wish to stay home, they get only 35 rubles a month until the end of the year. After that, their job is not held for them and they get nothing.

Once a Moscow woman talked to me about marriages and the Soviet divorce rate. As is true in America, one-half of all Soviet couples see their marriages end in divorce. She believes she knows one reason for this. According to her, "Men know little about how to satisfy a woman sexually. They sometimes act like animals, so after awhile, the woman would rather be alone." Alcoholism, so prevalent in men, is a big factor in divorce. In addition, most young people live with parents for awhile, so intimate relating is difficult.

After divorce, the mother usually gets the children, and there's automatic garnishment of the father's paycheck for child support: one-fourth of it for one child and one-third for two. American divorced mothers would like this rule!

May 28: The Chairman requested an "American dinner," so I worked all morning preparing it for him and his wife, Toli and Tanya, and Victor Party Secretary and his wife. First, we had bread and the kind of bean soup served in the US Senate cafeteria. The next course was roast pork, mashed potatoes and gravy, dilled buttered carrots, sweet and sour beets, tossed salad with oil and vinegar dressing, warm apple-raisin-nut bread, and for dessert—cottage cheese pie, tea, and coffee. I did the best I could with the available ingredients. Each couple brought a bottle of champagne, and when the Chairman opened his, the cork hit the ceiling and ricocheted around the room.

He liked the dinner, saying, "Well, you have some things to teach us."

But Ralph responded, "No, Ukrainian cooking is delicious, too."

Then the Chairman said something I didn't understand: "With a piece of meat like this, we need a bottle of vodka." Toli explained he meant the meat tasted good.

It became clear the Chairman would very much like to see the US. Also, he offered us one of the peacocks to eat, and said Johanna would fix it. We were horrified to think of eating our pets!

After the other guests left, Toli told us the Chairman announced today that the little church in Makov will be opened. Anna is overjoyed, and so are all the other villagers who've been working diligently toward this end for two years. They sent three delegations to Moscow only to be told they had to get permission on the local level. But local officials kept refusing. Just as they were preparing to send yet another delegation to Moscow, this time during the Congress of People's Deputies, the order came to open the church. People's Deputies are trying to be sensitive to people's demands.

"Who are the local officials?" I asked.

Toli's one of the 100-member village soviet, and the question of the church was never brought up there. "Perhaps the chairman of the soviet or the District authorities were responsible," he said. "The church belongs to the collective farm, and the Chairman has said the people could have it free of charge, but he hasn't insisted it be opened." He's gone about as far as a party member can go.

Though Toli doesn't like the church, he's glad the little church was opened because, as he said, "The people wanted it, and they should have what they want."

May 29: Today, one of the Russian Republic men stepped down so Yeltsin could be on the Supreme Soviet. A vote was taken. Gorby raised his card first, and all voted with him. Incidentally, the votes of each People's Deputy are not recorded, which Toli considers a great mistake. Constituents want to know how their representative voted. Also today, President Bush offered to reduce troops in Europe by 20 percent.

This morning, as we left just before nine o'clock for a big meeting at the Khmelnitski Region Gosagroprom, we saw about thirty people descending on Stupentsi—walking, riding bikes, and driving cars. They must have been coming to take the ducks and swans out of the large pond and put them over the fence into the tiny pool newly built for them. The Chairman wants the big pond for swimming, fishing, and boating, so it'll be stocked with fish after the fowl are removed.

The pond separates our house from the Chairman's dacha. He visits it daily, driving by our fence in his new Niva with its darkly-tinted windows all around the back seat. He sometimes jokes about taking me "to the forest."

At 10:30 A.M., we arrived in Khmelnitski, the seat of our Region, to meet Buddha and Mr. Chinik. They took us to an auditorium where 250 specialists from 20 districts were assembled. The soil conservation film was first, and then written questions began to come in. Ralph was a little nervous and very diplomatic in the way he answered. They wanted to know his thoughts on supervisors (most of them were probably supervisors). "What would you do? How many would you have?" they asked.

Toli asked Ralph twice if he could say, "None."

But Ralph answered, "Things here will change gradually, but I'm glad there are no supervisors on my farm."

One question Toli tried to ignore, but Buddha and Chinik insisted he ask it. "How do you like Stengach and Savkov?" Wow! What a question! Those two men are well-known and have enemies, and if Ralph were critical, he would be in trouble with our hosts. However if he praised them, he might lose credibility with the specialists.

Ralph answered truthfully, "I have a lot of respect for both men, but there's always room for improvement. I think they are progressive and willing to make changes." Toli told us later Ralph couldn't have answered better.

At one point, the specialists responded with amazement to Ralph's comment that his farm is never required to report to the government. Soviet farmers report every day!

When he gave the wage of the teenagers who work de-tasseling seed corn every July on his farm—about $4.50 an hour—they shook their heads in amazement. School children here are required to work on the farms for almost nothing during planting and harvest time. And college students also harvest and go to work in other republics.

Ralph talked at length about his own farm and about renting land, saying he and his sons come to mutual decisions. Then all join in the work, even if it's dirty work.

At the end, Toli gave a long description of our social and political work—for example, our work in peace and justice organizations in the US; Ralph's work as a conscientious objector; my 13-week course for the public, "Alternatives to Violence" (ranging from interpersonal to international relations); and especially our more than 300 presentations about the Soviet Union.

Toli also told what Ralph did on April 15, 1982: He took a large truckload of corn to the Dayton Federal Building and asked the IRS to accept it as tax payment, thus dramatizing his desire that his taxes go for constructive programs and not for the military. Sue made signs for the sides and back of the truck: "Taxes for Food, Yes! Money for Arms, No!" and "World Peace Tax Fund." Of course, the IRS refused to accept the corn, so he took it to an elevator and sold it. He asked them to make out the check to "Food for Poland." Then he sent on the $777 for just that purpose. His action was reported in the *New York Times* and on *Good Morning, America*.

After the meeting, we met for four hours in a large Gosagroprom office with Buddha, Chinik, and Leonid, the head of the Collective Farm Chairmen's Union and chairman of a nearby farm. They agreed with Ralph about almost everything, which prompted him to say, "We're preaching to the saved." Leonid was especially excited about the colorful and informative farm magazines, which are non-existent in the USSR.

Ralph broached the subject of meeting with potential renters, but the men said there weren't any. "No one's qualified," one stated.

Ralph countered, "Maybe they're afraid. We've heard that some renters' quarters were burned down."

But our hosts denied that officials have a hostile attitude toward renters. They claimed, "The state has offered poor land, equipment, and good prices to people, and no one takes them up on it." We know there *are* potential renters because we've talked with several.

There was a long discussion about their not having the freedom to choose their crops because farm chairmen are told from above which crops and how much of each they're to raise. They're hoping Congress will stop that. All agreed it's a handicap to have quotas and that price should influence the amount grown of each crop. Though there's no more command system about *when* to plant, they said, "It's still a habit to plant early, even when the soil is wet." Toli once told us wryly that it used to be the command system, and now it's the *request* system. Those who don't comply still run the risk of punishment.

We saw samples of the apple juice concentrate they're trading to West Germany for machinery. They said there's no hard currency yet to buy American combines and planters.

About grain storage, they assured Ralph there's plenty of capacity to handle the harvest. We've heard about crops being piled on the ground, but maybe that's not in this region.

Then Ralph asked, "What do you consider the biggest problem with Soviet agriculture?"

They all agreed it's the "organization" which to me means "the system." Nearly everyone—even some of those involved in the system—admits it's the biggest problem.

Before we left, Ralph gave them a set of photographs, and they gave us two boxes of herb tea, a box of cookies, roses, and a framed bas-relief of a flower basket made of straw.

On the way home, I told Toli about a Phil Donahue show I saw once demonstrating the power of systems. Phil Zimbardo of Stanford University (where my son Joel goes to school) did an experiment. He fixed up the basement of the psychology department like a jail and hired a number of average college men to take part in a two-week experiment. He gave them no other information.

When he had enough people, Zimbardo divided them into two lists—wardens and prisoners. The wardens were called in and told their duties. They were to be in charge of some prisoners and were required only to keep order. The prisoners were contacted differently. With no warning, local policemen in squad cars stopped them on the street, searched them, arrested them, and brought them to the jail, telling them nothing except the experiment had begun.

After six days, the experiment had to be stopped because dramatic changes had come over both groups. The prisoners were acting craven—as if they were worthless slime. The wardens had become harsh and dictatorial, abusing their power, and doing more than just keeping order. In some instances, they'd become violent, and one who had claimed strong convictions of non-violence before the experiment was one of the cruelest. Why did this happen? Zimbardo's conclusion: "Most people can be made to do almost anything if you put them in psychologically compelling situations, regardless of their morals, ethics, values, attitudes, beliefs, or personal convictions."

This prompted Toli to tell us a little about the economy and the shadow economy. The state subsidizes certain commodities, such as bread, meat, and transportation, and the money for the subsidies comes, of course, from the people. For example, the state procures grain from farms at the state price, and then the farms must pay double that price to buy it back for feed.

Shopkeepers have to gouge the public because their salaries are small, and they must pay for spoilage and pay suppliers and inspectors. They're either "honest" or "dishonest"—dishonesty meaning they charge much more than is needed to cover their expenses. This is one way a person with a tiny salary can have a lavish house. One of the shopkeepers in Makov is building a three-story house with fancy columns and verandas. The villagers cynically call it "The Symbol of Perestroika"—because there's little crackdown on corruption under Gorbachev.

Another way to get luxuries on a small salary is to be part of the nomenklatura. A third way was revealed to me by a beautiful woman who admitted she received her job, car, house, and dacha because she's the mistress of a district party secretary in a large city.

Some people hoard and control deficit goods. An oft-heard anecdote is: "The shelves are empty, but the refrigerators are full." In one Central Asian republic, people are reporting soap allergies from hoarding soap powder. One home had nine years' worth stashed away! No wonder the shelves are empty!

Bribes and favors are a way of life here, much to the chagrin of most people. They call it "managing to get" something. But I suppose it's that way all over the world wherever goods are scarce. Here people are so sick of it that when the *Moscow News* did a survey, asking people to describe the one quality they wanted most in the People's Deputies, the answer was a resounding "Honesty."

On the village level, everyone knows where everyone else fits into the system. There's strong resentment by ordinary citizens toward those who get special privileges and who cheat others badly for their own material gain. It's good that guns are not readily available to the citizens, for they might be used!

Toli explained that collective farm chairmen and state farm directors usually have to retire to another village or town so citizens do not take revenge on them when they no longer hold power. The members of their entourage become betrayers and will begin to serve the next master for his favors and protection. People call entourage members "leeches on the working people's body."

Chairman Stengach is particularly powerful, having been a Deputy to Ukraine's Supreme Soviet at one time. This gave him high connections, though many of his buddies were fired when Andropov tried to stop corruption. Several of the Central Committee members who were "retired" in March had been visitors to Stupentsi. "Now, the system of connections still works, but it works hard," said Toli. "Our Chairman isn't afraid, however, because he's old enough to retire." (Men may retire at age 60 and women at 55, after 20 years of continuous work. Many, however, keep working. This often creates a problem with the leadership—they're hard to move out of their jobs, even when they can't handle them anymore.)

"Savkov's position is unclear," added Toli. One thing we do know about Savkov is that in one of Ralph's few contacts with him, he indicated he hated the existence of Stupentsi. He called it a costly parasite on Ukraina collective farm. Perhaps he's basically an honest man. We know he works very hard at his job.

"Many chairmen of collective farms and directors of state farms make no improvements for their villages, only for themselves. Our Chairman has done a great deal for Makov," said Toli, "for example, the fine day care center and other facilities for the people. For ten years, it was the only village in the district with natural gas." Ukraina and one other farm in the district get half the available fertilizer. The other half is divided among all the rest. In actuality, Ukraina's wealth comes in large part from indirectly taking the profits of other farms.

The lucrative enterprise that makes Ukraina so prosperous is the feeding of calves to heavy market weight. Originally, someone helped the Chairman get the cattle deal. It has served him well. Calves are bought from dairy collectives at the same price per pound they're sold at a heavy weight to the state. In the US, a new-born calf may cost twice as much per pound as the market price for heavy cattle. Each year, Ukraina sells cattle for seven million rubles—a lot of money. Even at that, there would be no profit if the workers received decent wages. The 150 do-little supervisors on the farm have salaries twice those of workers. A saying about supervisors goes like this: "For everyone who works, there are seven others waiting with their spoons."

The *Moscow News* prints true sad stories of perestroika. A recent one was about a taxi driver in Moscow who left the state taxi enterprise to drive his own cab. Efficiency and profit rose dramatically, but he was badgered and attacked so badly by his old bosses he finally gave up. Why did this happen? "I had stopped feeding the hungry army of hangers-on," he explained. So he was made an example to other taxi-drivers that they'd better not try the same thing. Since the 1920s, the successful have been punished.

Enterprises cheat each other, too. We know, for example, about the way the sugar factory cheats the collective farm by false weighing and the way the farm outfoxes the state by cutting up its ear corn so the state can't remove the kernels for grain.

Chairmen who try to operate honestly are told when they ask for bricks or fertilizer they've all been spoken for. And so they have. The bribes were given long ago. So what's an honest chairman to do if he and his farm are to survive? Generally, he ends up making bribes, too. It's the same with ordinary people—if they're to have more than bare necessities. Some babushkas do have only essentials. Most villagers in the USSR, including their officials, live exceedingly simply. Makov is an exceptional village with an exceptional chairman. Soviet mafia pales beside ours, but it's still a blight. It's hard to say where the mafia ends and heavy bribers begin. Toli says there's a hierarchy: shopkeepers on the bottom; next, those people who do the dirty work (the Chairman's hands are always clean); then, those who protect them, like the Chairman; and finally, higher connections.

The District has a department to bring cases to court, but many never come to trial after phone calls from higher authorities. When cheaters are prosecuted in the USSR, it's usually those on the lowest level, such as shop assistants. Gdlyan was unusual. He tried to hit those on top. Ralph mentioned our IRS goes after the little guys and lets our Mafia go.

The Soviet system is favorable soil for crime to thrive. When sugar was rationed in 1988, who profited? The mafia, at all levels. It was noted when persons didn't pick up all their sugar ration. Then that sugar was sold for twice the price to moonshiners. They, in turn, sold their brew for ten times what they paid for the sugar.

Bribe-takers are afraid of the KGB, which Toli says is the least corrupted organization in the USSR. (We've heard that elsewhere, too.) When Gorbachev took over, the mafia pulled back on their activities, thinking a new offensive against high party privileges would begin, but when it didn't, bribers again danced with glee.

Americans look with dread upon the KGB, although in all our trips, we've experienced nothing ominous from them. In fact, Toli had many classmates at the Kiev Language Institute who ended up in the KGB because all agents have to be fluent in a foreign language. He says the young ones he knows are progressive and support change.

"Why didn't you become a KGB agent?" I asked him.

"I wasn't eligible for two reasons," he replied. "I have relatives in Poland, and I wasn't able to serve my time in the army because I was needed to teach English in a village. Most people who have a chance to take a KGB job take it, for it pays well."

"Have KGB agents asked you about us?" I asked.

"Yes," he said. "And I told them everything, because I wasn't ashamed of anything you've done. They just laughed at the bad rumors about you, and they were upset the Chairman hasn't had a meeting for you to speak to the people. They wanted to make it happen, but they don't have the power."

May 31: We got lost today, driving through little villages and poorer collective farms. The country road got worse and worse, more rocky and muddy, and eventually petered out in a field. Our good Niva took us through an orchard and meadow, past a cloddy, weedy cornfield and back down the hill to a cluster of houses in the bottom of a valley. Ukraine is five times the size of Ohio and has all extremes of topography, sometimes in close proximity.

At one very remote place where the roofs were thatched and there was no sign of anything less than several centuries old, I remarked, "Boy, this is really primitive living!" Just then we met a modern taxi on the rocky lane. Weird!

Once, we followed the ribbon road until it ended in a charming village. I wish we'd had our camera that day. There was a great shot of a woman walking the dirt road home, surrounded by her geese, nanny goat, and leaping kids.

Today I received my second letter from Andrei. I'd answered his first letter, and in it I'd enclosed a postcard from the Fellowship of Reconciliation with a "Prayer for Peace" printed on it in Russian and English. It says: "Lead me from death to life, from falsehood to truth. Lead me from despair to hope, from fear to trust. Lead me from hate to love, from war to peace. Let peace fill our heart, our world, our universe . . . peace, peace, peace."

Andrei had written back:

> If our peoples say to each other such kind things as you said, I think we will be able to break the thick wall standing between us. And the main key, the mightiest weapon, is your 'Prayer for Peace.' It is the prayer not only for peace, but for human love, for human right to be happy and healthy. That is why I have become another link [in the chain of people who pray this prayer]. I've prayed since the receiving of your letter. And I try to find other links among my students and teachers, try to be a continuer of your teaching. I can imagine your surprise during reading my letter, but from the first, you could learn that I am not the usual Komsomol leader. One can hear unexpected words from me. But they are unexpected for those who want to continue building of the wall. And there are many people in the USSR who want to break the wall. I am one of them."

He was right about my surprise. I could hardly believe my eyes to read that an "atheistic" Komsomol leader was now praying daily! One cannot judge.

The president of World Family Clubs talked with me by phone from Moscow and invited us to speak in Arkhangelsk, north of Leningrad, from July 25 to August 2. We accepted with pleasure, especially since an American friend had given us a *Soviet Life* magazine which chronicled the story of the famed "muzhik [rural fellow] of Arkhangelsk" we hoped to meet. The muzhik has become a very productive, independent farmer but has had tremendous problems with the old system fighting him.

Our zoo rarely has visitors, but today a whole class of third-grade children from Kamenets-Podolski came to enjoy the animals and do folk dances. Coincidentally (or was it?), just as we joined in the dancing, a film crew arrived to do a newsreel about us. So they filmed it all. Two of the dancing children in dresses and head scarves laughingly pulled up their skirts and yanked off their scarves to show us they were boys! There were many little girls who didn't get to dance in costume. Why were these boys chosen instead of them?

The newsreel people took us several other places for photographs. On the shore of Makov's lake, several men vacationing at the sanatorium were sunbathing and exercising. When I admired the spotless white cap one was wearing, with the word "peace" in many languages on it, he insisted I take it. I felt terrible, but luckily I was wearing one of our crossed-flag pins, so I gave it to him. From now on, I'll try not to admire anything at a Soviet home or on a person. Otherwise, I'll find myself the new owner of it!

While we were being photographed in the fields, I mentioned to some of the women workers I was happy the church was to reopen. One began to weep with joy and gratitude. It will be a homecoming for many of the older ones.

CHAPTER 5

Christine's Journal Excerpts

JUNE

June 2: On TV today we saw Sakharov receive a vicious verbal attack from Congress. Sakharov had told a Canadian media person Soviet troops fired on their own men in Afghanistan to keep them from being taken prisoner. Even the progressives didn't defend him. Sakharov was shaken and could hardly talk to defend himself but did say the actions are still being investigated. We heard on BBC that one of the People's Deputies called it "the moral lynching of a remarkable man." How ironic a young, disabled soldier, the very sort of person Sakharov tried to save from Afghanistan in the first place, should be the one to lead the attack in the Congress!

Tonight, we were thrilled to turn on the TV and see Phil Donahue and Vladimir Pozner at Notre Dame University. We like Phil, who got his start in Dayton. However, when he was Pozner's American counterpart on the Spacebridges, we were ashamed and embarrassed by the way he attacked the Soviets. We were sure he felt compelled to do this to prevent charges of "Commie-lover." Since then, the two men's friendship has had an effect on them. Here was Donahue tonight, saying risky things—in terms of American popular opinion—about the Soviet Union and the United States. Pozner, who lived in New York City when he was growing up, mentioned some things he likes about America—the freedom and the friendliness of the people.

The first time Ralph and I were with Pozner (summer, 1985), we were surprised to hear him criticize his government's policy on Jewish emigration. He said, "If it were up to me, I'd let them all go if they want to." We remarked at the time on his courage and fairness.

In talking about the Spacebridges tonight, Pozner told the audience he'd been attacked by letter writers in *Izvestia* for not following the party line on the shows. "I found the criticism funny," he said. "It's a question of doing what you think's necessary. Anything worth doing doesn't come easily. There's always a risk."

For his part, Donahue responded, "Nearly everybody in my business considered me a stooge, so I felt I had to go out like Rambo." At the beginning of tonight's program, Donahue nearly gave a sermon. He spoke with great feeling, saying, "Are there jerks in the Soviet Union? Yes. Also here in the US. Is there military? Yes, both places. We [Americans] are not being honest with ourselves about our economic reality, about jobs being lost and our poor and homeless. Our country needs more prisons, and we have to raise taxes to pay for them. We have a nation that's full time into denying reality. Increasing in numbers are people who don't care about any serious problems. *Time* and *Newsweek* look like *People* magazine these days. Few people are interested in my programs when we discuss serious issues. How can we possibly move toward healing relations?"

Towards the end, Pozner said, "Thank you for questioning what you always thought was right. That's what *we're* doing, and that includes our attitude towards the US. I hope *you* have the strength to reassess what you think about *my* country." (Standing ovation for Pozner.)

Donahue wrapped it up, "This is not about conservatives, liberals, Democrats, Republicans. This is about common sense. We are reaching out . . . for our children's sake." (Standing ovation for Donahue.)

June 3: We just returned from a fine dinner and relaxing evening at the home of Toli's school director and his teacher wife. We're beginning to notice when we're invited to someone's home for dinner, two things happen: there's a huge amount of food, and our hosts eat next to nothing. I guess they're making sure we get enough, but it feels strange to be the only ones really eating.

"We are small capitalists," said the school director, referring to his large house. Later, when discussing dental care, he said, "Before I go to the dentist, I say goodbye to my family and friends because I'm not sure I'll survive!"

His toast was especially heart-warming: "You have been here only a few weeks, but it seems you have lived here always!" We feel the same way. We've found ourselves immersed in this culture, and we believe we've made true friends here.

By this time, everyone must know how much we like strawberry juice. They gave us three jars of it, plus other remembrances, as we left.

June 4: Today we stopped to talk with an old lady we've never seen before. She said, "You got letters from America on Friday and Saturday, didn't you?" Oh, the joys of living in a village, where everyone knows everything about everybody, especially the two Americans! When a crew of women are hoeing sugar beets, they have to talk about *something*.

And tonight, we were eating roasted potatoes with Sasha Sportsman and two of his friends from Kamenets. When I discovered one was a hairdresser, I said, "I got a haircut in Kamenets."

"I know," replied the hairdresser. Even in cities of 100,000, word gets around.

When we arrived home, there were a man and a little boy on our doorstep. The man was holding the *Izvestia* article about us. They had come 150 miles on the bus and were tired. We brought them in and served them tea and cake.

The father said although he has a fine flat and a good job, he wants to be a farmer. He is sure he would be successful because he's had experience doing a variety of work since his father's death when he was quite young. He wants to rent 250 good acres so he can have pigs, make his own sausage, and raise crops. The authorities, however, keep trying to give him sandy soil. They also insist he have an agricultural degree. (Degrees are highly valued here, but in this case, it's only an excuse.) He wrote to the Congress to tell them of his poor treatment, and now he wants Ralph's advice. We agreed that the man will write questions, Toli will translate them, and we'll meet again.

Before he left, he asked if we were believers. When we nodded, he crossed himself and gave us a tiny icon. "You are good people; I could tell from your photos in *Izvestia*. God has brought us together," he said.

June 5: Two nights ago there was a horrible train explosion in the Ural Mountains due to a gas leak. About a thousand people died including many children on their way to Pioneer camps. Windows were blown out of homes fifteen miles away. Gorbachev visited the scene and likened it to hell. What suffering these people have endured! First Chernobyl, then the Armenian earthquake, and now this!

I think of a story I once heard about a Kiev TV commentator who was reporting the Challenger accident. "We had Chernobyl, and they have Challenger," he said. Then, after a pause, he corrected himself, "No, *we* have Challenger." The man had caught Gorby's spirit!

Early this morning Ralph, Toli, and I left on a three-hour trip west to the Ivanofrankovsk Region where we'd been invited to speak to the members of a fine collective farm. We hope no one will realize we took our car out of the Region.

On the way, we pulled into a gas station to top off our tank. There Toli recognized a man from Makov who needed gas but couldn't get any because the pumps weren't working. He asked Toli if we would give him some gas from our car, and Toli immediately replied, "Of course!" So the man and Ralph siphoned out a bucketful—another example of the way people help each other. We've often seen strangers give each other cigarettes and matches and share in other ways.

When we got to the collective farm, Mikhail, the barrel-chested young chairman, treated us to a sumptuous breakfast. Then he gave us the grand tour of the brand-new village "center" with its large Swiss-style brick buildings and lavish rose gardens. There were many amenities for the villagers—a volleyball court (where he plays twice a week), an Olympic-size indoor swimming pool, barbers and hairdressers, a clinic with a doctor, lounges, an auditorium, and a ballroom. It had all been completed within four years—an amazingly short time for USSR construction.

Mikhail then whisked us through the clean beef barn, saying, "Our barns are always this clean," and on to see the laying of blacktop roads on the farm and hay-drying. Finally, we rode to the top of a hill to see the special valley below which will be planted with herbs for badly-needed medicine and walnut trees. He borrowed money to do all this but thinks it will pay for itself.

Chairman Mikhail's most remarkable accomplishment, however, is the renting of his entire farm to groups of his people. "The renters keep half the profits," he said, "and the other half goes for village expenses. I also ignore some of the paper work required of me by my higher-ups." Would that more chairmen and directors were like Mikhail!

As we sat drinking coffee with him and his wife in his tiny office/kitchen, we discovered a small coincidence—Mikhail was in Cuba when we were—February, 1986. Also, I noticed he had a VCR, but it was Soviet-made.

At 2 P.M., we entered the auditorium (where about 200 farm folk were waiting), showed the film, and answered questions. At one point, Mikhail took the podium and said, "What is perestroika? I thought at first I was doing everything satisfactorily here on the farm, but then I realized I had to change my attitude. This meeting is to change attitudes, to see how others do things. We're late for this changing of attitudes, and we must make great changes. We're learning English here so we can go to other countries to learn their ways. All people should take part in perestroika. Many people just criticize, do nothing, and don't even have suggestions as to how to make things better. We need to admit our mistakes and move forward—for our children, for our grandchildren, and a little bit for ourselves."

During the question period, one question to me was, "What do *you* do on the farm?"

I answered, "Neechivo" (nothing). The women gasped and applauded.

Then Mikhail rose again and said, "Our greatest shame is the work our women must do. Their work is the hardest. But we must think of our children. We must read books and study culture, and our women could teach this to our children."

At this point, a young man from a neighboring farm, who had spent three weeks in 1988 on an Iowa farm, took the microphone and spoke enthusiastically about what he had seen. "In every way, there's much difference between American and Soviet agriculture," he said. "Everything there is just right. Corn and soybean technology is accurate. There's no corn left in the field after harvesting, and there's no need for student help. There are no trucks in the field [which compact the soil] because they unload the combine at the end of the field. And there's no waiting. It was great!" We sat back, smiling in satisfaction, listening to him tell the same things Ralph's been saying.

Other aspects of American life also impressed him. "In the high schools, they teach farming to boys and home economics to girls. Women have good equipment in their homes; I especially liked the washing machines and toasters, but I expected more from microwave ovens. Americans don't use fat in their cooking like we do," he said. "The American way of eating is this: take as much as you want, but eat it all."

At the end, we were presented with a large, intricately-carved, wooden, box, and each of us, even Toli, received a picture of a beautiful Ukrainian girl painted on metal. The box and metal pictures were all made by small enterprises in the village. Mikhail said, "These are from the people, too!"

When it was time to go home, we discovered our car had been washed and filled with fuel. As is the custom, we were escorted to the highway where we stopped for goodbyes. We were enthusiastic about Mikhail, and we started to hug him goodbye. He picked both of us up at the same time—our feet dangling—and hugged us back!

All the way home, Toli and I talked. We usually do this after these meetings, which energize and inspire us. We started with Sakharov. "Sakharov was searching for the truth," Toli said, "and most people aren't willing to do that because they don't want to accept negative truth. Some Soviets, however, may suspect our 'glorious' paratroopers are capable of doing horrible things, as some of your men did in Vietnam and as is done in most wars. Wars can bring out the worst in people."

In general, the military does not improve the human condition. Instead, it dehumanizes. We once heard a marine acquaintance recite two chants he was taught to march to in boot camp:

1. Napalm! Napalm! Sticks like glue!
    Sticks to the mamas and the papas and the kiddies, too.

2. Rape the town and kill the people.
    That's the only thing to do.
    Rape the town and kill the people.
    That's the thing we love to do.

    Throw some napalm on the schoolhouse.
    Watch the kiddies scream and shout.
    Rape the town and kill the people.
    That's the thing we love to do!

We discussed the military, which is nearly sacrosanct in both our countries. "Ralph and I see it as the single most powerful and inviolate enterprise in the world," I said. "In many countries, it has absolute rule."

Toli and I wondered aloud how a civilization from another planet would judge our level of development in human relations. Perhaps, we thought, if our allegiance were more to the human race than to one of its parts, we would stop making other people our enemies and take on our common enemies of poverty, pollution, and violence. If we were attacked from beyond our planet, we would quickly become a human family. We wondered why it's so hard for us to pull together when we're in danger from these evils within.

I told Toli about Ralph's lifelong work for non-violence, a concept that seems to be even less understood in the USSR than in the US. "Our American friend in Moscow, Bob Meyerson, is also a pacifist," I explained. "He came to that conviction by studying the Bible while he was in the Navy. Now he tries to give Soviets an understanding of pacifism: it doesn't imply passivity but is rather *active* work toward reconciliation. But he says it's slow going." (Russian and Soviet history are so full of horrible invasions they've developed a siege mentality—abetted, of course, by Stalin's paranoia. They are resolved to be ready to defend their motherland if they are invaded again.)

"All high school children here are taught to handle and use real guns," Toli said, "but only with defense in mind." One day I'd seen a group of the high school students marching down Makov's main street with wooden rifles over their shoulders, but this new information stunned me.

"Ever since my days at the Kiev Foreign Language Institute, I've been doing propaganda work," Toli said suddenly, as if making a confession.

"Is that why your picture is on the glory board in front of Headquarters?" I asked.

"That's because I'm a lecturer on international relations, but Viktor Party Secretary seldom asks me to speak. One of my purposes," he said, "has been to try to inspire people to be more spiritually-minded and not so materially-minded."

"What's 'spiritual' to you?" I asked.

"The most important thing is how we treat others," Toli answered. "I'm not a believer, but I think the Bible is the best accumulated wisdom on how to live. It's for more than reading. It's for study. Each verse holds so much. In my lectures, I sometimes said the Bible teaches the way to treat other people; it's the way of harmony in the world. My listeners have been amazed."

"How did you get away with that?" I asked him.

"The authorities rarely checked on my speeches, and when a few of them challenged me, they couldn't hold their own because I know so much about the Bible.

"When I was 13," he continued, "I discovered one family in our village who had one. They let me come to their house to read it. As I read it, deep chords sounded within me that I didn't know existed. I returned again and again to it and learned more each time. It's the greatest creation there is, but I can't say who created it. When I came to the place where Jesus was sentenced to be crucified, I was sure the people would rise up and save him. I was very upset when they did not. But when I got to know church people, I could see how it happened."

"What do you think about the Resurrection?" I asked.

"I don't believe it happened in reality," he answered, "but was a symbol of Jesus's teachings living on in the hearts of his followers.

"Many thinking persons now know," he said, "that Lenin's and Jesus's ideas for how to live and treat others dovetail. But we don't need the church," he added. "It divides people. It causes wars. And I see no difference between believers and atheists."

Toli is able to get books somewhere. "When propaganda was so bad against the US," he said, "I subscribed to a monthly journal put out by the Institute on US and Canadian Studies, written not for the people but for the experts. It tried to tell the truth about America. All information is available in the USSR, but it's hard to get."

The talk about spirituality prompted me to tell Toli about our beliefs. He knows Ralph and I are "believers" (as they say in the USSR) and have always been active church members. "But," I said, "we shrink from any religion that thinks it has the only way of life and others must be persuaded or persecuted until they agree. We think this attitude—be it in religious or political ideology—is anathema to Jesus' attitude of inclusiveness."

"I agree," Toli said. "An example of hard-headed political ideology is in El Salvador where both superpowers are supplying weapons. Nothing is being decided, and all that's happening is the death of innocent people."

Ralph joined in. "Forcing doesn't really work," he said. "Using violence is like sitting down on a waterbed; the problem just pops up somewhere else."

We finished the ride with a lengthy discussion of near-death experiences, which have been reported by about eight million Americans and many others around the world. There was even a recent meeting for Soviets who have experienced NDEs. Oh what a wonderful day!

June 6: Sasha Bekker, a Russian reporter from the *Moscow News*, and Wendy Sloane, an American reporter from *Time* magazine, arrived this morning. We invited them to stay with us for four days while they interviewed us.

Wendy speaks Russian fluently and is on a two-month joint assignment with *Moscow News* where she met our friend Bob Meyerson. While she was casting about for a story, Bob suggested she interview us. Besides, she wanted to see this part of the country and have a little vacation.

Slightly-built Sasha, who's thirtyish, speaks politely and with great intensity. He used to write for *Izvestia* and now writes agricultural stories for the *Moscow News*. We discovered he was the one who wrote the story in *Soviet Life* magazine about the muzhik of Arkhangelsk.

These two reporters were just beginning to know each other and weren't getting along very well. Sasha was trying to "take care of" Wendy, and she, being a capable, independent young woman, resented it. It turns out Sasha had been told by his superiors at the paper he was responsible for everything that happened to Wendy. Thus, he was doing his best to protect her.

In the evening five of the young people from the eleventh grade came to visit, as scheduled. It was a special treat for them to speak with Wendy, an American only nine years older than they were, not to mention an interesting man from Moscow. They liked the homemade cake I served (it was probably the cinnamon). Tonight blond, punk-haired Igor, who rides his motorcycle suicidally but is really quite serious, asked the best questions. He was especially interested in what Ralph and I thought we could do to help their country.

At one point, the conversation turned to sex and abortion. Natasha said, "We don't have any trouble with our high school girls getting pregnant here."

"Natasha, you don't know what you're talking about," replied Val.

One of the boys added, "Condoms are sometimes available, but they're of poor quality. Besides, everybody stares at you if you try to buy them." Pre-marital sex is frowned upon in the USSR.

I gave each of the students a blank audio cassette, a scarce item here. As the students left, they said words couldn't express how grateful they felt to be able to have a good talk with Americans.

June 7: Today was a full one. Ralph took the reporters and me to the fields, the stores, the rented beef farm, a chicken enterprise (where the chickens are in cages, as in the US), a forest, a cemetery, and a tiny village where we talked with an old couple. "We don't have much," said the old woman, "but we have all we need. We're very happy." Most people here want much more, though we've heard some people in Makov admit it's a pretty good life.

We picked up a hitchhiking woman today. She's the brigadier in charge of the vegetable fields on the farm. She invited us to her house to drink cold compote (cooked fruit juice and sugar with bits of fruit). Their house is being remodeled, and in the dining room was a piano, the only one I've seen in the village. This woman is dissatisfied with her life and begged us to take her and her oldest son to America. I wondered, "What about her husband and two younger sons?"

The woman's brashness embarrassed Sasha, and he kept saying to Wendy, "Don't translate! Don't translate!" Wendy did anyway, but Ralph and I didn't respond.

The evening found us at Toli's for dinner, with Ralph, Toli, and Sasha speaking vigorously about farming. The more excited Sasha became, the more Toli tried to soothe him. It wasn't that they disagreed about farming; it was Sasha's frustration about the problems standing in the way of change that agitated him so.

Meanwhile Tanya, Wendy, and I discussed our concerns about our children (Wendy has none) and our men. Wendy said, "I can see you and Ralph have a good relationship."

"Tolik and I do, too," said Tanya. "He's like a wall between me and the harshness of life. I can tell him anything, and he understands. If he weren't that way," she added, "I wouldn't be here."

About Vova, she said, "He's so quiet and dreamy. I wish he were studious and assertive instead. Sometimes I'm even mean to him because of it. I worry about his self-esteem because I'm always telling him to be different. He spends a lot of time with my mother. She accepts him as he is. Vova's always asking me to be with him, but I can't because Yura takes all my time and energy. But still, I think I understand Vova better than anyone, even Babushka," she concluded. Tears were in her eyes.

I felt a rush of memories, and suddenly, tears stung my eyes, too. I told Tanya, "There was a time when I could have given more to my youngest son, and I'm sure he felt it. I so regret it, but there's no way I can do it over again. Does Vova still ask you to spend time with him?"

"Yes," Tanya replied.

"Then do it, Tanya!" I said. "It may not be long before he'll stop asking. Anna can watch Yura for you occasionally. I think you'll be sorry later if you don't. Vova is precious just the way he is."

"I'm glad you think there's still time," replied Tanya. Our discussion would have been understood by women in any country.

June 8: Sasha woke up early to do his morning exercises, and he decided to wade in the Chairman's pond behind our house.

The pond was just drained and cleaned, and truckloads of white sand were spread on its concrete floor. Now, it's slowly being refilled, and the water is at a six-inch depth. Ralph and I have never inspected the Chairman's dacha close-up because it's behind the locked gates Johanna opens for him. Barbed wire blocks the shore around the pond. So the only other way to get there is by taking a boat. There are two, a rowboat and a bicycle-type paddle boat, but they're always moored on the Chairman's side of the pond. Besides, we wouldn't snoop around, knowing he wants his privacy.

Sasha walked through the water and came upon two naked men sitting in a sauna by the Chairman's dacha. As Sasha tells it, when they saw him, they nervously asked, "Who are you?"

"I'm a reporter for the *Moscow News*," piped Sasha. We giggled as we imagined their alarm in thinking they might be unveiled (figuratively, of course) in the *Moscow News*. It prints many exposes these days. Party officials are not supposed to have these special places. Their dachas are to be simple ones, like those of average people. They're *supposed* to be working toward a classless society. After this incident, the Chairman was especially solicitous of Wendy and Sasha.

Today was our fourth wedding anniversary, and Toli gave us red roses. Conveniently, Sasha and Wendy were gone all day to Kamenets-Podolski to be wined, dined, and shown the town by two party bosses. When they returned, they handed us more roses, sent by their hosts. And they brought cinnamon! Wendy knew it was running low in my cupboard. They said they got it at the market in Kamenets, but I've never seen any there. The Soviets I know aren't even familiar with it. Were their party hosts also responsible for the cinnamon?

Ralph and I spent nearly three hours that afternoon tape-recording answers to questions Wendy and Sasha had written out for us. We're glad they want to use our actual words because the articles will probably be more accurate that way. All the questions required thoughtful answers except one of Sasha's, which amused us: "Do you fight here more than you do at home?"

Wendy was annoyed at this and explained, "He asked that because he thinks it must be awful for you to live here, thus making you disagreeable."

Actually, we don't fight anywhere. Once in a while we don't agree, but we learn from each other. At our age, the sharp corners have been rounded off. Little things don't matter, and we treasure our moments together.

Sasha and Wendy intend to write an article together for the *Moscow News*. Wendy may submit a different piece to *Time*, but she doubts they'll use it because they recently did a whole issue on the USSR.

June 9: This morning Wendy decided to use her roll of film, so she snapped us cranking up the bucket at a pretty well in the village. The owner of the well was a tall, straight-backed old man who has lived alone since his wife died 20 years ago. His family's from Georgia, that area of the Caucasus Mountains where the people are so long-lived. His father lived to be 114, and he's hoping for the same. He has three children, all in different professions. A current *Moscow News* in English was on his table. I'll bet everyone in the village has fascinating stories to tell about their lives, if we only had time to talk with them.

Wendy also interviewed Valentina, who heard from Palamarchouk that when he returns to Ukraine, he wants to farm on his own.

Later, we drove Sasha and Wendy for one and a half hours through the pouring rain to the Khmelnitski airport. Wendy happily cradled a large box of sausages the Chairman had given her after she interviewed him. She also bought ten boxes of tea because it's scarce in Moscow right now. On the way to Khmelnitski, she and Sasha continued to trade insults like sister and brother, but I discerned a friendlier tone.

Ralph has decided the best way he can help Soviet agriculture become self-sustaining is to write a book for Soviet farmers and bureaucrats. So he has begun to write. I'll follow the original suggestion of the jolly newsreel-maker and write about our experiences here, and I'll put in a goodly amount about America, because people are eager to hear about it. It'll be two books in one. The title came easily—*Heart to Heart*.

Invitations are fewer now with the advent of summer. This is when most people take their 24-day or one-month vacations. Some spend these days at sanitoriums, like the one in Makov. It's famous for its healing mineral water and has a special program and equipment for those with liver disease. We've seen people walking the two miles from the bus stop to the sanatorium carrying a bag that looks as if it's holding only one or two changes of clothes. But just think! The women don't have to find food or cook during this time. They're served in a dining room!

Often city-dwellers go to their country dachas, usually tiny hand-built huts with no electricity or plumbing. They tend their vegetable gardens and rest their bodies and souls from the adversities of city life. Soviets aren't unique in receiving spiritual nourishment from nature; they just take more advantage of it. Forests and lakes are popular spots. And often we see Soviets enjoying robust games of ice hockey or cross-country skiing rather than hightailing it for home after work as we might do.

One thing that baffles me, however, is their zest for swimming in icy water. We've met several enthusiasts of that terrible sport. They seem extra-healthy, so maybe we're missing something. I remember seeing a Norwegian calendar with a small girl standing in the snow. It said, "Make friends with the cold, and it will be good to you." That appealed to me, and remembering it has rescued me at my coldest moments.

Mushroom-hunting is another enjoyable and useful activity for Soviet leisure hours. A potential mushroom-hunter will take a long stick, remove the bark, and rub the stick smooth. It is then the proper instrument for pushing aside leaves and grass to find the prize.

Once Ralph and I went mushroom-hunting on Maiden Island in the Volga River. We found one of those polished sticks in the grass, and after diligently probing the leaves, uncovered three large, white mushrooms. We proudly took them back to our cruise ship where I spent a long time removing the dirt. Then, as I made my way to the kitchen to ask the cook to prepare them for our supper, a fiery young Soviet man with a black beard, the resident environmental expert on our trip, accosted me and demanded, fortissimo, "Don't eat those!"

"Why ever not?" I asked.

"Because they sponge up pollution from our air," he stated. "If you eat those, you will have an extraordinary amount of contaminants in your body!" Then, pianissimo, he added, "But, of course, it's up to you."

By that time I felt so cowed I wouldn't have dared defy him. Sadly, I left them on the plate for everyone to see as an example of the functionless flora of that area. Later, I found them gone. Probably some reckless person had copped them, cooked them, and relished them immensely.

Another mushroom story comes to mind. In September, 1988, a Moscow co-operative obtained internal visas to take us north, three hours by car, to the Kalinin Region near the source of the Volga River. Much of the land there had been abandoned, The area was so poor local officials asked us not to take pictures. They showed Ralph a map of 150,000 acres and asked, "How much do you want to manage?" Ralph declined.

Later the men crowded into a jeep (the roads were too muddy for a car) to look at the fields. We two women—Marina, wife of the President of the co-op, and I—were to go to the dacha of a Moscow co-op member, so we climbed into his car. I was in the back seat, and he looked around and asked me, "Do you want to drive?" Startled, I declined. It took him about five minutes to get the car started because he couldn't work the clutch, and finally we were off with a jerk, rolling from side to side as the tires sunk into mud-ruts. It was a wild ride, with all of us laughing and exclaiming. Later, he admitted, "I haven't driven since I got my driver's license thirty-five years ago."

Finally, thankfully, we arrived. His wife was there, but she was asleep for she hadn't been expecting us. She quickly rose to the occasion and welcomed us with that typical Soviet hospitality which gives all. The dacha had been a regular cottage, but as the area was very poor, many people had abandoned their cottages to live in the city. Thus, the Moscow family uses it for a dacha each summer. She gave us a tour, and when she opened the fourth and last door, there stood a cow, quietly chewing her cud! Bossy had her own outside entrance, too.

As we sat talking, Marina asked me sweetly in English, "Do you want to go to the resting-room?" I did. The seat above a pit in the earth was in a separate room. The village is far enough north to make this possible, smell-wise. As in most homes, *Pravda* was being used for toilet-paper.

Then our hostess began to cook for us. Luckily, she had gathered mushrooms in the forest just that morning. She fried them and added sour cream from her family member, the cow. She also served wild honey and red-raspberry jam. Her husband had brought fresh bread and a sausage from Moscow. "This is all we have to eat," she told Marina. A great contrast to prosperous Makov.

June 11: Anna and Nina have been wanting to show us what they think is the most beautiful Russian Orthodox Church in the area. So this morning our Niva took the four of us up the steep, twisting, dirt roads to Verbka, a village several miles away. Anna thoughtfully gave me a new, flowered headscarf to wear. When we arrived at the church, Ralph and I thought we had the wrong place. There were no vehicles or any sign of activity. But we peeked inside and saw perhaps 150 people devoutly worshipping. As we entered, we caught the aroma of fresh mint and incense.

The congregation was comprised of about 25 men in black suit jackets, a few families with children, some young people, and many babushkas. At 5' 5" I was a head taller than nearly all the babushkas. One woman had a white patch over one eye, and another woman, with a stump leg and a crutch, sat on a bench against the wall. People were intensely involved in their worship and paid no attention to us.

As I looked closer at the women, I saw many were not really old; they only gave that impression, perhaps because of their headscarves and sun-worn faces. Americans often ask us why the women wear "babushkas," as we call them. It's tradition, of course, but the scarves also keep dust off and cover hair women haven't had time to groom. (By the way, though one of our meanings for "babushka" is headscarf, in Russian the word means strictly grandmother or old woman.)

As the offering was collected, little biscuits were passed out. Maybe they were the "Body of Christ." Then, the priest blessed the people gathered around him by touching an open book to their heads. He even blessed a baby in its father's arms. Anna led Ralph and me up to be blessed, too.

We knew Sunday services in the Russian Orthodox Church are over five hours long, at least in Makov. Consequently, I—a good, soft American—was hoping not to have to stay for the whole service. Anna must have understood because after an hour, she asked if we would like to leave. Ralph's back was beginning to hurt from standing on the stone floor, so we gratefully said, "Da." What wimps we are!

On the way home, I asked, "Anna, don't you ever get tired from standing all those hours in church?"

"Oh, no," she said rapturously. "The time goes quickly because I'm worshipping my Lord."

As we looked for a better route home to Makov, a policeman stopped us. It was a most unlikely scene—two Americans, driving a collective farm four-wheel-drive with two babushkas in the back, traveling through a stone quarry. As usual, Ralph didn't understand the policeman's request, so he handed over his Ohio driver's license. And, as usual, the officer studied it for awhile, said something, and we drove off. Soon the road took us under a railroad arch. As we drove through foot-deep water there, the rear-view mirror revealed Anna and Nina wide-eyed in the back seat.

Later, Anna asked us to stop so she could gather a bouquet of wildflowers from a field for me—scarlet poppies and delicate purple bell flowers. I jumped out of the car, too, and took her picture. Van Gogh would have loved the scene: bright-blue-eyed Anna, up to her hips in the rippling hay, with a chorus of colors around her.

As we explored by car, she said playfully, "I don't know this road. Maybe we're going to America!"

A bit later, Ralph pointed to a weedy corn field and said one of his fifty Russian words, "Kookoorooza [corn] kaput!" Anna pointed to another field, a bit better, and Ralph said, "Nyet!"

"Sovietski Soiyooz plokho!" (Soviet Union no good) she summarized.

I told her the US also has its problems. For example, there are many poor in our country. Anna asked, "Are they as poor as we are?" I had to admit most aren't.

In the afternoon, Toli came with Yura, and I babysat. I got a taste of Tanya's constant responsibility as I chased after Yura around the zoo. How can those little legs go so fast? They look like tiny wheels going round.

June 14: Toli received a letter today from Palamarchouk who said he was feeling overwhelmed by the abundance of goods in the US—and homesick. He mentioned American farm machinery isn't much more advanced than the Soviets' but is of higher quality. "The real secret, however, of the success of American agriculture," he said, "is that the farmers are independent."

After several days of my son Ted and me trying to call each other, he finally got through. One of the biggest problems with the phone is blaring music in the switchboard building in Dunaevtsi. Even if we get a line, we can hardly hear because of that confounded music. It's another of those illogical things that happen in the Soviet Union.

Ted and I talked about Joel, who's coming to the USSR with a youth tour led by the Fellowship of Reconciliation. I told him to tell Joel we'll do our best to rendezvous with him in Minsk, the closest he'll come to Makov.

I call Ralph the "Mad Writer" these days because he seems to spend every spare minute writing his part of our book. He wants to finish it here so Toli can translate it while he still has Ralph available to clear up confusing idioms. Toli knows agricultural terms in both languages. He also knows how Ralph thinks, so he would be our best translator.

Toli is especially busy at school now, finishing the year. Teachers here are responsible for the physical maintenance of their classroom—from washing curtains and shellacking desks to whitewashing walls, probably as our teachers were years ago.

This morning, I picked up Tanya and Anna and we went to the market at Kamenets-Podolski. The stands were full of people selling fresh, seasonal produce and flowers. All their products looked and smelled wonderful. The apples, however, are neither waxed nor as perfect-looking as those at home. We've learned to eat smaller fruits with blemishes, but they seem healthier. I bought peas in their pods, strawberries, apricots, and cherries. I've not needed to buy flowers because my vase is continually full of those that people give us, usually large, fragrant roses of all colors.

People were also selling roasted sunflower seeds for snacks. There's no junk food here, but people carry pocketfuls of sunflower seeds, cracking off each shell with their teeth before eating them. We Americans would be better off if our snack food were as hard to get at! The closest thing to fast food here is "shash-leek," delicious pork shish-ke-bobs occasionally cooked on grills by the side of the road to Kamenets.

Anna and Tanya bought big buckets of cherries to make into compote. Normally, the villagers go to market on public buses. These buses come by every half-hour or so on the road passing through the Shatava end of Makov. In addition, the villagers must walk to the bus-stop and home again, managing their heavy buckets and bags—an ordeal repeated dozens of times a year. If we were here all year, we wouldn't survive except by gifts from the people. I haven't done any gardening or canning, and that seems to be what villagers live on all winter. They can't count on what's grown on the farm, for that food's taken away to the cities.

Toli came to our home later, saying he was amazed I drove to Kamenets-Podolski. I've seen only two other women driving in this village of nearly 6,000. That probably accounts for his surprise.

He, Ralph, and I then dropped in on the machine-yard workers at Chechelnik. We had forgotten our photos, so the men simply didn't believe Ralph plants everything no-till. A couple of them said they'd like to be renters, but they didn't believe the State would give land to rent. One man with especially strong breath nearly used me for a leaning post. The only woman there shooed him back. The area around here is the 2,000 acres the Chairman wanted Ralph to farm—the hilliest and worst corner of the farm.

After that, we visited the family at the rented beef farm where Svetlana had interviewed Ralph. We then went to their house. Besides the four workers—father, mother, son and his wife—the family also includes a babushka and two children. They expressed their pleasure in having the opportunity to rent. They like what they're doing, with two exceptions: they don't like having to pay for manure to be hauled away, and they don't like the supervision they still have from the collective farm.

On the other hand, here's what they like about renting: feeling more independent, doing most of their own planning, and earning 16,000 rubles per year for their family (333 rubles a month for each worker), if the budget is met. We read their contract. It gives the collective farm most of their profit, just for "owning" the land and equipment. The renters' income is limited, but the collective farm's is not. This seems particularly unfair to me.

We've had rain for eight days so it's difficult to do the laundry. It's also strawberry season. We're gorging on them because when they're gone, that's it for strawberries until next year. But there'll be red raspberries and new apples soon.

Recently, I've been putting out milk for the wild, half-starved cats that occasionally appear. They skulk away as soon as they see us. Now three tiny, skinny kittens (two black and one gray) come to drink the milk, too. I hope this won't make life hard for them when we leave. I'd like to pet them, but they're too wild to get close to. They wait nearby until I'm a safe distance away, then approach the dish. Also, sometimes the peacocks poke around our house before they march to the lodge. I've seen them drink the milk, too, or clumsily upset the bowl by stepping on its edge.

And the ants are back. Now they've sprouted wings and are flying all over the place. Reluctantly, I'm spraying them with poison.

June 16: Today we had an excellent meeting with Chairman Ivan and his collective farm people, right outside Khmelnitski. To our delight, Buddha was there, too. There seemed to be especially good contact between Ralph and the people, perhaps due to Ralph's confident telling of the truth as he sees it. The mood went beyond mere curiosity to earnestness of purpose. At one point, when Buddha disagreed with Ralph's seeding rate remark, Ralph explained he'd actually measured that rate on three collective farms. Typical questions are: What's Ralph's education? How'd he get started? What's his profit? Does he ever have trouble selling his crops? What's a typical day during planting and harvesting? How does he raise his pigs?. How is the farm passed on? Why doesn't he need herbicide for wheat?

After the photos were passed around, one didn't come back—the one of the mother pig with her ten piglets. Luckily, we brought several sets of photos to the USSR. The meeting ended with gifts, flowers, and a hug between Ralph and Ivan.

Afterwards, we toured the impressive farm—the calf barn, the ginseng garden (eight years from planting to harvest), and the fabulous day care center which began not long ago with 5 children and now has 85. There was also an impressive complex for the people, with a swimming pool, sauna, canteen, medical rooms, game rooms (billiards and ping pong), and much more, including a large greenhouse for hydroponically-grown flowers. Ivan hopes these flowers will finance the whole complex.

We asked Ivan if he rented out any of his farm. He said he'd tried, but no one would rent. He then told two true stories about renters who wouldn't work—one who'd rented land for strawberries and didn't even get them planted, and another who let his goat nearly starve. We saw the goat grazing there; Ivan was rehabilitating her. "You can put these examples in your book," he said. He's obviously negative about renting.

Ivan has visited Britain and Hungary. He has a West German corn planter and hopes to sell furs to Austria to get more equipment. He's also very interested in no-till. During the tour of the farm, we came to a stretch of muddy ground, so Ivan just picked me up with one arm and carried me over the mud! Every Chairman we've met so far has been big and powerful. Is that a prerequisite for the job? (Just kidding.)

Ivan said he was at Kiev Gosagroprom when our letter and pictures came in. It tickled him we had cut through all the red tape and just come. He had asked to host us but was turned down, so he invited us to come next year to stay on his farm. He'd also like to work for a month in Ohio.

Ivan then asked if we wanted coffee, and took us to a room with a round table laden with food. It seemed to me the two men were good friends, so I asked Buddha if that were true. "You felt that, didn't you?" he replied. Then he added, "Ivan is something of a poet."

That became evident when one of his toasts brought tears to my eyes. It was a special tribute to citizen diplomacy and how important it is. Ivan said, "You two are true patriots of your country because you are making real contact with the Soviet people."

Later, he told us, "Anatoli [Buddha] hasn't been promoted because of the way he is. He knows verses and likes to read, especially history." (Buddha may be an example of the better-than-mediocre who are often passed over.) Ivan continued, "Truth will always be revealed, no matter what country it's in. The truth will overcome!" Buddha agreed. For the second time that afternoon, my eyes were damp.

As usual, Toli and I talked all the way home. He objected to Ivan's saying, "The reason few people have come forward to rent is that the habit of not working hard is ingrained in the souls of our people."

"We should have talked with the *people* to get their version of the rental situation," Toli said. "The people are not lazy but are afraid the government may cheat them again." Ralph and I agree.

Toli and I also talked about new ways of thinking. I told him about Virginia Satir, the psychologist who was a pioneer in family counseling until her death in 1988. The last emphasis in her life was peace—inner peace, peace between people, and international peace. She believed the old way of thinking reached its final, logical conclusion in Hitler's thinking and actions. This old way—characterized by hierarchy, violence, fear, conformity, a feeling of us versus them, and win/lose situations—has been in the ascendancy since humankind began. This old way, of course, has been epitomized by the Soviet Union, but most countries have some of these aspects. The old way, however, is giving way to a new one characterized by equality, democracy, negotiation, risk-taking, individual expression, win/win situations, and a feeling of us *and* them. Of course, Jesus said the same things 2,000 years ago.

Virginia Satir believed critical mass is building. Soon, a big enough percentage of the population with this different attitude will exist to trigger a change. Eventually all of humanity will make the leap. I told Toli I believe it's beginning to happen already. In any case, we see people all over the world striving for their true rights as equal people.

June 18: Last evening Ralph and I went to the House of Culture for the eleventh grade's graduation. It was a dreary affair with only adults speaking. During the graduation, Toli was engrossed in a book a friend from Philadelphia sent us. It was called *USSR: From an Original Idea by K. Marx* by Marc Polonsky and Russell Taylor. It's a humorous guide to tourism in the USSR. Toli showed me a passage: "Karl Marx invented it, V.I. Lenin put it into life, and the Soviet people have to live with it." He laughed and laughed and said the book would be very popular here. I'll leave it with him. Perhaps he'll translate it sometime. We can get another back home.

Afterwards, we enjoyed the graduates' ball with them—eating, dancing, and talking—until we left at 11 P.M. It was in the gym again and very much like their prom, without the speeches. All the girls looked fresh and pretty. I wonder if a few years of hard labor in the fields will make them look decades older.

Most of the young people we know, however, plan to go on to some sort of higher education. One will be a doctor. Another will study child-care so she can work in a day care center. Several will study agriculture, one will learn how to repair TVs and refrigerators, and Igor will train to be a sailor on a ship that sails the world. Natasha will try to get into the same Kiev Language Institute Toli attended. Each has plans.

I invited Toli and his family to dinner today because Lusa and Valeri are here from Kiev. People are more casual about time here, and since most don't have phones, a hostess takes what she gets. Today, however, was an extreme example. I expected 10 people for dinner at 3 P.M., and 4 showed up at 5:30. They were late because of Yura's nap and other problems. I was slightly annoyed but soon got over it. I try to remember two rules to relieve stress:

1. Don't sweat the small stuff.
2. It's all small stuff.

Besides, something amusing happened: We've always brought pantyhose to the USSR as gifts because we were told they're hard to get. Today, Lusa gave me a gift—a pair of beautiful pantyhose with roses on them—the prettiest I've ever seen!

Right after all but Toli left, the Chairman and his wife Lydia arrived with a big box of chocolates and a full-page article in the *Silski Visti* newspaper (Agricultural News) about Ralph. (A small symbol of the difference between our two cultures: a box of chocolates here contains identical candies while an American box usually has a large variety.)

Discussing the article, the Chairman said, "Four years ago, directives were written giving collective farms nearly complete freedom from their higher-ups. But there's practically none of that freedom left. Ligachev [USSR party boss of Agriculture] might have had something to do with that. He doesn't know agriculture," he added.

"I was told you were coming only four days before you actually arrived," he went on. "Earlier, I was told you were to come in October or November of 1988, so we built a house in the village for you. But as you didn't arrive, I sold it to someone else."

"How did we end up on your farm?" I asked. "And how was Palamarchouk chosen?"

"I don't know," he answered. "I was told only to receive you."

"We recently met with Chairman Ivan near Khmelnitski," I said. "He said he asked to have us on his farm but was refused."

"The authorities help him build a showplace," said the Chairman somewhat bitterly. "It's close to the center of the Region and can be easily reached, whereas Makov is not often visited because it's far away."

He changed the subject. "Why don't you travel and see things while you're here? Perhaps to the beautiful city of Lvov in western Ukraine? Also, I must tell you—on Tuesday, the Jewish hosts of my granddaughter who's in medical school in Chernovtsi will be staying in the lodge next door to you for 10 days. They want to discuss with you whether or not they should emigrate to America."

He left us wondering what our new neighbors will be like.

June 19: Though Khrushchev was progressive in many ways, he was very hard on the churches. It was he who closed the little church in Makov. Today, three large crosses that were on its roof before it was closed are to be restored to their former perches. We went over to watch. The crane hadn't arrived, but the church was open. We went inside. Dozens of women and a few men were standing, singing among rough vertical timbers—the scaffolding for painting the inside.

After awhile, Anna appeared at my side and asked me to sing a solo. Gazing at their ancient icon of Christ surrounded by flowers, I sang a verse of the haunting Negro spiritual, "Were You There When They Crucified My Lord?" Ralph said the people really liked it, even Toli, who's not easily impressed.

We sang two or three more numbers with the people. Sometimes I heard a rich baritone behind me. I turned to see a white-haired man, rapt in song. Later, we joined Toli. He was talking outside with a large group of old men, all believers. The baritone was among them. We were particularly drawn to him because his body language seemed to personify the quality of humility. His name is Zhenya, and he told us the history of the church. It was built in 1756, closed in 1958 "due to structural weakness," and then damaged by an earthquake in 1976. In 1982 the authorities decided to destroy it. They put three large cables around it, each attached to a caterpillar tractor, and gave the signal to pull. The people surrounded the church, praying. It held! Next, the decision came to blow it up. But the dynamiting crew deliberately charged such a high price it was decided to let it stand. Finally, the church was repaired, painted white inside, and used for a picture gallery.

As Zhenya spoke, he did so with the greatest sweetness I've perhaps ever encountered. Each gesture was an act of reverence, of worship. He said, "We think President Reagan influenced General Secretary Gorbachev to change the attitude toward the churches."

"Gorbachev made those changes before he met Reagan," I replied.

"We are not against anyone," he answered simply. What a beautiful lesson in peace and love!

We noticed as we were talking with Zhenya that some of the men began to snicker about him. Toli said later, "Zhenya is a very unusual man, and some of the people don't understand him. But they call him 'Little God.' It's not a derogatory term; it's descriptive."

June 20: Ralph and I have been wanting to talk with Anna and Nina about some of their experiences, such as the Nazi occupation during World War II. Nina, who's 65, began. "When the invasion was announced on the radio at 11 A.M. on June 22, 1941, people were greatly afraid. No one expected it—so much so that the school balls were held the night before. The next day, all the village men between 18 and 40 were mobilized, loaded onto trucks, and taken away. Anna was 12 then and lived in a village 95 miles north of here. I was 17 and lived in Makov. My brother and five cousins fought on the front lines. My brother survived, but my five cousins perished. My father fought in World War I and was a prisoner of war in Germany. Then he took part in the Great Patriotic War (World War II) and survived it all.

"On July 6, the Nazis moved in. Fighting was heard around Shatava, then separate from Makov. Party and Komsomol members ran when they knew the Germans were coming. Those who didn't were hanged. Many gypsies and Jews—and even those who looked like gypsies or Jews—were killed not far from Makov.

"The Germans put a detachment of 50 Hungarian soldiers in charge of Makov. The Germans themselves were based in Dunaevtsi, and they came here only occasionally—to get sugar from the sugar factory."

"Everything was taken from our village," Anna said.

"The same was true in Makov," added Nina.

Anna continued, "Machine guns were used so there would be no hint of resistance. People worked the fields as usual, but the Germans took all the food. It was too dangerous to try to hide any. We ate mostly barley bread.

"People were told to bring all their radios and arms to the police station, and if they disobeyed, the punishment was death. I don't know of anyone being killed in Makov, but people were shot and hanged in Kamenets-Podolski and Dunaevtsi. Near the hospital in Dunaevtsi, the Germans had a POW camp for Soviet prisoners. All the prisoners were later shot. In a neighboring village, prisoners were locked in a barn which was then burned down. Women used to take food to prisoners.

Nina and Anna in Makov, talking about their lives.

"After two months, the Hungarians left, and a Ukrainian mayor and 10 Makov policemen were appointed to be in charge of Makov. Of course, they were required to answer to the Germans.

"In the spring, German soldiers came with dogs and trucks and began to take away teenagers to work in Germany. People were afraid to go to Kamenets or Dunaevtsi because a net had been organized to capture young people. First, they took the oldest teenagers. Eventually, even boys of 13 were taken. They'd been told they were going to study in Germany."

Then Anna spoke. "When my brother Vasily was 16, he and my 19-year-old sister were taken, and my mother nearly went mad. Luckily, both of them survived and returned to Ukraine. My sister, however, nearly starved to death because she worked in a factory. Those who worked on German farms were often better off. There was more to eat and sometimes the farm families were kind. During this time, my five-year-old sister died at home. And as for my father—he was taken at age 44, *after* the liberation of our village, to fight with the Soviet army. He was killed, and after victory was declared, we all cried because we realized he wasn't coming back."

"Early on," continued Nina, "the Germans came to Makov to take Jews to Dunaevtsi. Older Jews and children were shot in Shatava. Many Jews lived in Shatava before the war, and more than a hundred were killed there. They had hidden in the forest. Somehow the Germans learned of it and found them. Approximately 300,000 people, including over 200,000 Jews, were killed in Kiev at a place called Babi Yar [which Ralph and I visited in 1985].

"Savkov is half Jewish, and he was five when the Germans discovered it. At the time, his Jewish father was divorced and was living in a different place, so a brave non-Jewish man from Makov stepped forward, claiming to be the boy's father. In this way he was saved.

"I remember two Jewish children, a boy twelve and his four-year-old sister. They were ordered to go to Dunaevtsi. It was too far for the little girl to walk, so her brother carried her—to their deaths. I knew their handsome father.

"My boyfriend had escaped army recruitment because he had a crippled hand. He and I were not registered anywhere, and we stayed together. We went from one village to another, hoping we wouldn't become known. We married in 1942, and he died just last year.

"Soon, people began to conspire, and the guerilla movement was born— a great help to the regular troops. The Ukrainian POWs who worked at the sugar factory communicated with the guerillas at night. In Makov, the guerillas only kept accounts of the activities of the mayor and policemen. But in other areas, those guerillas who knew German and were especially brave took forged papers to those places where young people were to be taken to Germany. They saved many youths from that fate. At the time of liberation, a guerilla headquarters was at my house. Once I heard a German POW say he was afraid of our guerillas in the forest.

"The mayor and one policeman in Makov were particularly cruel. They beat people. Early on, they also swept waste into piles and forced Jewish people to eat it while they laughed. A couple of the policemen, however, warned us when someone came to take our cow so we could hide it. Later, the mayor was arrested by Soviet troops when Makov was liberated. If he had not been arrested, the people would have killed him.

"The village people, having no radios or newspapers, knew almost nothing about the progress of the war. But in the winter of 1944, it became clear the Germans were retreating because we could hear the roar of the front lines. Makov was liberated at the end of March, 1944, two months before the US beached at Normandy, but retreating Germans took old men and young boys to use as shields on the front lines."

"Was there fighting in Makov?" I asked.

"There was virtually no fighting either when the Germans arrived or when they left," said Nina. "This is because when Soviet troops liberated a town or village, they always surrounded it on three sides, leaving one side open for an easy retreat by the Germans. This ensured less destruction. There was severe fighting, however, in Dunaevtsi."

"There was much fighting in my village," said Anna, "when the Germans arrived in 1941. We had a defense line three and a half miles from our village. My father and brother fought, but we children and the women ran from the village. There were shells everywhere!

"Those were difficult years," she continued, "with no salt and hungry people. And we didn't know how long it would last. But after the war, it was even worse! People starved to death in the 1947 famine, caused by a severe drought; there'd been no rain or snow the entire fall and winter of 1946-47. People ate leaves and grass, small children cried, and our neighbor died of hunger. I remember not being able to sleep because I was so hungry. Even though I knew Mother had no food, we'd beg her to cook something. During the war, there were no new clothes and even no way to mend torn ones. But when my sister returned from Germany after the war, she brought some clothes with her."

Ralph and I are quite aware of the horrors the Soviets went through during WWII. And we mention them in our slide show presentations because most Americans don't know their extent. Still, it becomes much more real after hearing our Soviet friends' experiences.

Before we came to the Soviet Union in 1983, we were ignorant of the war sufferings of the Soviets. Yet we quickly learned they are sincere when they say they want no more war! Our emphasis is "freedom;" theirs is "peace." The difference comes from our histories. Many of our ancestors came to the new land to escape the chains of persecution; thus, we prize freedom. But Soviets have had many invasions since 1800, usually from the West. They value peace. They think we glamorize war in our movies because none of us has experienced war on our own soil.

Next, we asked Nina and Anna, "How did the people react during Stalin's reign of terror?"

"I remember a little of that," said Nina. "During the famine of 1933, which Stalin created, we had a cow. Because of this, we were better off than most. About the disappearances—people on every level of society just disappeared in the night. Strangers would come to the house and say, 'Get your clothes on and come with us. You are an enemy of the people.' More than 70 people were taken from Makov, many sugar factory workers, even women, also an assistant of the priest. No one knew why, and no one knew who would be next. People lived in constant terror during all those years. Sometimes the fear would lessen temporarily—until the next person disappeared. It started in 1935 and seemed to come in waves. And it continued after the war, too. Once a delegation of people went to Moscow to tell Stalin what was happening, but, of course, they never returned."

"No one blamed Stalin for anything," added Anna, "and people cried when he died, saying, 'What will we do without our Papa Joe?'"

Later, Toli said, "Socialism was proven successful once—during WWII. "Why did France fall in two weeks, and the Soviet Union, sustaining enormous suffering, prevail for so long and finally achieve victory?" he asked. "Socialism had taught us to work together." Perhaps, but I maintain it might have been for another reason. For example, the fact that Russians have lived for centuries under very hard circumstances—repression, hardship, and frigid weather—and have learned to press on through any adversity.

On the other hand, there's always that nagging question of whether the adversity, death, and destruction would have been less with a non-violent, non-cooperation resistance to attain the same end result. There weren't enough Germans to run the world by themselves.

This evening, seven of the graduates came for a relaxed evening. I served strawberries on cake, with milk poured over. Their tradition is sour cream with strawberries, but the students gamely tried the dish and liked it.

"Do you have any family stories about Stalin's repressions?" I asked. Two did.

Val began. "My great-grandfather was taken away. My grandfather was not there when it happened, because he was in another town applying to enter an institute. (There he discovered they had a paper prohibiting his acceptance.) The charge against my great-grandfather was that he was a German spy and had a radio in his attic. Since he owned no radio, it must have been planted. We know little about his fate except he was badly tortured and perished somewhere in a camp. One of the tortures used—perhaps not on him—was to put the prisoners' legs in fresh concrete, which, of course, hardened. They were left to starve to death."

"My grandfather was taken away," said Natasha, "when he was the chief bookkeeper for a railroad. He was in prison for 10 years. When he returned, he had lost his memory and was very sick. He died soon afterwards. My family thinks he may have been taken because he was Latvian."

We talked about religion, and I asked the students in turn if they were believers. Only one was, the tall young man who said "Good morning" to us in the evening. He wore a cross around his neck tonight.

"Remember," said Toli, "you're all Komsomol members which requires you to promote anti-religious propaganda."

"Why do you join the Komsomol?" I asked.

"Tradition," one said.

"What do you like about it?" I continued.

"Nothing!" exclaimed Natasha, a disgusted look on her face.

Toli once told us that at Komsomol meetings the young people are supposed to harangue each other into becoming better members of society. However, they won't do it.

Ralph then launched into the proven health problems caused by smoking. Nearly all Soviet men smoke, including Toli, who says it gives him a chance to be alone. So far, we've seen only one woman smoking. "Do you girls like it when the boys smoke?" Ralph asked.

"What is a man without a cigarette?" answered one of the girls.

"How do you feel about Jews?" I asked. As I went around the circle, all answered that they considered Jews to be the same as other people. But when I got to Igor, he said, "We've been indoctrinated to dislike Jews."

"Why?" I asked.

"When a Jew gets into power, he brings in all his family," answered another of the boys.

"That's for sure!" said another.

At that point, our get-together deteriorated into anecdote-telling. We've been surprised Ukrainians tell anecdotes even about themselves. They must be confident in their identity. I wrote down some of them:

1. A Russian, a Jew, and a Ukrainian were each given a million apples. The Russian ate as many as he could and brewed the rest. The Jew ate as many as he could and gave the rest to his relatives. The Ukrainian ate as many as he could and took a tiny bite out of all the rest.

2. Q. Why don't Chukchas eat pickles?
   A. Because their heads won't go through the neck of the jar. (Soviets love to make fun of these Siberian Eskimos.)

3. Q. Why do Moldavians plant potatoes at night?
   A. So the potato bugs can't see them.

4. A Russian is bragging. He says, "We have the world's biggest subway, the world's biggest department store, and the world's biggest computer chips."

5. One doctor says to the other, "Shall we treat the patient or let him live?"

6. Q. Why don't Japanese and Soviets have AIDS?
   A. Because AIDS is a disease of the 20th Century. Japan is in the 21st Century and the USSR is in the 19th.

7. Perestroika is like a lot of wind in the forest blowing the tops of the trees. But on the ground, it's calm.

8. Perestroika for dogs—the chain was lengthened and barking was permitted, but the food dish was put farther away.

9. A collective farm sold 20 calves to the state and reported that to the District. The District said, "Let's report to the Region that they sold 30." The Region said, "Let's report to the Republic that they sold 50." The Republic said, "Let's report to Moscow that they sold 100." So in Moscow, it was reported that they had 100 calves. They said, "Let's send 20 to Vietnam and keep the rest."

10. Latvia asked Moscow for independence for one year. The answer was no. So they asked for independence for two weeks. Still, the answer was no. But when they asked for independence for two hours, Moscow said yes. Latvia then declared war on Sweden and surrendered to them five minutes later.

11. Q. What's the difference between the US and the USSR?
    A. The US will soon be the one with a legal Communist Party.

12. A Soviet man was ordering a car, and the official said it would be delivered in 10 years. "Will that be in the morning or the afternoon?" asked the man. "Why do you ask such a thing?" responded the official. "Because the plumber's coming in the morning," the man replied.

Earlier today, the Chairman called Toli and said we would have to get our own food from now on because Nikolai's work is increasing. Ralph accepted that explanation at face value, but I think the Chairman is angry at us for some reason. I have no idea why. He also wanted back the art books in our living room. Luckily, I've looked through all of them.

"Perhaps you're scapegoats for Stengach," said Toli. "He may connect you to the higher authorities who ordered him to receive you on his farm. Just yesterday those authorities told him he must cut 80 of his 150 supervisors. He won't cut them, however; he'll only shift them around. Maybe instead of one being responsible for the right leg of the table, he'll now be in charge of the corner."

After the young people left, we went to see Nikolai. We asked him where he gets the food, and to please make one more food delivery. The supplies are needed for the big dinner I'm planning for the Greenhouse Gang and their families on Friday night. Though Ludmila wanted to obey the Chairman to the letter, Nikolai, a kind man, agreed to one more delivery.

June 21: Last night, two specters disturbed my sleep: the obvious prejudice in the minds of the young people and the Chairman's arbitrary cutting off of our food supply. First, I despaired of our human race ever ridding itself of its intolerance. On the second matter, now I know the helplessness people feel here when decrees from above are handed down. Actually, we're glad it happened because we've wanted to live more like the people. Soon, we'll experience first-hand their problems getting food. I'm thankful, however, I've had this long to develop some working language.

This morning Toli, Ralph, and I visited the dairy barn and the Chairman's meat place to make arrangements for getting milk and meat in the future. The meat-processing enterprise is in one of the farm's more remote villages. It supplies the Chairman, his entourage, his guests, and perhaps villagers who can pay extra. In addition, trucks loaded with meat go from there to other areas of the country every night.

The parallel state meat store in Makov has little or no meat, so people rely on their own pigs, chickens, geese, and cows. Or people hear through the grapevine that a villager is going to slaughter an animal, and try to buy some meat. Also, people buy home-grown meat at the daily Kamenets market, or the Makov market, which is open only 5 to 7 A.M. Sundays.

Meat is highly prized in the USSR. Guests are sometimes served three kinds. White 1-inch squares of raw pork fat are sometimes served, too, like thick bacon with no lean parts. People just stick their forks in the cubes and eat them plain. I can't watch! The way they *really* like their fat, however, is frozen and then sliced thin, with garlic. Eskimos, of course, eat much blubber, and the USSR is a northern country. I was surprised to see on a map that the 40th parallel, which goes through Ralph's Ohio farm, touches only the southern tips of the USSR. Most of the Soviet climate is like Canada's.

While we were at the meat place, we watched the men making sausage. They put pork into the grinder-mixer and added lots of pure fat. The man in charge offered us some sausages, and we took two without the fat added. He also gave Toli some sausages and meat because he owed Toli a favor. The man, part of Stengach's entourage, occasionally has Toli translate the English instructions on his new foreign electronic equipment.

When we returned home, there on our doorstep was an old man with long white hair and beard. He was a Russian Orthodox priest who had come on the bus from Odessa, 300 miles away. He wanted our help in getting an American co-producer to help make a film for believers. He hopes the film will be shown on national TV. He already has a Soviet producer, but he wants the American to film actual scenes of the Gospel being preached all over the world, a feat nigh-impossible for a Soviet.

The priest had a kindly smile, and he brought us a large, round loaf of bread and a sack of plums. "I am close to the angels," he said, "because I constantly say a prayer of the Holy Trinity—'Holy, holy, holy.' In fact, someone once took a picture of me that shows an angel's head above mine with his chin touching my head.

"Do you have that picture with you?" I asked.

"Unfortunately, no," he replied.

Then he told us an anecdote:

> There were two men in a prison cell. "Why are you here?" asked the one. "I killed a man," said the other. "Oh, that's nothing!" said the first. "I killed 12!"

He explained, "Some people are really wicked and boast of their wickedness, and they will go to hell." (I could tell that Toli was getting bored.)

Odessa priest visiting us in Makov.

"I'm 68," he said. "I grew up in a non-religious family, and my mother wanted me to become an engineer. Sufferings and the war shocked me and made life hard for me, but if I hadn't had those hard times, I probably wouldn't be a believer now. After the war, I became a chauffeur. I kept asking myself questions: 'What is the meaning of our lives? At every turn, we can be insulted and hurt. What is the truth?' Then I answered myself, 'The world cannot exist without truth, and truth is in belief.' For two years, I couldn't decide whether or not to become a priest. This sinful world attracts people," he continued. "and it's hard to give up. Eventually, however—at age 32, the same year I married my 16-year-old bride—I had the will to go to seminary. There, I heard these words from the New Testament for the first time—'You don't have the right to call someone else a fool.' For me, it was enough! I had found the truth, and the truth is everything!"

We ate lunch together. I was the only interpreter, as Toli suggested I practice my Russian. The priest and his wife have 11 children because she doesn't believe in having abortions—the main method of birth control in the USSR. A Moscow friend once told me Soviet women average about ten abortions in their lives. They get them because other birth control methods are virtually unavailable and because they feel they have neither the money nor the energy to raise more than one or two children. The abortion itself is a horrible process, with the doctors showing contempt for the women and treating them roughly. There is no anesthetic, and the women are shuttled out of the clinic after a five-minute rest. If one pays a hundred rubles, however, a doctor will come to the woman's home and perform a painless abortion.

As the priest left, we gave him a peace button and a peace prayer card. While we waited together for his bus, he told Toli, "You know, don't you, that smoking prevents the Holy Spirit from coming to you."

"It prevents nervousness!" Toli retorted. "I'd rather smoke than kill someone!"

I wrote immediately to Billy Graham and to Clyde Weaver of the Church of the Brethren, both of whom have visited the USSR several times, to ask for help for the priest.

Later today, we watched a TV program about two Soviet combine-manufacturing enterprises trying to outshine each other. A joke about combines goes like this: "It takes two men to run a combine, one to drive it, and one to walk along behind and pick up the pieces." It really isn't that bad.

We then discussed with Toli the two lines of agricultural thought now prevalent in the country. Before the March (1989) Plenary meeting, everyone thought radical changes would be made in agriculture. Some regional Gosagroproms and collective and state farms prepared by setting up a few rent arrangements. But when the Plenary meeting did little, the fledgling changes and rent contracts were repressed. These two lines of thought—renting land to farmers versus continuing the collective and state farms—are in Congress, too, so the Deputies declared that collective farms, state farms, and rent contracts are equal. But declaring them equal does not make them equal. Renters have no place to get supplies, for example. Now some people are insisting on real reform for this *declared* equality.

June 22: Last night, our toilet overflowed into the bathroom. Ralph wasn't able to fix it. So today, the village fire truck came, removed the toilet, put the hose into the sewer pipe, blew out the clog, and left, leaving a stinking mess—splattered walls and two inches of filth on the floor. As Ralph cleaned it up, it reminded him of his hog house-cleaning days, only worse. He detests human waste but doesn't mind animal manure. Apparently, our mistake was putting toilet paper into the commode.

A letter from Bob Meyerson came today from Moscow, with an article from the International Toastmasters' magazine about Bob's starting the first Toastmasters' Club in the USSR. He had a horror of speaking in public when he was younger, so much so he once dropped out of college when a speech was required. His association with Toastmasters, however, cured that. He went on to get his master's degree and has spoken to large gatherings in the USSR—the Pushkin Institute and the Soviet Peace Committee. He challenged this latter group in ways it did not want to hear. He has also spoken on national Soviet TV about Toastmasters. Bob has been a real pioneer in citizen diplomacy, having lived here since 1983, when the livin' wasn't so easy.

Eda, the woman who hosts the Stengach granddaughter, has moved in next door with her son Edward, his wife, and their young son, who were visiting her from Vladivostok. This evening, we spent an hour having coffee and delicious cakes made by Eda, who can't use her left hand because of a stroke.

June 23: I cooked most of the day, and in the evening the Greenhouse Gang and their wives, all looking beautiful, came walking down our driveway as a group. Oleg was carrying roses. "Late for your anniversary," he said.

Of course, Toli and Tanya were here, too, and they brought us a large samovar to remember them by. It was inscribed in Russian—"When you drink tea, remember us and our region. Anatoli and Tanya." I was delighted and immediately filled it with water to heat for the tea and coffee we had with dessert. (A samovar is a large, usually ornate, metal urn to heat water in. A little teapot sits on top filled with a strong solution of tea. When the water is piping hot, the hostess pours a small amount of the strong tea into each cup and then turns a little faucet on the side of the samovar, allowing the hot water to fill the cups. Today's samovars have an electric heating element inside.)

Stepan took the lead in the conversation. It was a good, honest, serious time, with questions about blacks, Native Americans, banks, American attitudes about Soviets, volunteerism in the US, Soviet hospitality, peace, accusations that Ralph and I are communist sympathizers (we're not nor ever have been), the slowness of the democratic process, and the importance of non-violent revolution. (We feel violence is self-defeating because when those on the bottom get to the top, they tend to use the same tactics used on them).

After three hours, everyone left. We took Toli, Tanya, Oleg and his wife home in the car. All the others live in Kamenets, and Stepan and Nikolai have cars. The young women sat on their husbands' laps, all crowded together in our back seat. Oleg said something about getting hot feelings because he and his wife haven't been married very long. I told them those feelings can stay, even for an old grandpa and grandma. At that point, Toli remarked, "I don't know about feelings, but I'm getting just plain hot!"

June 26: While we were in Dunaevtsi today, we went to meet the telephone operators who help us with our long distance calls. As they sat working, I asked to take their pictures. One of the women objected, probably because in the past, foreigners were not allowed to take pictures of communication facilities. We complied, but we noticed their switchboard was like those in our country when we were children—not a secret Americans would be interested in. Besides, we'd seen one just like it in a Soviet movie on TV. But how was she to know? She didn't want to get into trouble.

This evening, Zhenya, the gentle, white-haired man we met at the church, came to our house, as I had asked, to talk about his life and the church. He brought me one branch of small, white, Easter lilies and two branches of wild red roses. As we sat down, I said, "Please tell me about your life."

"I was born in Makov 51 years ago," he began. "I'm divorced and live with my mother, and I have two grown sons. My job is in construction work, but I went to drama school for three years after high school. I also learned how to direct choirs. I directed a drama group in Makov from 1964 to 1975 and received many diplomas, medals, and honors.

"I paint portraits—I've done two of the Chairman—and landscapes. Sometimes the Chairman sends me to the village of his birth to paint some of the scenes there for him. Have you seen that large landscape in the lodge next door, featuring a deer? I painted that."

"Yes, it's beautiful," I said. "Also, when we were at the Chairman's house for Easter dinner, I noticed an excellent portrait of the Chairman. Was that yours?"

"Yes, that's one of two I painted, but the other is missing. In fact, most of my paintings disappeared from an exhibition. I also paint icons and like to sing.

"But my biggest love is the church. When I was seven, I was taken to church, and I 'knew' immediately. The art was so beautiful to me! And I have never doubted."

"Do you pray or meditate much?" I asked.

"There's no need, for God is always in my heart," was his beautiful answer. "For me, the way to live is to be kind to others. Otherwise, why would we be here?

"I love people, but I also like quietness and peace. Someday I shall have that quietness, but for now my job is good for me because I want to make sure my mother and sons are taken care of first. I gave my older son a big wedding. I'll do that for the other one when the day arrives."

"Do you like your nickname?" I asked.

"What nickname?" he responded.

"The people call you 'Little God,'" I replied.

"I didn't know that, but let it be!" he answered.

"Please tell me more about the churches here," I said.

"The other church in the village used to be a watchtower, and I don't know much about it. When the little church is reopened, I think there will be about 500 people attending each of the two churches. When the church was closed, people took the three big crosses and 'hid' them on graves in the cemetery, and they took the icons to their houses. Now they're returning everything. However, the authorities are still trying to close the church. The day before you were there, a man from the Region came and ordered us to close it. But the Chairman told us to resist. He's a very good man," said Little God.

Late in the evening, I went outside. Edward called me from the lodge next door and asked me over. Eda said she'd been calling me in her heart to tell me they have to leave tomorrow because her grandson is ill.

While Ralph and I enjoyed her homemade cakes again, she told us a little about herself. "I, a Jew, married a Russian when I was at the institute at Kiev," she said, "and my father acted as if I were dead. He actually performed my funeral service. My mother died when I was 2. During the war, my husband and I moved to Siberia, where there were many women with no men. They stole my husband when Edward was 11 months old. So we were divorced. Being a Jew, I wasn't able to get a very good job, so I worked in a day care center, eventually becoming a specialist in methods. When Edward was 16, I married a kind, Jewish man. But Edward rebelled. He left home at 22. For awhile I didn't even know where he was. But he's a good son now.

"I have a fine two-room flat in Chernovtsi. But I'm alone there, except for hosting the Chairman's granddaughter and another medical student during the school year. My niece and her husband want to go to America, but I don't know whether I can go along because now, after years of calling on our country to let our Jews go, the US has put a quota on them. It isn't fair!

"Edward says when he finishes building and selling his apartment in Vladivostok on the east coast, he and his family will come to Chernovtsi to be closer to me. But he said the same thing last year, and he has not yet come. I'm very undecided as to what to do."

"Maybe things will become more clear," I offered.

"Yes," she said. "God will decide."

"But I thought you weren't a believer!" I exclaimed.

"Oh, my sister, who lives in Israel, is a great believer," Eda said. "She says if I allow my son to live with me, she'll cut off all contact with me because he's half Russian and is married to a Russian."

When we said good-bye to Eda, I said, "God be with you," and she said the same in reply.

Then she added, "I'd like you to visit me. I'll show you Chernovtsi, my beautiful city."

June 28: Ralph has had no official visits to pig farms yet (though he's looked around some on his own). Today we started out early to inspect a modern pig farm near Dunaevtsi. After a long, productive conversation at the veterinary headquarters in town, word was sent we were not permitted to visit that pig farm—for health reasons. What's more, we were told we were not allowed to see any *poor* pig farms either! So, instead, we went to visit a poor collective farm in the area (though the fields looked productive). Ralph talked to a young brigadier there, asking him if he wanted to rent. "There aren't any opportunities," he answered, "and if there were, I wouldn't rent."

Ralph countered, "If someone else rented and made a lot of money, would you rent then?"

"Yes!" he answered enthusiastically. Ralph thinks it's important that renting be profitable for early renters, thus encouraging others to take the leap, too.

In contrast to the surplus workers on Ukraina farm, this farm has few workers. Some of the buildings looked primitive and centuries old. The mud roads were nearly impassable. We entered one of the low, stone buildings and found an old carpenter who lamented the abandonment of the village. "The old are dying and the young are leaving," he said. "I retire next year, and after I go, there'll be no one left who can even make a coffin."

There are 35 farms in this district, and only two are prosperous. One, of course, is Ukraina. In the Russian Republic, most farms and their villages are exceedingly poor.

When we got home, I called the *Moscow News* to talk with Bob Meyerson. He said he'd seen Joel yesterday. So Joel and his group are in the USSR! I also talked with both Sasha and Wendy. Wendy said *Time* magazine agreed to print our story in its "American Scene" section. She also said, "Sasha is now my best friend!"

Eda called from Chernovtsi—"Just to hear your voice," she said. Ironically, she could barely hear it. Bad connection.

Later, my curiosity was piqued when I saw Johanna and her helper wearing hats like chefs wear. I've never seen them without their ubiquitous headscarves, except once when I came upon Johanna brushing her long, thick, black hair. I saw the two women coming from the deer field carrying between them a large cloth filled with meat, ribs, liver, etc. Later I saw them capture all the ducks, put them into cloth bags, and load them into a truck. I hated to see that. But I eat meat, and I've been protected from the process that comes before the meat gets to the grocery store. It was amusing, however, to see they changed hats when they changed jobs.

In the evening, Toli had to visit Natasha's parents, so we went along. We discovered her father is from Latvia and her mother is Ukrainian. Natasha is Russian though because she was born there. When Soviets turn 16, they get internal passports. If they have mixed parentage, they may claim one or the other or the republic where they were born, for their nationality on this passport. People who are half-Jewish, for example, sometimes have trouble deciding what nationality they want to declare because if they put "Jew," they may be discriminated against, but if they put another, say "Russian," they have less chance of being invited to emigrate. Soviets are allowed to emigrate only by invitation, usually from family in another country. But I've heard rumblings there may soon be legislation allowing Soviets to emigrate without invitations.

All this time, I've been spraying our flying ants with poison. But more appear the next day. Today the solution struck me. I just opened the nearest window, and, in no time, they all flew out!

The little gray kitten let me gently pet her today as she lapped her milk.

June 29: This morning we met for two hours with about 50 children, half from Toli's school and half from Bulgaria, the Eastern Bloc country with which the Soviets have the most exchange. It's like summer camp, held in and around the school building. Toli's neighbor, Ola, helped with the children, and is very good with them. Unfortunately, she has no children of her own. Because she's slightly crippled, she and Sasha have decided it would be too hard on her to have any. They often play with Yura.

Toli told us Valarovsky of the District called, upset we had visited the poor collective farm. He must be one of the "old guard," those who want to pretend everything is wonderful, hiding the undesirable. It's embarrassing, if nothing else, to expose one's soft, ugly underbelly.

The chairman of that poor farm came to Makov after we'd been there and asked Toli what we were going to do with the information we got. "Are they going to tell it to the Region, the country, the world? Will they name names? I've been chairman just one year, and I'm doing my best to build up this farm. I don't want any trouble."

"The Americans will do nothing to harm you," said Toli.

Late this afternoon, we took Toli, Tanya, and their neighbor Nelya to Kamenets to shop while Tamara cut my hair. Nelya has one child, and she always buys him several pieces of bubble gum at the market—at 1 ruble each! Tamara asked if I would be godmother to her little son who is to be baptized in the Makov Russian Orthodox Church. I said I'd be honored.

When we returned home, the Chairman arrived and asked us if we could get an American wedding dress in size three for his "niece" to wear. "When is it needed?" I asked him.

"In three weeks," he replied. I was relieved there was not enough time to get one. Wedding dresses here are just as pretty and elaborate as ours. The Chairman understood and called his "brother," saying it was impossible. But he gave us invitations to the wedding anyway. Toli told us later Stengach thinks we're rich. "He keeps talking about millions of dollars," said Toli.

Later, we returned to Kamenets to hear a boys' choir from near Cleveland, Ohio. Andrei, the bright-faced Komsomol leader, had told us about the concert. He and his friend Sergei were waiting to sit with us. The choir sang beautifully, first religious pieces, then after changing their costumes, Ukrainian songs. They received a standing ovation.

Afterwards, when the Ukrainian-born director and I were talking, he said, "I want you to know we sing only *Ukrainian* national songs, not Russian. *Ever!*" We can understand his bitterness, but we think this attitude of blaming doesn't help anyone. My favorite child psychologist used to say,

"We don't blame, we find solutions." A strange feeling engulfed me when the Americans' bus pulled away from the curb, leaving us behind.

Andrei and I talked. At one point he said American policemen are good men, that they learn to deliver babies because poor people (I think he said black people) can't afford to go to the hospital.

"Where did you learn that?" I asked.

"I think I read it in one of my books," he replied.

I responded, "Only part of that's true. Policemen do learn to deliver babies because they sometimes have to, but only if the women can't get to the hospital in time. It's also true many Americans don't have money or insurance for a hospital. But often there are helps, such as the hospital's charging less or setting up a schedule for them to pay a little at a time. Sometimes there are organizations or government aid to help pay their bills, too."

During the concert, Andrei again told me he was praying daily. He whispered during one of the choir's sacred numbers, referring to the boys, "They are good pray-ers!" He said he thought he'd stay with the Komsomol and see if he could make changes from the inside.

CHAPTER 6

Christine's Journal Excerpts

JULY

July 1: Last night we drove to Khmelnitski to pick up Sergei and Marina, a couple coming from Moscow to spend the weekend with us. Sergei had originally written to Ralph, asking to work on his farm. I'd written back, inviting them to visit us in Makov and discuss it. We waited for them at the train station for an hour or so. They never arrived. What had become of them?

About 2 P.M. today, as Ralph and I were sitting down to eat lunch, in they walked! They had come on the train to *Kamenets-Podolski* not Khmelnitski, and had taken a hotel room there so they could go see that historic town as well as visit us. Our trip to Khmelnitski was the result of incomplete and faulty information we received.

Marina and Sergei are a bright, attractive couple, both 27. They speak English and will soon receive degrees in nuclear materials science. Neither wants to work in that field, however. They want to live in a village with several other couples, friends of theirs, and grow vegetables and livestock. In preparation, they'd like to spend six months in America to learn farming methods. Their three-year-old daughter would stay in the USSR with her grandmother.

Yesterday afternoon, we learned Joel and his group will soon be in Minsk, 500 miles away. (Minsk is the capital of Byelorussia [White Russia], the republic north of Ukraine. It received the first dose of Chernobyl's radiation. Then the wind changed, contaminating Ukraine. Certain areas, such as Makov, escaped.) The Chairman gave his permission for us to go, but after our experience with Kiev, I braced myself for what an attempt to go to Minsk might bring.

Sergei and Marina traveled from Moscow to Makov to see us.
They spent several months in Ohio in 1990.

So we began. First, I called Eda to see if she could get us train tickets
from Chernovtsi to Minsk. She called back, saying she could get only third
class tickets, "which are horrible," she said, so she didn't take them. (Third
class means riding in extra cars added for the summer—on crowded,
uncovered wooden seats or bunks.) Her neighbor will try again tomorrow.
I'm to call Eda at 10 a.m.

July 2: The Red Tape Saga continueth. This morning, Toli—afraid of
punishment for himself or difficulties for us if correct procedures were
ignored—said in addition to the Chairman, Buddha should also give
permission for our trip. Accordingly, he and Ralph left for Khmelnitski at
7:30 this morning. No problem with Buddha. However, Ralph and Toli had
to return to Makov, pick up written permission from the Chairman, and take
it back to Khmelnitski. A phone call wouldn't do.

Ralph called me from Khmelnitski at 10 A.M., while my call was going
through to Eda, to tell me we don't need train tickets. Buddha said we could
get there any way we liked, so Ralph thought we'd drive. I hated to have
to tell Eda we didn't need the tickets. She and her neighbor had gone to so
much trouble. But she was gracious and said they would just return them.

About 3 P.M., Wendy called from Moscow to say the *Time* photographer
was on his way and would arrive by plane at Khmelnitski at about 4 P.M.
Our plan had been to leave at 5 A.M. tomorrow for Minsk, but I told Wendy
we'd wait until noon.

Ralph returned home about five, tired from two round-trips (six hours of
driving) to Khmelnitski. Then Toli said we had to have the Chairman's

permission to drive the farm's Niva. He happened to be driving from his dacha a bit later, so I asked him, and he said, "No." I asked him why not and who said so. He replied, "Valarovsky [of the District]."

The *Time* photographer arrived by taxi at seven; we arranged for him to stay the night with us. We spent three hours this evening posing for pictures. He'll need more time in the morning. It was midnight before I made supper.

In the meantime, Valentina told us about a man in Kamenets who would probably rent us his car for $100, money he could use when he visits the States. She went to Kamenets to discuss it, but he was out of town. So she kindly offered us her car. Now that may work!

July 4: Oleg came to congratulate us on our Independence Day. We saw the American ambassador, Jack Matlock, on television. He spoke about the holiday in fluent Russian. We've heard the Soviets consider him down-to-earth and are flattered he speaks their language. We had met with Matlock's predecessor, Arthur Hartman, and his wife in their elegant Moscow residence, Spasso House, on two of our trips. Donna Hartman has a Quaker background. She used to take flowers from her garden into the streets and give them to Soviets as a gesture of peace. On one occasion, she opened her garage door, backed out her car, and took us where we needed to go.

Shortly after Oleg's visit, the photographer began his picture-taking again. This must have been a dull assignment for him; he'd recently returned from China where he covered Gorbachev's visit. He finished up about one o'clock and left.

Valentina said she would need the car until about five. That time came and went. So did the next six hours, with us wondering what in the world was up. Farmer Ralph has patience, but I've needed to learn it. The USSR is a good school for this. At 11 P.M., Toli called to say Valentina and Tatiana had been picking cherries at a distant place and would bring the car over for us as soon as they washed it! So at midnight, Toli, Ralph and I left for Minsk, 19 hours later than planned.

July 5: Ralph drove all night, and I drove for awhile after dawn. There were a few trucks and fewer cars on the road. One approached us too wide on a sharp curve, and when Ralph dodged it, Toli woke up, a little startled.

The other crisis came when we were almost out of fuel at 3 A.M. A fuel station attendant said "No" to Toli's request for gas, with the next station about an hour away. But Toli detected a slight hesitation in the man's "no," so he pressed on. Finally the man consented to sell us fuel from a pump only for state-owned vehicles. He probably pocketed the money and did some creative bookkeeping because state vehicles don't pay cash. Toli was our navigator and savior through the night on the mostly unmarked cross-country course.

We were all very tired, and finding where Joel's tour was staying was a problem. Finally, we walked in as they were eating lunch in their remote hotel out in the countryside. But our problems were not over. The huge hotel would not give us a room, saying they were full (which I didn't believe). So I'm staying with the two young women who are leading the group, and Ralph is bunking with two young male participants. Toli will sleep in the car tonight and then try to find a room in town for three days. He plans to spend most of that time shopping for his family. It was too difficult to arrange for extra meals at the hotel, so Ralph and I are eating what the young people leave behind. There'll be enough, I think, because they don't like the food very much.

Joel and I spent a wonderful evening talking, although by that time I had a terrible migraine. He brought us lots of mail, slide film, popcorn, etc., and some things from Viktor for his Valentina and Tatiana. Poor Joel thought he was going to get rid of some weight, but we gave him our large suitcase of winter clothes to take to Ohio.

July 9: This morning, we left at 6 A.M. for the 13-hour trip home. All in all, these last few days were physically and emotionally exhausting.

We did some interesting things, however, while we were in Minsk. Mostly we accompanied the group in their activities, such as visiting Khatyn again, the war memorial not far from Minsk. (Khatyn is often confused with Katyn where hundreds of Polish officers were murdered by Soviets under Stalin.) We remembered Khatyn well from our 1983 visit. It's a poignant monument commemorating the nearly 200 area villages burned to the ground by the Nazis. It was there we learned the Nazis had concentration camps in the USSR for Slavs, some camps just for children.

A few days after that experience in 1983, we had the exciting experience of eating with the "black" Metropolitan Filaret. His black hair and beard give him that name to distinguish him from the white-haired Metropolitan Filaret in Kiev. (The Russian Orthodox Church has one Patriarch, the highest official of the church, and several Metropolitans on the next level down.) A group of us had attended the Russian Orthodox Church in Minsk one evening, and lo and behold, Filaret, Head of International Relations for the Russian Orthodox Church, was officiating. After the service, we were invited downstairs. The jolly Metropolitan sat at the head of the table. It was the first time we had held hands and sung peace songs with Soviets. Even though it was rather official, we were thrilled.

One of the kids in Joel's group told us of a disturbing experience they just had at the American Embassy in Moscow with an assistant to the ambassador. Even though the man was young, his comments represented the old cold-war attitude. An example: "We saved their butts in WWII, even though they hated our guts!" Boy, is he uninformed!

This story reminds me of when Ralph and I were in the same Embassy, and the elevator stopped at the wrong floor. We went around the corner and faced a commercially-made sign on a door—"Russia Sucks." Though it turned out to be the door of a US Marine, we found the slogan's presence in a diplomatic mission inexcusable. We complained about it at a party at the Ambassador's home that night. The sign came down.

Along these same lines, not many years ago Wendy's fast-food restaurant had a nasty advertisement on TV. It featured a fat, militarized, poorly-dressed woman who was supposed to be a Soviet fashion model. First, she modeled a drab house dress called "day-wear." Then she came out in the same dress, carrying a flashlight. This was "night-wear." Finally, in the same dress, she carried a beach ball. Now she wore "beach-wear." The point: "At Wendy's, you don't have to have the same old thing. You can have a choice." Ralph sometimes ate lunch at Wendy's, so he wrote them saying he wouldn't eat there again until the ad was canceled. They wrote back saying they hadn't intended to make fun of anyone. For whatever reason, the ad soon stopped.

Also in Minsk, Toli, Ralph, and I met one evening with the young people of Joel's group to talk about our experiences in Ukraine. Their Intourist guide was there, too, and it was great to see him and Toli playing off each other as they spoke passionately about life in the USSR.

"What can we do to help the situation here?" asked one of the young people.

"Tell the truth back in America," stated Toli. The guide echoed him.

When we arrived home from Minsk, Ralph washed Valentina's car. I returned it, and brought her the box from Viktor. Viktor had sent dozens of photographs. When Tatiana saw her dad in one of them, she began kissing it, crying, "Papa! Papa!" Tears streamed down her face. Then she tried on the two outfits he sent her. Valentina grabbed Viktor's letter and began to read it. It must have been very hard for the family to be apart for so many months. Ralph thought we'd put a lot of wear and tear on Valentina's car, so he gave me 100 rubles to leave with her. I laid it on her television.

July 10: Ralph and I rested today, quietly visiting the fields. The workers were having a lot of trouble cutting the wheat because so much had fallen over. This often happens when too much fertilizer is applied. The corn looks good though—better than Ralph expected.

The rest of the day he wrote while I slowly worked, giving him a haircut at one point. What fun! It reminded me of what Ralph says whenever I'm discouraged about facing a very busy day back home. He says, "Try to have fun today!" After all, we have to do the work anyway. We might as well try to enjoy it. Today Joel and his group leave for Warsaw, where President Bush is now.

Toli called to say Valentina was offended we tried to pay her for using her car and she'll be returning the money. We feel bad. She's a dear friend and the last thing we want is to hurt her.

There must be different customs about gifts, money, etc., here. For example, once Tanya asked me, "Do your sons help each other financially?"

"Well, once my oldest son borrowed some of the college savings of his three younger brothers to buy a car," I said. "He paid them back, with interest, before they went to college."

"With interest?" exclaimed Tanya. "That sounds like Americans!"

"His brothers hadn't asked for interest," I explained. "But my oldest son wanted to be fair and compensate them for the interest they lost when they took their money out of the bank."

Soviets seem to help each other with no questions asked. We know of several instances of older parents buying a car but allowing one of their children to use it full time. They remodel and live in apartments together, etc.

In the evening, Ralph and I walked to the greenhouse where all five men were building a storage barn for their apples. They invited us to Little Michigan on Sunday.

I'll put down my thoughts about these five good friends who are renting two old greenhouses and 185 acres of apple trees around our house. All are 36, except for Sasha Sportsman; all are married with children; and all are kind, sensitive, and intelligent.

Blond, burly Stepan, a professional mechanic, holds the contract for this hard-working creative group. He's steady, careful, thoughtful, solidly grounded, and speaks seriously. At times, though, a wry smile betrays his sense of enjoyment.

Nikolai is the tallest. He has a jaunty, comfortable way of lightening the atmosphere with his smiling openness, musical speech, ever-present quick wit, inquisitive mind, and strong personality. Stepan and Nikolai were party members. But they turned in their party cards before we arrived—some of the first to do so.

Sasha Professor is shy and endearing, always smiling, alert, and modest. He is usually quiet, except when he contributes a humorous or helpful summary with a brief, direct phrase. He and Oleg speak a little English, Professor's specialty being numbers.

Oleg, who looks like a dark-haired Baryshnikov, is complex, with a good heart and deep, intense emotions. He's happiest, I think, when expressing himself through music or art. At different times, he's as delighted as a child; dramatically telling anecdotes; or brooding openly, with a hint of tears.

Sasha Sportsman, 27, has a perfect body, roasts the world's best potatoes, and is always good-natured and self-confident. He's truly a fine athlete. He does the Triathlon, a grueling three-part event: 3800 meters of swimming, followed by 180 km of bicycling, and ending with 42 km of running. (That's two and one-third miles of swimming, 112 miles of bicycling, and 26 miles of running!)

Their humble quarters, a small room in one of the greenhouses, present an aura of peace. There is tea instead of vodka; a vase of roses on a sturdy homemade table; and, at night, a campfire under the trees illuminating a tent. Sasha Sportsman supplied the tent for cozy sleeping when they take turns guarding after dark. A stereo radio is often heard playing music or the proceedings of the Congress of People's Deputies. Oleg has painted colorful animal and clown faces on the inside entrance of the greenhouse, each a birthday gift for one of his partners' children. Their tomatoes, potatoes, cucumbers, roses, apples, and sweet corn thrive, and they keep our table full of them. Once Nikolai even taught me how to make pickles.

The Greenhouse Gang—from left: Sasha Professor, Stepan, Nikolai, Sasha Sportsman, Oleg.

We are isolated here, and as I need more company than Ralph does, I occasionally walk over to the greenhouse in the evening and talk with whoever's on duty. I've usually drawn Oleg or Sasha Sportsman. They're patient with my poor Russian, and I like getting to know them.

Sportsman told me one night about his time in Czechoslovakia, serving in the army. He said, "They live much better than we do." He always displays a hard, muscled chest; cut-off jeans; and a smile. One day when the temperature was 52 in the middle of summer, I wore my heavy coat when we visited the Gang. There was Sportsman without his shirt, as usual. Ralph took a picture of us together. Sasha worked in Siberia for three years, spent three more in the mines of Ukraine, then worked as a swimming instructor. He wants to work two or three years at the orchard, save his money, and then build (with a bank loan) a 25-meter indoor swimming pool in Kamenets. He hopes to rent it out. One day his mother was at the greenhouse, and she said he was wasting his life there. He should be practicing his sports. He might have been in the Olympics.

One night Oleg confessed to me he had been in prison for nearly seven years. "My sentence was unfair," he said. "My girlfriend and I were dancing in a public place, and another man kept cutting in. When I finally told him to leave us alone, he attacked me. In defending myself, I beat him pretty badly. The police said I started the whole thing, so I was sent to prison in eastern Ukraine."

"What was it like in prison?" I asked.

"We worked eight hours a day doing metal work," he said. "Our food was bread and water, but two or three times a week we got 20 grams of fish, and soup made of water, bad potatoes, and cabbage. When I was there, 20% of the prisoners were political prisoners, and 10% were religious prisoners. My record was good—hard work and no fighting—so when Gorbachev came in, I got amnesty several months before my term was up. If I ever fight again, though, I'll go back to prison. So when people steal apples from the orchard, I can't fight them."

"Who steals the apples," I asked.

"Everyone in Makov," he answered. "Since everything belongs to the state, people have always taken apples from the collective farm. And even though we're renting it now, they still steal apples."

Another night he told me, "Twelve years ago, a load fell on me, crushing my back. They thought I would never walk again, but a Korean doctor taught me a kind of Korean kung fu, and it has brought me back to normal. I still do it daily, beginning with a five-minute meditation."

He also said, "When I was working in Siberia, I killed a bear, a wolf, and a reindeer to eat, but I don't have the heart to do that now."

Once Oleg said, "I love my country, and I love my people, but I don't like the ruling communists." He often indicates the terrible dominance of the party by raising his fist in a gesture of power and saying resolutely, "Red!"

"Someday I will come to see the United States," he said once. "I don't know how I will, but I will!" Also, "We want to have a daughter, and if we do, we will name her Christina, after you."

"I can't speak," I said. It was a great honor.

July 12: Most of our days are a series of small adventures, and today was no exception. It's truly fascinating to wake each morning, not knowing what's on the horizon. We feel very blessed to have this experience.

Toli came about 10 this morning with an editor of the English-language *Ukraine* magazine, which is sold outside the country. Also along was a bouncy, friendly photographer. I gave the photographer a packet of sweet corn seed in an old envelope bearing the symbol of Crosscurrents International Institute. The logo caught his eye, and he said enthusiastically, "I know that symbol! Bill Shaw [President of Crosscurrents] is my good friend!"

We spent several hours in the fields being photographed. One place we always seem to go is the beet field, where the women hoe weeds. We always enjoy talking with them. Today one of them asked me, "Isn't it true blacks in your country have no rights?"

I replied, "They have all the same *legal* rights as whites, but prejudice still poisons certain situations. In general, though, life is better for blacks since the 60s."

The *Moscow News* came out today with two articles about us—one each by Sasha and Wendy. We liked both articles, except for Wendy's emphasis on our accommodations in Makov—a car, rubles, a good house. We're afraid Soviets may get the mistaken idea we think all collective farms are like Ukraina.

About noon, a 27-year-old, long-haired, English-speaking guitarist arrived from Moldavia. He volunteered to work on Ralph's farm. He said during lunch that there's plenty of heroin use in the USSR. I'm sure drug abuse is more prevalent in America, but there's at least twice the alcoholism in the USSR. Makov, by the way, means "poppy"; they grow wild here.

The editor of *Ukraine* magazine gave Ralph eight written questions to answer at his leisure today. Ralph answered the first seven, and I answered the last one: "What is Your Life Credo?"

This evening, we relaxed near the sanatorium while the editor questioned Ralph some more. While we were there, we saw Val with his older brother and their uncle, strolling the sanatorium's shady grounds. Val's brother was identified as a gifted student when he was young. At 14, he went to a special math school in Kiev. Now he has a fine computer job with the army.

I'll record our Life Credo, borrowing the title from my first childhood hero, Albert Schweitzer: "Reverence for Life is our credo. This means wishing all people well, and trying (often unsuccessfully) to live and think as non-violently and lovingly as possible. We are believers, and we think every person is part of God and very precious. Every person should have the right and responsibility to develop into the best unique person he or she can be. In our view, diversity is good and beautiful—as is each flower. Differences are not right or wrong, just different.

"We think the best way to live is to try to follow the Golden Rule, found in all seven great world religions: 'Treat others as you would want them to treat you.'

"Violence is anything divisive or exclusive, repressive or exploitive; and part of our 'Reverence' creed is to come together with others in understanding and acceptance. We try to see God (or good) in others and ourselves, though we may disagree on many things. Underneath all the differences can be a heart-to-heart contact, which is more basic than the differences and demonstrates the deep connection among us all. We want to knock down walls and build bridges."

The last slide in our Soviet slideshow is a quote from Einstein, "Peace cannot be kept by force. It can only be achieved by understanding." Then Ralph says, "There is one world, not to be one world under Moscow or one world under Washington, D.C., but one world allowing great diversity in economic and political systems, a world absent of name-calling, violence, deception, hatred, and national arrogance. Peace is not a vacuum, but a working together of all humankind."

July 15:   On the way to spend the day with Eda in Chernovtsi, we stopped at the market in Kamenets. It was the first Saturday we'd been there. It was extremely crowded, with the street blocked off to make a mall. Though most wares were being sold in open stalls or on the pavement, in one building flowers of all kinds were displayed. A man had cages of live pigeons, guinea hens, and other fowl for sale. Goldfish were available, and one little girl sold baby guinea pigs. People from Poland were there selling clothes and other non-edible wares. The meat building held quartered hogs, hog heads, regular cuts of meat, and a small amount of butter. No one ever shouts their wares; they just wait.

I bought the only cottage cheese I saw, tiny plums, and wax beans to give to Eda. Whenever we go to Dunaevtsi or Kamenets, we get ice cream which is always vanilla and sold in cones from a sidewalk booth.

When we arrived at Eda's, she had a fine dinner waiting for us in her comfortable flat. I noticed a Russian Orthodox icon on a shelf. I asked, "Is that yours, Eda?"

"No," she replied. "It belongs to Stengach's granddaughter."

Would this be why the Chairman has tried to help the church people? We know he's a capitalist, for he once told us so. Maybe he's a Christian at heart, too.

One day he told us of his own personal tragedy as he sat in our living room. He said, "I was deeply in love with my first wife—we were extremely happy—but she died of cancer after 20 years, and I've never found anyone to take her place. Lydia is okay; we have a calm, normal marriage, but it's not the same. These things happen," he concluded sadly.

Toli told us later, "The Chairman's first wife was extremely kind, and all the people remember her with great love. He always becomes sad when he speaks of her. When she was alive, the Chairman was very kind, too."

After we ate, we toured the city. We visited beautiful St. Nikolas Russian Orthodox Church, the fine university, an ice cream cafe, and a working Jewish synagogue. Here, Eda wept as she thought of her dear husband, who had attended the synagogue.

At the synagogue, a man in his thirties accosted us and begged, "Please help me to come to America. This is my situation: I went AWOL when I was in the army, so 'Schizophrenic' was put on my internal passport. Now no one will hire me. I get along as best I can, which isn't very good."

We told him we'll give his name to the Jewish Family Service of Greater Dayton. They have brought dozens of Soviet Jews to resettle in Dayton.

We've had many Soviets ask or hint to us to invite them to the States "just to take a peek." They say, in essence, "We love our country, and we don't want to leave it. We just want it to be different." We're inviting a few people to the States for specific purposes, not just to sightsee or buy electronics.

Chernovtsi is a beautiful city—much like those in Eastern Europe—but recently the children there have been losing their hair. The people suspect a chemical or nuclear spill from a train passing through, but the authorities claim a thorough investigation has turned up nothing. In fact, Chernovtsi is quarantined. We used Valentina's pass to get into the city to see Eda.

Eda showed a better attitude toward Gorbachev than most people. Many want to blame him for all their ills. She said, "Gorbachev is the first head of our country who wants to make our life a little easier. He wants that, but what can he do? Some people don't want to give up their places of power."

On our way home after supper, we picked up a hitchhiker at the edge of Chernovtsi. She was a young, pretty, blond who smiled a lot, cried a lot, hugged me a lot, and occasionally slapped Ralph on his shoulder. This induced Ralph to get a death-grip on the steering wheel in case she should grab it. I could hardly understand what she was saying, and we decided she was either distraught, emotionally unstable, or drunk, though her breath seemed all right. She put my fingers on her swollen lip where, she said, her husband had hit her. And she cried when she talked about her 10-year-old daughter.

I kept asking where she was going, but she wouldn't answer the question. When we were quite far from Chernovtsi, Ralph began to think she was going wherever we were going. Shortly after that, she looked out the window, became alarmed and exclaimed, "I don't know where I am!" So we turned around, drove a long way back to a village we had passed through, and stopped at a restaurant where there were other people who might assist her. I opened the car door, stepped out, and told her to get out. But she drew back, looking distressed, and shook her head. I insisted, however, and when Ralph opened his door to get out to help me, she finally left. As we pulled away, we saw her waiting to hitch another ride.

About that time we picked up another hitchhiker—a rainbow that traveled with us until sundown.

Four miles before we reached the gas station on the Makov side of Kamenets, we ran out of gas. It was nearly midnight. Ralph flagged down a man in a jeep, while I stayed with the car. The cheerful, young man took Ralph to the gas station and brought him back with a can full of gasoline. While they were gone, a man wandered over to the car, looked in, and shuffled on. We've gotten used to seeing people walking anywhere at any time.

Ralph told me the station attendant refused to sell him any fuel. But then he realized the man must want a deposit on his gas can, and he pulled out 20 rubles. That did the trick! Characteristically, the jeep driver wouldn't accept any money from Ralph, and the station attendant returned the deposit when we stopped to fill up the car.

July 17: A couple from Khmelnitski found us getting our car repaired at the truck yard today. They said an uncle, who had lived in the United States but left there in 1930 to return to the Soviet Union, left a lot of money—"either 2 million or 20,000 dollars"—in a Philadelphia bank. Before he died in 1972, he told them they could have his money. But they haven't been able to get it. We promised to look into it though we're sure after 60 years the bank has absorbed the money.

As we wandered in the car today, we saw a paved lane off to the left. We took it, driving a mile into deep forest. The road ended at a tall, sturdy gate set in an elaborate fence. We sat there awhile, and then, seeing no one, drove away. Someone told us later we'd been at the gate of a secret military base.

After leaving the forest, we picked up a hitchhiking babushka who, on discovering we were Americans, began to weep and talk about peace. It was quite touching.

July 18: We had an excellent meeting today at Headquarters with Savkov, Viktor Party Secretary, and 30 journalists from nine regions. Savkov repeated the tired, old story about the Chairman's expecting Ralph to take land here and all that's being done for us (house, car, etc.).

Toli finally had enough! He informed the reporters, "That's only half the exchange. Chris and Ralph and his family are paying out of their own pockets for all the same amenities for Viktor and Nikolai in Ohio, which includes giving each of them pocket money of $200 every month!" Toli insisted the international understanding aspect of the exchange was at least as important as the agricultural part. The journalists agreed.

Savkov then said the reason for the difference in agricultural production between the US and USSR is the machinery. But the reporters had taken sides and didn't buy it. At the end, Ralph related Palamarchouk's statement that the secret of US farm success is the independence of the farmers. Afterwards, the reporters asked for our autographs.

Earlier today, we drove through a very poor farm and then a good one, where they welcomed us with open arms. "We're not as productive as Ukraina, though," they said at the good farm.

We also visited Toli's son Vova in the Makov hospital. Vova has a short-term lung ailment. We gave him gifts of chewing gum, little ceramic animals, and a handkerchief with a dog embroidered on it. Whenever I see animals, especially dogs, I think of Vova. He loves them so. The three-story hospital seemed deserted. We saw only Vova, lying on his bed in the six-bed room; a little girl whose babushka was sitting on the bed with her; a nurse far down one hall; and a yellow cat roaming in and out of the rooms. Tonight, Grandma Anna will stay with Vova. Mama Tanya will give the doctor coffee, butter, and condensed milk as a tip and to ensure good care next time.

Few villages in the USSR have hospitals. Most people from Makov go to the clinic in Dunaevtsi for medical care. Soviet health care does not begin to compare with ours, but it's freely available to everyone. To get *careful* attention, however, one gives deficit goods or rubles to the doctor, especially if one is going to have surgery! Doctors have very low salaries— about 120 rubles a month—and tips are simply part of the system. These tips are like those Americans give taxi drivers, table servers, and hairdressers.

The Chairman visited us today and mentioned the problem of bureaucrats. But he admits he's one. He said there are no real renters, repeated his desire to visit the US, and said Gorby is bright. Some of his talk was contradictory. Toli, confused, had some trouble interpreting it. We think the real reason he came, however, was to suggest we give $500 to the bride and groom whose wedding we'll attend Saturday. He made it sound like a joke, but we knew he was serious. It's legal for us to give dollars, but so far, it's illegal for Soviets to receive them. We don't even have that much with us.

For the last couple of days, when I ask Johanna for eggs, she gives me a cold, hard stare and says, "Tomorrow." I wonder why.

July 21: Today we visited the poor collective farm where we'd talked to the old carpenter. We found the chairman working on the farm with his shirt sleeves rolled up. He'd just returned from the funeral of his best woman worker. At 57, she'd been in excellent health. However, shortly after her brother died of a heart attack a week ago, she began to feel poorly. She went to the hospital and there died of a heart attack herself.

The chairman was happy to talk to Ralph, and he asked many questions and took notes. But when I took his picture, he became afraid we might include it in our book for Soviets. I assured him we would neither do that nor mention him in that particular book.

His farm was operating at a loss when he took over two years ago. Now it is profitable. He said, "I'm pleased our milk production has increased from 4,000 to 8,000 lbs. per cow a year. For 13 years I worked on a neighboring farm, and I was elected by the people to be chairman here. It's happening now that the party doesn't always get their person in. The bad news is I can't get nitrogen for my corn. Last year we didn't have it for our wheat. I've been to Khmelnitski six times to beg for it, and the answer is always no. I can't imagine what it would be like to be in America and have as much fertilizer as I want!

"My son is the chief agronomist for us," he continued. "He graduated from the Kamenets Agricultural Institute. In March, he was told to get ready to go to an American farm for six months. Then he didn't hear anything more." We wonder if the intention had been to send him to Ralph's farm.

"I know this farm," put in Toli. "When I was teaching in another village, I brought children to this farm to pick apples."

At the end, the chairman said to Ralph, "I want you to come back and talk to my people and inspire them to work harder."

July 22:   Today I found myself inadvertently a part of the shadow economy. I tried again to get eggs from Johanna.

"I don't have any," she said, glowering at me.

"Where'd they go?" I asked, knowing there are at least a hundred chickens at Stupentsi.

"I gave them away," said Johanna.

At that, I went back into the house, considering it a closed case. A minute later, I heard the front door bang. When I got there, I saw Johanna retreating down the path. She had left two dozen eggs in the entrance way. I was thrilled she'd been kind enough to somehow get eggs for me. I thought, "I'll go out and thank her and give her that fatty sausage someone gave us. Maybe she'll like it."

After thanking me for the sausage, she asked, "Do you have laundry soap powder?"

"Yes," I said. "I have lots. Thanks, but I don't need any."

We chatted some more, and she asked me the same question. Then I realized she wanted *me* to give *her* powder. I said, "I'll give you some. Come on." She followed me and sat on the back steps while I went to get two boxes for her. Shortly afterwards, I heard the back door bang. When I went into the kitchen, there was a bowl of buckwheat and three dozen more eggs. No eggs, indeed!

I resolved to find another source for eggs. I don't want to get into this game of favors. As Providence would have it, Toli told me later today Anna had extra eggs she wanted to give me.

About meat—Ralph and I have decided to be nearly vegetarian while we're here because we want to use only food sources available to the people. Besides, the meat at the market is too fatty for us. We have access to the Chairman's good meat place, but we used it only once (when we were given two sausages). We don't plan to go again. I do have two good pieces of meat left in our freezer which Nikolai brought when he was still supplying our food. I'll use them only for guests.

Both of us have lost weight, though Ralph can hardly afford to. Our diet of abundant fresh fruits and vegetables, brimming with vitamins; few meats and sweets; and no junk food is doing it. We feel satisfied, too. We'll try to continue this way after returning home.

A group of young people from Khmelnitski and their sister city, Modesto, California, came to Makov today. This group didn't know we were here. They were amazed to see a village woman (me) walking toward them in

Birkenstock sandals. It all became clear when I said, "Hi! We're Americans!"

We met with them at Headquarters and were astonished to hear Viktor Party Secretary say, in this era of glasnost, that the Chairman is elected by all the people, with everyone sharing equally in the profits. That, of course, is how a collective farm is *supposed* to be run. Toli, sitting in the back row next to one of the American students, told him, "You're hearing a fairy tale." The Chairman *is* elected, but by hand vote. Woe to him or her who dares dissent. They might lose their job.

But, worse than that, the group's Khmelnitski guide stood up and said, "Soviet farms were collectivized *at the wish of the people*"!

We made arrangements to see the group again in Modesto when we go to California in December. We want to tell them how it *really* is, at least on this farm, with the Chairman and District party officials wielding all power. I've always wondered how the party managed to control the people far from Moscow. Now we know each little area has its own party apparatus to run it, and each area fares according to the character of its leaders.

But things are changing. We were happy to hear from the chairman of the poor farm the party people are sometimes not getting their way. We also know a woman in Volgograd whose husband was elected director of his factory over the party's choice. In Makov, however, conditions are much like they've been in the past. Our chairman takes few orders from above since the advent of perestroika. But he hasn't passed on that freedom to his underlings.

With the youth group was a slender woman from Khmelnitski named Raisa. She taught in Modesto for several months in 1988-89. We liked each other immediately and agreed to get together before Ralph and I return to the US. Raisa confided to me that she greatly misses her American friends.

Shortly after the meeting, Ralph and I went with the Chairman, his wife, and Toli to Khmelnitski to attend the wedding reception of the Chairman's "niece." The couple were married at a Wedding Palace, a large building for that explicit purpose. There the couple signs a book, an officiant says a few words, the two exchange their rings (which are worn on the ring finger of the *right* hand), and the sterile ceremony is over. Then they hurry out, making way for the next couple, and leave their flowers at a war memorial.

As we walked from the car to the reception, we passed a war memorial where I spotted a couple in all their formal wedding finery. The tall groom carried the tiny bride in his arms. Thinking they were our couple, I rushed over and snapped a picture, feeling very pleased. Later, I discovered they were *not* our couple.

The reception was held at a restaurant resembling a modern hotel lobby. It was very similar to wedding receptions in the US. At one point, we were asked to speak, with the suggestion Ralph talk about agriculture—a strange subject for a wedding reception, we thought. As part of the crowd watched from a balcony, he obliged, saying only that the USSR has good resources and someday there would be surplus production. I spoke a little. Then we harmonized to one verse of "Tell Me Why."

Food and drink kept coming for hours, much of it prepared and served by relatives of the couple. At one point, a big man at our table asked me to dance. I declined (as I'm not much of a dancer), but when the bride's mother led Ralph onto the floor, I changed my mind and danced with the man. Then two pretty young girls asked Ralph and Toli to dance. The head of a medical school asked me. And so it went. Finally, when the Chairman declared it would soon be time to leave, we danced with the bride and groom. We did give them American money, but nothing close to $500. I was sorry to go because I was just getting warmed up.

Tonight, Ralph's son, Mike, called to say the Dull family is so pleased with Palamarchouk they want to pay Valentina and Tatiana's airfare for his last two weeks in America. Dirk Harms, the dairy farmer on whose farm Nik works, has already begun the process for Nik's wife.

Later tonight, Toli called Moscow for us. When he told the woman who answered the phone Americans wanted to speak, she didn't believe him. She exclaimed, "Go and dry out!" and hung up.

July 23: We had a rare occurrence today—the woman on our doorstep was English-speaking. She said she was Jean from Canada and someone would be inviting us to dinner today. Sounded mysterious! We ended up eating with Jean and her niece's family at their large tiled home. The niece told us, "I don't know what this village will do when our wonderful Chairman retires."

When I told Toli later what she'd said, he remarked, "She means she doesn't know what she and her family will do!" Toli recently repeated his request for a larger apartment, and again the Chairman refused. Toli said to get a bigger apartment, he'd have to act stupid, be obedient, have no opinion, flatter the Chairman, or have other connections. This is not to suggest Jean's niece does this. Perhaps her husband is part of the entourage; we don't know their situation. She was surely lovely to us, however.

Sixty-six-year-old Jean was born in Makov, was hauled to Germany by Nazis to work during WWII, and afterwards she married and moved to Canada. She's now visiting her family in Makov. One of them is her 61-year-old sister who looks ten years older than Jean because of her hard life here. And what else did the sister have to show for her hard work? A pension of only 50 rubles a month! She still must work in the fields to make ends meet. The contrast between Jean and her sister in aging, standard of living, and condition of teeth is striking. Jean was disgusted that in most of the beautiful, intricately-tiled houses in Makov, people still have no indoor toilets. We know, however, that Headquarters and the apartment buildings have toilets.

I was restless tonight while Ralph was writing. I decided to talk with friend Bill Shaw, who's now in Moscow. Not knowing where he's staying, I called another Moscow friend, John Nicolopoulos (Greek correspondent for an Athens newspaper), to get Bill's phone number. John didn't have it, but he said, "Coincidentally, right now in my living room is the president of Vladimir Cooperative who wants to set up a model American farm outside Moscow. He's looking for a foreign manager, and perhaps he'd like to talk with Ralph." After speaking with the man for a minute, John returned to the phone and stated, "They'll come to Ukraine to see you, and they want to show you their land when you're in Moscow." This could prove interesting!

I also called the president of the World Family Clubs because we'd heard nothing from him about our upcoming trip to Arkhangelsk. He said, "Oh, you can't go there because of a recent submarine incident." Our hoped-for trips to Arkhangelsk, Krasnodar, and Stavropol have fallen through. The latter two are the result of the co-operative's failure to get an invitation to us. Soviets are doing the best they can in this new environment, sometimes promising more than they can deliver. Restrictions still abound and lack of know-how is rampant. But we've had other nice surprises. Perhaps Providence has improved on our expectations!

July 25: We had a great day today with Kamenets students Andrei and Sergei when they came for their planned visit. We ate and talked, and they read our *Time* magazines at length. In 1983, we'd talked with a young man who had a stash of *Times* hidden in his flat. He knew it would be dangerous to be caught with them. Now, they may be read here with no problem except they're difficult to get.

It pleased me Andrei liked my cooking. "You're an ambassador of the stomach!" he said. He and Sergei will go to work in Bulgaria for the rest of the summer, making wooden crates.

After Ralph left to take Sergei and Andrei to the bus, I was startled to see a woman right outside our living room window. She was Jewish, and she and her handsome son had come to ask our help in contacting their relatives in the US in hopes she and her family can emigrate there. I promised to write immediately.

We were told today some land outside Moscow is to be made into 50 family farms. One thousand people applied, but so far only seven have been accepted. That should be proof people want to rent land!

July 26: Anna's brother, 65-year-old Vasily, told us long ago he would come to Makov to talk with Ralph, but he hasn't come yet. We decided to drive to his village today. Ralph, Toli, and I took Anna along so she could see her birthplace in that area, 100 miles from Makov.

While riding along together, she told us how the little church was finally opened. "A telegram was sent to the Congress, and a message came back immediately from Moscow saying to open the church. The Chairman and the head of the local soviet keep asking who sent the telegram, but it's a secret. It will be much better to have two churches in the village," she added, "because now some of the villagers walk seven miles one-way to church.

"I remember when the bells stopped ringing—about 1938 or 1939—just before the war," she said.

"How did you become a believer?" I asked.

"My father believed in God but disliked the church. Because people were required to take two kilos of wheat every time they went to confession, he thought the priest had an empty sleeve that would never get full. But my mother loved God *and* the church. She took all seven of us children when she went.

"I was the middle child, and I went alone to Makov at age 19 because my family had no food or clothes. The sugar factory employed me, and I worked there until retirement, but for years I also had a job with a wealthy merchant in order to make enough money to raise my two daughters by myself."

"Anna was extremely honest," said Toli, taking up the story, "but one day the merchant lost a package of gold, and Anna was accused of taking it. That offended Anna. She stayed home from work for two weeks. It was then her boss came bringing champagne and caviar. The merchant herself had found the package. When Anna was working for this woman, sometimes people would tell her to steal from her boss. They said, 'Take it! It isn't hers, anyway!' But Anna never did. She made 67 rubles a month when she worked at the sugar factory. Now her pension is 60 rubles, and every fall she still works there for three rubles a day, to supplement her income a bit."

When we got to Vasily's village, we discovered he had gone to Makov! We had unknowingly passed his bus on the highway. But we visited his house anyway, a cozy cottage with a full apple tree and a grapevine canopy over the entire front courtyard. Vasily is a widower. But we met several sets of his and Anna's relatives, eating dinner at the home of a brother. This man is married to a woman 11 years older than he is, so Americans didn't start that.

After dinner, we took Anna to the place where she was born. She hadn't been there for 40 years. Even though she knew the house and even the forest were gone, she wept a little to see the spot so changed. We took a picture of her as she drank water from her childhood well. A couple walking past on the dirt road turned out to be old friends of Anna's. After talking with us for awhile, they said what Americans often say after being with Soviets for the first time: "Why, you're just like us!"

Anna visited with another neighbor, a nearly blind 85-year-old woman, and her son. In the course of the conversation, he made a sad comment on the meaning of his life, "I built two houses and three barns, and then I died."

July 27: I'm sick today with sore throat, headache, and fever, but we still asked Vasily (and Toli, of course) to come for a long, homey conversation.

Vasily wanted to talk about agriculture. "I did several kinds of jobs on the farm during my working life," he began. "I know different tillages, how to plant, and crop rotation. I've worked with little pigs, with horses, in the grain yard, and I've driven machinery." Vasily mentioned fertilizers are not spread evenly over the fields. When Ralph asked why not, he replied, "No one cares."

"What was your life like in Germany?" one of us asked.

"My sister and I both worked in an airplane factory there during the war."

"How were you taken?" I asked.

"The day I was sixteen and a half, policemen arrived, and we were taken away that very day. Nobody wanted to go. Some ran away, but they were caught. We were taken to the District where we had health exams. If anyone tried to escape, he or she was shot. Later, we were loaded like cattle into cargo trains and put into locked cars with small barbed-wire windows. The train stopped only once, after six hours, for people to relieve themselves. When we arrived at Frankfort, we went to distribution camps where buyers came to take us away to farms, railroads, or factories. I went to the town of Nereopeen and was put into a storage place. This place was surrounded by two rows of barbed wire and guarded by police. Every ten minutes, patrols with dogs came by.

"We got up at 5 A.M. and had breakfast: thin soup, artificial coffee, and bread. The bread was 25% flour and the rest sawdust. We had 200 grams of this bread each day, soup for dinner, and bread and coffee in the evening. Once in a while we'd have a small ear of corn. Men and women were not together in the camps. The girls did lighter work but had the same amount of food.

"We were allowed to write letters and receive parcels from home, and people were especially glad when they received tobacco. The Germans were rationed to two cigarettes a day, so there was a bazaar in the camp every evening where tobacco was traded for margarine or bread. People who tried to get food from the garbage died of dysentery. I preferred to be hungry, dividing my daily bread into three parts.

"We were always sure we'd be liberated. Germans—kind people or anti-fascists—kept us informed about what was happening on the front.

"At 7 A.M. we began work, often unloading ammunition from trains. Each person had to unload two railroad cars every day. Even if we were taken at night to unload cars, we still had to get up at 5 A.M. for our regular work. Once, I had to carry 130 lb. bombs, and I weighed only 110 lbs. Another time, we were carrying artillery shells that weighed 125 lbs. each, and the wagon turned upside down. Thankfully, the shells were not ready to explode at that point, but four people died from the crush. My leg was broken, and after that I got light work—chopping firewood.

"When we were liberated, I was inducted into the Soviet army right then and there. In the army, I saw my friend who'd served in the military before being taken to Germany as a POW. After being questioned for 45 days, he disappeared. If a person was a POW and survived, he was considered to be a betrayer because he didn't kill himself to prevent being captured.

"For a week and a half I served by the River Elbe. After Yalta we were moved 550 miles to the west. For eight months we were there on the border, with the Americans opposite us. The Americans brought us cigarettes and white bread, and we were friends. But then, for some reason, we were made to stop visiting. Soon afterwards, we were replaced by the national guard.

"During the war, the Americans helped our country with food and war equipment, and after they and Britain entered on the second front, it was easier to fight on the Eastern front. However, the Americans didn't fight with their breasts as we did. They fought with aircraft and artillery. When I was 150 miles from Berlin, I witnessed them bombing non-stop—24 hours a day. Once, they bombed a railroad station where there was a train full of oil and artillery shells. The cars with shells exploded, making a huge pit that could have held a four-story house. I can't say the Americans won the war, but they helped. The Soviets really won the victory; we liberated our own territory. I think the Americans were afraid if we were captured, they would be next. Russian soldiers can tolerate worse conditions than any other army in the world. We fight better when we're hungry. Americans won't fight on an empty stomach. This is my conclusion, based on my life's experience.

"Our people usually called Germany 'he.' 'He' captured . . . etc. The fascists did horrible things to people. If they had not, there might not have been such a strong guerilla movement. After the war was over, I served for three more years in the infantry, in a detachment near Moscow. During that time, I was allowed to visit my home only once. But I was released early for good work."

We asked, "Did you ever consider not working while you were in Germany?"

"I tried to escape once," he answered. "When I was sick, I was put into isolation, where there were no bars on the windows. A young man and I decided to escape together, so one night we went into the forest with no food and walked many miles to the east. Exhausted, we lay down to sleep in a clearing in the forest. When the sun rose, a forester who was mowing grass mowed up to us and told us to get up. I knew some German words, like 'eat bread,' and I asked him for food. He took us to his house, and his wife gave us potatoes and bread while he secretly called the police. In 15 minutes they came, took us back to the district camp, and asked why we had escaped. We said we wanted to work on a farm because the food was better there. My friend was big, so he was taken to a farm. But I was put into an isolation cell for three days where I could only stand. I was not beaten but was simply taken back to work."

"What happened after the war to the POWs who were Soviets?" I asked.

"Some were taken to the army, but those suspected of collaboration with the Germans spent 15 to 25 years in prison," Vasily said.

I said, "I read in the *Moscow News* women who served in the war were looked down upon later. Why would that be?"

Vasily replied, "That isn't true. Only fools would have treated them badly! We had many women pilots and women using anti-aircraft guns. But most of our women worked in factories."

That made me think of a story our guide in Volgograd told in 1985. She said her father had gone to the army and had been declared missing. Her mother worked in a factory and lost part of her hand there but kept on working. When she could, the mother went to find her husband. She died in the process, but he later came home.

After that, we turned to Vasily's remembrances of collectivization. He told us, "My grandfather had 2 sons and a daughter, 47 acres of field, and 7 horses. When the daughter married, she was given almost 20 acres and 2 horses. So 27 acres and 5 horses remained. In the opinion of the state, my grandfather was still a kulak [wealthy farmer]. So as not to be sent to Siberia, my grandfather and one son took half, and my grandmother and the other son took the other half. Collectivization began in 1929, and in 1930, the authorities became insistent. By 1931, more people than not were collectivized. By 1932-33, all the rest were in—or in Siberia.

"During the time of total collectivization, a man came to our village. He liked my father and asked to stay the night with us. Even though we had a small house and five children then, Father agreed. While we were eating supper together, the man advised my father to join the collective farm the next day. 'Otherwise,' he said, 'everything will be taken anyway, you'll be sent to Siberia, and your children will be under the snow.' My father didn't have an education and couldn't write an application to the collective farm. So the man wrote it for him, and Father signed.

"In the morning, Father took the application to the local soviet. He had only two horses and two wagons. Up until this time, when people were taken to the collective farm, there'd been no barn for their horses. So the council decided to make our yard a department of the collective farm. Now, they could use our barn for horses. Father entered the collective farm in December, 1931.

"We had a neighbor who had given everything to the collective farm. But he was accused of keeping some remnants. The very next day, he was taken away and no news of him ever came. His sister and wife were driven out into the snow, and everyone was ordered not to take them to their homes. They went to another village and found lodging. The collective farm used his place and ours for horses and wagons for three years—until they built their own barns.

"Those were hungry years. But we did better than most because we were allowed to have two cows and pigs, due to our having feed for the horses. We survived thanks to that one man who warned us in advance. The famine of 1933 was not natural; Stalin ordered all crops taken away, up to the last grain. Those who had cows [which ate grass] survived; those who didn't, died. Forty percent of the people around us died."

Before we ended our talk, Vasily told us a joke:

    Q. What's a good way to discourage religion?

    A. Take down the icons and put up pictures of the Central Committee of the Communist Party.

July 28: We went to Khmelnitski today to take a stack of letters for the California group to mail for us in the States. While there, we decided to get spark plugs for our car. Hmmm . . . how to find out where to get them. We drove around, finally stopping at a small shop where we saw tires being put onto bikes. I found "spark plug" in my dictionary and asked the men where to get them.

When we got to where they'd directed us, no one was there. But adjacent was a window where a man was taking money for gasoline, so I asked him about spark plugs. He responded by asking us if we were tourists. "No," I said. "We're living for six months in Makov, but there are no spark plugs there."

Immediately a look of recognition crossed his face, He lit up and started talking and smiling. "You're the Americans! I've read about you!" he exclaimed. He then left his booth and locked the door, leaving several customers waiting to pay for gasoline. He took us over to the order building and told the attendant who we were and what to do for us. After several comings and goings, paper signings, and the payment of seven rubles, the second man handed Ralph four new spark plugs. (By the way, at the gasoline station, the fuel is always paid for first; then, the attendant turns on the electricity for self-service.)

After that, we went to the market. A woman, on discovering we were Americans, heaped beets and herbs into our bag. One young man kept hanging onto Ralph, wanting to buy his shoes, pants, anything.

People are always asking us if we're homesick. We really aren't, though we miss our family and friends, and Ralph misses his farm and his work. It's beautiful here. We're enjoying the slow life, and people are wonderful. We're learning a lot and are having interesting experiences. We also hope to do our part for Soviet agriculture with our book. What more could one ask from six months? We would no doubt gain more respect if we worked beside peasants in the fields though.

We spent some time with Toli, who was depressed today. I really don't know why. He told us one of the main goals of the coal miners who've been striking for two weeks is to become independent, to make their own decisions about the use of the mine's profits.

He also talked about the apparatus/nomenklatura. He said, "They are gray people—a kind of mafia—and they try to surround themselves with those who are grayer than they are. Some are good-intentioned but incompetent. There are intelligent members of the party, but rarely are they in positions of leadership. I've never met a party leader I can respect. They're usually full of pretensions and have low intellect. The existence of the nomenklatura may be the main reason for our backwardness. They've lost the ability to function successfully, and it's a closed system.

"Makov has five primary organizations of nomenklatura—the collective farm, the school, the sugar factory, the sanitorium, and the state chicken enterprise. Once, our school music teacher was with a group of the rulers of Makov at a birthday party at Stupentsi. The Chairman made a toast: 'To us, the elite! None of the chaff are here.' It made the teacher feel very bad. In this society, those who do nothing live well, and those who work get little."

Here's an example of how the system ruled by nomenklatura doesn't work: The country has 60 or so ministers in charge of various areas. But they don't co-ordinate, so two trainloads of lumber, for example, often pass each other, going to where the other originated.

We dropped off Toli and picked up our mail at his place. As usual, there were half a dozen children playing at the rear of the apartment building near the door. Sometimes Tanya leans out the third floor kitchen window to give instructions to Toli, Vova, or Yura, or toss something for Toli to catch. Just inside the building, there's a set of mail boxes. Toli pulls them away from the wall to get at the mail from the back rather than take time to unlock his box from the front. Monday instead of Sunday is the day off for the post office here. The Makov carrier is a woman who simply opens envelopes and takes out money. If she's confronted, she returns the money. Yet she keeps her job and does it again—with no prosecution.

As we walked towards the car after getting our mail, an elderly woman whom we'd never met walked over and handed us a bag of pears. Kindness overflowing!

This evening, I watched the American country singer Roy Clark on TV. I never cared for him back in the States, but I enjoyed hearing him sing tonight. It made me feel surreal and impersonal. Where am I? Who am I? What universe am I in? There seem to be no boundaries.

July 31: I walked over to talk to the guys at the greenhouse during their dinner time today. While we were talking, a young woman came in and sat down. She was well dressed, with several necklaces. When I asked the men who she was, they whispered they'd never seen her before. Oleg showed me a word in the dictionary which meant "an impudent person." Stepan calmly filled a plate for her, which she accepted but barely touched. After talking to me for awhile, she began to sweep up the place, probably as payment for her dinner.

The girl and I left the greenhouse at the same time, going in opposite directions. Half an hour later, she was at our door, asking to be a guest. I invited her in.

All at once, she asked, "Do you want to see an interesting mental hospital about 45 miles from here?"

"Of course!" I responded.

"The people aren't really mentally ill there," she said. "They're people who speak the truth and are put away."

"But surely I wouldn't be allowed in," I said.

"I have a doctor friend who would give permission," she replied.

Ralph went to get Toli, so we could understand her words more in depth. Toli could hardly make sense of what she was saying because it was so illogical and fragmented, but he translated as best he could. With tears in her eyes, she said, "The mafia recently shot to death two of my friends in the Democratic Front movement—one in Lvov." She also said, "I'm divorced, and I have a five-year-old son. Now I'm engaged to the son of Valentina Shevchenko from Kiev [Chairman of Ukraine's Supreme Soviet]. I'm a chemical engineer in a lab, and I make 130 rubles a month.

"Only Oleg and Sasha Sportsman at the greenhouse are renters, she stated. [At first she had told me all of them were janitors.] The two with cars [Stepan and Nikolai] are KGB men. I can tell their rank by their license plates. They tried to take me to Kamenets-Podolski, just so I wouldn't visit you. However, the KGB is not bad. Once, when the militia roughed me up, some kind KGB men helped me. The reason I'm here in Makov, she added, is that once a militiaman brought me here to compromise me, and I wanted to see the place again.

"I travel on foot because I have no money. See?" she said, emptying her pockets and purse, which contained no money, only blue beads. "I pay my way by working or by selling the stones from my necklace."

At first, I thought perhaps she *was* one of the people who'd been put into a mental hospital because of speaking out. And maybe that did happen, but at this point, I'm sure her mental problems are real. The final proof came when she said, "The accident at Chernobyl made everyone speak Ukrainian."

Afterwards, she and Toli walked over to the greenhouse where the men laughed at her. But Oleg, after listening carefully to her, took a board and told her to leave fast or he would beat her.

Later, at the greenhouse, Nikolai told me, "We're sorry she bothered you; we tried to prevent it. She's a charlatan, and you're kind. We didn't want her taking advantage of you."

About the KGB—our friends in America have always been worried about our getting entangled with them. Friends often asked, "Have you been followed by the KGB?" We've never feared the KGB because we don't change money on the street or sell anything. Only once in our six trips did we have an experience of being watched. We were meeting with a Jewish refusnik in Armenia, and a man stood right by our table in the restaurant, listening to us. When we left, he followed us, but soon disappeared.

We've met several times over the years with the Moscow Trust Group, an independent peace organization. Some of their members were harassed by the KGB very early in the Gorbachev Era, but their meetings weren't broken up. One of the members was sent to Siberia on a trumped-up charge. He later emigrated with his family to Israel. We know two others who were put into a psychiatric hospital for two weeks. These brave people knew the KGB could have destroyed the group. But they never did, probably because of Gorbachev's new way. Now, things are so changed that two Trust Group members were asked to speak to the huge government-connected Soviet Peace Committee.

Anna gathering poppies near Makov.

Toli's extended family in his Makov flat. Foreground: Yura and Tanya. Back: from left: Vasily (Anna's brother), Valeri and Lusa holding their 2 sons, Ralph, Chris, Anna, Vova and Nina. Oriental rugs on walls is the custom.

Breakfast at Victoria's restaurant our first day in Makov. From the left: District Gosagroprom official Valarovsky, Ukraina collective farm chairman Vitaly Stengach, Christine and Ralph Dull.

Valentina Palamarchouk and Toli brought homemade Paskha bread and cheese-stuffed rolls to our Makov house on Easter Eve. Note Ukrainian painted eggs in dish—also a gift.

Christine and Anna
in Anna's cottage.

Tatiana Palamarchouk
at Last Bell ceremony.

Sasha Sportsman at "Little Michigan."

Makov teachers, including Toli's friend Vanya,
dance in Ukrainian costume.

View from Makov school window.
Preschool children play in the little houses.

Bake sale at Makov school.
Day care center in the background.

Second graders.

High school graduating class.

Christine and a Makov resident.
It was good for us not to have a car the first month.

Anna's back door and root cellar.

One of the tiled houses in Makov.

Thatch-roofed houses on a collective farm near Makov.

Every family has a private garden, and 1 in 12 families has a cow.

One well for every 10 houses in Makov.
We used a well for drinking, cooking, and laundry.

Eighty-six-year-old Makov man approaches Ralph.

Ralph and same elderly man exchange greetings.

In Ukraina sugar beet field.

Ukrainian veteran meets Americans for the second time:
1945 at Elbe River in Germany, 1989 in a corn trench-silo.
Both were happy occasions.

Babushka 100 miles east of Makov in Anna's birth village.

Woman with beads, 66, born in Makov but a resident of Canada since 1946, next to her 61-year-old Makov sister.

Christine and Ralph chatting with women hoeing weeds out of sugar beets, Ukraina collective farm.

Women spreading asphalt near Makov.

Gathering hay from a private plot.
Most plots contain only
fruits and vegetables.

Makov girl enjoying
bread and jam.

Food store in small Ukrainian village.

Market in Kamenets-Podolski where we did most of our food shopping.

Picnic in Makov park with Toli's friends.

Makov mill, over 150 years old,
used only by families.

Little Russian Orthodox church in Makov:
closed in 1958, re-opened in 1989.
Zhenya (Little God) is framed by doorway.

Redecorated inside of the same church.

Dimitri came from far away to visit us.
He's impressed by photos of Ohio agriculture.

USA-USSR cake baked by teacher for reception following Christine's
final lecture at Kamenets-Podolski language institute.

Corner of hay field on collective farm made available to families to cut with sickle or scythe for their privately owned cows.

Big bows are often worn by little girls.

Scene from one of our train trips.

Ralph observing Niva combine on Ukraina collective farm.

Ukraina corn field. Several strips were planted twice after the driver
thought the planter had malfunctioned.

Mowing and windrowing peas on Ukraina.

Grain yard in Makov at time of wheat harvest. While waiting to be dried in white shed, three days of rain fell on it.

Fishing in the Moscow River near the Kremlin. Office buildings and cathedrals are inside Kremlin.

Carpathian mountains in Ukraine near Czechoslovakia.
Region where Nikolai Zubyets lived before coming to Ohio for 7 months.

A girl with her grandmother in Tbilisi, capital of Georgian Republic.

Christine came upon this Soviet boy.

Ralph and Christine near Moscow.

Zagorsk, a main center of the Russian Orthodox Church.

Wedding in Moscow Baptist Church, 1986.

At Armenian Orthodox church, this live chicken was taken into the sanctuary and blessed. While we watched, it was dressed nearby and taken home for Sunday dinner.

Statues in Tbilisi, Georgia.

Estonian geography professor telling woes to Christine, 1985.

Market in Yerevan, Armenia. Private enterprise for families with gardens.

Christine speaking with Central Asians on Red Square with the Kremlin in background. Kremlin means "fortress." Several Russian cities have Kremlins hundreds of years old.

Hikers at Lake Baikal, Siberia.
This lake is one mile deep, the deepest lake in the world.
It is purported to hold one-sixth of the world's fresh water.

Cottage near Baikal.

CHAPTER 7

Christine's Journal Excerpts

AUGUST

August 1: Today we saw a long line standing outside the hardware store. When we asked Toli what was happening, he said, "It's the first day of the month, and the laundry powder is in. It's rationed. The ration is adequate, but people are afraid it'll run out before they get their month's portion."

On a different subject, Toli said, "Voice of America said that at Ternople, not far from here, a riot broke out. Also, I heard that in Dunaevtsi, people planned to demonstrate in front of party headquarters. But the first party secretary went around making promises to various industries, averting the demonstration, at least temporarily. People said his lips were trembling."

I'd been wanting Toli to tell me about the schools for a long time. He agreed to make some time for it. He's soured on the schools. "Our schools are in poor shape," he began. "Education's not a priority in our country. You spend much more money on your schools than we do. [Toli often refers to his book of US statistics.] The main disadvantage of our school system is it's too authoritarian; it smashes the initiative of both teachers and students. Teachers have a few choices. We may bring in supplemental material only if we do not deviate from the program. Every school in the country uses the same books. We're all supposed to be on the same page on the same day.

"Our schools need to be more democratic. Recommendations on how to teach the children come from above, and usually those high authorities never worked as teachers. They issue recommendations, sometimes stupid ones. The teacher is last in the chain of command. The teachers sometimes want to revolt, but the school director must make them obey regulations—sometimes by persuasion, sometimes by tricks.

"For example, there are different promotions a teacher can get to gain a higher salary. And obedient teachers get promotions. Also, the director decides how many lessons teachers may teach, which affects their salary, too. And the director can control the teacher by visiting certain classrooms every day, or by having administrators from the district or the region do it. I'm not afraid about my lessons; anyone can observe what I do.

"The school director is responsible for everything at school, including getting money for building maintenance. His deputy's [assistant director] job is scheduling. The director must have good relations with the Region and District. He must beg for financial help from the Chairman, the sanatorium, the sugar factory, the hospital head, and many other places. Our school head and the Chairman have a personality conflict, so the Chairman gives little to the school. Every school is supposed to have a greenhouse to help with the school's food supply. The Chairman has a greenhouse which he could give the school but hasn't.

"School directors can be fired more easily than teachers. A director, as he works in the district, may have access to good food. So he gets some and delivers it to the district school heads, securing his position. He gets other benefits, too. He receives money, caviar, or cognac from certain teachers so they can get better salaries in one of the ways I told you. He also gets money or favors from parents who want their children to get medals. Medals almost always insure students' acceptance into certain institutions of higher learning. The brightest students receive medals, but so do those whose parents bribe. People say the parents of one girl who visited you at Stupentsi paid 8,000 rubles to get her into medical school. She'll benefit later by being a doctor, even though her salary will be low. The other students who visited you wanted to talk to you about this shadow economy in our lives but didn't, out of deference to her. Most schools don't have the honors and connections of our Makov school.

"Our salaries are low—teachers average 207 rubles a month—and many teachers have poor training. In our district, there are 53 schools, so you can see how many English teachers there are. And only 12 have Institute training like mine. The others have taken two or three years of correspondence courses, which are inferior. All teachers are required to take updates every five years. Our salaries are based on the number of classes we teach. The basic number is 18 a week. I teach 24, so my salary is 300 rubles a month. Because of low pay, there are shortages of teachers in the village schools all over the country. There are even some schools where certain subjects are not taught. Out of the 115 who graduated with me at the Institute, only 15 work as teachers. The rest do other work. Some had a 'hairy arm' [connections] which gave them a promotion. There's little in my job to challenge my intellect. Tutoring is more satisfying because those students are interested in learning.

"Sometimes the kids, at 15 or 16, try to express what they really think. I tried that once. There were two marks on my paper. My mark for literacy was perfect, but I received a very low mark on content. This is how children are treated when they show their creativity. Our schools don't prepare independent workers or scientists who can defend their thoughts. I try to teach my students where to get knowledge. And I encourage them to get extra information so they can learn all their lives.

"The school is organized like this: We have four quarters, with school in session six days a week. The first day is September 1, the last May 25. Then students work in the fields, planting tomatoes or cabbage. Or they take exams—starting with the fifth grade—until June 17. At that time, many go to Pioneer camps, but some stay home with grandparents. Shifts at the Pioneer camps are one month long, so a child may go for one, two, or three months, depending on family circumstances. Most children would rather stay with their grandparents.

"We have one week of vacation in the fall, two over the New Year, and another week in the spring. In the fall, there are only four hours of school, then dinner. The next three hours is spent harvesting vegetables and fruits on the farm. Lenin believed using the head *and* the hands is necessary to develop a well-rounded person. Older students from the Institutes spend September in the fields.

"The children start to school at age 6 and graduate at age 17. Thus, there are eleven grades. They're required to attend school until they finish 9th grade, usually at age 15. A child can get five marks: 5 is highest, 4 is good, 3 is average, 2 is failing, and 1 is seldom used.

"The primary grades have reading, writing, arithmetic, arts, handwork, physical training, and music. From the fifth grade on, the subjects are these: Ukrainian language and literature, Russian language and literature, math, English language, history, geography, arts, music, physical training, and handwork—first aid and home economics for girls and wood and metal work for boys.

"Biology begins in fifth grade, physics and algebra in the seventh, chemistry and geometry in the eighth. There's one year of technical drawing. In the tenth grade, they have ethics, psychology of family life, and computer engineering—without computers. Next year, however, our school will have computers for a class of 30. In their last year, they have Development of Society and astronomy.

"In the last two grades, five lessons a week on trades or professions are taught. Also, all students take military training their last two years—two lessons a week. They learn to parade; shoot; take apart and assemble a machine gun; and general notions about attack, defense, and civil defense—how to protect themselves. Personally, I think the best thing to do in a nuclear attack is don a white sheet and go to the cemetery."

"How much emphasis is put on Lenin and ideology?" I asked.

"There's not much about Lenin and socialism in the schools. About capitalism—they used to be taught there are a few rich and millions of homeless, unemployed, and starving. They've seen photos of those conditions on our TV. What's taught depends on the teacher. There are a few older teachers still teaching outdated things about America. Most people, however, know life's better in Western countries, though they can't always say why.

"I can't explain it all to the little kids. However, this is what I tell the older ones: The problems in the Soviet Union stem from many things. First, the centralized command-and-administer system is no good, and the selection of leaders is poor. A market economy would be better, slightly controlled for the good of the people. Prices should be according to costs of production. Stalin's repressions put us behind; he killed off the best minds in the country. Industrialization was done at the cost of agriculture. There's no personal interest in work here. The system may have worked well during the war, but it hinders our development during times of peace. The District is ruled by one person. Also, it's strange that gifted people can't get a decent post.

"I tell them capitalism has changed greatly over the years. It gives people what they want. People can influence their government. And—this is strange for students to hear—people living in capitalist countries don't want war. I also tell them Americans live with the same ideas as we do. Common human values are formulated in the Bible.

"As I see it," he continued, "the negative things about capitalism are the following: the producing of arms because it's profitable, the striving so much for profits that life and relationships are forgotten, and not considering the question, 'What would this lead to?' This last can be dangerous. A person is not well-protected under capitalism. If he does well, he's okay, but if he does not, he falls out of the system. It's survival of the fittest. Neither capitalism nor socialism is good enough for people. Both should think more about the people, securing for them a certain level of life, even for the worst representatives of society.

"Here are two anecdotes:
1. Capitalism is the exploitation of man by man, and socialism is the reverse.
2. Under capitalism, those who have money, rule. Under socialism, those who rule, have money.

"I speak much to the students about the socialism we have, compared to what Lenin thought. The students are taught to be honest, But they see the striking contrasts between what is taught and what is done in Makov, a center for the shadow economy. Parents also don't talk about reality. The students get so they don't trust anyone, especially the teachers. For example, every year, our school director says, 'This year we'll be honest.' And then the students see the school janitors working on the director's house and yard. It's horrible what happens when the students start to see what's what. They usually laugh at ideals and lose trust in words."

"I thought the students and teachers seemed close to each other at the school functions we went to," I said.

"It only seemed that way," said Toli. "They're polite but not close. A recent poll showed if a student is having problems, he'll first talk to his friends, then to his parents. Teachers were practically never mentioned. The whole situation in society makes everything seem negative. Everywhere they look, students see unfairness. The school is a reflection of society."

"Do you have much paperwork or many meetings?" I asked.

"Yes, we have *much* paperwork! We must write a plan for half a year. We also have to write a plan for how we're going to work with the class that's been assigned to us for seven years. Every lesson must have a written plan, and we'd better not be caught without it! No one cares what kind of lesson you give, just so you have a plan. Then we have to write about the students' development.

"Meetings seem interminable. We've been fighting against this for three years. There are regular meetings for many things—with the Pedagogical Council of Teachers; with the school director; production meetings, when we discuss school stuff; and trade union meetings. From October 1 to May 15, there's the so-called School of Scientific Communism, twice a month. It's horrible, rotten. Last year we studied changes in education. They really are trying to change the school system. In 1988, the history books were thrown out, and the students didn't have to take history exams. They were told history had been written up wrong and they would get new books. Also, we're experimenting with a five-day week.

"One other thing," added Toli. "Sometimes the party committee has required teachers to act against the churches. In the past, each year the teachers sent to the District a list of students whose families attended church, though there's never any persecution. This year, the teachers refused to send the lists. It was usually only the Baptist students who were reported. But those are our best students, and a crew of Baptist workers are the best workers in the village."

"What do you do with the class for whom you're responsible for seven years?" I asked.

"Every Wednesday, for half an hour before school," he said, "I meet with them. They must speak about the current events they've heard on TV or read in the newspapers. For another hour each week, we discuss problems, the behavior of different kids, plans, and moral problems. And they ask me questions. Then I have to meet with the Pioneer organization once a month. I hate it. We talk about the ideals of the Communist Party. They're supposed to organize events like concerts, and we talk about that."

"What about after school?" I asked relentlessly.

"The school day goes like this," said Toli. "Lessons start at 9 A.M. After two lessons, breakfast is served. Then school continues until 2:40 P.M., when dinner is served—sandwiches and tea, brought in by a co-op. Most children then stay after school with caretakers, though they don't like it. It's said to be voluntary, but students and parents are pressured to participate. They play games after dinner until 4 P.M. Then they do homework and have activities such as reading, band, and singing. They go home at 7 P.M. Vova begged me to let him out of staying after school. I was able to do so because Tanya is home.

"You know, when I was at the Institute in Kiev, the best students were sent to Great Britain. I was chosen to go, but I was not allowed to because I wasn't a communist and didn't serve in the army. We had American teachers for three or four months at the Institute, but Jimmy Carter messed that up. When he started that human rights stuff, the majority of Soviets didn't even know what he meant. But now we know about the 'persuading' of dissidents in mental hospitals and other tactics."

We finished by talking a little about army life. "Army men get only 14 rubles a month—for soap and cigarettes. Parents help the soldiers' wives and children," Toli said. "If they can't, the government helps them. However, it's a pitiful amount of money."

On another subject, Ralph was stopped by police today. Ralph has been pulled over several times for routine checks, but today it was for speeding on the highway at the outskirts of a distant village. A traffic policeman standing on the side of the road put out his white stick to indicate Ralph should pull over. Then the officer took his sweet time sauntering over, probably to give the culprit time to figure a bribe. We once heard an anecdote about this: "Our militia men are sheep who graze on the asphalt." Today, as usual, Ralph was waved on, leaving the sheep hungry, thanks to our being Americans.

At Kostya's tonight, we stuffed ourselves with ridiculous quantities of food. His wife, Meela, made three fancy desserts! We conversed for a long time. Most thirtyish men we talk to—and Kostya and his guests were no exception—have tremendous resentment against the nomenklatura, bureaucrats, supervisors, and mafia (these overlap) who enjoy special privileges and extra money. Yeltsin is beloved by the people because it's said he has given up his privileges.

Kostya's apartment in Kamenets has three bedrooms, a living room, two balconies, a kitchen, bathroom, and hall. It looked wonderful until I realized two families live there—Meela's parents; Kostya, Meela, their three-year-old daughter; and, in the summer, Kostya's nephew. Even then, it's not bad. Meela's parents bought the apartment for 15,000 rubles and remodeled it—most people spend much time building or remodeling the inside of their apartments when they get them. We have seen some beauties in Moscow. The crumbling outside of apartment buildings can hide fine furnishings.

We talked about why Americans have so much more leisure time than Soviets. One reason is Americans spend only an hour or two a *week* buying groceries. Soviets spend at least two hours a *day*. People even leave their work place to go shopping for a while. And it's accepted. Families who can, have one person working full time just shopping.

This continuous shopping affects other aspects of Soviet life, too. We've noticed people in Makov don't wave when greeting each other, for example. They nod, probably because their hands are always carrying something. However, Makov children have learned to smile and wave vigorously as soon as they see our car. They're a delight!

For two weeks, there have been guests in the lodge next door. Oleg says they're officials and their families from Kiev, friends of the Chairman. Johanna takes the women and children mushroom-hunting every day. The men play cards outside every evening, amidst lots of good food. Large black or white cars from Khmelnitski sometimes park there for the evening. Occasionally the Chairman joins them. It's not a luxurious vacation by our standards, but it's better than most Soviets get.

The Chairman dropped by with a prescription for medicine. He wants us to get it filled in the US for his granddaughter who has a skin problem. I sent it to my surgeon brother in California.

All these months, I've seen no hard cheese. But today in one of Makov's two restaurants (they sell some food to people out of a refrigerated display case), there was a large round of white cheese. I bought a hunk—a real treat!

August 5: Something extraordinary for the local people occurred today. Baptists from Dunaevtsi spent the day by the Makov Lake, singing, praying, preaching, and finally baptizing 40 new members in the lake. A traffic jam resulted as curious people from Makov and Dunaevtsi stopped their cars, trucks, and tractors to watch. Tears came to my eyes as the new converts lined up to be photographed. How wonderful they can now follow their hearts without fear! During the proceedings, small New Testaments were given out to anyone who wanted one. I was surprised Bibles are so available these days.

August 6: Back home in Dayton on this Hiroshima Day—it's 10 A.M. there and 6 P.M. here—our friends will be standing at the gates of Wright-Patterson Air Force Base. They are gathered to demonstrate opposition to the military approach to conflict. Though we can't be with them this year, we are part of the world-wide mourning for the Japanese victims of 1945, and for the victims of all wars, as we watch remembrances of the day on TV. The questions continue: Was it predominantly an atomic-bomb experiment? Was it done only to save lives? Was it done to end the war before "Russia" could enter that theater and claim the spoils? And why did we drop the second one?

Forty Baptists from Dunaevsti ready for baptism in Makov lake.

Baptist Church of Dunaevtsi baptizing new members in Makov lake. Traffic jam on road to Shatava.

Toli's face was badly swollen this morning. He's had a toothache for some time and has been avoiding the dentist. But he could put it off no longer. We went to the clinic in Kamenets where my black teeth were examined in April. First, we told the dentists my dad, a retired dentist, had written to say my problem wasn't systemic. It was only on the surface of the teeth. They had been right to want to polish it away. There's still some gray, but it's gradually disappearing.

About that time, a flamboyant, young dentist named Sasha waltzed into the room. He wore a tall white hat (like Johanna wore when she carved up the deer) and gave Toli a shot of novocaine. While Toli was numbing, Sasha went to a small closet and pulled out a huge, unwrapped fish he had caught. He handed it to me for a present. (I was glad I had my plastic bag! I've learned to always carry bags as Soviet women do because they never know when they'll see something they need.) Then Sasha proceeded, without washing his hands, to the dental chair to pull the tooth! No harm done.

Ralph picked apples for a while today with the Greenhouse Gang. He intends to do more of it. In return, they gave him a 10-ruble bill. He returned it to them, asked each to sign it, and he pocketed it while handing them a fresh one.

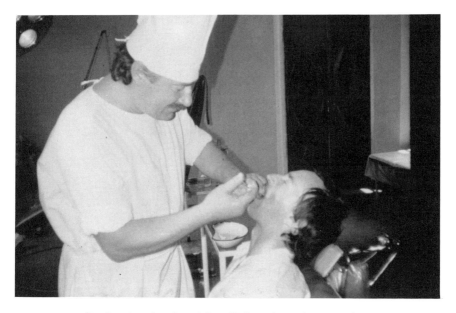

Sasha the dentist giving Toli a shot of novocaine.

Toli asked me to call Kiev Language Institute to see if Natasha was approved for entrance. She was! And she got in without a bribe. She studied hard and did it honestly, but I think few villagers will believe that. Both she and Alla won awards in the District: Alla, first place and Natasha, fifth. Alla didn't apply to the Kiev Institute, however, because her parents were afraid she wouldn't get in. She entered the Institute at Kamenets instead. Now I think she'll wish she had tried for Kiev.

The last few days, a man has been phoning me, just wanting to talk. I don't know who he is or where he lives, but he continues to call and hang on the phone. One morning he called at 6 A.M.

August 10: Oleg came this morning to give me a souvenir—a fountain pen. I'll treasure it! All the Greenhouse Gang say they want to give us mementos. Stepan has already given us a fine old coin.

Later, as Ralph and I sat writing in our living room, we heard the roaring of cars. Ralph remarked, "Here comes Vladimir Cooperative!" He was right. There were four men in three cars—Vladimir had a chauffeur. With Toli's help, we talked enough to realize they're not ready for Ralph yet. They're still in the beginning stages of planning their model farm. What they really want is for Ralph to solicit hard currency in the States and for him to manage a farm near Moscow. But Ralph can't manage a Soviet farm. He doesn't have the necessary connections. Also, he doesn't like to solicit investors. The language barrier would be another handicap.

Being a consultant, however, and helping to analyze and plan, would be something Ralph might consider. "Even more important than hard currency," Ralph told Vladimir, "it is necessary to have competent Soviet people manage the farm. A very successful farm could be had without hard currency or foreign machinery—if the organizing is different. Also, I would caution you against choosing an enterprise just because it's the most profitable one now. The price could go poof! It's better, in the long run, to do what best suits the particular land, climate, and the country's greatest need."

We tried part of Sasha the dentist's fish tonight. It was one of the best we've ever tasted!

August 12: About midnight last night, a pleasant couple arrived from Lvov in far-western Ukraine, a gift of champagne in hand. They were apologetic about disturbing us so late. The couple wants to re-establish contact with relatives in Toledo, Ohio. I promised I'd do my best to find them. They also offered to show us around their beautiful, fervently-Ukrainian city. I hope we can go.

This evening, Tanya and I spent a couple of hours talking. Tears came to her lovely almond-shaped eyes as we talked of Ralph's and my return to the States. She made me promise to write once a month.

Tanya wants to go to work—only part time, because of Yura. She wants to work as a bookkeeper, the field in which she was trained. "But even if I can't find work," she said, "I think our lives would be completely happy if only we had a bigger place to live. Nelya and Nikolai have one child and two rooms, and Sasha and Ola, with no children, will soon move to a new flat." Tanya chafes under her family of four having only one room for living, eating, and sleeping. She and Anna often push Toli to ask the Chairman "one more time" for a bigger apartment.

But Toli finds it hard to ask. He knows if the system were different, if he were not dependent on higher-ups, he could do just fine providing for his family. He knows it is necessary to humiliate himself to get what he alone should be responsible for. He has too much pride and principle to do much of that. But he feels sorry for Tanya having to care for super-active Yura in one room. So he's torn.

It will be about 5 years before he and Tanya can save the money needed—perhaps 20,000 rubles—to build their own house. Vova will be 15 by then. At least, they don't have to ask the Chairman for land to build on. Tanya inherited a bit of land from her grandmother, who had a cottage there. The grandmother left it to Lusa who's older. But Lusa, because she lives in Kiev, gave it to Tanya. Tanya applied to the collective farm to keep her land, and they gave consent, with the stipulation that she pay 35 rubles a year. So she wouldn't have to pay the tax, Tanya gave the land to Toli, who, as a teacher, is allowed to have one-half acre of land free.

Tanya also talked about the day care center next door to their apartment building. "Yura needs a strong hand, which he gets there," she said. "He attends five days a week from 9 to 5, but then he's wild until 11 o'clock every night and all week-end. The kindergarten teachers make the children sit still," she said, "although some teachers are kinder and allow movement." I think she wonders if the kindergarten helps or hinders Yura's wildness.

She and I went to get her regular order of dairy products from a woman with a cow. The woman was so delighted I came along that she gave me a quart of milk and some cottage cheese.

Usually, Ralph goes to the dairy barn to get our milk every other day. Once I went. The milkmaid was still milking, so I watched. She wiped off the udder with a well-used rag before she began. When she noticed the cow's flanks were filthy, she used the same rag to wipe the leg and then again the udder. It's a wonder we haven't gotten sick on the milk. Some people here boil their milk before consuming it. We've been lucky.

BBC said tonight that as of August 15, any reading material may be brought into the USSR except for pornography or anything advocating the overthrow of the government. The announcer also said the Soviet summer grain production is about 210 million tons this year—10 million less than expected. Still, this is 20 or 30 million more than last year.

August 15:   For two weeks, we've been trying to track down the supervisor in charge of sugar distribution so we can get our ration of 22 pounds. Today we grabbed him when we saw his car parked near the sawmill. He immediately opened the warehouse. After Toli and I entered, the man stood in the doorway and pointed to a large bag of sugar on the floor. I was shocked that he stood there watching as I began to scoop out the sugar. Toli insisted on doing the job for me. Then it dawned on me I was experiencing personally what we've been hearing about: supervisors do no hand labor. I didn't mind scooping. It's just that, as an American, I'm used to the seller packaging the product.

I've also seen the supervisor of one of the cow barns letting the grass grow under his sandals while women, squishing in their shoes, shoveled out the barn. One said no matter how hard they scrub, they can never rid their bodies of that manure smell. She also told us the supervisor makes twice her salary.

I'm understanding more and more the enormous resentment people feel for their bureaucratic supervisors. People here say Palamarchouk is a supervisor who likes to get his hands dirty on the machinery. He sometimes does, but then he endures a scolding by the other supervisors. They don't want his example to ruin their inactivity.

We needed to talk to Wendy (who's now in Vienna) to try to make sure the *Time* article is accurate. While Toli was making the call, the Kiev operator asked him, "Why do the Americans go around taking pictures of bad things?"

Toli countered, "Did you see them do that? How do you know?" We have heard this unfounded rumor about us several times. In one version, we took a picture of a drunk man lying in the mud. We haven't even seen anyone like that. Toli thinks the rumors may have been started by a District bureaucrat.

This led to an interesting discussion. "We Soviets are hungry for social justice," said Toli, "even more than food and goods. People would be less angry about suffering through these hard changes if *everyone* suffered."

"I get discouraged when I hear people bad-mouthing Gorbachev," I said. "I think their expectations are unrealistic. They want everything *now*. But I can understand their frustration and agony. Many have waited a lifetime—suffering, sacrificing, believing, and even dying. It must seem like empty promises are being made again. Their ideals, hopes, and very lives have been contorted by people who were selfish or who got caught in an inhumane system and became corrupt themselves. It can happen to nearly anyone. But to blame Gorbachev, in my opinion, is to misplace the blame.

As I write this, I'm watching an interesting segment of a TV program called "Rainbow." Africans, their dark bodies painted with psychedelic paint, are dancing to weird music in near-darkness. A large, luminous moon and blinking stars glow in the background. The dancers seem to be telling a story. At the end, they're all reaching skyward against the yellow moon crying, "Hope!" "Hope!"

All over the world, people are hoping, hoping for goodness to prevail—for love, peace, and justice to be in the ascendancy. We can all hope and work for this—and I believe that every good thought or act helps—but utopia is not likely.

Does my attitude come from being married to a practical farmer who never has a perfect year but must continually cope with various problems? Or am I just showing my age? I wonder.

August 16: About 4 P.M., Ivan from Yalta arrived unexpectedly. Earlier, after reading about us in *Izvestia*, he invited us to visit him and his family. We declined because of our difficulty in leaving the Region, and instead, asked them to visit us. So he came, bearing many gifts. He brought wine and cognac which we'll take to my family's Christmas dinner in California next December. Ralph and I don't drink, but I shall have a taste. "This is how I got these two bottles," he said, weaving his hand forward like a snake.

We were talking about his country's difficulties, and Ivan said, "It's not just that we had Stalin for so long; the whole system is wrong. Eastern Europe didn't have Stalin, and they live poorly, too. If I were Gorbachev," he continued, "I would have Western experts come and show the people how to do things, such as in factories. I don't care about capitalist or communist. We just need to relate as human beings."

Ivan told us about his family. "My grandparents lived in Siberia and escaped to a better place there. From Siberia, a neighbor of theirs went to America. My grandparents wrote to them about the possibility of their going to America, too. But the letter was opened, and my grandfather was taken away. He died in a labor camp or a prison.

"My father lost a hand in the war, but he worked with cows and animals, and we children helped him. Later, I became a mechanic, responsible for 106 cars and drivers. But I found it easier to work with animals than with other mechanics.

"I worked for awhile in Kazakhstan. Where do you think they put the wheat after harvest? First, they piled it in the fields because they had no shelter. Then, they carried it to the railroad station and piled it without shelter again before they loaded it onto railroad cars. There were no roads at all, so when it rained, everything stopped. What they managed to put onto railroad cars, went. The rest spoiled. It was put back onto the field.

"In 1978, I had to sign a paper saying I wouldn't have any contact with foreigners, because of the black market and other things. Now, I work as a fire truck driver and a chauffeur for Intourist. I don't smoke, but my liver is bad, so I haven't had any liquor for two years.

"My mother's 85. She worked until she broke her hip two years ago. She was a very hard worker, and got many awards. But now she's an invalid, and I wanted to buy a car to take her around. I was ready to pay. Twice, I wrote to the military department. Twice, I wrote to the Minister of Defense. I heard nothing. Then I wrote to Raisa Gorbachev on behalf of my mother. I knew she didn't distribute cars, but maybe she could help. I got a letter back saying that my letter, along with the personal documents I'd enclosed, had been sent to the Central Committee. I don't know why. The Central Committee sent my letter and documents to our local party committee. They said they couldn't help. Most recently I wrote to Biryukova, the woman who's an alternate member of the Politburo. The letter was sent to authorities in my region. First, they answered that my mother was third in line to receive a car. Then I got a letter saying she wasn't in line anymore. It said, 'If you want to be in line, you must send us your documents.' But the local party committee had kept them, so now my mother isn't even in line anymore.

"I have two children. My son is an excellent student and doesn't drink or smoke. He entered an Institute to learn radio technology but left after three and a half years, as did many of his friends. He made no explanation as to why he left, only that he thinks the Soviet Union doesn't need engineers. My wife became very upset when he said he didn't need a diploma or a trade. He's working now as a construction worker. He's not depressed. He has good friends, and he reads and listens to music. Maybe it's this: if you want to have a higher salary, you have to beg, be friendly, and play up to people. Maybe that's not his nature.

"My daughter is a tenth-grade student, and my wife is a nurse."

"How much training did your wife have?" I asked.

"She had just one year of study after high school, but now nurses must have three years of training. Nurses take regular improvement courses, too." he responded.

"About six years ago," said Ivan, "society began to get extremely dishonest. [That must have been after Andropov died.] Cheaters have no fear now. My brother, a police captain from Siberia, went to Yalta on a vacation and was given a room with three other men on the sunny side of the building. When he complained, he was advised to prepare a package with 25 rubles, cognac, and some other things, and give it to the proprietor. They didn't fear even a police captain!"

Toli said, "The real problem is moral *values* have changed. Bad values are now a way of life, and people who can get away with dishonesty are admired. 'They really know how to live!' is sometimes said of them."

August 17: Ivan stayed all night, but he said he didn't sleep because so much was racing through his head. I really enjoyed talking with him. And I think I understood everything he said because he spoke slowly and used simple words.

Before Ivan left, I handed him some small gifts for himself and his family. As we all embraced good-bye at the bus stop, he burst out, "My brother-in-law said, 'Those Americans won't give you the time of day!'"

August 19: There's a beautiful Russian Orthodox holiday—day of forgiveness—when people say to each other, "God forgives all." Then they forgive each other. Today, however, was a holiday for blessing fruit.

Though we could only guess at the significance (harvest thanks), we planned to go to the church for the ceremony.

Instead, Viktor Lesik, 25, a reporter from the Dunaevtsi District newspaper, came to interview us. He brought good holiday muffins his mother had baked. Viktor collects stamps from all over the world.

He began his interview. "I think it's important to know what's going on in people's heads, not just in the fields," he said. "Don't you think you're too isolated to write a book?"

"A person could come here for a month and talk to people and not get the picture," answered Ralph, "but we're here for *six* months, and we're looking at everything and talking to people on all levels."

"But you have to drink to find out what people really think," opined Viktor. "Ukrainians need to get drunk and angry to say what they think. They're not so open as Russians."

"We don't believe you have to get drunk to truly communicate," answered Ralph.

"Creating initiatives for people to change the economic system is the only answer," put in Toli. "Not all this psychological stuff."

Viktor continued, "Please give your impressions of the USSR."

"Democratization and glasnost are working quite well," said Ralph, "but the shadow economy is tragic."

"The people are taking more initiative now," I added.

"What do you think of our ideology?" he asked.

"I'm sick of ideologies!" I said, surprising him.

"Why?" he asked.

"I think they've caused more problems than they've solved. In both our countries, many things aren't done if they don't fit the prevailing ideology. I think countries should be pragmatic and do what works, as long as it harms no one," I answered.

"In Dunavetsi, they were frightened about your visit to the poor farm," said Viktor. "They thought you might publish pictures with a note at the bottom identifying it, and then our District and that collective farm may be punished."

I thought to myself, "Maybe I misjudged Valarovsky. He's probably motivated by fear."

"It used to be people who were out of favor with the apparatus were called, 'enemies of the people.' Now they're called 'extremists,'" Viktor continued.

Together, we explored the word "liberal" and discovered it has a bad connotation in both countries. In the USSR, it means "soft and indecisive," as opposed to the "strong Communist spirit." In the US, Ralph and I prefer the word "progressive." Actually, we prefer no categories, for everyone is different and has mixed opinions. Pigeon-holing people dehumanizes them.

Viktor's a member of the party, but his girlfriend is a Baptist. "She got divorced," he said, "and the Baptist Church expelled her for it. But she still believes."

"Why'd you join the party?" I asked.

"I was 20 and in the army. That's the way boys usually join the party," he said. "But in these last five years, ideas have changed greatly. I published an article about a communist turning in his card, and the officials say the man did it because he had no laundry powder and no one listened to him. But now, the atmosphere is tense at one factory in Dunaevtsi. Six people have refused the party—three turned in their cards, and three refused to join. The authorities think maybe my article helped that happen, and they were angry at me. Even though I'm a party member, I can be fired."

"What are the duties of a party member?" I asked.

"To follow the rules and all demands," said Viktor.

Then Toli spoke. "Once at a so-called meeting of People's Deputies at the District party committee, a man insulted the young People's Deputy for whom I campaigned. Viktor here wrote about it, and the insulter took him to court. But Viktor had great support from the people. He won the case. He's quite brave."

"I speak out because I believe in truth and I support Gorbachev's reforms," said Viktor. "I also enjoy risk, although I wake up every morning wondering if I'll have problems that day. The Regional newspaper is very controlled. It's easier to write risky things for our District newspaper in Dunaevtsi, so I'm glad to be working for it. Our editor is a woman, the only woman editor in the Region. It's difficult for her."

Viktor kept trying to stir up controversy and incite Ralph to say bad things about the authorities. Ralph was too wise to do so.

Before Viktor left, we made arrangements to take him and his girlfriend to Kamenets-Podolski to a Baptist choir concert tomorrow night. He'll buy the tickets. Dunaevtsi authorities had prohibited its performance there.

Tonight Roza, Viktor (the school director), and their young son came from Kamenets to have dinner with us. We talked a little about school systems.

"Do you like being a school director?" I asked Viktor.

"Does a person like to have a toothache?" he answered. He didn't want to talk much about what his position requires him to do.

But Toli said to us, "Viktor gives his teachers as much freedom as he can. He's able to be democratic, and he speaks up for the best ones to receive awards in the Region. I'd like to work for him, but my salary would be much less."

August 20: This evening, we picked up Viktor Lesik and his girlfriend, as scheduled. He'd kept it a secret we were going to the concert together, so she was astonished to see us. I, too, was astonished. She's the pretty young woman I talked to at the Dunaevtsi veterinary clinic.

The Baptist choral concert in Kamenets-Podolski was superb. In addition to music, dramatic readings were interspersed throughout. The head of the church from Khmelnitski prayed and spoke, telling about his recent visit to their church's congress in Czechoslovakia. Ralph could hardly believe he was hearing prayer in a Soviet public auditorium. Another man on stage talked about the "new" practice of charity in the Soviet Union, exemplified in the world by Mother Teresa. He said the proceeds from the tickets would go to the Red Cross. Most of the 800+ people attending were nonbelievers. I could tell because only a few women wore the filmy headscarves of Baptist women. Towards the end, the main speaker said, "Everyone who's willing to try to live every day and moment in the spirit of charity, please stand for one minute." Everyone stood. I recorded the concert and gave the cassette to Viktor's girlfriend.

Leaving the concert reminded me of another of the illogical inconveniences of Soviet life. Namely, when there's a pair of doors, only one is open. This makes it difficult for people, with their inevitable bags of food, to squeeze past each other. But tonight, as we were leaving the concert, we saw *both* exit doors open! Strangely, however, the crowd was still moving slowly, with that steady pressure of body against body. Finally, we discovered why: the *outside* exit door had only one side open, as usual!

After stopping at a cafe for ice cream, we headed back to Dunaevtsi. On the way, Ralph stopped to help a man whose car had broken down. He turned out to be a veterinarian who worked with Viktor's girlfriend. Ralph hooked up the car and towed it 20 miles to Dunaevtsi. Once we got there, the veterinarian invited us to have supper with his jovial family.

August 21: This morning, we witnessed a strange occurrence. We dropped Toli off at a potato field for one of his teaching duties. All the rest of the teachers were already there, picking up dug potatoes for their school food supply. American teachers would strike, I think, although such duties may have been expected of our teachers decades ago. Many aspects of life here are like American life was over 50 years ago or like some of our Appalachian and rural, deep-South areas are now.

We've made arrangements to go to Volgograd for a few days to visit a state farm. We'll stop in Kiev on the way to see an American friend who is on a Dnieper River Peace Cruise. Our friend doesn't know we're coming. We haven't been able to make connections with her since she arrived in the USSR. Her daughter, Torie Scott, is now in the middle of an amazing bicycle trip across Siberia from Vladivostok to Leningrad. There are seven cyclists, Soviets and Americans, participating. They'll live off the land and the kindness of people while a movie is being made of them.

We still have the signed and sealed six-month invitation to the Volgograd state farm we received the day before coming here in April. We can use it to visit because it says we're invited "anytime." Consequently, this time it was easy to get permission to travel. All we had to do was make one round-trip to Khmelnitski to get our visas stamped for Volgograd.

Sasha Professor drove us and Toli in our car to the train in Kamenets. To top it off, Oleg had him give a bouquet of roses to the train attendant so she would treat us especially kindly. So it's good-bye to Makov for ten days!

August 22: We've traveled probably 10,000 miles on Soviet trains and enjoyed them (except for the dirty toilets). But this one had wooden beds with thin pads over them, and we slept little. Toli didn't sleep much because he read late into the night, as usual. Soviet people and commerce depend much more on rail systems than do Americans. A unique condition is the different gauge of rail between the USSR and Poland. For instance, on a 1983 Sunday journey to Warsaw, our train stopped at the border for two hours while hydraulic jacks raised the entire train three feet into the air. All of the undercarriage was rolled away and replaced with a different width. This condition also slowed down the invasions from the west.

We got into Kiev at 5 A.M., and Toli took us to Lusa's apartment where we napped and ate before meeting the ship. Our friend was happily surprised to see us, and the cruise directors arranged for us to have a room and meals, as their "honored guests." Quite a different reception from the one in Minsk! Many people were eager to talk with us about our experiences.

Toli was doing errands and arrived later. And what a surprise he brought! Today's *Izvestia* contained a long letter from Palamarchouk, sent from Ohio, all about Ralph's farm. Ralph was thrilled! He said, "That's the best thing for agricultural reform that's happened in this whole exchange!" *Izvestia* has a circulation of 10 million, and the story mentioned dozens of aspects of US agriculture that are good for Soviets to read about.

Toli spent two hours translating the article to me while I wrote as fast as I could. Then we put the newspaper and the translation into the package of Soviet newspapers Valentina had sent for our friend to mail to Viktor when she gets to the States. Viktor's always eager to get in-depth news about his homeland.

Earlier today, we visited a new village for Chernobyl victims not far from Kiev. There, a man told us he'd been liberated by the Americans from the German concentration camp he was in. He and his comrades had knelt down and kissed the American tanks. I felt his joy as he spoke; it had been one of the most important events of his life. I can hardly imagine the confusion and sorrow he must have felt when not long afterwards he was told his American friends were now his enemies.

On the other side, in the US, we once heard an American veteran of WWII say the army manuals did a complete about-face immediately after the war. In it servicemen were instructed to consider the USSR their enemy. Such are the wounds of cold war.

World War II memorial, Mother Russia (200 feet tall) calling
her people to defend their motherland. Volgograd (formerly
Stalingrad).

August 24: After breakfast, Ralph and I said good-bye to the cruise people and to Toli (who went back to Makov) and got on the train to Volgograd. We have fond memories of that city from our visit there in 1985. Of all the war memorials we've seen, the one at Volgograd is my favorite. In addition to the sheer enormity of the statue of Mother Russia and the beauty of the surrounding statues—created by the sculptor who made the famous *Swords Into Plowshares* sculpture at the U.N.—German music (Schumann's "Traumerai") is included as part of the memorial. The music moved me deeply; I interpreted it as a symbol of forgiveness. One of the statues is in the form of Michelangelo's *Pieta*—a mother holding her dead son across her lap. What is different is this son has a cloth over his face: he could be a man of any race, religion, or nationality.

Our Volgograd guide in 1985 had been helpful and open. From her we got a taste of the fear of Germans many Soviets feel. She said when she was leading a group of Germans, sometimes a feeling of horror would come over her. She imagined the people behind her were German soldiers. The woman had nearly starved to death during the horrible siege of Stalingrad, now renamed Volgograd.

She was proud of her country and its progress. "My grandparents had only a few years of education. My parents got through high school. I had five years at the language institute. Now my daughter is studying to be an interior decorator," she said. When one of our group brought up Afghanistan, she had simply told us, "You know very well that if we're not in a certain part of the world, you are, and vice versa."

This guide had taken us for good visits to our first day care center, school, Pioneer Palace, and dental clinic. Again I'd been moved when the head of the dental clinic smiled and said, "Please take the love of the Soviet people to the American people!" Ralph and I have often felt the love of Soviets for Americans. And now, since Gorbachev has reduced Americans' fear, Americans tell us to take their love to the Soviets, too. I think most people are relieved to see the end of the cold war. It takes energy to hate.

On the train today, our first roommates were a couple from the Ukrainian city of Kharkov, sister city of Cincinnati. The young woman and I enjoyed talking, and she was characteristically generous, giving us a big box of candy and a bag with Russian and English peace words on it. She wrote in the front of my dictionary, "A mother loves her baby, with all its vices and shortcomings. We love our native land, as you do yours, with all its goods and bads, and always we hope for it to be better. If all Americans are as friendly and nice as you, we can feel secure for the future, that our children will live in peace."

She was worried because three years after Chernobyl, their food is still contaminated by the soil. Several inches should be taken off the top of millions of acres of soil, and that's impossible. Most people here are quite concerned about the radiation. Someone told us Kiev higher-ups get their food from Ukraina farm, which is considered clean.

Toli's sister and family live in Kiev. Her little daughter's immune system has been damaged, as have all children's there. It takes a good month for a child to get over a simple cold. Luckily, vitamins are available, but that's all the help they have.

Our next roommate was a handsome young man who used to play rugby for Kharkov and had played against the Boston Bruins. We'll send our roommates photos of themselves.

August 25: Luckily—because this train has no dining car—I brought some food. I'm learning the ways of my Soviet sisters. But we would have been all right anyway. At each tiny train stop, people sell their ripe melons, apples, cherries, apricots, and tomatoes.

Today, our roommates on the train were a young couple who don't live together half of the year because their living quarters are so bad. The man, Vladimir, graduated from a five-year institute, but he makes only 160 rubles a month. He has only one room—in a prison for criminals who work in the city during the day and come back at night. He, however, is not a criminal but works in a tractor factory. His wife and baby daughter live in that room with him part of the year and with her mother in a village the rest of the time. The couple was lovingly spending the weekend together, while Babushka watched the baby.

What shocked me most is discovering they must share a kitchen and toilet with *40* other people! Naturally, both these facilities, not belonging to anyone in particular, are in a deplorable condition. We've noticed that, almost without exception, people take immaculate care of what they actually own. Incentive! I asked the couple if we could visit them while we were in Volgograd. She agreed, but he was too ashamed to allow it.

Then came another shock. As Vladimir gently played with a young child in the next compartment, he told us, "I'm a Stalinist." Then he added, " We need a good, strong dictator to straighten everything out."

"Do you mean it's okay with you that Stalin killed millions of people?"

"Yes," he said. "I don't like Gorbachev because he doesn't act."

"Whom do you like?" I asked.

"Yeltsin," he replied, "but he can't do anything. I liked Andropov, too. He acted."

"Who in history has been a good dictator?" I asked.

"Peter the Great," he responded. I remembered Peter had his own son killed.

"Well, what should the Soviet Union do while they wait for such a man?" I asked him.

"Nothing," he replied.

"You realize you're utopian in your thinking and all countries have problems, don't you?" I said.

"But we have worse problems," he answered.

Personally, I'd prefer the Soviet Union to such places as Ethiopia, El Salvador, or India. In 1986 in the Philippines, we saw thousands of people living on a garbage dump. "You know, in a democracy," I remarked, "it takes longer to get things done because all opinions must be considered." At my words, the young couple hung their heads; they didn't want to hear that. Our hearts went out to rail-thin, young Vladimir when he tearfully said, "Life is very, very hard. There's no meat in Volgograd. I work so very hard, and I have nothing to show for it while others, who do little, have much."

We enjoyed the young couple, sharing food and talking about many subjects. They are good people but feel helpless. Naturally, they yearn for someone who can change things for them.

Our friend Volodya Chernov, consultant to the Volgograd Journalists' Union, and another man who was party secretary of the state farm, met us at the railroad station. We were covered with sweat and grime after two days on the train, so we were delighted when they took us to a hotel for a bath, rest, and dinner. I grieved as I thought of the couple on the train, just as grimy as we were, who must go to one room and a filthy toilet and kitchen.

August 26: After breakfast at the hotel, Volodya took us through the city market. The fruits and vegetables looked great, but I didn't see any meat. He told us people prefer to buy from those who have private plots, so their food won't be treated with so many chemicals. (We hear that everywhere.)

After that, we went with him and the state farm party secretary to the town of Gorodishi. There a monthly festival was being held at the market-place. Also with us was the head of onion production on the farm. At the market we met the leader of the town soviet and had a good talk. In order to increase democracy and get people's input, the local soviet has a representative from each of the 96 streets in town. These 96 people have street meetings to get other street dwellers' opinions. These they bring to the soviet meeting, held once every two months. The soviet often gathers between regularly scheduled meetings, too. I asked if, ultimately, the party or the soviets would have more power. He said the soviets hope to gain power as they get more support from the people. Ralph talked about Soviet agriculture, saying he thinks it has great potential and could export in the future.

The two state farm men are interested in more grain storage and drying facilities. They say they don't have enough trucks to transport all their crops, so much sits outside and molds.

The onion man also talked about the onion harvest. He said there are 600 workers on the farm, and when the 100 who are responsible for the onions have too much work to do, the rest don't pitch in and help. Every worker on a Soviet farm is a specialist; he has one job to do. So if you're a truck driver, and there's one short haul that day, that's all you do. The rest of the day you might sit around chatting and drinking with other idled workers.

Ralph advised, "It works best if persons do a variety of jobs."

"I'd like to do the whole onion process from beginning to end, including the selling," the onion man replied.

The three accompanied us to the hotel for dinner. We talked at length and showed them our photos, which interested them immensely.

Later, six people arrived from the English club. Some we had met on other trips to Volgograd. They've formed a Citizen Diplomat Club. They hope to have unofficial exchanges with people from English-speaking countries, housing them in homes rather than hotels. They plan for visitors from each side to pay their own way across the ocean. Then the hosts will take care of expenses in their home country. Together, we walked along the Volga riverfront and talked, changing partners from time to time. We ended our evening together with ice cream.

August 27: Today was lovely. We spent it picnicking, swimming, and talking with our friends on Mother Volga's sandy shore. Every now and then, when Ralph talked farming, Volodya would whip out his little tape recorder as he had done during each meal at the hotel.

Volodya mentioned people are dropping out of the party. He thinks this might be good because those who are left may be more effective. "People join the party for a variety of reasons," he stated. "Some are ambitious, some want to live better, some are true believers, and some are persons of service. Communists are supposed to do more work but get no extra pay in their work to improve society. That's what I try to do," he said.

He also said, "The bureaucrats may be causing the deficits, to erode people's support of Gorbachev [which we have heard from many people], though a few of the bureaucrats are truly trying to support perestroika.

"Stalinists who want a strong hand haven't grown to know that people must take responsibility," he added. "They're waiting for a savior." He mentioned many good changes: Bibles being printed for everyone, more journalists in the Congress, and the election of new blood. "We'll see what happens in the local elections next March," he mused.

"Gorbachev doesn't want to get rid of Ligachev," Volodya speculated, "because the conservatives must be dealt with. I think Gorbachev consciously invites criticism to make people active. When people accuse him of being too soft, he says he doesn't want to employ methods used and abused in the past and which are now repudiated. Method and outcome are related."

That's what Mahatma Gandhi always said: one should not fight violently for a non-violent outcome. Ends do not justify means. To my mind, this has been one of the biggest problems with communism. Bad means (force and terror) have been used for good ends (the well-being of people).

Volodya witnessed the destruction of the INF Treaty missiles. He saw Americans there also, but the press was kept at arm's length. He related how at 15, he'd voted for changing the name of Stalingrad to Volgograd, even though he didn't know the extent of Stalin's evil. It was only recently that Khrushchev's famous speech exposing Stalin's heinous acts was printed in its entirely. In aspects of wrongdoing over the years, Americans have known more about the USSR than Soviets have known.

About his own living conditions, Volodya said he lives well but is frustrated he can't get a telephone—a real handicap for a journalist. When I brought up the horrible living conditions of the young couple on the train, he said, "Millions of Soviets live in barracks or hostels like that."

Just before we arrived in Volgograd, there was a conference of American and Soviet ecologists held here. Volodya attended. The Volga Region is one of the most polluted areas in the world. The Americans were shocked at the extent of it. "The USSR has environmental laws on the books," Volodya said, "but they're not enforced." This is certainly true. Yesterday we noticed smokestacks across the river pouring out pollution, adding to the pervading layer of haze. This country has gotten by with its bad ecological habits because of its large land mass. But now its practices are catching up with it.

August 28: This morning, Sergei took us from our hotel to the small guest lodge belonging to the Volgograd Agricultural Institute. There we settled in for three days. At 2 o'clock, we met with the director of the Institute and a dozen experts for discussion. Next we were given a tour of the Institute's programs. Their test plantings, machinery, and science museum were all impressive. In one of their research buildings, we saw a sleek ice cream maker. We thought of buying it for Makov. Also, we sampled good-tasting noot, a cross between peas and soy beans. Noot is our guide's pet project.

While talking with our guide, we mentioned that many Soviets have asked us about non-chemical remedies for the Colorado potato bug. (Ralph responds to the question with, "What should we do about the Russian thistles?")

"I know of one," our guide offered, "which our Institute developed and which I've tried for three years on my own garden. At first my neighbors thought I was crazy. When the potato plants have three or four leaves on them, I burn them to the ground with a welder's torch. They grow back again, and there'll be no potato bugs. It probably kills the eggs. They recommend doing this every two or three years. Now my neighbors are also trying it."

August 29: We spent the day at the state farm, meeting the brigadiers and touring the farm. Each field held a surprise. In the wheat field, Ralph liked the brigadier so much that as we left, he gave him a big hug. In the onion field, we kicked up several metal remnants from WWII. We took some to show Americans. Sadly, every year a child or two is killed on finding live ammunition in remote places from 47 years ago. In another onion field, we were amused to see a man chopping holes in the bottoms of shiny new buckets to be used for collecting onions. This was, of course, so people wouldn't take them home to carry water.

Lunch had been prepared for us at the village home of a local driver, his wife and three children. They were obviously a model family because we also visited their home in September, 1988, when our Crosscurrents Cruise docked at Volgograd. The father really pushed Ralph to drink, saying, "We can't be friends unless you drink." It did him no good to push Ralph, but we were friends anyway. The alcohol flowed freely—so much so our young translator, Boris, was admittedly drunk all afternoon.

He managed to translate, however, after lunch at a day care center. I really liked Irma, the director. She and I had a long discussion about how to deal with children. She explained she and other teachers need to change their ways. But it's difficult because they're still tied to the book that tells them what to do and what children are supposed to be like. She said a psychologist had come and said children need to learn through play and moral lessons. Then she wondered out loud, "Why is it, when I try to teach children to be kind, they are not kind?"

"They're too young," I said. "Learning true kindness can be a lifelong process."

The facilities in Soviet day care centers are impressive, but the regimentation of the children is excessive.

Afterwards, we ate with the 6'5" director of the state farm and two other men. They asked Ralph about seed corn and grain drying, being very attentive to what he said. Ralph promised to draw plans for a seed corn processing facility, which he'll send from Makov. When Ralph invited the director to send someone to his Ohio farm for three months to learn the seed corn business first-hand, he immediately chose, coincidentally, the brigadier Ralph had hugged in the field.

August 31: Last night our Volgograd friends saw us off at the train. One of them, who speaks flawless English and is a correspondent for Moscow Radio, interviewed Ralph until two minutes before the train pulled out. We sprinted to make it.

There were no roommates, so we went to bed immediately. We had trouble sleeping though because the bad-tempered female train attendant scolded people at the top of her lungs. We've tried to find out why Soviets are usually ultra-kind in their personal lives but are often brusque and imperious on the job. One explanation we got was this: Since they have to follow and pass on stupid regulations to subordinates, they intimidate their underlings so there will be no questions. Also, I think it could be a way of spewing out their anger at the meanness of their lives in ways that wouldn't affect their personal relationships. Friendships and loyalties run deep here. We know of an American woman who lives in Moscow by choice for this very reason. She once told us, "Life here is physically hard, but I cannot get in the US the rich friendships I have here."

The windows on our train car wouldn't open, so we sweltered all day. The Russian Republic's continental climate serves up very hot summers in addition to very cold winters.

We talked at length with a gentle, kindly English teacher who lives 90 miles from Kiev. He sympathized with Gorbachev, saying, "He has a very hard job." When we showed him our pictures, he got excited about the one of Pozner and me, calling him "a clever man." And he liked the photo of my kitchen, saying, "It's my dream to have a kitchen like that! Five years ago, one could find everything in the shops. That's still possible in Kiev but not in Volgograd." I also spoke to two beautiful, oriental-looking Kalmic girls on the train. They are from an autonomous region near Volgograd and were vacationing with two young Russian men. They gave me a large fish. I wondered about it's not being refrigerated, but our teacher friend said, "It has been preserved with oil and salt, is very hard to get, and is absolutely prime. It's delicious sliced very thin and eaten on bread, with beer." The girls asked me to send them a picture of me as a souvenir. This I'll happily do.

CHAPTER 8

Christine's Journal Excerpts

OUR LAST MONTH IN THE USSR

September 1: Our new friend the English teacher had planned to visit his sister in Kiev this morning and then travel to his village where he would begin teaching tomorrow. Instead, he insisted on standing for hours in the mob at the Intourist office, waiting to get us tickets to Kamenets-Podolski. His is just another example of the Soviet generosity of spirit.

Our companions in the waiting room were a blond, young couple who'd come from East Germany to study philosophy. In addition, we had good conversations with dark young men from Tunisia, Sri Lanka, and Nigeria, who'd come to study engineering for six years at a Kiev Institute. One had been accepted at an American university but couldn't afford the $10,000 tuition. Now he's here in Kiev where he'll get free schooling. When I spouted off that ideologies were unimportant and we think what we do because of where we're born, the young men agreed. But the East German couple turned up their noses and wouldn't talk anymore.

There were gypsies hanging around the railroad station, begging and holding strangely quiet babies and little children—I wondered if they'd been drugged. I hadn't seen gypsies dressed like that since I was a child. The bangles and full, colorful skirts the females of all ages were wearing fascinated me. At one point, I heard a ruckus outside. I joined a crowd gawking at two gypsy women who were yelling and waving their arms at each other, surrounded by other gypsies who had taken sides. A policeman soon broke it up.

At 3 P.M., I tried to call Toli to tell him we were on our way home, but the woman in charge said there would not be an open line to Khmelnitski Region until 6 P.M. Our train was to leave at 5:20. Then, when I tried to send a telegram, she said it couldn't be done before tomorrow. It wasn't crucial, though, because I'd called Oleg a couple of days ago, giving him the approximate date of our return.

Again, Ralph and I were lucky; we got the last spots in our train car. All evening we shared food and conversation with a seamstress and two young men who repair refrigerators. During our conversation, a man sat outside our open door, listening intently. I'm convinced he was not KGB but only curious.

A special treat during Soviet train travel is the mugs of hot tea (actually clear glass tumblers in silver filigree holders). The train attendants also serve packages of cookies mornings and evenings. When I went to the end of the train car to get more tea, I stopped to talk with the young train attendant, his girl friend, and another friend. They became overly friendly, speaking suggestively and putting their hands on me, so I left. I've had only one other Soviet man talk lewdly to me. That was a few days ago in Volgograd. I ignored his comment, ending his fun. (The southern republics are known for their aggressive men.)

September 2: This morning we disembarked at Kamenets-Podolski at 3:40 A.M. It was raining, but a friendly private cab driver said he'd take us to Makov for 10 rubles. We were delighted and gave him 15 when we arrived at Toli's. The cabbie had graduated from a Lvov institute and now works at an institute in Kamenets. But since the advent of perestroika, he has been able to be a cab driver to make more money, and he's grateful.

Toli had our car, the key to our house, a large bouquet of roses for us from Oleg, about twenty letters from the US, and three from the USSR. When we got to Stupentsi, there were some withered carnations at our door. Who had brought them? We stayed up the rest of the night reading our mail and then went to bed. Altogether we've received over 100 letters from American friends and 55 from Soviets.

Toli came at 4 P.M., wanting to know everything about our trip. He said he hadn't told us there was a nasty word used at the end of Viktor's letter in *Izvestia*. This word gave the impression Ralph and his family look down on Soviets and are paternalistic, which is absolutely not true. He wrote to Viktor asking about it.

There was a small change in Makov while we were gone—only the children of the collective farm workers are now allowed to go to the day care center. Previously, all children could attend, but the collective farm was the sole support. In this way, the Chairman is coercing financial help from the sugar factory, the sanatorium, and the Kamenets factories. All employ Makov residents. Yura is home 24 hours a day. We'll see whether he becomes more or less of a terrorist.

While we were at Toli's apartment this evening enjoying Tanya's *blini* (thin, rolled Russian pancakes, usually filled with soft cheese), Anna described how glad she was to see me: "like the sun suddenly coming out after a rainy day." Dear, sweet Anna! She told me, her eyes full of tears, that she'll miss us very much when we go home. Tanya concurred. They and Toli are truly like family now.

September 4: Though we can get free gasoline at Ukraina's truck yard, we've bought about half our gas from filling stations. But now that it's harvest season, fuel is scarce everywhere. People carry around gas cans and fill them at any opportunity. While waiting in line, the car's engine is turned off. The driver pushes the car forward to save gas.

The Soviet Union is the world's largest producer of petroleum. Still, there's a shortage of gasoline. The same with paper in this heavily forested country. Also, though there are millions of cows here, one can hardly buy a leather jacket. We've heard an anecdote about this:

Q. What happens if the bolsheviks take over the Sahara Dessert?
A. For 70 years, nothing happens, and then there's a shortage of sand.

Toli, Ralph, and I have all managed to get fuel at different times, but the way Tanya did it was the most amusing. On our way to Kamenets today, she and I picked up a couple of hitchhikers and pulled into the only gas station in a 40-mile stretch. The sign said, "Benzine nyet" (no gas), but we noticed a man there. So Tanya got out of the car and spoke to the man. When she came back, I asked her what we should do. She just said, "Shas" (wait). So we sat there quietly. After a while, I asked her again. Same answer. A few more minutes passed. Then the man approached our car, told her to get some gas, and said to hurry up and leave. Later, when I asked her what she'd said, she replied, "I told him an American was driving, and I couldn't communicate with her. She didn't have enough gas to get anywhere, so she was just going to sit there!"

Later, she and I walked arm in arm through the market, feeling very close.

Tanya resents cooperatives. Since some charge exorbitant prices, all cooperatives are suspect in the minds of many. Whenever we're browsing and she sees a stall—selling clothes, for instance—that belongs to a co-op, she quickens her pace. She says she doesn't like their wares.

Palamarchouk called from Ohio and said we have tickets to return to the States on October 2. Also, he told Toli he didn't use that nasty word. *Izvestia* must have added it. It didn't seem to be Viktor's doing because the whole tone of his letter had been friendly before that word appeared.

About 5:30 P.M., Toli arrived at Stupentsi accompanied by a huge, pleasant man, no taller than Ralph (5'9") and not fat, just enormously square, with large bones and a great, deep voice. He was Philip from Kamenets, and I think he just wanted to meet the American farmer before we left. His plans are to return to his home near Odessa and farm with his two cousins. He hopes the second Congress of People's Deputies in the fall will make a law that land can be given to the people. When Philip asked Ralph if there was any difference between peasants in the US and USSR, Ralph remarked, "They're bigger here!"

Philip asked how Ralph could manage to have his tractor still working after 37 years. Ralph said it did 15 years of very hard work, but since then it's only used around the buildings.

"Still, it works." Philip said, "That's the thing!"

He told us some of his background. "I grew up in agriculture, graduated from mechanics school, then did my obligatory two years with the army. Finally, I became a miner. Now I'm retired and single. But I'm only 50, and I'm strong and healthy and I want to be engaged in agriculture. The chairman of the Odessa farm was a classmate of mine. He invited me to come there to farm, saying he'd help me get my own farm of 500 acres. My mother died, leaving the house where I was born, so I'll live there. One of my cousins is a teacher in Moldavia. But now that they're shifting from Russian back to the Latin alphabet [Romanian language], he'd have to learn everything over again. So he wants to return to Odessa and farm with me. We're a strong family. My grandmother lived to be 115 years old, and my grandfather died at 105." Then he added, "I'd like to have 10 kg [22 lbs.] of soybean seed to start up with."

"I'll send you some," said Ralph.

"The land is hilly—good for grazing—and I'd also like to have pigs," continued Philip. "Where do you get your boars?"

"We get them from other farms, because if we use boars related to our females, we'll get freaks. Every two years, we get new boars for the young females we've raised."

This evening, Ralph and I took a long walk at sunset. The unbelievable beauty of the vast rolling landscape of forests and multi-colored fields struck us again in a way it doesn't when we're driving. We felt immersed in it all, as in a Chinese landscape painting where humankind is just a small part of creation, not the dominant figure.

September 7: We met with the specialists at another Ukraina collective farm, an hour or so away. In the audience was Anton, the farm's distinguished-looking economist, who spoke some English and asked excellent questions. One of them was, "Do you go to church because you really believe in God or because it's the custom?"

Ralph believes in simplicity. He answered, "We're believers."

Typically, too, my response was, "To us, God is a great, loving mystery within us but much more than that. If we try to define It or put Her in a box, we may be only partly right. We believe we cannot explain Him with our minds but only know Him with our hearts."

Several of the men responded, "We think the same."

"Our church is called the Church of the Brethren," I continued. "It encourages its members to serve others with their time, energy, hearts, and money. It's also an historic peace church, which means that officially it takes a pacifist stance. We believe one should never kill another human being. Ralph was born into the Church of the Brethren, and I chose it halfway through my life. In our particular church congregation, half of us are black, and half are white."

"Do you sit separately?" someone asked.

"No," I answered. "We're good friends. Also, I'm in a women's vocal quartet—three black women and myself. We love each other. But we think nobody has a corner on truth," I continued. "Do you know the story of the blind men and the elephant? Each of the blind men touches a different part of the elephant—tail, legs, trunk, side, ears, tusks. 'Oh,' one says, 'he's like a rope.' 'No,' says another, 'he's like a wall.' 'No, No!' says a third, 'He's like a tree!' And so on. Each was *sure* he knew what that elephant was like! And each was right in a way, but they needed to listen and learn from each other to get the whole truth."

After the meeting, we had a long dinner with the farm's chairman, Buddha, Anton, and Ivan, the first party secretary of the district. Ivan didn't look like a party secretary; his face and bearing were more like a good-natured professor's. Also, he seemed modest and unobtrusive. He kept things lively with his astute questions about the farm pictures, because he'd originally been an agronomist.

On the way to the collective farm, Toli had translated a letter he'd received from Palamarchouk, which was for us also. Viktor related that he'd met several of Ralph's and my friends and liked them very much, so he was sure he'd like us. He also liked the six newsletters to our friends and six newspaper articles we'd written, but he thought we had made them a bit too soft in comparison with the real situation in the USSR.

In addition, he wrote about Gorbachev and the fact people are turning against him. "Who said Gorbachev is ideal?" he asked Toli in the letter. "It will take more than our lifetime to straighten out our problems. But look at what he has begun and already done!" Perhaps Viktor's visit to the US has given him a broader comparative perspective on those problems than many of his countrymen have.

At the meeting, we talked about the *Izvestia* letter. The men said they could tell it was *Izvestia* and not Viktor who had said that unfriendly word. Others have told us the same thing. During the evening, we finally told Buddha our nickname for him, and he didn't seem to mind at all.

Anton was surprised there are no economists, as such, on American farms. He said humbly, "Here in my country, I have a job. But in your country, I am no one!" He also said, "In the cold war, our differences are emphasized, but when we meet here, we are people—very much alike, wanting the same things."

Ivan added, "We need to do more of this! We can read about the other country, but when we actually meet each other, then we know. May there be many more of these meetings! We're building a foundation so our children can meet and not be afraid of each other. And it can happen in our lifetime! Maybe some of us believe in God. Maybe some of us don't. But we're all human beings."

"Under the same moon," added Ralph, as he noticed the full moon rising behind us.

"You know," continued this unusual party secretary, "we can change things quickly, but what really must change are the attitudes in the mind." He smiled. "We have no secrets from you," he said. "Anything you want to see, we'll show you. You know, they're now selling army tanks for use on farms. Yesterday I got a letter from my friend in Vladivostok, asking me to buy some tanks for use on the farm. I will, and when I come to Ohio someday, I hope I'll see a converted tank being used on *your* farm!" Swords into plowshares! Tanks into tractors! Tanks are probably too heavy for farm work, but at least they wouldn't be harming people.

Agriculturists speak a language of their own. Earlier, as Ivan guided us around the grain yard and seed corn fields, Toli didn't need to translate, because Ralph and Ivan knew just what each other meant—through gestures.

September 8: Today was the first of three lectures I'd been asked to give to about 100 English-speaking students at the Pedagogical Institute at Kamenets-Podolski. When Roza first asked me to "lecture," the word intimidated me. But as long as I think of them as talks, it seems okay. This first day, I spoke for the entire hour and a half on the American educational system. I think it went all right. Still, I know the students didn't understand everything I said, though maybe the teachers did. Afterwards, one of the teachers asked me to send her American history and geography books, which I promised to do. The comparison of American and Soviet history books should be fascinating. Sometimes the descriptions of WWII don't sound like the same war. In return, I requested she try to get me a book in English on the ideology that's taught to the Pioneers and Komsomol.

Volodya, the student who had spoken to me about the possibility of emigrating sometime, talked with me about the Soviet army. He said older recruits are cruel to the younger ones until the latter step up to a higher rank. "Some young men commit suicide," he said, "and one killed eight of his torturers with an automatic weapon."

Ralph and I have heard that soldiers of the various republics are cruel to each other, too. Volodya is gentle, and I'm sure he dreads his required two years in the army. His words reminded me of the American movie about Vietnam, *Full Metal Jacket*. The superior officer was especially cruel to a new recruit, and it built up in the young man until he finally killed the sergeant and himself with his rifle.

On another note, the Chairman visited us today. He asked us to give $100 to one of his friends to buy a used car—an amount worth at least 1000 rubles on the black market. We refused. Toli later told us the man and his family already have three cars. And the villagers were angry because of it.

The Chairman also said, "I think perestroika will fail because of the bureaucrats. But we need capitalism in this country." He must be feeling guilty about not having a meeting for us on the farm, because he said, "I've asked Savkov to arrange a meeting for you. He refuses."

September 9: A disturbing letter came today from Ivan, who visited us from Yalta. He wrote:

I'm still thinking about our meeting. I'm glad you were born in a free country and can live and go as you like. You don't have the problems we have. We may only dream about such a life. When I visited you and we talked about corruption, I said it began six years ago. But it really began in 1917. In a recent issue of our magazine *Ogonyok*, it was well-described how the Romanovs, including five innocent children, were shot without a decision of the court. That was when the period of lawlessness began. The leaders were sure they wouldn't be punished. And today's communists are sure they won't be punished either. For 72 years of Soviet power, our government cheated us.

In 1939, we began a war with Japan. In 1989, we withdrew troops from Afghanistan. For 50 years, we participated in wars directly or indirectly. After Germany, it was China, Indonesia, Albania, and Vietnam. History will tell us what our expenses were in Vietnam, Egypt, Cambodia, Syria, Nicaragua, Cuba, Afghanistan, and Bangladesh. I think our interference didn't bring anything to people except suffering and grief, as in Afghanistan. Where did they get the money to interfere in those countries? I don't think it was from the dead Lenin. That money belonged to the people, and it was not used for the benefit of mankind.

Izvestia told about Gorbachev talking with workers in a Leningrad plant. He said, "We live the way we work." It would be better to say, "We live the way we are ruled." Those words are closer to reality.

Gorbachev's best merit is his fighting for disarmament and getting closer to other peoples of the world. I don't think the communists were compelled to do this through intelligence but because of misery.

Why am I so hostile to our leaders and to our system? It's because today is the first of September, and the children in holiday dresses, joyful and with flowers, went to school. But my daughter went to the hospital. It is not for the first time. The diagnosis is something with her blood vessels and nerves. She fell ill in 1984, and the disease is progressing. Her treatment is no good. In our country, good treatment can only be had in the Kremlin hospitals, but not everyone can get in.

I'm sure our country wants only healthy people. Mama worked until she was 82. She got bonuses and gratitude. But after she became an invalid, no one needed her. During the three years of her illness, no trade union or Komsomol member visited her. They didn't congratulate her on holidays. It was as if they said, "Take your 52 rubles of pension, and live as you like." It's the same with my sick daughter. "The best of everything for our children!" goes the slogan. For whose children?

So, dear Ralph and Chris, I'm sorry I'm so sharp about my country's leaders, but I can't help this because since my mother became an invalid, I've asked many times for them to help her, and no help came. I have the feeling they didn't even read my appeals. When you speak out your grief, you feel better.

Thank you for the presents for my wife and daughter. We were so looking forward to hosting you, but impossible means impossible. Dear friends, goodbye. Best regards from us to your children. Let God give you health and a happy return home. Say hello to Toli. Come to see us sometime.

He had enclosed two small newspaper articles. One told about an incident in 1920: "At the end of the revolution, many thousands of officers in the Crimea who had fought against the bolsheviks thought they must flee the country. But they didn't want to leave their native land, so they appealed to Red Army Commander Frunze. Frunze guaranteed life for those who stayed. Later, he nearly committed suicide when he learned all who stayed—tens of thousands—were killed a few days later. They were either shot with machine guns or thrown into the sea with stones tied to their feet. In good weather when the sea was down, rows of standing dead people could be seen through the water."

Today went from sadness (Ivan's letter) to celebration. This evening, we met our Pedagogical Institute student friend Sergei at the Old Town in Kamenets to enjoy a Ukrainian folklore concert. My anticipation was dulled when I realized that officials had planned the event. I'm sure it was a diversionary tactic because Rukh is holding a Congress to promote perestroika this weekend.

But the setting sun looked spectacular behind the old fortress where all the singing and dancing were to take place. We walked with a crowd of people, dressed in their finest clothes, across a decorated bridge spanning a deep gorge. Then we went up a hill for a good view of the stage. A Kiev TV van was there, too, to film the excellent entertainment. Fireworks at the end rivaled ours on the 4th of July. Then, the crowd made their way back across the bridge. Some danced along; others sang Ukrainian songs. All were happy.

We enjoyed being with Sergei. He likes English, "more than girls, more than cars," he said, and would like to visit our country. He said it's hard for young people to get good-looking clothes, although he had on a handsome denim outfit. He got it person-to-person on the black market. "More and more people are now speaking Ukrainian," he said. (He's obviously a city boy because in the villages, it's always been Ukrainian.) He also said, "I must go to the army as soon as I finish my degree. If I had tried for the Kiev Language Institute and failed, I would've had to go immediately."

During the concert, a pleasant man of about 40 told us he had read a book by an American nutritionist, Paul Bragg, who lived to be 92. Like Paul Bragg, this man eats mostly fruits and vegetables and runs six miles a day. He asked how we liked his town, and I answered, "It's very beautiful."

"That's only words," he responded.

Then I realized he wanted enthusiasm. So I said with passion and gestures, "I *love* it!" He smiled broadly.

He had read about us in the paper. He asked Ralph what Ralph had learned here to take home for abundant harvests in the States. We were amazed he didn't know the US has a surplus of food, and our government pays most farmers *not* to grow so much.

September 10: This morning Toli went with us to Dunaevtsi to attend a service at a small Baptist church packed with around 200 people. The atmosphere was reverently alive. The minister, talking about God's love and his gift of salvation, said we can't buy it or do enough good works to earn it—just as I learned in my Lutheran catechism. I think Toli was moved by the sermon. The service also included several vocal numbers, hymn-singing, and the reception of a new member. The latter was a woman who came to the front of the church, fell to her knees in tears, and asked forgiveness for her sins and for the opportunity to become a church member. She was embraced by a woman member who gave her flowers and a Bible.

After the service, I gave out some peace prayer cards. There was much embracing. A few men kissed Ralph full on the lips. He said later he could have done without those wet kisses! Many people spoke with radiant faces about their gratitude to Gorbachev for giving them religious freedom. One said, "People used to consider us illiterates, but now they respect us." Also, "Now we do not have to worry about being put into prison on some pretext." I asked them to tell me more about that, and one said, "We don't want to think about it because we're so happy now with our new freedom. That's all behind us! We can do anything we want to."

"Do you have Sunday school," I asked.

"No," they said, "we're waiting for the new article Gorbachev ordered on freedom of conscience now being readied for the Constitution."

Currently, the Soviet Constitution has this to say: "Citizens of the USSR are guaranteed freedom of conscience, that is, the right to profess or not to profess any religion, and to conduct religious worship or atheistic propaganda. Incitement of hostility or hatred on religious grounds is prohibited. In the USSR, the church is separated from the State, and the school from the church."

Worship has always been permitted; any *propagation* of the faith over the years has been forbidden and punished. But the clause about "incitement of hostility" has been flagrantly violated. Komsomol members are required to promote anti-religious propaganda as part of their duties. Val told us shamefacedly that when he was small, he once blurted out to his believing babushka, "There is no God!"

In our country, it's the first amendment to our Constitution which guarantees freedom of religion: "Congress shall make no law respecting an establishment of religion, or prohibiting the free exercise thereof."

"We have many more Bibles now," continued the young minister. "Our national headquarters in Moscow has ordered 8 million Bibles and 20,000 children's Bibles from Sweden. We've even heard there will be two lessons in the schools on the Bible as literature. Also, the local officials of Dunaevtsi gave permission for us to give our choral concert here. And now we'll give our concert for a third time—in Khmelnitski."

The Baptist Church is an umbrella name for several evangelical Protestant denominations and is the fastest-growing denomination in the USSR. Numbers are increasing at the Russian Orthodox Church, as well, at least for baptisms and weddings. The Dunaevtsi Baptists told us there are 20,000 Baptists in Ukraine and 50,000 in the USSR. Unlike the Russian Orthodox Church, which doesn't record membership but claims 50 million adherents, the Baptists apparently keep a membership list.

We had an unforgettable experience in the Moscow Baptist Church in 1983. Our group came in late, so the ushers emptied the first row of the balcony to seat us. After awhile, we were asked to sing. Our group sang "In Christ, There is No East or West." When we finished, the people below us, so crammed into the large sanctuary that they flowed out the doors, began to sing in Russian. They sang "When the Roll Is Called Up Yonder, I'll Be There." We joined them in English and our voices blended. Those dear souls turned their faces up to us, their eyes wet with bliss-tears, and threw us kisses. Soon we, too, were weeping. As we left, they grabbed us and kissed us mightily. That day we knew Soviets, Americans, and all of God's creation are one!

Seventh-Day Adventists have a goodly following in the Soviet Union and recently opened their first seminary here. Methodists are headquartered in Tallinn, Estonia.

I like to think of the last time Ralph and I met with Rev. Olav Parnamets, head of the Methodist Church, and his wife. After a good talk, I asked, "Can we do anything for you, Rev. Parnamets?"

"Oh," he said quietly, "My old car, which takes me to see parishioners and other congregations in my charge, needs a new tire. Would it be too much for you to get me one?"

"Of course not," we said. "Where can we get it?"

"In the *berioska*" (hard-currency store for foreigners), he replied.

So, after a good laugh, we took Rev. Parnamets to the Tallinn *berioska* where we found a tire. Ralph, the tourist, picked up the tire, paid $100 for it, and carried it out of the store. While we were there, we met another couple from our group. They had the Baptist minister in tow, buying something for him! Obviously, the powers-that-be encouraged this. Otherwise, why would there be tires in a store where only foreign tourists can buy? This is just one way the government gets badly needed hard currency.

But back to Ukraine . . . . We bade farewell to the Baptists and hurried to Makov for dinner at the home of Viktor Party Secretary and his teacher wife. They had invited a roomful of guests. There was lively conversation the whole time, and, of course, we showed our photos and magazines. One man, Nikolai, looked at the picture of Ralph's three sons and one son-in-law. "You can tell which one's the son-in-law," he remarked sourly. "He looks exploited!" We were amused because we know Jim enjoys wearing the oldest of clothes. But Toli told us Nikolai was rejecting *everything* we said about Ralph's farm. "A person would have to live there a year to know what it's like," the cynical fellow stated. Also, "You can't tell me those sons aren't overworked!"

Toli whispered, "I hate a know-it-all attitude!" (We, of course, have met Americans who've never visited the USSR but know everything about it. The subject is never open to real discussion.)

At one point, a woman teacher stood to make a passionate toast to the time when women wouldn't have to work anymore. At the other end of the table sat Tanya and another young mother who are bored staying home with their children. They wish they could be out working. As in America, the grass is greener . . . .

I asked a general question. "How do you envision the future of your country?"

"Within ten years there'll be a market economy," said one. At that, Ralph raised his teacup and toasted the party men at the dinner that they would help make it come true.

Many people can't understand why Ralph and I are here. "There must be some kind of profit in it for you," said Nikolai.

"No financial profit," I said. "We can't do much with rubles. But we get personal satisfaction because we're doing what we think needs to be done—learning to know, understand, and trust others in the world, especially those dubbed 'the enemy.' Besides, it's fascinating and enjoyable."

When the talk turned to the shadow economy, they assumed there are as many bribes and favors in America as there are in the USSR. Ralph said, "Bribes aren't a part of the everyday lives of most Americans, as they are here, but we do have some big-time cheating."

Nikolai spoke up again. "I know all about bribes on a governmental level in America." he said. (The FBI would like to talk with him!)

Toli told us later that Viktor Party Secretary wishes he could go back to teaching because he feels useless. He said to Toli, "I'm finding Christians are kind and forgiving when you do something wrong or make a mistake. But party people punish you if they don't like what you're doing."

This evening we had fun conversing with personable little farmer Dimitri, 49, who looked jaunty in his Swiss-style hat and backpack. He'd waited several hours for us to come home. Dimitri had written, asking to meet an American farmer, so we extended him an invitation. First, he looked at our photos. He could hardly believe Ralph's farm is the way it is. He was especially excited when he saw the picture of the 37-year-old tractor. He laughed and laughed, shaking his head in mock disbelief at everything. But most surprising to him was the fact that Ralph's four sons decide for themselves what to do. Dimitri thinks the market system and perestroika will never happen in the USSR because of the bureaucrats.

He asked about divorce. "Why do American marriages break up?" he asked. We've met several people here whose spouses were unfaithful. In their cases, this led automatically to divorce. Dimitri divorced his wife for that reason. However, I've also heard that women often put up with unfaithfulness because they have nowhere else to go.

Dimitri has married again and says he's happy. "I've always had enough to eat and a roof over my head. What else is there to want?" he asked. "I have two granddaughters, five and three years old."

"The very ages of my grandchildren," I remarked.

"My wife and I do odd jobs on our collective farm, the poorest one in our district," he continued. "I was born in the village in which I work, and I've known no other life."

He also said, "All my life I've doubted religion, but now I'm starting to believe." Ralph and I have heard this from several people. In fact, a recent *Moscow News* poll revealed half of all Soviets consider themselves believers.

September 12: I got up early today, nervous about my second lecture. However, it went fine. I listed topics on the blackboard, and the students asked questions about them. The hour and a half went fast.

Andrei regretted he had to be gone much of the time. As Komsomol leader, he was conferring with the principal. The principal wanted to expel a student for wearing the yellow and blue ribbons of the original Ukrainian flag at the folklore celebration last Saturday. Andrei said later he told the principal, "Don't punish him. Because we're free now, he did nothing wrong. Besides, the students might riot."

Andrei and I also talked a little about US politics. He was interested in how one joins a political party and if there are dues.

After the lecture, student Sergei took Ralph, Andrei, and me to have dinner with his family in their two-room flat. Considering that his father is one of a committee of men who give out flats in Kamenets, their apartment was quite modest. It did, however, have a prime location—a block from the market and stores. Both of his parents were home and also his cultured grandmother, who speaks some English.

I was rude to Sergei's pleasant father. But I was aware our time in the USSR is short and decided not to mince words. I asked bluntly, "Are you a party member?"

"Yes," he answered.

"Well, is it the party who's responsible for this mess the country's in?"

He didn't blink an eye as he answered, "The party made the right choices, but the people didn't carry them out." Then he changed the subject. "How long do you think it will be until Soviets can live like Americans?" he asked. "We're tired of being poor! We want our children to live as your children do—with computers and electronic equipment."

I thought of Yogi Berra's (or Casey Stengel's) quote: "Predictions are dangerous, especially those involving the future."

"No one can say when," I answered. "The thing is to begin and to keep moving toward the goal. Actually, we hope you don't live quite like Americans," I said. "We live with great excess. Half of our houses are too big for the number of people living in them. We're burdened by too many possessions. We're always throwing them out or selling them second-hand to others who want to sell or give their stuff to us. Our trash dumps are nearly full. Recently a train loaded with garbage from the east coast went back and forth across the country trying to find a place to dump its load and finally had to go back to its starting place. Most people have three times the clothes they need. We have about 5 percent of the world's population but use one quarter of the world's resources.

"We hope you'll have our advantages but not our problems. For goodness sake, don't let your citizens have handguns around; they are often used in anger against family members. Ralph thinks it will be a generation until the farm system is really changed, but your electronic supply and political changes will come faster." It was probably not what he wanted to hear.

Wendy called us today and said, "The September 25 international edition of *Time* magazine will carry your story. But I think it's dry because it's only about agriculture. The article for the American *Time* is set in type for Oct. 2 and is somewhat different because it has a different editor. I've been able to express some opinion in the article because it's in the 'American Scene' section."

It's cold now and has been rainy for two weeks. Because Ukraine is farther north than Ohio, the days were quite long in summer, with daylight until 11 P.M. But now, as fall comes on, the darkness curls around our days on both ends. It's so cold, I'm worried about leaving my three little kittens. One looks so very tiny. I don't know where they'll get food. They usually stand by our door and want to come in—one did once. But I can't let them get used to warmth; they need to grow heavy coats.

Toli and I waxed philosophical today. I said, "We've found that people all over the world have the same human nature. Comparatively, history and culture are superficial layers."

He replied, "I think there are different ways of being. Americans approach goodness and kindness in one way. Soviets approach them in another—maybe a more difficult way. But people everywhere are trying to fulfill those ideals." Beautiful!

This conversation reminded me of what our artist friend, Slava of Leningrad, once expressed, "People all over the world are being drawn up into God, whether they know it or not."

September 13: We turned on the TV today to see Peter Jennings on a Spacebridge called *Capital to Capitol.* The Congresses of the two superpowers were discussing the electronic system of the US Congress, and then, global environmental problems. Thank heaven for Gorbachev who's changing the cold war mentality so we can begin working together on our global problems. Perhaps just in time! Someone had to do it, but isn't it strange the world leader who speaks of spirituality and has the greatest global vision came from an officially atheistic, closed country? Such is life, always surprising us!

It's possible Gorby's work in his country essentially may be over. If so, others will pick up the standard and carry on. Perhaps he needs a radical Yeltsin to help him push the reforms forward. Like Moses, Gorbachev may not be the one to lead his people into the Promised Land. Still, I hope he is.

I gave my third and last lecture at the Pedagogical Institute—half on problems in America. I allowed 20 minutes for questions. Beginning on a controversial note, I said psychics have predicted for years the US and Russia would be great friends eventually. I've really enjoyed doing these lectures! I didn't know they intended to pay me—95 rubles. At the end, Andrei gave me flowers. I kissed him on the cheek, and everyone went, "Ooooooo."

Afterwards, a tall young woman who looked a bit older than the other students spoke briefly to me. Indeed, she was not a student but had come to hear me speak and to invite us to attend her organ concert at noon on Saturday in Kamenets.

Then, a beautiful "studyentka" (female student) approached me and said, "If I were in the US, I would be so happy to have all those opportunities! Why do your young people take drugs?"

"The answer is complicated," I responded. "The main reason is peer pressure. And some drugs can be addictive after only one or two doses. But, why do our young people give in to peer pressure? For one thing, altering one's consciousness has gone on in every culture and age. There's a physiological reason for this, and it has to do with the pleasure receptors in our brains.

"Another reason is our culture has become one of instant gratification and attempts to get happiness from the outside. Because we have such an array of wonderful opportunities and things to buy, many people get caught up in acquisitiveness of some sort. Then their children think this is the way to live. In many ways, we're products of our mass media. TV commercials promote the idea a person must immediately get whatever he wants, including feeling good.

"An important reason, too, is, there's not as much family unity and stability in our country as in more agriculturally-oriented cultures. Many American families move far from where they were born so the father (or mother) can take a better job. Grandparents are seldom nearby to provide stability and extra nurturing for the children. Sadly, some children end up feeling alienated, especially if their parents are divorced. In addition, parents are caught up in their busy lives and may not be emotionally present for their children. This lack of community feeling can lead to drug-taking with friends."

I noticed our Jewish student friend Volodya was writing on something. Shortly afterwards, he gave me a record album with music by Claude Debussy, my favorite composer. I was glad I remembered to bring a Michael Jackson cassette for him.

Inside the album Volodya had written a note to us:

I have lately been betrayed by the only woman I loved. But I forgave her. So, now my back's against the wall. And I'd like to say to you: Let us forgive everybody who makes us hurt, who betrays us, even, who does not love us. Let us love each other. Do you remember the words of Jesus Christ, "All people are brothers"? If one is angry with somebody, let us say: "Let bygones be bygones!" Let us believe in kindness, in love, in hope, in God. I want to finish this short letter with words by John Lennon: "All we are saying is give peace a chance!" Let us live in peace! I wish you luck! P.S. Tell everybody you meet in the USA our people want to live in peace. I will remember you forever. Your Russian friend, Volodya.

Ralph and I then retired to a small room with eight of the teachers. They had prepared a tea for us with home-baked cakes. One had USA and CCCP on top.

Someone asked me to talk a little about things I hadn't had time to mention. One subject was abuse: spouse abuse, child abuse, and sexual abuse of children. I said, "Only recently has it come to light that these abuses are not rare in the US."

"They're also common here," said one of the teachers, "but they aren't discussed openly yet." Surely he's right because alcoholism, male chauvinism, and general frustration in the USSR would result in the abuse of other people.

The teacher who wanted the history book handed me a book in English called *Young Masters of the Land*, published in 1988 for the Komsomol. Janna, the woman who had been fearful to talk with me, chattered with enthusiasm. She gave me a letter her 14-year-old daughter had written, to be passed on to an American pen pal. In it, the girl said, "I think friendship and understanding are the most precious things in the world." Out of the mouths of babes . . . .

Janna has "healing hands." During our party, she rested her hands on the aching head of a colleague, and the headache disappeared.

(Psychic or spiritual healers are very popular here. On the morning show out of Moscow, *120 Minutes*, several minutes are given daily to such a spiritualist. The man makes healing motions with his hands, reads letters asking for help, and gives answers. Also, there's a famous man who heals with his hypnotic eyes. We've seen him on national television. Both men are considered to be effective healers. Herbs, too, are used more in the Soviet Union for healing purposes than in our country.)

Roza told me, "All the boys are in love with you, and the girls, too, but they are more shy." Also, "You will go down in the history of our Institute as our first American guest lecturer!" For me, my friendship with these teachers and students is a highlight of our stay here.

After our tea party, Sergei, who'd been patiently waiting, got into our car and directed us to the railroad station. He secured tickets to Kiev for us for the night of September 25, the day we leave Makov for the trip home.

Then he helped me buy bread. He told me to speak English through the door of a bakery, though a "closed" sign was on the door. It worked. I dislike trickery and special favors but . . . I wimped out.

Finally, we went to a village right outside Kamenets to see Sergei's family dacha. The old two-room cottage was where Sergei's grandmother lived and died, his father was born and raised, and Sergei spent his boyhood. His family had been able, with great difficulty, to get a little more land around the cottage. Now they're in the midst of building a new house and a couple more cottages for Sergei's five uncles and their families to use during vacations—a family holiday complex. It's really a small amount of land and a simple place, but it's highly prized.

Sergei climbed high in the apple tree to find the best apples for us, and he gave us many gifts. One was his father's officer cap from his army years.

Since Sergei and Joel are both the same age, 19, he thought Joel might like it.

When we got home, I looked over *Masters of the Land*. The names of the chapters are "The Tasks of Soviet Youth," "Work is an Honorable Duty for All," "To Study—the Must of Our Times," "Our Youth's Participation in Arts and Sports," and "Youth Struggle for Peace and Friendship." One of the tasks of Soviet youth is "to learn communism." I turned to that section, and here's what I read:

> To learn communism today means to be an active participant in the renewal of our socialist society, to search for new and more effective ways to do one's work.

> To learn communism means to study the theory of Marxism-Leninism, to understand the great historic cause for which the Communist Party of the Soviet Union and the Soviet people are working and to be ideologically convinced that this cause is right.

> To learn communism means to be active in social life, to uphold the interests of Soviet society, of the Soviet state.

> To learn communism means to strengthen the standards of communist morality by word and deed.

> To learn communism for Soviet young people means to be a real Soviet patriot, to be always ready to give all one's strength, and, if necessary, one's life for one's country, for the happiness of one's people.

> To learn communism means to educate oneself in the spirit of proletarian, socialist internationalism, in the spirit of fraternal friendship with the working people of our country and of other countries.

> The task of learning communism is a historical task and becomes concrete with the social changes taking place nowadays.

I'm sure not many young persons groove on that stuff. And what does it all mean in practical terms? Another quote from the book:

> The Komsomol educates young Pioneers in the spirit of devotion to communist ideals, readiness to defend their Motherland. Young Pioneers must study well, be honest, brave, polite, must set a good example to all children. Many serious and fascinating affairs in the life of the Young Pioneers could be listed. For example, pioneers gather scrap-iron and waste paper, they take an active part in all workdays. They organize such expeditions and marches as "We Are Devoted to Lenin's Behests," "Always Ready," "A Little Grain," "Kindness," and others.

The rest of the book talks about studying well in school and working diligently. There are numerous examples: Komsomol members working hard in Siberia building the BAM railroad, or "Admitted to the University at [age] 12," or "Samantha Smith and her Counterpart, Katya," or "The Right

Man for a Woman's Job" (a man who taught kindergarten and loved it), and other stories. Under "Young Scientists and Technologists Helping Perestroika," it says, "Until now the real share of Soviet youth in promoting scientific and technological progress in our country has not been satisfactory. The young wanted more rights and less formalism." It all sounds like boring pep-talk to me. Toli says it makes him sick.

Late this evening, Oleg came, handsome in his sweater. This after spending the day digging a hole much deeper than his height for his family's septic tank. I was disappointed he hadn't brought his guitar, but we talked for a couple of hours. And he gave me another souvenir—an antique pocket watch. It needs work, but he hopes it can be fixed for Ralph to use.

September 14: We spent several hours today with Anton, the economist at the other Ukraina farm 40 miles away. At one point, he admitted, "We are not commanded from on high so much anymore, but old habits are hard to break. Inertia is the worst problem. Gorbachev can't do it all. Each person must help make the changes. Our farm could start to make changes."

In the corn trench-silo, we met a man who told of his happiness at the end of WWII when, as a Soviet soldier, he met the American soldiers at the River Elbe. The soldiers had kissed, embraced, and rejoiced together. I gave him one of our small pins with crossed American and Soviet flags, and Ralph hugged him. It was the second time he had embraced Americans, both times in a trench. The encounters were 44 years apart.

After leaving Anton, we risked going on our own to a seed corn processing yard a few miles away. Ralph wanted to investigate the equipment. It's a little scary driving through a gate and past a watch house. We went a hundred feet beyond the watchman and parked at an office. There was an anxious moment as he strode toward us, but when he learned we were "the Americans," he indicated all was well. Ralph explored every corner of the seed factory.

While there, we showed our Ohio pictures to a group of people who began expressing their opinions. Naturally, there's great variety of thought. Like Val, some idealize America too much. Others still believe the old propaganda. One asked the question we've been asked most often—"Where is life better, here or in America?" We've always answered, "In America, because life here is hard." And the response would invariably be the same, "Very hard!" But today, one man answered simply, "Mozhna" (But one *can* live here). The great majority of people want more than they have. Still, a few are satisfied—usually because they know nothing else. Or perhaps this attitude of contentment is a sign of high spirituality.

On the way home, we picked up a hitchhiking policeman on his way to work. He soon recognized us, and he began enthusiastically spouting fact after fact about Ralph's farm. His source was Palamarchouk's letter in *Izvestia*. He sounded like he'd memorized it! Then he asked us to give him a photo and write something on it so his comrades wouldn't think he was crazy when he said he'd been with us. We happily complied.

This evening Ralph took Toli to visit some of his students' parents. The parents of one girl didn't have enough money to buy her gym clothes. So tonight Toli gave them the news that he'd talked the farm into helping. Accomplishing this lifted a great weight off him, he said. Another task was to deal with a boy who'd recently been out until 4 A.M. He'd also once stolen a bicycle.

Valentina is trying to get exit visas for herself and Tatiana. She went to Khmelnitski where they said it would take 45 days. When she told them she needed to be in Ohio for the first two weeks of October, they said they could do it in 30 days. What good would that do? Viktor would be leaving just as they were arriving. Ralph's son, Mike, tried and failed to get them on Finnair with us, so he got them Pan Am tickets for Sept. 30. Now she must manage to get exit visas earlier.

September 16: This morning a film crew shot footage of us to be used in a documentary about agriculture. The artistic director wanted Ralph to say, "If people would just respect farmers, who do eternal work, it would improve agriculture immensely." Toli scoffed at this, and Ralph refused to say it. For the film, our desk and two chairs were put out on our tiny upstairs porch—so the interview could have the orchard in the background. It all took several hours, and the kind director encouraged us to visit him in Kiev on our way home. He wanted to show us the film he'd made about the Russian Orthodox millennium in 1988.

While Ralph was being interviewed, I began removing items from drawers and bookcase in preparation for packing. The Chairman was interested in everything, and in a cavalier manner, just took what he wanted for himself. He especially liked the large thermometer which Ralph had secured outside our upstairs window.

At noon, Ralph and I attended the Kamenets organ concert of the young woman we met when I spoke at the institute. It was held in the Old Town in an ancient church with a fabulous organ. Her two friends, a soprano and a violinist, were as talented as she. One thing about this country we can all agree on—its performing arts and sports are outstanding!

Both of us loved the music. Tears streamed down my face, partly due to the exquisite music, but partly, I'm sure, because of the poignancy I've been feeling about leaving. A man standing nearby observed this, and afterwards, spoke to us. He introduced himself as a Catholic priest from Poland. He's a friend of the young musicians. After they joined us, we talked awhile and agreed to work for peace in our three countries. Then we embraced and parted. Ah! The universal ties that bind us together are so much stronger than the petty differences that separate us!

September 17: On our way to Kamenets today, we stopped at the home of Toli's school director. Hanging in the house was a big homemade banner.

It announced his wife wouldn't have to cook all day because it was her birthday. But when she discovered we hadn't had lunch, she quickly brought out chicken, meat, and other delicacies and served us. There was a birthday torte for her—their cakes are European-style, with multiple thin layers. While we were there, her mother and other family members arrived with kisses, flowers, and gifts. We took a group picture of the family, which we'll send them.

When we got to Kamenets, we bought fur hats at a store. Mine's fake fur; Ralph's is rabbit. I think my hat will go with the black, crushed-velvet babushka coat I got in a Makov clothing store for 35 rubles.

Next, I went into the post office to send three 8" by 11" registered letters. One had been returned from Volgograd because the address was slightly incorrect. I corrected the address on the same envelope and tried to send it off for its second trip.

"This envelope has been used, so we can't take it," said the woman behind the counter. I tried to explain to her what had happened, but she wasn't buying it.

All of a sudden, like an angel out of the blue, there by my side was Komsomol leader Andrei! He quickly explained everything, and my letters went. Andrei remarked, his round face shining, "This is like a dream!"

Our final destination was the Kamenets flat of Nikolai of The Greenhouse Gang. The five families had planned a farewell dinner for us. As we were shown around the flat, we could see a spectacular view out one window. The cathedral steeples and fortress turrets of Old Town were silhouetted in the distance. In addition to Toli, Tanya, and the five Greenhouse families, Nikolai had invited a couple who teach English to his two little sons.

There was much drinking and toasting as the evening progressed. And because of the large number of people, there were many individual conversations. As I showed the female English teacher pictures of my sons, she looked at my third one, Neil, who lifts weights. She said, "All American men look like that, don't they?" She also said, "We used to be taught to dislike Americans, but that has stopped." Same in America.

After dinner, I gave each family a packet of American products: toilet paper, shaving equipment, little bandages, gum, rubber bands, American coins, tape, bubble gum, balloons, "make-ups" for each wife, two peace buttons, a prayer card, small plastic bags, and an envelope with our US address on the front.

I also called each family into the bedroom so I could take a portrait-type photograph of them. By this time, several bottles had been tippled, and the male English teacher was not in good condition. Though he talked sense earlier in the evening, he had become paranoid. As I took his picture with his wife, he said, "That picture is only for you to see. Don't ever send it to us in the mail!"

"Why not?" asked his embarrassed wife. "I'd like to have it." But he continued in that vein. I'll send it anyway.

Later, a new couple arrived—somebody's godparents. Ralph talked with the man, who explained in detail how the head of the Chairman's meat place cheats people. Many babushkas like Anna and Nina buy young pigs and calves and raise them to maturity. The meat man then comes to buy them, "estimates" their weight, and pays accordingly.

I asked if we could have a song—Oleg had his guitar—and that started a long, vigorous, rather off-key round of songs. We were sad we didn't know any of them. The only Russian songs I'm familiar with are "The Volga Boatman," "Dark Eyes," and "Meadowlands," not likely to be included at this party. Soviets and Americans do share the Beatles' songs, however. They also know the West's Bon Jovi, Billy Joel, Pink Floyd, Deep Purple, the Jackson siblings, Jethro Tull, and others familiar to rock aficionados. Several times we've been asked the embarrassing question, "Which of our rock bands do you like?" We know not one!

Toli surprised us by taking the lead in singing old songs—from his institute days, I think. In fact, Toli and Oleg sang loudly in the back seat all the way home! Toli was a tad embarrassed. When we dropped him and Tanya off, he said, "I wasn't drunk. I was only singing." Sure, Toli!

September 18: After midnight last night, many young men in their cars roared along the unpaved ribbon road, one by one, in the first annual Makov car race. Each was timed, and Toli said some cars went up to a hundred miles an hour! He told us the Chairman's car nearly got hit as he left Stupentsi's long lane and began to turn onto the village stretch of the ribbon road.

Yeltsin is in Baltimore, Maryland, now. An Italian newspaper said he is doing much shopping and drinking. *Pravda* immediately printed the article, hoping to help Gorbachev. But it did more harm than good because the people don't like Yeltsin to be criticized. Today *Pravda* apologized to him.

About six this evening, Ralph and I arrived in Khmelnitski to have dinner with Raisa, her woman friend, and a young man from Modesto, California, who is teaching English in Khmelnitski for a few months. We nearly missed each other though. I'd remembered the name of the street wrong—it was Marx, not Lenin!

As we walked toward a restaurant, the smell of gasoline became stronger and stronger. We entered quickly, thinking we'd escape the stifling odor inside. But no! It was worse! They had cleaned the floors with gasoline, of all things! Naturally, the restaurant was empty. Eventually we found another, a happy choice. The band there played American tunes for us: "Feelings," "I Just Called to Say 'I Love You,'" and "When the Saints . . ." —Satchmo style.

We talked and talked as if we'd known each other for years. When we asked Raisa what she liked about America, she answered, "What I like the most are the choices and freedoms Americans have. I like the level of living, and I love American men! They're so kind and helpful to their wives. I also like it that when Americans are asked, 'How are you?' they answer, 'Fine,' whether they are or not. However, it shocked me that Americans are as open as they are about their personal lives. They sometimes tell intimate details even to strangers. We don't do that here."

Soviets do not call every acquaintance their "friend" as many of us do. For instance, once we picked up an old woman hitchhiker who lived near Anna. She pumped us for information about Toli. When I told Anna we'd picked up her friend, she said, "She's my neighbor, not my friend."

The Modesto teacher told me the Khmelnitski school where he's teaching doesn't have enough books for the students. He also said, "I think half the population here is chronically depressed." Toli thinks they're not—they're too busy surviving. On the other hand, a psychologist once told me America is a depressive society, with its fast pace, competitiveness, and materialism. Maybe Soviets and Americans could learn *dukhovnost* (spirituality) together.

September 19: Toli and I went to Kamenets to get our new samovar fixed. There was a defect in the way it was assembled. The frustration of the experience is worth recording.

We arrived in Kamenets at 8:45 A.M. Toli had brought some home-brew—as a bribe, of course. He told me how it's done. He just says one word to the repairman: "marioche," meaning "extra pay, probably strong brew."

First, I went to see if Tamara could cut my hair. (I had tried for days to call her, but the beauty shop's phone wasn't working.) "She'll be in by 10 o'clock," one of the hairdressers told me. While I was at the beauty shop, Toli stopped at the samovar repair place. This shop was supposed to be open but wasn't. We shopped at the market and the bread store, where the just-delivered bread was still warm. Then we learned Tamara was still not in as scheduled. So we went again to the samovar place. We were told the man in charge of repair wouldn't be in until tomorrow, though he was supposed to be there today. The attendant sent Toli to another establishment to get a part for the samovar. That place was closed for dinner.

But hurrah! By that time, Tamara had arrived. She gave me one last beautiful haircut and a long explanation about her husband being ill, as an apology for being late. Her little son has not been baptized yet because both she and her husband have been away on their vacations. (Soviet couples often take separate vacations, usually for practical reasons, but also so the woman has a break from serving the man.) She'll write on the record that I am her son's godmother, even though I won't be here for the baptism. When she finished the haircut, she waved away my five rubles. Then she took off her clip earrings, put them on my ears, and hugged me goodbye. She blew kisses as I left. Toli watched sadly. "That's probably the last time you'll see each other," he said.

He, too, needed a haircut. Unfortunately, the men's line was so long, he gave up. We got some ice cream and went home at about 3 P.M. We were told to be back at the samovar place by ten the next morning.

Buddha, Toli, and Ralph. Photo of cat consoling Buddha's granddaughter.

Buddha came by late this afternoon. We made final arrangements for sending soybeans to him for the Regional test station. Before we parted, he gave us a photo of his baby granddaughter and her cat. They were sitting quietly opposite each other on a bed, gazing into each other's eyes. He explained, "When Valeria cries, the cat comes to console her. Understanding can come between animals and people, so it can be that much more between humans." Then he added, looking directly at Ralph and me, "This picture is a symbol of the understanding between us." What a sensitive gift! He had written on the back, "See you in ten years."

Finally, a meeting was hastily arranged on Ukraina farm for us today. For five months, we have wanted this. We were never invited to the day care center, the sanatorium, or the sugar factory, places we would have enjoyed seeing. (This isn't to say we haven't been in a day care center and sanatorium though.) We'd have liked to sit in on a village soviet or farm meeting, too.

Savkov still didn't want the meeting. He argued with Toli about it this afternoon right in front of us in the Chairman's office. "What did he [Ralph] say about our corn in his book?" he asked Toli defensively. Stengach looked on quietly. Finally, Savkov grudgingly agreed to hold the meeting.

At 6 P.M., 35 specialists were sitting in the auditorium at Headquarters. Savkov, who really is a famous agronomist, was in the front row. He looked at the floor or out the window, and otherwise studiously avoided looking at Ralph. Ralph, Toli, Viktor Party Secretary, and I sat behind a table on the platform in front. Ralph began to speak in his quiet, unassuming way. First, he said, "I feel, in general, Soviets think too highly of American agriculture." As Ralph spoke, I watched Savkov intently. His eyes continued to go either to the floor or the window. Before long, however, they were casting quick glances at Ralph. Finally, they were fixed completely on Ralph as he talked. Soon Savkov was asking questions. And when Ralph asked, "What do any of you think should be done to improve agriculture here?" Savkov was the first to answer. As the meeting progressed, the possibility of growing soybeans on the farm was elaborated on, and Savkov took a few notes.

Ralph has the kind of *ahimsa* (harmlessness) Gandhi spoke about. I've watched him with his grandchildren and once when he played Santa at a nursery school. He has a gentleness and a dignified humility which gives a safe feeling to those around him. I can surely attest to that. Even towards those who have aggressively opposed his peace stand over the years, there is little antagonism in him. This *ahimsa* radiates from his soul. To me, it was beautiful to watch him gently disarm Savkov. I wish I'd had a hidden video camera to show the dramatic change. Later, when I told him about his effect on Savkov, he said, "I didn't notice that, but I had him in mind during my opening remarks about his farm and ours."

Savkov wasn't totally transformed, however. Towards the end of the meeting, a tractor driver Ralph is especially fond of asked, in fear and trembling, "Which is better—collective farms or independent farmers?" Immediately, Savkov turned around and growled at him.

At the end of the meeting, the Chairman rose and announced to his people, "We are a good farm. We do everything right, and we're not going to change anything. And I'm glad we have no dissidents on this farm who want to do anything differently."

Ralph whispered to Toli, "You need a new Chairman."

September 20: Toli and Ralph had good luck this morning. They managed to get the repaired samovar and a haircut for Toli.

Today we celebrated Toli's birthday with him and his family by giving him a gift and enjoying Tanya's good cake. Toli had said, "Let's just be together. No toasts or anything."

Toli told us Shcherbitsky, First Party Secretary of Ukraine, and two others were retired from the Politburo. A new KGB chief was put onto the Politburo, so Gorbachev is continuing to strengthen his support. For the first time, he actually has a majority.

At the end of the evening, Nina burst into tears, thinking she might never see us again. I love the rich emotional expression of Soviets! A few times

I've even observed huge Russian men with tears on their cheeks as they parted with new American friends.

September 22: This morning Ukraina's economist spent some hours with Ralph and talked about crops. He wanted to know only Ralph's total cost per acre of each crop. But Ralph insisted on breaking everything down because he has some expenses Soviets don't: rent, high wages, and bank interest rates.

Later, Ralph and I made some farewell visits. We stopped one last time at the rented beef farm. I hugged and kissed the women, and then the young father grabbed me and planted a big one right on my mouth. No sooner had I escaped from him than his father did the same thing! That's a gesture of friendship I could do without!

At 3 P.M., we met for a couple of hours with the gentle TASS man who interviewed us our first week here. He's a kindred spirit, and we were glad to see him once more.

Then, towards evening, we surprised the telephone operators in Dunaevtsi by giving them a thank-you gift of champagne and chocolates. It turns out they *had* gotten in trouble for letting us see their switchboard, even though they didn't let us photograph it. Old ways die hard.

On the way home, we stopped to see wheat being planted. We also met a small-sized chairman! He admitted the soil was mistreated by too much tillage. He also said he's hoping to bring his poor farm to prosperity in three years.

When we arrived at Stupentsi, an unfamiliar white car was parked by our front door. Reporter Misha Alexeyev had arrived with an attractive colleague, Anya. Misha had promised he'd be back for one more interview with Ralph before we left. He's a young man of his word. So I cooked, we ate, Anya did the dishes, and then we were off to bed.

September 23: This morning, Oleg and a young musician came to see if there is anything I could do about the man's loss of hair. He's completely bald and wears a shortened woman's wig because he can't get a man's hairpiece. I decided to send him one from the US, and this pleased him greatly. When he asked what he could do for me in return, I asked him to sing for me. He and Oleg sang in turn, accompanying themselves on Oleg's guitar, while I taped them. Meanwhile, several other people made me happy by dropping in to say goodbye.

Ralph took Misha and Anya on a trip around the fields this afternoon (an American showing Soviets the USSR) while I stayed home to nurse a raging migraine.

Come evening, my head was no better. But Anya wanted to have a party, so she and I went to Victoria's Restaurant where she bought champagne in the back room. Then she set up a pretty table in our living room with a cloth, champagne, chocolates, and apples.

Misha Alexeyev, Kiev journalist, (right) talking to man who wanted an American wig.

We gathered there after supper, and Misha entertained us with his lively guitar-playing and singing. As I taped him, he sang in both English and Russian. Misha is a fine journalist and very knowledgeable. We enjoyed talking to him and listening to some of his large fund of anecdotes. But Anya was displeased he was getting so much attention and became petulant. Despite the sweet music, the evening ended on a sour note for her.

Anya doesn't think life is so hard in the USSR. It's her opinion the new freedoms will all close up again in two or three years. She and Misha will leave tomorrow. He'll write another article about us for *News From Ukraine*.

September 24: Today was our goodbye dinner with Toli and his family. First, we went to Anna's cozy little cottage where she was waiting for us with candy and her life's photographs laid out for us to see. I was very moved when she gave me her two best shawls. I'll give one to Becky who hosted Viktor in her Ohio home.

We finally succeeded in giving something to Anna as well. A month or two ago, Anna had a some front teeth pulled. She's been reluctant to smile ever since. I offered her 120 rubles to get her teeth fixed, but, of course, she refused them. So Ralph said, "Well, Anna, we have extra rubles we can't do anything with. I guess if you don't take them, we'll just have to burn them!"

Anna quickly responded, "Oh, I'll take them!" She couldn't bear the thought of burning rubles after having worked so hard all her life to earn kopeks (100 kopeks make a ruble). Today we handed her an envelope with 120 rubles for her teeth and 100 more to help renovate the new little church.

The three of us then walked a block to Toli's. He, Tanya, Vova, Yura, Nina, and couples Vanya and Tanya and Sasha and Ola were waiting. We exchanged gifts, and Vanya gave us a lidded glass pitcher. He had made it to look as if it were covered with tree bark—very unusual. He also presented me with a beautiful, many-colored butterfly lapel pin which he had crafted out of metal. Smiling Ola had made and embroidered several cloth napkins for us. Gifts of the heart and hands!

We relished our last of Tanya's fine dinners. Of course, there were toasts. But Vanya and Sasha didn't drink because both were recently diagnosed with heart trouble. That's unusual because both are in their early thirties.

Later, other friends dropped by. We spent a long evening talking. Tanya served tea and sweets twice, and Vanya serenaded us beautifully, accompanying himself on his guitar. He has outstanding artistic and musical talents and is completely self-taught.

Tanya asked, "Whom do you want to see first when you get home to Ohio?"

Ralph said, "My grandchildren and Palamarchouk."

"My son Neil and my California brother who will be traveling through Ohio. They'll both be at the airport," I said. "My other three sons are living in California."

Then Ola asked, "What will you do your first day home?"

Ralph responded enthusiastically, "I'll be driving the seed corn picker!"

"I'll talk with Neil and my brother, call other family members on the phone, and start going through seven months of mail," I said.

"When will you be coming back to visit?" someone asked.

"We have no plans to return," Ralph said. "But we might come back to work if there's an intriguing project."

"I'm sure we'll be back in the USSR," I answered, "but we don't know if we'll get to Makov."

On the way home, we stopped at Valentina's to see how she's coming along with her visas. Success! She managed to get them, thanks to Savkov, who has connections. I called a friend in Moscow to find out what comes next. Valentina must stand in line at the American Embassy for a day or two to try to get a US visa. Then she'll go to a Moscow bank to exchange rubles for $320.

September 25: Today's our last day in Makov. We picked up our final mail delivery. Farmer Dimitri had sent us a photo of his two blond little granddaughters. An inscription read: "We hope these girls will have a common language with your grandchildren, the language of sincerity and unity. For Ralph and Christine to remember always the granddaughters of Dimitri."

Hearts full of emotion, we packed our suitcases. Tanya's sister Lusa has managed to get us train tickets from Kiev to Moscow. Ralph went to the fields for his last two hours there. Two friends let him drive a six-row corn picker.

We wanted one last photo of the little church with Anna, Nina, and the saintly Zhenya in front of it. The church will have its official opening two days after we leave. We gathered Nina and Anna and were about to look for Zhenya when he came running down the street, carrying a hoe. I asked if he would take a minute to pose for us, and he said, "Later. The Chairman wants to see me now." He continued down the street, red-faced and panting.

At about 3:30 the Chairman and Viktor Party Secretary came with Toli for a brief visit. We talked and toasted. The Chairman said he was finally told from on high that our mission was different from what he had expected. It took six months for him to get the official word! He also said we were nice people. Viktor Party Secretary mused, "When Palamarchouk returns, he will either turn the farm upside-down or secede from it." Before we all said "do sveedanya" (goodbye), the Chairman graciously offered us a month's visit in "our" house in the future. After the officials left, Toli told us Savkov had asked about us in a friendly manner.

At 5:15 P.M. we left Stupentsi, stopping at the greenhouse to say a last goodbye to Stepan, Nicolai, and Sasha Professor. They said we had opened their eyes to many things. Then, on to Oleg's house to bid him goodbye. Finally, we arrived at Tanya and Toli's for one brief togetherness with our Soviet family, though Toli's going to Kiev with us. All three babushkas (Anna, Nina, and I) wept. Finally, making our goodbyes perfectly complete, Sasha Sportsman arrived to hand us a big bag of pears and wish us good health.

We left Makov as we had arrived: in the farm taxi-van with Toli, all our suitcases, and the same driver. But oh! How different we are from when we first entered Makov! What new poignancies we carry within us! In large part, we've not only learned the life of the people, we've lived it—exactly what we wanted to do. We've had an unforgettably rich, unique experience, and we're deeply grateful.

Our van arrived at the train station in Kamenets-Podolski, with only 15 minutes to spare. And there on the platform—we might have known!—were fifteen of our Kamenets friends waiting to say goodbye. Most were from the Pedagogical Institute. Roza had cookies and caramels for us to eat on the train. Janna gave us a jar of honey and a letter. Janna had given her class writing assignments about my lectures, and she quoted from their essays in the letter to me. Students Andrei and Sergei carried our luggage onto the train, and Toli arranged the luggage and made the beds. We felt supremely well-loved and cared for! There were hugs all around before we boarded. Right before the train pulled out, I tried to take some photos of that group of beautiful people standing on the platform. But the train attendant put her stick in front of my lens, a reminder of the waning ugliness in the lives of Soviets which ravages their innocent human joys.

At 10 P.M. we stopped for ten minutes in Khmelnitski. Standing on the platform were Raisa and her two friends with a gift of farewell flowers. Thank goodness we still have Toli with us! There would've been too much grieving all at once. Can we sleep tonight with hearts so full?

September 26: At 4:45 A.M. the train pulled into Kiev. Waiting for us were Valeri; Kostya, who's now taking extra schooling in Kiev; our photographer friend; and two publishers. We were mighty surprised they'd all gotten up so early!

They told us an anecdote about Ralph that's going around Kiev:

> When Ralph meets the Chairman of the collective farm, he says to him, "What do you do?" to which the Chairman replies, "I'm the Chairman of the collective farm." Ralph answers, "Yes, but what do you do?"

After breakfast at Lusa's, we went to the publishers. We talked for several hours about our book. But we didn't commit ourselves to them because we want to talk with Progress Publishers in Moscow first.

While there, we talked with a Komsomol leader in his twenties. He said, "The youth of the country will save it. A full 95 percent are in favor of going the way of the West, while the rest want to return to Stalin. The deficits are caused because the old ways just aren't working anymore." This young man sounds like Misha who said of the deficits, "That's the way the system is built—it doesn't work."

Ralph told the publishers the anecdote we've heard most often:

> Q. What's the most anti-communist country in the world?
> A. The Soviet Union.

We noticed they weren't smiling.

Afterwards, we went to see the kind film maker who shot footage of us in Makov. As promised, he showed us his stunning film on the thousand year history of the Russian Orthodox Church. We were impressed to hear it had been shown on nationwide TV. He said. "The next time you come to Kiev, I'll show you the film I'm making about you and take you for an airplane ride over the city!"

Lusa served us a fine dinner. When it was time for toasts, I made one to Toli. I said he was "the single most important feature that made our mission a success!"

"Wait a minute . . . " Ralph teased Toli, "after the car!"

Just before time to leave for the train, someone said, "Oh! We must sit!" So we sat quietly together for several seconds. This ensures we'll all meet there again in the future. Then the nine of us went to the train.

Surprise! Misha and Anya of Kiev were waiting for us on the platform. Misha handed me two Paul McCartney albums (*Back in the USSR*) for sale only in this country. As we talked, Misha remarked in his wonderful British accent, "There's simply no petrol in Kiev!"

"I saw a gas station today with a line of about 40 or 50 cars," I responded.

"*Where*?" asked Misha excitedly, pouncing on my words.

Soon, it was hugs and kisses all around. The saddest moment was having to part with Toli, our loyal friend and advocate for six months. The train took off at 9:26 P.M., bound for Moscow. Toli and Kostya ran alongside. We looked back until we could no longer see them . . .

September 27:   At 9:19 A.M. Bob Meyerson; Nikolai Sapozhnikov, a kindly professor from a Moscow Agricultural Institute; and the professor's son met us at the train. They took us and our bags to Bob's apartment, where we settled in for five days. Nikolai had written to Ralph in Ohio in 1988, after seeing an article about us in *Pravda*. I wrote back to thank him, and he invited Ralph to speak at his agricultural institute.

A couple of weeks ago, I also wrote to Jack Matlock, asking if we could meet him, as we have mutual friends. So Ralph, Bob, and I went to the Embassy, and made our way past a long line of people. Many of these people were Armenians, waiting for permission to leave the country, temporarily or permanently. We were disappointed to find that Matlock was back in the USA with Shevardnadze.

But our letter had been sent to the agricultural attache, and he said he wanted to meet with us. He was interested in what Ralph had seen on the farms and even more interested in how long Ralph thought it would be until the farming system would be more productive here. That's part of his job—to evaluate whether or not the Soviet Union will need to import as much grain as always. "Will things be changing quickly here on the farms?" he asked.

"No way!" answered Ralph.

For dinner, we went to the flat of friends of Bob's, a couple about our age. The husband's 92-year-old mother lived there, too. She has a great sense of humor and flirted with Ralph. The wife speaks excellent English and has been in the US. We even discovered we have mutual friends. The man is retired and does the cooking while his wife, Nina, teaches. He fried potatoes, mushrooms, and onions together in sour cream. Delicious! Our conversation was about the world being a neighborhood and the Soviet Union is a neighbor in trouble.

September 28:   This morning, the three of us went with Vladimir, head of Vladimir Cooperative, to see land outside Moscow he may be buying. The land is owned by an agricultural institute, and we spoke with its director. Vladimir asked us if we would like to live there for a while and take over the management of raising beef and dairy cows. Again, we had to tell him Ralph will do consulting but not management.

We also met Sasha, who has a fabulous art collection and would like to sell in America some of the paintings he has acquired from contemporary Soviet artists.

We arrived back at the Moscow Agricultural Institute, just in time for our appointment. Ralph spoke to about one hundred faculty and students there. They seemed to really like him and asked good questions for nearly three hours. Our translator, who had been with the Soviet Embassy in Washington, was tops, but we missed Toli.

As we were leaving the institute, we literally ran into a group of Soviet army officers who write for *Red Star* newspaper and some American army personnel who are on the staff of *Army Times*. This is the way to get our armed forces together! When the enemy has a human face, it's nearly impossible to kill him.

Later, Ralph and I had dinner with our good friends, film maker Viktor and his music-professor wife, Dina, who speaks English. They are thirtyish, childless, and very affectionate with each other. She's taller than he is, and when he goes out, she lovingly plops his hat on his head and kisses him goodbye, murmuring little sweetnesses to him on his way out.

When I think of Soviet kindness, I always think back to the time I asked Viktor if he had a piece of wire so I could fix my glasses. A screw had fallen out of mine. He immediately whisked his own glasses off, took out a screw, and put it into my pair.

Dina has lost a lot of weight (deliberately), wears contact lenses now, and looks great! For her doctoral thesis, she developed a test to judge innate musical talent. I asked her if she's optimistic about perestroika. "I am not," she said, "and no one else is, either. Viktor and I think that something very hard may happen," she added ominously, "like a civil war that starts in the nationalities. Communism is dying and must die, and capitalism must be established."

September 29: We talked with Valentina and Tatiana, who are now in Moscow. They were able to get US visas and must now exchange their money before they leave on Pan Am tomorrow at noon. All this time, Valentina seemed to go through her preparatory activities without emotion. I asked her in Makov why she wasn't more excited about visiting the States. She said she wasn't sure it would happen. Now it looks like a certainty. It'll be a nice transition to have the three Palamarchouks in our home in Ohio for two weeks.

I had telephone conversations with several Moscow friends. Then Ralph, Bob, and I went to see Dale Posthumus who works for Ciba-Geigy, an American pesticide company. He used to work in the US Embassy in Moscow but had to change jobs when he married a Russian girl. We noticed his attitude toward the USSR has softened since we spoke with him at the Embassy in 1985.

Our next stop was Progress Publishers. There we spoke with a man who was nearly hysterical with busy-ness because he's going to the US tomorrow. We decided we might be lost in the shuffle at Progress, so we decided to sign a contract with the Kiev publishers.

In the lobby of Progress Publishers, we met a friend of Bob's who had just been in North Korea. He reported it's a very poor country. However, the people are satisfied there because they aren't aware of what life is like for the rest of the world. Stalin's use of this tactic was successful in his country, too. But many forces worked together in this long-suffering country to bring on perestroika—educated citizens, an easing of the Bear's paw, improved communications, the failure of the economic system, a growing emphasis on human rights, the prayers and acts of people of good will, and a brave Gorbachev and others who were willing to speak the truth and work for improvement.

Finally, we put our remaining rubles in a bank account, which will pay 2% interest. When we return someday, they'll come in handy.

At the flat of our friend Marina this evening, we met Irina, who is staying there temporarily. She and I discovered we have migraines in common. We exchanged remedies—mine was a pill, hers a fruit like a date. Irina is a party member, and when I criticized the party for its special privileges, she got a funny look on her face. She said emphatically, "I've never had one privilege because I was a party member, and neither have any of my friends! We got only extra work!"

I thought, "Well, this confirms our understanding that it's only the high party officials on various levels who have these privileges." There's a great difference between ruling communists and the other party members, who are really just like the rest of the people.

Irina continued, "I was a good student, and I was taught to love my country. I believed that it was a great country and was doing good things, working for peace, and trying to make the United States understand we didn't want war. It was natural for me to join the party to show my love for my country. So I did. But my father told me when he lived in the villages, those who did nothing took power. I chastised him, saying, 'How can you say that, Father?' But my father said, 'I saw it!' Now we know all these things are true! I'm reading Alexander Solzhenitsyn's *Gulag Archipeligo*, which is being serialized in one of our magazines, and I see that not only Stalin but also Lenin sent people to the gulags! I am dumbfounded, confused. I honestly don't know what to teach my child."

"This must be happening in the minds of many Soviets," I thought. Ralph thinks the party is built on sand and could easily go down because most people don't join it for the right reasons.

September 30: This morning, Vladimir of the co-op drove us to the Moscow *Time* Bureau where we picked up a copy of the international *Time* carrying our story. The photo they used was one of us in the sugar beet field with the hoeing women.

Then Ralph, Bob, Vladimir, and I were picked up by Alexei, whom we met two days ago. We rode in his shiny, black Ford Scorpio to see some land he's going to develop. We wondered why the Scorpio could go twice the speed limit and not get stopped. Finally, the police did stop us after our Armenian driver drove down the wrong side of the road to pass a long traffic jam. A police car was in the jam and reported ahead.

Alexei is used to running things and is exceedingly overbearing. He told us he plans to have bulls and crops on the land. He will also move the babushkas out of their homes into apartments and restore the churches. I suppose he thinks he's doing well by these women, but I asked him, "What if the babushkas would rather not go?"

As Alexei was telling us all his plans, Ralph asked him, "Have you asked the people what they want?" He hadn't. This is a good example of the attitudinal changes that must occur along with structural changes in the Soviet Union. Russia has had very little democracy in its history, so leaders aren't used to asking the people what they want. As the editor of a progressive Soviet magazine says, "We are like a legless man learning to walk."

October 1: This afternoon, we walked and talked with our friend Elena on the Arbat—an old street in Moscow which has been restored and turned into a shopping mall. We watched one young man speak to a gathering crowd. "We must get rid of the slave, the bolshevik, inside ourselves," he said. "Only we can do that work . . . . This system is not humanitarian for people. I want to be independent and live by my conscience." Other groups on the street were arguing passionately. Glasnost in full flower!

We've seen great changes since we first came here in 1983, though the pot's been coming to a boil for fifteen years or so. In Leningrad on one of our trips, we met with a group of artists and intelligentsia. They proclaimed, "We've been speaking out for ten years now, regardless of the consequences. We cannot live any other way." The critical mass was building.

Elena is, like most others, afraid of the much publicized, growing crime rate in Moscow. There are now a handful of murders everyday in Moscow, a city of about nine million (eight million registered). She said, "People, especially the young, are pessimistic. There is something terrible in the air. We can feel it. Life is horrible—no food, no good medical care, and people are poor. And I'm still afraid of the KGB because I don't know who they are or what they do."

Fear of an unknown future is a very powerful emotion right now among Soviets. And it seems more evident in the big cities because people don't have the security of growing their own food. Western freedom is not attractive to some Soviets because they see complete freedom as chaos. And so it is, compared to what they've had. Eventually, freedom will be

accompanied by responsibility and full regard for fellow humans. It's going
to be productive and satisfying.

Glasnost in action. Moscow man "on soapbox," saying, "We
must get the Bolshevik out of our souls."

Leaving Elena, we met our ski-trip guide, who spent two months in the
US last summer. He loved his time in America. But he did say, "Americans
are good people, and they are so free, but they're soft intellectually; they
don't read and they don't care. They have so much in the way of material
things that they don't need their friends' generosity, as we do here." He
added, "I think the Soviet Union is going to be like the US was in the 20s,
with speculation, mafia control, and crime."

Ralph and I continue to be optimistic and feel perestroika will eventually
succeed—due to increased participation of citizens in politics and government. Tomorrow, we shall leave Moscow on Finnair, change planes in
Helsinki, fly to New York, and then on to our dear families and friends in
Dayton.

Strangely, I feel a change within me. Now I notice that I care very little
for material things. All I see is shining spirit, connecting people—people
similarly caught in their diverse circumstances, people doing the best they
can.

Goodnight, all our Soviet brothers and sisters whom we love so much!
Peaceful night to you! How beautiful that it is peace the Russians wish each
other at night! May it soon be so!

From left: Toli, Lusa, Tanya, Valeri (waving goodbye).

CHAPTER 9

Letters from Soviets
by Christine

As a result of our media exposure, Ralph and I received 55 letters from Soviets while we were in Makov. I answered every letter except one and had quite a correspondence going with a few people. Some we ultimately met. I told each one whether or not we could help them in their requests. Here are some examples:

Two people asked to work on Ralph's farm. One was a man from Siberia who invited us to visit. He wrote that he wanted to work with Americans. Another—a retired helicopter pilot with a family—said he was quite impressed with the *Izvestia* article. He wants to be engaged in personal farming and asked to work on Ralph's farm at no pay. However, only experienced labor is needed on the Ohio farm. Still, if Ralph is ever a consultant on a Soviet farm, we'll contact these men to see if they can work there.

One of the stranger requests came from a man who wrote a card addressed only to me. He asked that I send two full-length photos of myself. If I did, he said, he would tell me more about what he wanted. This letter I did not answer.

Another letter came from an author who wanted information about the life of coal miners in Pittsburgh between 1907 and 1922. He had been working for many years on a documentary about a friend who became a hero and great scientist. This friend had spent his early years with his family in Pittsburgh, PA. He also sent two books of stories he had written, hoping we'll be able to get them published in the US. I'll see what I can do on both counts, but it may take a while.

A man who's in charge of a Museum of Bread wanted pictures and some of Ralph's writings for display there. He asked for the address of a similar museum in the US. A Museum of Bread seems strange to us, but bread is a near-sacred symbol in the Soviet Union, due to the famines and wars. Then, bread must have seemed divine.

Also, an inventor wrote about his "microsaturator." This device turns ordinary well water into a carbonated version, "meeting all the needs of a farmer." I explained how difficult it is to get an invention into production in the States and said we couldn't help him.

A loader wrote about the wonder medicine he had concocted. He claims it eliminates backache, warts, fungus, two kinds of heart diseases, baldness, alcohol and smoking addiction, cockroaches, moths, and worms. He said we probably had at least one of those problems and asked, "Would you like to try some?" He also wanted us to try to sell it back home. I explained such selling isn't easy and is out of our line. Thus, we wouldn't be able to help him.

One letter came from a renter. He wanted a copy of Ralph's "Considerations for Land Renters" and answers to his questions about pork production. He ended by saying, "It's a pity we don't have *real* rent relations. Rent contracts don't give high results, though it's a step forward." He lives the problems of renters, and Ralph sent a lengthy reply.

I had quite a correspondence with a woman who has the prettiest handwriting I've ever seen. We thought she was a young woman because of the energy in her letter. Later correspondence revealed she was actually 75 years old. She first wrote asking us to find the address of a 93-year-old man in Philadelphia, a Charles Osborn. Ralph said we'd better hurry. We'll try to find him, however.

Then she wrote about religion, saying she liked the program entitled "Religion in Our Lives" on Voice of America. In one letter she talked about the great theologian Paul Tillich and his book, *The Courage to Be*. I wrote asking her how she knew about him and his works. She explained—people get their religious education from books on atheism! These books, she said, usually have some brief information about the Bible or religious books, followed by a long criticism and "Many people just ignore the criticism." Also, she said, "In religion, compassion for people is the most important thing."

She was interested in nature, natural processes, and agriculture. She talked about the "geobiological web of the earth," the effects of music on plants and animals, moon phases and planting time, starting a goat farm and giving the milk to a hospital, organic farming, and finding a medicine to combat AIDS. She's one lively babushka!

The last two people I'll mention wrote heart-breaking letters. A woman wrote saying she had read in the *Izvestia* article that we wanted to know more about the Soviet people, their life, salaries, etc. She wrote:

> You've been given a two-story house, a car, and expensive furniture. I am a teacher and my husband is a worker—we worked since we were ten—and we were honest and got awards. But our whole life has been misery. There was never enough food, we've never seen a color TV, had a car, good footwear, or expensive

furniture. We aren't paid according to our labor in the USSR. Those who don't do anything get high salaries. We were surprised at how much you pay your working people. My husband worked in a factory and liked to work. But then he lost his health—he's an invalid—and our state considers people like this the waste of society. There aren't enough hospitals—not even stinking barracks—for medical treatment.

Our rulers hate the people, and what they say beautifully are only lies. You can't speak the truth in the USSR; they'll kill you for it. I'm also an invalid. The medical service took away my most precious thing—my health—and crippled me. When I started to tell the truth, they stopped treating me and stopped my pension. It's now 33 rubles a month. Can a sick person afford to live on this kind of money? Our life has reminded us of a concentration camp because we have to depend on stupid supervisors. But what can we do?

Our communists live like millionaires; they don't work, they only go abroad on the pretext of learning about capitalist countries. Please help us to see your country and how you live, at least for a few days. My husband will work and help.

I wrote back, saying how extremely sorry I was about their suffering. But I said I thought Gorbachev and some others in power really cared about people and were trying to make life better for them.

I wondered how an invalid like the woman's husband could work. However, I know now there are three classes of invalids in the USSR. The least handicapped are people with heart trouble or high blood pressure.

Her second letter was also pitiful. She told of being persecuted for her honesty on the job:

I was a teacher by training and taught kids to be honest and just. All my life I was persecuted for this by our authorities. I've never hurt anyone, not even a cat, and I worked honestly. I could not adapt to life because it meant to cheat someone, to sell, to speculate, etc. It's very hard for me to live in the USSR both morally and materially. You cannot even imagine that. I cannot lie or cheat, but no one needs my truth, my honesty, my soul. Finally, I wasn't allowed to teach. I saw how the ruling Communists cheat, steal, and speculate with our nations' wealth, and I could not keep silent about that. That's why I was persecuted.

Her third letter contained these words:

I'd like to live just one day in a free country to see the order in life, where people are paid according to their work. I'd like to eat real food. It would be a happiness in my life. But we are exploited slaves and always will be. Our people are angry. They are tired with life, and that's why they're cruel. They adjust to life as they can.

The last writer mentioned here is Alexei. He also had read the *Izvestia* article about our fine provisions as guests of the collective farm. He wrote:

In our country we have a model of everything; this is done for foreigners, to make them think we all live well.

Now I'll write about *our* collective farm. There are no black-topped roads; only caterpillar tractors can go on ours when it rains. On our farm the fertilizers have no roof, so they are washed away by the rain to the River Don and the Sea of Azov. As a result, the fish die. During corn harvest, more than half remains in the field—15 centners per hectare [24 bushels per acre]. They don't allow people to take it but quickly plow it under so no one can see it. Vegetables, watermelons, potatoes—thousands of hectares are not harvested—and there's little in the stores. Why plant? There's nothing to feed cattle in the winter. They harvest corn for silage poorly, and hay is left in the fields. They get two or three liters of milk a day from a cow [one-eighth the average of American cows]. There are long lines in the stores at the milk department, but there is not enough milk for everyone. Many cattle die.

In 1933, I lived in Ukraine during the famine. People ate crows, dogs, cats, turtles, everything alive! It's a wonder I survived. Of 520 households in my village, half of the people died. There were even cases of cannibalism. I write the truth to you. I think people are telling you much about the famine, and any Ukrainian will tell you about it.

In my dreams, I often see your country. I'll never be able to see it because it's expensive to go, and I can't save any money. Prices at the co-op stores are three to four times higher than at state stores. At the co-op stores there is some food, but at the state store the shelves are empty.

We live on the same planet, but how do each of us live? You live in a civilized country where you can buy everything. I live in Stalin's creation. For 62 years I've been living in boiling oil. I think my life is coming to an end. In our country there's a film called *Life Goes By*.

If you have a farmer of Ukrainian origin, I would like to get acquainted with him. God bless you both.

Alexei said in his second letter to us:

Gorbachev does his best to improve the life of the working people, but we have many bureaucrats, bribe takers, and drunkards.

Before 1917, we had the same as you have now. But in 1930 we were collectivized. Those who didn't want to join the collective farm were "enemies of the people," and most were forced to join. They were summoned by the people responsible for collectivization and were told to write an application to be a member. When a man refused, the one in charge took a gun and directed it to the head of the refuser, and under fear of death, he wrote the application as if he were joining voluntarily.

They closed all the churches. The priests, as enemies of the people, were sent to Solovetsky Isles where they died from hunger, disease, and hard work. Dear friends, even the fascists, our deadly enemies, did not do what was done by order of *dear* leader Stalin. I was in occupied territory and saw everything myself.

We now have full democracy. I would like Bush and Gorbachev to meet and make an agreement on trade, reductions of nuclear weapons, and improvement of agriculture, especially in Russia, because we have hundreds of thousands of abandoned villages. No one works on this land, the weeds are two or three meters [yards] high, as high as American corn.

I think that in your book you will mention how corn and wheat are harvested here. On wheat, we have 10 percent losses. It's done today as before, only "quicker and more." Our Gorbachev has often spoken about that, but there are no changes.

We invited Alexei to visit us, but he felt too frail to do so. He did arrange to speak with us by phone one day, but (alas!) that day, all the phone service was out in Makov. Our hearts went out to both of these last two letter-writers.

So it is with life in the Soviet Union. People are content and discontent, happy and sad, energetic and lazy, rich and poor, optimistic and pessimistic. Sounds like American life, only in different proportions. The people want to secede from something, perhaps from the past and present more than from the Union of Soviet Socialist Republics. They need each other, but under a structure that works for human fulfillment for everyone. Don't we all? If misery loves company, Soviets can look to the south of them. But they're looking to the West, and they feel restless and cheated politically and economically. The USSR has more than adequate human and national resources. When will the roadblocks be removed?

CHAPTER 10

Soviet Potpourri
by Ralph

When Chris and I present slide shows or talk about our visits to the Soviet Union, certain questions invariably arise. Americans, it seems, are just as interested in Soviet lifestyles and their political and economic systems as the Soviets are in ours. This chapter addresses the topics people ask us about most.

How do elections work in the USSR? Soon after we arrived in the USSR in March, 1989, there was an "All-Union" election of the 2,250 People's Deputies who constitute the Moscow Congress. Fifteen hundred were elected from equally-populated districts. Another 750 were chosen by various organizations and groups. This Congress met twice that year for several weeks at a time. Early on, 542 of its members were elected to the Supreme Soviet—a body that meets most of the year to debate and legislate. (The Supreme Soviet elected Gorbachev President.) Members of Congress take turns serving in the [national] Supreme Soviet. In addition, each of the 15 republics has a Supreme Soviet of its own. We arrived in a history-making year: 1989 was the first time this entire election procedure was carried out. It was also the first time most ballots listed more than one candidate per position. In fact, a run-off of top vote-getters for each office was often necessary to ensure that every elected deputy had a majority vote from his district.

In future elections, all 2,250 People's Deputies will be elected by districts. This change will satisfy complaints that many of the 750 deputies elected by organizations represent very small groups. Competition meant many candidates campaigned hard. (Toli was campaign manager for one successful candidate.) The voting public rebelled in forty cases where the party managed to restrict the ballot to a single candidate—always an old party functionary. Voters turned down these lone candidates, and new elections were held. This happened to an old pol in Leningrad. When he complained, Gorbachev told him, "You can't *make* voters want you."

On that March election day, there was a ninety percent voter turn-out, though response was lower for the runoffs. A strange situation developed when the deputies in Congress elected the Supreme Soviet. Boris Yeltsin, leader of the Moscow liberal faction, didn't make it in. Another man dropped out so Yeltsin could take his place.

The Congressional proceedings were so new and exciting, Soviets were glued to their TVs tighter than Americans are during the World Series. Eventually, day sessions were tape-recorded and shown at night because many citizens were staying home from work to watch Congress! Although some debates were heated, order was maintained. Procedures seemed to work as well as in the US—one difference being that in Moscow, Congressional seats are full. Their committee work is similar to ours.

When the 542-member Supreme Soviet was formed, sixty journalists (11%) were among them. We think this is good because, as a whole, Soviet journalists are bright and progressive. Seventeen percent of the Supreme Soviet were women, nineteen percent "workers," and eleven percent farmers. There was also an increased number of intelligentsia compared to previous Supreme Soviets. As in the past, many aren't members of the Communist Party. Of course, the Central Committee and the Politburo are all party members.

In the spring of 1990, elections were held to form new local, district and regional soviets (councils). Democratization hadn't reached the local level yet when we were there—the hierarchical system was very much in place on the farm and on up the ladder. However, Toli has been nominated by the Ukraina collective farm machine yard workers to run against the Chairman for a position on the District soviet. He could very well win. Perhaps that's why the local party secretary has tried to intimidate the machine yard workers, without success.

Are Soviet cooperatives like American ones? The word co-op doesn't have the same meaning in the USSR as it does in the States. In America, a co-op is an association of many people who join together in cooperation to own, sell, or buy the goods they produce or consume, or the services they give or need. Its purpose is to save money for members by combining orders or sales. Also, a group of families may set up a credit union bank to make loans to each other.

Most co-ops in the Soviet Union, however, look like private businesses. They manufacture or purchase wherever they can, and set prices much higher than state stores charge. Many consumers are hostile toward co-ops because some buy out a state store item, take it across the street, and then triple its price. In the future, when there are more co-ops and items for sale, competition will keep prices in line. But how do co-ops go from no competition to complete competition without chaos?

Some USSR cooperatives are really large conglomerates. The co-ops have been given a wide range of failed factories by the state. These factories now pay high wages, demand maximum effort from employees, and become profitable. However, most co-ops are the one-family type or are owned by a small group of friends who share profits. A typical co-op is a single restaurant, or small clothing store.

Greedy co-ops give co-ops a bad name in general and may cause the state and consumers to squash them all. If that happens, economic perestroika is over. Moving from complete state ownership—with its central planning, price setting, and administering—to private ownership—and thus individual planning, pricing, and administering—is one gigantic step. Toss in the need for making the low-value ruble convertible into hard currency, and we have to feel sorry for the promoters of perestroika. Soviet planners are curious about the formation of US cooperatives and how a similar structure might work for them.

It's also a big challenge for the USSR to establish a system for small and big farm loans which is fair, encouraging to farmers, and beyond corruption. Where money is involved, dishonesty lurks just around the corner. Money must not be used as a tool to force farmers into doing what officials want them to do. Loans should be a tool to help responsible Soviet farmers advance the country and themselves at the same time. Several US farmer cooperatives established between 1917 and 1935 are still going strong. Perhaps they can provide a workable model for Soviet cooperatives.

How is construction handled? Two heavy horses were plodding round and round the front yard of a house under construction in Makov. An old man was riding one horse while leading the other with a rope. They were walking knee-deep in mud—a mixture of layered clay, straw, and water—in a boxed-in area 30 feet across. Why? The straw-mud mixture would be used for an adobe-like ceiling in the new house. Boards had been propped up to form a temporary ceiling ready to receive the mixture. The mud is then carried in buckets up a ladder to the attic. There it's poured onto the loose-fitting boards. Days later, after the water has evaporated, the props and boards are removed.

The man with the horses seemed to be a specialist for hire. At one point, he took the horses out of the mud to rest them and added more straw and water to the goop. He struggled to get back on his horse, but was too old or too intoxicated to get his right leg over the top without the assistance of two boys who rushed to his aid. Back into the 12-inch-deep mud they went, the horses struggling to thoroughly mix in the new layer of straw.

In the Soviet Union, building a house takes two to five years. The work is done by the family or a private crew hired by them. A village culture-center building has been under construction for 13 years. By now, the roof leaks and interior damage has occurred, creating controversy as to who will fix it. Many windows are also broken before construction is completed. Nobody cares. There are no American-type lumber yards to go to for a wide choice of building supplies. Materials to build a house are available via the collective farm chairman or through private deals using the *managing-to-get* technique. Incidentally, there are few apartments in the villages and almost no individual houses in the cities.

Truck cranes are numerous because pre-cast concrete is used, not only for Berlin Walls and dairy barns but also for houses. For individual residences, the concrete cubes are typically four feet long, two feet high, and one foot wide. They are planted in the earth for a foundation. Sometimes this pre-cast concrete is set all the way up to the roof by a crane, leaving openings for doors and windows. It seems like a waste of material to have interior and exterior walls of solid concrete a foot thick. Other houses have eight-inch brick walls starting from the foundation. The bricks are crude and unfinished, so the houses require a covering of stucco or glazed tile. This finish is very attractive—until it starts to fall off.

Whitewash tinted with pastel colors, especially blue, is plentiful and is generously applied to stucco walls every year. Both stucco and tile exteriors are sometimes relief-decorated by skillful masons. Interiors are attractive and quite comfortable. In summer, the colorful houses are complemented by flowers, fruit trees and sometimes vegetables in the surrounding small yards. The large gardens are out back. There are no smoothly mowed lawns here. These descriptions fit poor villages as well as prosperous ones.

The houses are owned by the occupants, and the people do a nice job in their private domain. However, public amenities such as streets are often neglected. Some villages can't get asphalt or other material for street construction. In contrast, Makov received enough asphalt to cover an acre in front of Headquarters—even though the old blacktop was still in good condition. We only hope there will soon be enough of everything so strings won't have to be pulled for basic needs in the future. Smooth, hard-surfaced village streets would raise the morale of the people tremendously. For now, the houses, trees, and flowers are pretty, but the streets in most villages are muddy or dusty with moon-crater features.

A new dairy facility is being built by state crews at the edge of Makov near the apple orchard. It will be occupied by 200 milk cows and 700 calves. (The infant calves will be purchased from other dairy farms.) An office building just for this dairy has 28 rooms, and there are additional employee rooms in the cow barns! Ohio cows could never pay for facilities as extravagant as this two-story brick office building covered with decorative glazed tile. You can be sure the dairy complex is close enough to the road to be seen by passersby. What disgusts me may impress tourists though, I, too, believe buildings should be neat and attractive. However, it's not fair to ask cows or tax payers to finance a beauty contest between collective farms, even if the luxuries are "for the people." These frills can come after basic needs are met. The total cost of this project is 2 million rubles. (For comparison, the average monthly wage on the farm is 160 rubles.)

We saw a second dairy setup being built on another progressive farm 70 miles to the east. Both dairies will use the tie method (in which animals are tied in stalls with neckchains) rather than the modern, milking parlor method employed in America. The Khmelnitski project started before the new chairman arrived. Now he's stuck with it, although he prefers the loose-housing milking parlor system. However, he's interested in extravagances as well. For instance, he was excited about the American computerized system of feeding varying amounts of grain to each cow automatically according to her milk production. I had to say many other economies need to be achieved in the USSR dairy business before fine-tuning with a sophisticated computer feeding system. He is to be complimented on his creativity and desire to develop the best of everything for his farm and its workers. But it seems to be *his* farm and his show. He doesn't believe *his* people can shoulder management responsibility. The contrast continues: 10 percent of the farms are full-speed-ahead, getting resources from somewhere, and 90 percent are just existing. In the US, the reverse may be true.

Because construction workers are employed by the state and wages are low, there's not much concern about how many people it takes to build a structure, how long construction goes on, or how many people it takes to operate it. (This isn't necessarily true for private houses which are privately built.) Therefore, a multitude of women are employed to move wet concrete to build the new dairy, for example. Also, there's no factory in each region to make roof trusses for houses and barns. That would be a tremendous labor and wood-saving technique, but I saw no factory-made trusses in the USSR.

We saw piles of broken pre-cast beams wasted because reinforcement iron in the concrete was not correctly positioned. Six concrete posts, 18 inches square by 20 feet tall, were planted in concrete down the center of a new hay-drying barn. Later, they were pulled down and broken when the building plan changed. Who pays for such mistakes? The state and the collective farm; ultimately, the people.

The state designs and builds new facilities and then turns them over to the people to use. The designer should personally experience building, using, repairing, and paying for one of these systems.

On the Dull farm, I design the buildings myself with these factors in mind. I know my sons and I will be doing the construction, paying for the material and equipment, operating the facilities, and doing the repairs ourselves. Also, we don't want half-built structures sitting around unused for years. Then fixed costs of interest, insurance, and depreciation continue with no income to offset them. Soviets don't worry about such expenses because it's the state's money. Interest rates, if there are any, may be only three percent.

Personal profit or loss is the key to efficiency. Central planning and state ownership are supposed to be good for ecology and non-exploitative, but they don't seem to get the job done.

Construction in cities is more sophisticated. Stationary cranes seem like permanent parts of the skyline. Major cities limit their population to match the orderly growth of housing—mainly high-rise apartments on the fringes of the cities. Urban growth swallows up farm villages, and cottages are replaced by these high-rise buildings. We've never seen a Western-style suburbia in the USSR. Farmland is adjacent to the last high-rise apartments (flats).

Hotels built by Finland and Sweden are luxurious. Other structures erected since WWII usually have stucco falling off and contain drab halls and elevator shafts. The flats themselves though are usually quite nice. Many are remodeled by their occupants, though the plumbing remains inferior. Flat roofs are common, and drain pipes extend from roof to sidewalk.

Is Soviet electricity like ours? Gazing across the rolling landscape of Ukraine, I know this patchwork of green corn, golden wheat, and dark-green forest unfurls under the same sky, sun, and spaceships that are over the USA. The only flaw marring this peaceful scene is the presence of concrete-and-wood poles, holding up the power lines. All farm buildings and houses are in the villages. Lenin was big on electricity. Even remote reaches of this vast country have it. Most electricity comes from hydro generators, like those I saw operating on the Volga River near Volgograd (I was permitted to go down a ladder and touch them) and nuclear generators, like Chernobyl's.

There was little concern for the farmers' inconvenience when these poles were consistently placed in the middle of fields. Farmers hate utility poles, especially since crop-growing equipment has gotten large. We dream of spacious, uninterrupted fields, especially when near the end of a long day of planting, with a marker extended 30 feet out to the side, a utility pole marches up to hit the marker. Then the farmer says to himself, "I can't believe I didn't see that pole" before he solemnly heads for the heating torch and welder. Experiencing this even one time is once too often. In the USSR, wooden utility poles are strapped to concrete stubs in the ground.

Soviet current is 50HZ, so American exporters of motorized equipment need to take note. The central (what else?) heating system of our Makov house was electric. Electricity heated water for radiators in each room. A rhythmic banging began every time the heat came on. Our control looked like a clock behind glass. I frequently had to set its two hands with a screw driver for upper and lower limits.

Although electricity is plentiful, the street lights past Headquarters in Makov automatically turn off at midnight. I enjoy the complete darkness of country nights. My childhood nights were spent in the black velvet that existed before outdoor lighting became popular in rural areas to scare away thieves. Sometimes I long for the abolition of artificial lights. Then we would go to sleep with the sun and get up with the rooster. We could dis-invent the telephone, too, and live in peace forever.

What about telephone service? Phone service in rural Ukraine is often primitive. There is direct dialing within the district, but few people have phones. A second phone must be dialed for operator assistance when calling outside the district. Then the operator uses plug-in equipment to transfer calls like I saw in my Ohio village in the 30s.

High officials have phone access however. The Chairman has four phones, each a different color, lined up on his desk for various purposes. One day we were in his office. After the Chairman stepped out for a moment, a phone rang. We took a photo of Toli, hand hovering above the phones, anxiously trying to decide which was ringing.

Although Toli is one of the highest paid villagers and is very busy with community work, he had no phone before we arrived. Even as a teacher, he couldn't visit with his students' parents over the phone. Instead, he periodically borrows a bike and rides to each home for parent visits. None of the teachers have a car to use. Toli asked us several times to take him around in ours, just to save time.

(The lack of cars is apparent in other ways, too. For instance, it's odd for us, as Americans, to approach a village school or church and not see a single car there. The villagers were amazed at our photo of an American high school. It revealed a parking lot full of teachers' cars and an even larger lot behind the school packed with the students' automobiles.)

The officials and farm leaders on the collective farm all have radio phones in their jeeps to keep in touch with Headquarters. It's common for the Chairman, the party secretary, the chief agronomist, and the District and Regional officials to have a driver sitting in their jeeps at all times—in case a call comes over the radio phone.

Almost everything about the United States is fascinating to the Soviets, even a discussion about telephone books. Our phone books with thousands of names in them, our Yellow Pages, and our direct dialing to anyone in the country is unbelievable to villagers.

Even when villagers have ready access to telephones, very little business is done by phone. Further, permissions and deals have to be hand-delivered in writing and signed by the proper officials. Toli and I experienced this for a whole day on one occasion. In Ohio, similar tasks could be accomplished over the phone in five minutes. For instance, when Viktor and Nik planned to go out of state, my son called the State Department only to inform them, not for permission.

When our Makov phone was out of order, which happened frequently, Toli seemed to know where to find the guy who knew how to fix it. Once, all the village phones, including Headquarters', weren't working for three days.

Due to this lack of phone service, it is common to see cars, bicycles, or motorcycles stopped along the streets and roads while their occupants or pedestrians conduct business with each other. Deals are made or information about desired purchase items is garnered—all transactions Americans would do over the phone. To get sugar, for example, we had to track down a man driving a red car with a certain license number. It was like a treasure hunt.

Even when phones are available, communication isn't easy. Toli and Chris had to yell to be heard on the many long-distance calls. Because some calls to Moscow or the US take days to arrange, hanging up and trying for a better line is out of the question. One day we needed to make an urgent call to Austria to a *Time* reporter who had interviewed us, because the article was going to have an adversarial twist. The operator said she couldn't get through. Then Toli told her his American friends needed to complete the call to avoid an international incident. Pronto, the lines opened up!

RANDOM TIDBITS: As I wrote about Soviet Agriculture, many random memories and opinions came to mind. Since people in both countries are curious about these topics, here are my thoughts on 16 of them.

Will the Soviet Union Survive? There is much talk about the secession of several of the fifteen republics that form the Soviet Union. As a result, Americans often say, "The USSR is falling apart." Of course, this statement suggests each republic will completely sever itself from Russia. Americans were shocked to learn even the republic of Russia wants more sovereignty. The language we prefer is "Each republic will have a high degree of political and economic independence." This phrasing allows room for economic cooperation and perhaps even a little political federating.

For instance, we hope the Baltics can sell their excess production at a fair price and govern themselves. Still, they're lacking many resources that logically could be purchased from the Russian and other republics. The republics need each other, but under a better arrangement than they've had in the past. In visualizing the new arrangement, we picture a large tree stump labeled USSR. It has at least 15 new branches, one for each republic, growing up from its sides. The old has been cut away, but the sovereign republics are still joined together.

We refuse to predict the future of the USSR. But let us hope for the above-mentioned relationship of republics—with a spirit of cooperation for mutual benefit. Secession will not eliminate frictions because within each republic are Russians and other nationalities.

The Russian bear has come a long way since Stalin in how it treats neighbors. However, in the case of those who dissent, the USSR still has a long way to go. Still, it behooves Americans to remember that Washington, D.C., didn't take kindly to the departure of the South in 1860 either.

We feel the desire for independence by various republics is justified, however. Sometimes drastic actions must be taken to shake up an unjust system and change it for the better.

In a sense, the USSR is an old oak tree that has had a couple of sticks of dynamite (people power) under it for years. Gorbachev came along and lit the fuse. Two sticks of dynamite will shake a sturdy oak tree, but won't blow it to pieces and cause it to die. If the Soviets can reorganize to use their available mental, spiritual, and physical resources, they will be a true superpower in the best sense of the word. In these hard times, it's natural for each republic or nationality group to be angry with somebody. Moscow, or an adjoining nationality, is a likely target.

In addition to the Baltics, our impression is that Moldavia would like to be a part of Romania again. Georgia is rebellious and so are Armenia, Azerbaijan, and Uzbekistan. Ukraine is starting to boil as well. And Central Asia has many fundamentalist Moslems who identify with the Middle East.

How are babushkas cheated? Most village families raise animals for meat to supplement their food supply or income. The situation frequently arises that a widow, for instance, has a cow or pig to be butchered. She can't do it herself, so the manager of the butchering house comes to buy the animal. The problem is *he* estimates the weight of the animal and *he* sets the price. He's also the only buyer in the district. The widow isn't skilled at guessing weight and price, so she accepts his offer. This explains why butchers have cars and big houses. The question is, why aren't the animals weighed? Every village has scales to weigh everything from cattle to grain to manure to silage, for daily reports to the government.

Who will motivate the people? Americans often notice the number of posters and amount of haranguing that goes on in the Soviet Union. Posters and speeches urging people to work better and harder are not effective anymore, if they ever were. Reorganization from the fields to Moscow is the greatest need. When power comes from the people, self-motivation develops, and more is accomplished.

What about Soviet regimentation and laziness? After working on the Dull farm, Viktor Palamarchouk was enthusiastic about farmers' deciding for themselves when to start the day's labor and what jobs need to be done. Considerations such as the weather, season, type of work involved, or the level of ambition all play a part when making work decisions for American farmers. On the collective farm at Makov, however, Palamarchouk went to the machine yard at 7 o'clock every morning whether there was work to do or not. The fact that many categories of workers are on a job site without enough work to do leads to idleness. Drinking and low morale are the likely results. Specialization (such as drivers who only drive trucks) also contributes to idleness. Soviets are not inherently lazy.

American farmers may waste time, but you won't see them just sitting in a truck, lying on a grain pile, or snoozing under a tree on the back forty, like we saw workers do in the USSR. It's also common for Soviet factory workers to drink and play cards, even when there's work to be done, because the state-run system allows it. Some workers who begin working for co-ops (private enterprise) complain because they're not allowed to drink and play cards on the job. According to the *Moscow News*, even though co-op wages may be double those of state wages, some workers go back to the state factory where they can loaf.

Many people on the farms, though, work long and hard and take pride in their work. However, the temptation is to loaf and be careless in a state-run operation.

How important is ideology? Poland's Lech Walesa says, "We want to develop an effective market economy, and approach this pragmatically rather than ideologically. Of substantial importance is the reconditioning of the values of social justice."

Too many bureaucrats? The USSR needs bureaucrats, but not so many. Further, they need to become servants of the people. There are currently eighteen to twenty million bureaucrats. A Soviet anecdote illustrates the difference between workers and higher-ups:

> A foreigner is watching people walking at 7 A.M. in their work clothes. "Who are they?" he asks. He's told they are "the people." At 9 A.M., he sees men in ties go by in fancy black or white cars. "Who are they?" asks the foreigner. "They are the servants of the people," was the answer.

Why the Soviet fear of mistakes? The fear system is still in effect in the USSR, so many Soviets are reluctant to grant a request in case it results in punishment from a superior. It's such a waste of time for bureaucrats or business people to have to consult a superior—who, in turn, must consult his or her superiors—especially for routine matters. Americans find all this puzzling as we tend to delegate responsibility. If the employee makes too many mistakes, the manager will help him or replace him because a person is hired to make decisions.

Command or consult? Most Soviets are still entrenched in the approach that in order to get something done, a strong command must come from somewhere. Arriving at a plan of action by the quiet discussion route is uncommon, whether it be a political or agricultural question. People were surprised to hear that decisions on the Dull farm are made by equal input from all workers.

Is the party over? Of the 19,000,000 Communist Party members, few joined the party for purely ideological reasons, especially in recent years. We've met many people who've left the party, many members who are indifferent, some who have benefitted materially and have special privileges, several who are confused, and a surprising number who are critical of the party. Some members would rather be capitalists. We didn't meet anyone, however, who defended the present system, not even a current party member.

People who joined the party long ago for noble reasons are becoming disillusioned as they hear more about the actions of Stalin and others over the last seventy years. This leads us to two conclusions. If all Soviets, including party members, could express their true thoughts at the same moment, there would be no one left to do the punishing for such statements. The system and ideology would disappear—poof! That's close to what happened in the Eastern Bloc countries. Not only would the command-and-administer system be gone, but so would the Communist Party as the dominant force in government. Because of the soft, less-than-dedicated membership of the party, it's like a structure on a jelly foundation.

Ordinary members don't receive big privileges. They join hoping their lives may be made a little easier or because it's the natural progression for many young people—Pioneer to Komsomol to party member. New party members are required to put some effort into the organization. In return, certain career advancements, for instance, are more likely if one is a party member.

The party could lose its hold on the people in another way, too. It's inevitable as the Supreme Soviet in Moscow takes more power, and democratization shifts more power to local soviets in the villages and cities, the party will automatically have less power. These governing groups are increasingly made up of non-party people who are elected from multi-candidate ballots. However, party bosses don't give up easily. We know they are still strong in Ukraine.

In a sense, there were three parties in Moscow in 1989: the Yeltsin-types on the liberal side pulling for faster reforms, the Gorbachevs in the middle, and the Ligachevs on the conservative side, resisting serious reform. The Politburo and Central Committee are not the only shows in town anymore.

How can there be rich and poor in a socialist country? When the shortage of everyday goods in a socialist society brings on a favor system, that system has the worst feature of *pure* capitalism—the rich get richer and the poor get poorer. Since it's inevitable that he who has, gets more, the US has developed a controlled capitalism. But President Reagan opened the floodgates again.

Are Soviets concerned about the environment and clean food? During our stay, many Soviets were talking and writing about chemical-free food and cleaning up the air and water. Not much has been done yet, but we know of co-ops that want to produce clean food for foreigners living in the USSR (in embassies, etc.). Many foreigners will pay hard currency for food that meets international standards. Also, environmental groups are analyzing the rivers and air. We haven't seen any lead-free gasoline yet. Laws and an enforcement effort on manufacturing is beginning thirty years after a similar effort in America. An example of this new environmental concern occurred when our orchard friends in Makov had to send a sample of their apples to a laboratory for testing for contamination before they could sell a truckload in Moscow.

As for clean food, both countries have a long way to go. Organic farming exists in the US, but not on a large scale yet. There's a modest market for natural foods, and they bring a high price. It's difficult to test all the produce that claims to be naturally grown—a necessary procedure to keep everyone honest.

For our part, Dull Homestead wants to quit using herbicides to kill weeds. Unfortunately, we don't know how to control weeds naturally and still produce the crop volume and income needed for five families. No-till farming conserves soil, fuel, water, etc., but herbicides are necessary for weed control. On rare occasions we use insecticides, though this doesn't make us any different from most Americans. One-third of the nation's pesticides are used in and around the house. It needs to be stated that some chemicals are not so poisonous. For instance, insecticides are much more hazardous than herbicides, fungicides, or manufactured potash and phosphorous. To use the word "chemical" or "pesticide" with a wide paint brush approach can confuse the issue. Just for the sake of definition, insecticides kill creatures and herbicides kill plants, and both are pesticides.

What do Soviets think of Americans? As we visited with Soviet people, we realized it must not be possible for them to be free of resentment towards Americans, although they don't show it. Seventy years of cold war in the minds of Americans and Soviets isn't going to be erased suddenly. Anti-American and anti-Soviet sentiments were taught by both our governments and other groups. These brain wounds will linger for a while.

Soviets appear to be less affected by what they were told than Americans were. We hear most Soviets never disliked ordinary American citizens. Soviets knew their own government sometimes lied, about other things, while Americans tend to believe their government.

We're thankful great strides have been made in recent years to reduce these prejudices and misconceptions. It's almost a miracle Mikhail Gorbachev appeared on the scene with all his efforts for improvement. Even if the Soviet nation's domestic problems are never resolved, it shouldn't detract from this remarkably good man who is giving it his all outside the borders.

What about McCarthyism? No book should be written about a communist country without mentioning Senator Joe McCarthy. This man caused many a would-be reconciler with the Soviet Union to run for cover, by fanning the flames of anti-communism into an inferno. I got a little scorched once myself. In 1950, another volunteer and I were leading discussions in churches and schools about peacemaking in the world. A Keyser, West Virginia, newspaper called us communists after we held a session in a local high school about making peace with the Russians. If you weren't called a communist during the McCarthy era, it meant you were either a Russian-hater or hiding under a rock.

In 1991, we've shifted to a smaller foe and from cold to hot war. We can't seem to accept the no-communist dividend. Ironically, as many predicted, the falling of communism has nothing to do with Joe McCarthy or anyone else from the West fighting it. Will the West self-destruct, too?

Do Soviets need American-style insurance? Soviet wages aren't quite as bad as they sound because the state provides many services for them: free higher education and medical care, low food and insurance costs, and other benefits.

A major reason salaries must be higher in the US is simply to pay the insurance bills. There's medical insurance; disability insurance; liability insurance; life insurance; house insurance; car insurance; retirement insurance (in addition to Social Security deductions); fire and windstorm insurance on barns, livestock, and equipment; debt insurance; and crop insurance. The Dull farm pays about $60,000 each year just to insure five families and the farm. We hope the USSR can come up with a better insurance system than we have.

Do Soviets pay taxes? Soviet taxes are difficult to figure. Of a 300-ruble-per-month wage, 40 rubles may be withheld. However Toli figures since the wage should be 600 rubles, the state also takes an additional 300 rubles to pay for all the services it provides, including the military.

In America, taxes and death are certain. Sometimes taxes even continue after death. Americans pay estate tax, inheritance tax, property tax, sales tax, vehicle license tax, federal and state fuel tax, liquor tax, cigarette tax, tire tax, garbage tax, street light tax, highway use tax for truckers, telephone tax, federal Social Security tax, federal income tax, state income tax, city income tax, federal unemployment tax, and state employment services tax—just to mention the most common varieties! We are grateful there isn't still a poll tax to tax a person before voting.

How did we get so many kinds? To keep from raising existing taxes, politicians often invent new taxes. I think many of these could be consolidated, which would simplify everyone's life. The Soviet system has taxes, too, but nothing as ridiculously complicated as ours. They have ten times as many farmers, but we have something they don't have: a zillion tax attorneys and accountants.

As in the case of insurance, we hope the USSR can develop a simpler system to pay for public needs. Two ways to ease the strain on Soviet national finances are to continue reducing military spending and get agriculture straightened out so subsidies aren't necessary. That can happen when Soviet workers earn more, because they produce more, and then they can afford to pay for food what it costs to produce it. (Even with higher wages for farmers and agriculture-related workers, food production costs may not need to rise, because of higher production and efficiency per worker under a new system.)

What are sales and service like in the USSR? In the Soviet Union, people work hard just trying to find something to buy. In the US, hundreds of sellers work just as hard trying to find us. They spend fortunes trying to convince us we need to buy their item or service. They are in our living room by way of TV, they knock on our door, they call us on the telephone, and they stare at us from huge billboards while we walk or drive our cars. Their goods are fancifully displayed in large store windows. Their slogans are on blimps and banners pulled by airplanes above sports events, and they look up at us from magazines just before we go to bed at night. What a relief to spend six months in Ukraine. Not once did we have to tell a salesperson, "Don't call me; I'll call you." When we traveled, there were no billboards cluttering the roads. All we saw were cows, chickens, ducks, people, and the beautiful landscape. Of course, walking a mile to a store only to find bare shelves isn't much fun, either. Maybe there's a happy medium.

Another big difference between US stores and USSR state stores is the Soviet stores don't worry about servicing the items they sell. The Soviet consumer has cause to celebrate if he just *finds* what he wants—let alone expect future repairs on it. When he walks out the door, it's for better or worse. If an appliance or piece of farm equipment doesn't work, he must hire someone to fix it—or fix it himself. For example, take the new samovar Toli gave us. Weeks and gifts later, it was finally rebuilt by a metal worker because original parts were unavailable. Sometimes farms virtually overhaul equipment fresh from the factory before they can use it. And we've heard the same about cars.

In the Soviet business world, everyone is suspect. Thus transactions require many signatures and permissions, and deals aren't normally made over the phone. The shadow economy rolls on anyway. An American businessman once told us a sort of dance goes on before a deal is closed. Once a businessperson in the USSR is sure the other party can be trusted, there is no better partner than a Soviet, this American said.

SUMMARY (as published for the Soviet readers, also): My intention while writing this multitude of opinions is simply to critically analyze the Soviet system. I do this because all Soviets are at risk if stagnation persists. It's not my intention to analyze or blame people, though. Directors, chairmen, other bureaucrats, or workers—we are all products of history. None of us sets out to be selfish or to mess up the economy and society. Thus, I restrict my observations to an analysis of methods, existing conditions, and organizational structures.

We want to cooperate with Soviets in an effort for social justice everywhere on earth. Too often American politicians reject a plan because it looks too socialistic. Other reasonable and logical solutions are rejected in the USSR because they look too capitalistic. Perhaps social justice can be the ideology of the world instead. In this world, everyone can climb the ladder without having to step on the fingers of others.

The necessary resources to build a better life are in the USSR right now, but resources are never unlimited. Agricultural resources, for example, are being wasted: people, soil, water, iron, fertilizer. Tradition, growing out of a certain type of collectivization for sixty years, is the biggest handicap . . . a pattern of thinking . . . or not thinking . . . waiting to be told . . . fear of punishment . . . for doing nothing wrong . . . perhaps for doing something right . . . for being too successful . . . fear of being sent away . . . starved . . . opinions not asked for . . . power and privilege only for the few.

What happened to creativity, adaptation, fearless criticism, industriousness, productivity, and the evasive high standard-of-living? Why hasn't the government and party trusted the people to make wise decisions? Why hasn't skill and knowledge been rewarded? Will collective and state farms be willing to sacrifice their old life for something better by helping independent farmers and granting democratic control to the community? Will young men and women, and some not so young, have enough self-confidence and the opportunity to venture out on their own? Some *have*, and many more want to.

The old command and administer system must go . . . peacefully, we hope. An abundance of food will be produced enthusiastically by Soviets working freely, while enjoying friendly cooperation from the rest of the world.

Part II

The Ukrainians: Sojourns with Americans

CHAPTER 11

The Other Side: Soviet Undercurrents
by Anatoli Kushnir

On the 10th of March, 1989, in the apartment of Viktor Palamarchouk, the telephone rang. The operator told us we could speak to the USA. I would do the actual talking while Viktor listened on the parallel phone, testing his English to get answers to his questions. Over the phone I heard a clear and distinct woman's voice, later joined by a profound and confident man's. I could hear well, and I asked about the weather, grandchildren, and plans for the future. Then I said Palamarchouk was to arrive in the USA on March 16, and we said goodbye.

I had just talked with an American farmer, Ralph Dull, and his wife, Christine. For me, it was something unreal, fantastic. I had met some Americans before at the institute where I studied. Guest professors from the USA gave us lectures there. But over the phone, I spoke—for the first time in my life—across the ocean . . .

There were rumors about an American farmer coming to work on the collective farm in Makov starting in September, 1988, but nobody knew for sure.

At the beginning of November, Palamarchouk, the chief maintenance engineer of Ukraina collective farm, asked me to help him with English. He had been chosen to work in the States. So we started. The whole procedure of sending him abroad was clouded by so much mystery that until the last day, he wasn't sure if he would go. Now I know how things went on the American side of the exchange, but who made the decisions on the Soviet side? I don't know even today. As it has always been in my country, the decisions were made at the misty heights.

At the end of March, Palamarchouk left for Moscow to fly to Washington. In Makov, everything was quiet. Suddenly, on the afternoon of April 5, I was summoned to the Chairman. He asked me to go to Kiev to meet the Dulls and bring them to Makov. I was supposed to be their interpreter. When I told this at home, my wife and mother-in-law became frightened; they realized the responsibility of my future job. I didn't think my English was wonderful, but I wasn't afraid. I had been a good student and had grown up in a village where I had learned about farming.

I expected some instructions about what I could and could not do with foreigners, but there were none. We were used to somebody else making the decisions, so when it was I who had to decide, the situation somewhat troubled me.

Everything went all right at the railway station, and also with visas. Late that afternoon we started to Makov in the collective farm's van—a long drive. At first, Ralph and Chris seemed a little anxious. They looked with interest at the fields and villages along the road. What was in store for them during the next six months? Later, when it became dark and only the lights of the van searched the road, it seemed to me the four of us were not Americans and Soviets, only people. Mostly Chris led the talk, with Ralph remaining silent. But when we got to some complicated questions, Ralph joined the conversation.

I think our friendship originated that night. I realized the Dulls were unusual people—those who form their own opinions and decide for themselves, people interested in a better fate for humankind. I became acquainted with a vision of the world I had only read about. I was meeting people who saw the earth as one big community. They considered themselves citizens of the world. It was midnight before we arrived safely in Stupentsi.

There is no need for me to tell you about Ralph and Chris day by day. Chris did that in her journal. First, I want to tell about the people of the village—about the people themselves, how they live, and what they think. They are the heart of the rural area, the eternal source of any nation.

I have never been taught to hate American people. Our people have always had deep sympathy with them and have considered the American nation to be very close to Soviets. We have always listened to, read about, or watched with interest our common fight against Hitler, the historic meeting on the Elbe River in 1945, and the Apollo-Soyuz space flight. Mark Twain, O'Henry, Jack London, William Faulkner, and J.D. Salinger are known and loved by Soviet readers. For many years, Ernest Hemingway has been a favorite writer of many here. (In fact, his writings are what inspired me to learn English.) We know your movies well, and now many people think an American movie means a good one.

Everything bad in America—homelessness, unemployment, crime, drugs, national arrogance—we thought resulted from capitalism and greedy capitalists, not the people.

The vast majority of villagers and other people were friendly and kind to the American couple. At first, it was mostly traditional hospitality. But later, when people got to know Ralph and Chris, they loved them and befriended them for their own personal qualities. Everywhere the Americans stopped, people came up to them and asked about their impressions, their farm, family, friends. Often Soviets wondered if the Dulls missed their home. They sympathized with the couple who were staying for so long in a strange country.

It's true that until recently, contact with foreigners wasn't welcomed by the authorities. The contacts were restricted, and those who had such contacts were suspect. One of the guest professors at our institute was a woman from the States who wanted to teach us American folk dances. At our meetings with the woman, there was always somebody from the party bureau. During the last rehearsal, the American gave us a tape of dance music and a booklet on folk dances. A woman from the party bureau snatched them out of my friend's hand, with the American woman desperately witnessing the scene. She asked, "Are they sure to get the things back?" The answer was, "Sure!" We never saw either gift again.

But party people weren't the only ones who didn't trust foreigners. The rank and file were constantly indoctrinated to suspect them (and each other) as well.

For instance, in 1984, a group of Americans came to Makov just to see the village. They visited the collective farm, the school, and the day care center. When they were about to leave, an American in his late 60s noticed a group of second-graders walking to the school dining hall, and he ran up to them. First, he took some pictures with his Polaroid. It was good the children's teacher was not at a loss and met the Americans with a smile.

Then the man remembered something, rushed to the bus, and elbowed his way in. Seconds later, he was out again. He took frisbees from his bag and threw them to the kids. The children got excited and ran to catch them. The American was excited, too; it was obviously quite fun for him to watch the happy kids. But on the way back to the bus, he felt the reproachful looks of Soviet officials, became embarrassed, and got on the bus, murmuring, "I didn't mean to hurt anybody."

A few hours later, some of the teachers expressed their indignation with that American's provocation. They thought he had thrown the frisbees as bones to a hungry dog. They objected to the kids rushing to the frisbees as though they had never seen any.

I felt sad to hear this response. I had seen how his face lit up. I told my colleagues, "I think that old grandpa only remembered his grandchildren and wanted to do something pleasant for the kids. And our kids acted as kids should—they were offered interesting toys from America, and they were glad to accept them. It would be horrible if they just stood there. It would give the impression that they are small, well-trained soldiers devoid of the joys of childhood."

When the village children first saw Ralph and Christine, they stood amazed. But Chris taught them to cheer and wave their hands. The children were always friendly and interested. I think for them and for many other people, after Ralph and Chris had been around a month, they weren't strangers anymore. People called them, "Our Americans." The teachers made real friends with the Dulls. Even now, a year later, the teachers often ask how they're doing.

I can't say why, but old people expressed the most generous feelings to the Americans; they were extremely kind and friendly to them. They couldn't know much about America. For many years, they had been told the USA was a hostile country. Maybe these elderly had already reached the height of human experience, and having stopped the race for getting things (which is usual for the young), they realized a simple but very important truth: we who live on the earth are people, first and foremost.

There were people indifferent to the Americans as well. Maybe they thought, "Some strange Americans have come, and they do nothing important here. Don't they have anything to do at home?" Those were people busy making money and settling their own lives. They weren't really concerned about peace and friendship among the nations. Most were the people of the establishment—the District party committee, Kiev Gosagroprom, etc. There were such people among the rank and file, too, but very few.

I was always disappointed when someone approached the Dulls, hoping for special favors. As I remember, about a hundred people asked Ralph and Chris to invite them to the States. Evidently, these people were only interested in pleasure or shopping trips. Some expressed their wish plainly; others made obvious hints. I felt uncomfortable interpreting these requests, but that is what an interpreter has to do—to let both good and bad come through. Still, I was never able to become just a machine, transforming Russian into English or vice versa.

In the case of the invitations, I was embarrassed by people's impoliteness. Sometimes I got indignant with their impudence. For me, it was absolutely obvious: if people want you to come to their home, they'll ask you themselves. I felt uncomfortable because I knew it wasn't easy for Ralph and Christine to say, "No." Ralph was simply resolute, but Chris immediately started explaining why they couldn't do it. It was annoying for me to hear how those who wanted invitations poured dirt on everything in my country and praised America to the skies.

In spite of the stupid system which has led our country into misery, there has always been friendship, love, generosity, mutual assistance, unselfishness, and honesty. My country has had wonderful successes and achievements, and there have always been wonderful people. America is a rich and free country, but it's not perfect either. I'm absolutely against our system of repressing people and our absurd economy. But Stalins come and go. People and the Motherland remain.

Ralph and Chris were placed in Stupentsi—a site hated by most Makov people. It's a small forest reserve a half-mile from the village. There are three houses, barns, a zoo, and a man-made lake. By name, it's a reserve and summer place for a day care center. But in essence, it's one of the thousands of "hunting lodges" all over the country. It is in these places where the elite used to gather, where the selected "finest" decided how to rule the people, where the "servants of the people" had rest and fun.

When perestroika started, people pressed for the lodges to be given to hospitals, rest houses, pioneer camps—that is, to be returned to those they belonged to by right. But the Stupentsi fortress stayed. Even now, those who pound their chests, saying they have no special privileges and work 16 hours a day for the benefit of the people, come in big black or white cars to have fun. The house where they usually gather is hidden by trees and separated from the rest of the reserve by a high fence.

Devoted servants and caretakers assure the high-ups' privacy. Once when reporters interviewing the Dulls wanted a well-lit place to take pictures, they noticed such a place behind the fence. When they asked the caretakers to unlock the gate, they were absolutely refused. There was nothing else to do; it was a sacred place. I can say many of the officials who had access to that paradise did not welcome the Dulls' stay on the farm.

As far as I know, at first our Chairman was glad he was offered the chance to host an American farmer. He thought he would be able to get better machinery and supplies for the farm. He also liked the idea of all the newspaper and television coverage. It was obvious the Americans' stay would attract a lot of reporters.

But later, he realized the reporters could also be nosy and that the farmer would see more than he wanted him to. So he tried to stop the affair. However, by that time, the decision had already been made—and in a place high enough the Chairman couldn't stop it. To top it off, the Dulls just appeared in Kiev on April 4 and said, "Here we are. We want to accept your invitation to live in Ukraine."

When the Dulls arrived in Makov, stupid talk started about Ralph's taking land to farm. The officials said they expected Ralph to bring equipment, seed, and even sons to show them how to farm. I think those who stuck to that idea realized its absurdness. I thought such talk would stop after Ralph explained the situation once. But no, that idea, taken up by some reporters, was in action the whole time the Dulls were in Makov.

In fact, local, District, and perhaps Regional agricultural officials realized that Ralph, with his idea about independent farming being the most effective system in agriculture, was a threat to their positions and well-being. Ralph could undermine the command-and-administer system in Soviet agriculture because independent farmers don't need millions of supervisors living at their expense.

I consider it necessary to explain the general situation of Soviet agriculture at that time. Prior to the CPSU (Communist Party of the Soviet Union) Central Committee Plenary Meeting on Agriculture, which was held in March, 1989, renting was begun because Gorbachev was resolutely for it. People expected much from the Plenary Meeting, as food is the USSR's number 1 emergency.

But the Plenum didn't meet the expectations. No radical reforms were approved, so the officials started to curtail renting. The system found even restricted renting to be dangerous, to say nothing about Ralph's ideas of independent farmers. As a rural resident, I can say that no serious changes have occurred in Soviet agriculture since 1985. In many respects, the situation is much worse.

Savkov, the chief agronomist of Ukraina, was against the Dulls' stay. He thought collective farm supervisors had enough knowledge, that the farm only needed better machinery. The chief bookkeeper and the chief economist tried to convince me Ralph could not be useful for the farm because the yields of Ukraina were the same as on Dull Homestead. Then I asked how much food was produced by one worker on Ukraina farm and told them how much was produced per worker on Ralph's. We compared only those actually engaged in field work. The difference was striking. Then they played their main trump card: "American farm machinery is better."

I answered, "Yes, it's better, but not ten-fold."

Equipment was also made the most important reason for Soviet agricultural failure by the former Politburo agricultural boss, Yegor Ligachev. He explained away the inferiority of Soviet agriculture compared to American farming by claiming that each American farmer has five times more energy at his disposal than Soviet farmers do. I think his comparison is inaccurate because there are many more workers in Soviet agriculture. To my mind, the comparison would be more correct if we consider how much horsepower is used for 250 acres of cropland. Viktor Palamarchouk calculated that on Ukraina, 80 units more horsepower per 250 acres of cropland are used than on Dull Homestead.

What's the real reason for Soviet agriculture's inferiority? Ralph asked that question many times. At the agricultural institute the professors say it is the system. At Regional Gosagroprom the officials say it is the organization of agricultural production. Palamarchouk wrote the same from Ohio. Everybody seems to understand. But who will do the work to make the changes?

Our collective farm officials were against Ralph's ideas about independent farmers, but they received the Dulls quite cordially as persons. However, the Dulls brought a lot of trouble for the District Gosagroprom's chief, Valarovsky. He did his best to prevent their seeing poor farms. When Ralph and Chris visited a poor farm anyway, the next day Valarovsky shouted in his office, "Those American spies have too much freedom! They poke their noses everywhere!"

Ralph wanted to visit a modern pig farm. He wasn't allowed to, under the pretense of possible infection. As I understand it, the real reason was different. This farm raises 7,000 pigs and has 3,000 acres of land—50 percent more than Dull Homestead. But there are 250 workers! The comparison would have been telling.

Later, after Ralph and Chris returned to the States, the spy story continued. At one of the District party committee plenary meetings, a young chairman, who already realized the position of chairman is a wonderful feeding trough, took the floor. With the other members applauding him, he said those Americans looked for only the worst places on the farms and then took pictures of them. He also stated the reporters should have exposed those tricks instead of praising the Americans highly.

But by then, the Dulls already had many friends in the District. These friends organized a good rebuttal to the fabrications. I wrote a letter to the local newspaper, and it was published. My thesis was that the Dulls had come to our country hoping to help agriculture, to learn the life of the people, and to contribute to the development of the Soviet-American people-to-people movement. In the letter, I proved my point with facts. I also wrote that our officials were used to the notion that if something bad was not made public, then it didn't exist. But people who live in those neglected areas see the problems every day.

Although the officials were afraid of the Americans, they thought our people could be dismissed as if we were a herd of mute cattle. But the time has come when our Communist Party bosses have to be afraid not just of Americans but of their own people. The time has come to make the ruling party responsible.

I think it's worth mentioning that our bosses, and the chairman of Ukraina as well, were used to feeling they themselves were the carriers of the final truth. They were accustomed to people begging them for favors and being obedient. But Ralph and Chris felt independent, and I could see that independence annoyed our almighty chairman. Under the trifling pretext the farm was going to reduce its staff, he stopped food deliveries to the Dulls. Later, Chris told me she saw Nikolai delivering food to somebody next door to the Dulls' house in Stupentsi. And that was called reducing the staff!

The farm's officials wanted to make people hostile to Ralph and Chris. In 1989, Ukraina wasn't as prosperous as it used to be. Sometimes there was no money to pay farmers' wages. Rumors started about the Americans' getting too much. That trick didn't work though. All it took was the simple explanation that the average monthly payroll for all Ukraina's farmers is about 200,000 rubles. Did the 900 rubles a month the Dulls received really affect the farmers' wages? Everyone agreed this wasn't the problem.

Also, I had to explain that the expenses of hosting the two Soviets on Ralph's farm were out of the Dulls' own pockets. By the way, it was clear to everyone how Nikolai Zubyets got to the States—his father is a big boss in Ukraine Gosagroprom. Then why were the expenses of hosting Ralph and Chris paid only by Ukraina and not shared by the farm which sent Zubyets to America? Savkov asked me that question, but I was not the one to answer. He should have asked Ukraine Gosagroprom.

When the Dulls visited Ukraina, the supreme authority in our District was the District party committee. (Not now! They were voted out in the March election.) The attitude of the committee toward the Dulls' stay was expressed by Viktor Party Secretary: "I was categorically told by the District party committee not to mix into the affairs of the Americans." A very strange position. What would party leader Gorbachev, who is in favor of developing Soviet-American links, say if he knew the attitude of that party committee? I'm sure with Chris' and Ralph's energy and willingness to promote Soviet-American friendship, there would have been wonderful opportunities to contribute much more to peacemaking than they were able to do without the party committee's help.

During the first month of the Americans' stay, I felt I would take them to my home and organize everything myself. But in my apartment I had no place for them, nor had I the right to do so. I was just an interpreter.

The ordinary people were tremendously interested in the Dulls. I often got very tired just telling so many people about Ralph's farm, their peacemaking activity, family, and lives. Sometimes I would say, "Ask your supervisor to organize a meeting with Ralph and Christine. They will be glad to come and answer all your questions."

Our Makov officials seemed not to care about international friendship, nor did they care about their own people. Later, when after the Dulls' departure I became involved in political activity, I realized the system wasn't able to accomplish anything for the people. The system's leaders were busy defending themselves and fighting for survival. Though the system was in agony, it kept standing. The people behind the system are the notorious nomenklatura. When at work, they usually settle their own private problems. And most of all, they are afraid to take risks. But when Ralph and Chris were in my village, I wasn't yet aware of all this.

Never in my life have I heard of an American couple living in a rural Soviet place for half a year. It was clear this unique experience would get broad coverage in the Soviet mass media. The representatives of the press, radio, and TV were excited at the chance to interview the Dulls. They were very friendly to them—though a few tried to sensationalize their articles, which neither the Dulls nor I liked.

For example, in some articles, the reporters said Ralph had radio-telephones in his tractors to call home and ask how things were going. In fact, there were no such telephones or radios. Or they stressed how the collective farm provided a big house and a car for the Americans, even though neither were of great importance to the Dulls. They would have preferred to live as most of the village people did, their car was not a new one, and their presence wasn't depriving anyone on Ukraina farm.

Also, except for our District newspaper, no reporter gave proper attention to the peacemaking activities of the Dulls, which, to my mind, were not less important than agriculture.

Worst of all, when Palamarchouk wrote a letter to *Izvestia* about Ralph's farm and it was published, the editors added a sentence of their own. One could believe from the sentence that Ralph came to preach at Soviet farmers. In reality, nothing of the kind happened. Ralph hadn't come as much to teach as he had to learn; he wanted to learn about Soviet agriculture and to offer his considerations for improvement.

It was interesting for me, and I'm sure for the Dulls as well, that while the reporters agreed with Ralph about many things, their articles did not properly reflect this. The mass media at the time was tightly controlled by the system, and the reporters knew quite well what they could and could not write.

The first article in *Izvestia* about the Americans in Makov was published in May, and it helped much to improve things. Shortly after it was published, interesting meetings started. And there were many letters from Soviets. The Dulls' life in Makov became much more intriguing, though they had a lot of work.

Conservative officials in Soviet agriculture used to intimidate farmers, saying they would have to work hard without breaks and holidays if they become independent farmers. I really liked the words of the chairman from the Ivanofrankovsk Region after he had invited the Americans to his farm: "I wanted my farmers to meet with the Dulls mostly because I wished to convince my people that an independent farmer is not a slave to his land and animals. He is a man living an interesting life, educated, confident, and having time for holidays and even traveling."

It's natural, with all the interest in the Americans, that rumors would start about what they said and what they did. One of the first rumors was that the Dulls came to help reopen a church in the village. Ralph and Chris were ready to help if they could, but I advised them not to step in because I thought our people had enough power to cope with it themselves. And, eventually, the church was opened.

Later, people gossiped that Chris had said: "You Soviets are happy because you don't know how poor you are." The fact is, that phrase was in one of the Soviet magazines a year before the Dulls came to Makov.

Once I had a talk with some village people who told me they were sure Chris and Ralph knew Russian, and that the C.I.A. had sent them to Ukraine. I doubted that and reminded them Palamarchouk was staying on Ralph's farm in Ohio with Ralph's sons. The answer was the C.I.A.

probably bought the farm and placed its agents there. I tried to convince them this wasn't so, but I don't think I was successful. The main reason for their suspicions was the belief a real farmer couldn't write a book and do so well with the press. There are always and everywhere people too confident in their own knowledge. I didn't pay attention to the rumors because I knew such talk often happens in the village. When I came to the village 13 years ago, almost at once it was rumored that I was a drunkard.

As an interpreter, I sometimes had to change some rough words or make sentences more polite. I didn't do that on my own initiative; people asked me. For instance, the Chairman asked me to do this on his second meeting with the Dulls. Chris gave an American dinner for the Chairman, and the atmosphere at the table was pleasant. There were many jokes and much laughing. The Chairman wanted to take a photograph of Chris. When he was ready to push the button, Chris made a face and then said she was probably the first woman to make a face at the Chairman. He immediately answered, "That's nothing! At least 200 women have showed me their naked bottoms." I knew it was true (and not only their bottom), but I didn't translate this.

Also, some people close to the Chairman used to say the Americans did nothing—they came here just to rest. I would answer that in our country, we had already done almost everything that could be done with our hands. It was high time we used our brains. Ralph had a lifetime of experience as a farmer, and he was ready to share his knowledge with Soviet farmers. Our farmers should have studied Ralph's experience because we'll have to solve in the future the very problems that have already been decided on his farm. Take, for instance, no-till planting. We don't have any. But someday we will. Ralph had more than 20 years' experience in no-till, but again it was the system which was hostile to anything new and wouldn't listen.

Ralph and Chris learned a lot about our country and people during their visits to the USSR, but there is still more to learn. There is much to be told before Americans have a better understanding of people's life in the USSR.

I am not pretending to give you the full picture. That's impossible for one person. But I think you have to know the following facts: The percentage of wages in the cost of newly-created national product in the USSR is about 40 percent. In the USA, it's 64 percent. This means in my country, the state takes more from the workers. But because the state uses the money for the people, distributing it through its budget, there would seem to be nothing for our workers to worry about. In the USSR, medical service, higher education, and social security are free. The state also gives huge subsidies of 80 billion rubles a year for food production, keeping food prices low.

But let's have a look at how all this works. Medical service standards vary much in the country; in rural places, it is usually considerably inferior to that of urban areas. Also, school equipment and often even the teachers' training are much better in the cities. Another problem is only people living in big cities have the opportunity to buy food at subsidized prices (though it's not easy). Villagers can do this only when they come to the cities for shopping. (And now many cities have closed their stores to nonresidents.) As there are no state stores in rural areas, peasants have to buy food at Consumer Cooperation Union stores where prices aren't subsidized and are much higher.

But the money taken by the state doesn't come only from the urban population. It comes from rural people as well. Yet the country people who produce the food have to pay more for it than city dwellers. That's why people in rural areas have gardens and grow fruits and vegetables. Many also raise cows, pigs, or other animals. But this means much work at home after their regular jobs are done.

Another difference concerns housing. In the cities, most people don't buy their apartments, though there is some cooperative construction in which people pay for their individual flats. In the rural areas, however, the vast majority of people build their own houses, and, of course, they pay for them.

The party and state bosses have special hospitals, sanatoriums, resorts, and special stores as well. The financing of all these special accommodations comes from the state budget; moreover, the facilities, treatment, or goods are of much better quality. Thus, officials may not know how ordinary people live, or at least they don't have to endure that life. All these inequities happen in what is called "a society of social justice"! (However, this is changing. In the summer of 1990, the president of Russia abolished all the special privileges in that republic.)

About 20 years ago, high-ups and not-so-high-up communists made a special kind of communism for themselves, and they live in it. Much effort by the whole nation is needed to remove this huge spider from the nation's body. In the USSR we often say it's not easy to take our "finest" away from the feed trough, which is the command-and-administer system. The only solution is to abolish that feed trough. Some people say we are in danger of a new civil war. I think we can avoid another time of bloodshed if the republics are more independent and are allowed to take care of the problems of the people on their own. It is no use, to my mind, to try to settle conflicts from Moscow alone.

For many years, the Soviet Union has been and still is a hard place to live. A man in my country is helpless, a gear in the horrible state machine. Our law enforcement bodies, courts, and prosecutor's office are oriented to punish people instead of protect them. In many places, especially rural regions, the party preserved its control over law enforcement bodies, courts, and procurators. Lawyers are few, and most of them still serve the system. People have little legal redress.

The most depressing aspect of the system is this: for the majority of people, it's impossible to have a decent standard of living with a job as the only source of income. Many people have to work extra. Doctors work at other hospitals or do more work in their own facilities. Workers have to take other part-time jobs, farmers sweat over their large private gardens after their main job on the collective farm is done. For the rural population, these private plots are the only source of better income and extra food for their families.

The most difficult problem for many people trying to supplement their food supply is getting feed for animals. In very many cases—and I can say it's true nationwide—people have to steal. In general, low wages and the impossibility of earning a decent living on the job force people to pilfer. If they work at a meat-processing plant, they steal meat. From factories, they take parts. From sugar mills, they steal sugar. I tell you, people are forced into it.

Because so many people are pilferers, it's easy to rule them. A man who regularly violates the law is completely at his superior's mercy. If he disobeys, the supervisor can fire him or put him in jail for stealing. If he's purely honest, then his family is doomed to struggle at poverty level. A supervisor is also at a higher supervisor's mercy, and so on. I really don't know where this chain ends.

This brings us to politics. One may ask why so many communist supervisors were elected to the different levels of soviets. The answer is, I believe, many people are still threatened and are afraid to vote their minds.

I feel it's absolutely humiliating our people have to beg everywhere. We beg for a good job, for apartments, for vouchers for sanatoriums or resorts, for different goods, supplies, allocations, and what not. So I assume you've guessed how great is the power of those who distribute.

Until recently, only the various party committees decided the appointments of supervisors on all the levels—from the principals of schools on up to the president. This is what we call the nomenklatura, the most horrible product of the Stalin epoch. Once somebody gets into it, it's next to impossible to be fired out of it. You can be promoted if you fit the system, or at least you stay at the same level. There have been many cases when, for instance, a chairman of a collective farm—due to incompetence or some other problem—was fired only to emerge a week or so later as chairman of another farm or in a new position. Still, he remains within the nomenklatura.

The choice of people to be on the selection list is often not because of their special knowledge or abilities, but because they've made connections through relatives, special services, personal loyalties, or bribes. This system provides rich soil for wide-scale corruption, the flourishing of bribery, and violations of the law. Those selected have the opportunity to get whatever they need. These people distribute everything in the country, and they never forget about themselves and their families in the process.

Farmers in the country were and still are the most helpless group of people. This is especially true in villages where there is only the collective farm and no other enterprise. (Makov has a sanatorium, sugar factory, and beef and chicken enterprises.) In many villages, the farm's chairman is an absolute ruler, and the farmers are his serfs.

There are striking contrasts in the standards of living among those who work on the same farms. A chairman and his entourage live similarly to members of America's lower middle class. Of course, they don't have the diversity of food or all the electronic equipment the Americans have, but, in general, they're not very far from it. Officials on Ukraina farm use more than 20 cars belonging to the farm. The chairman himself uses two cars (until recently, he had three).

Meanwhile, the rest of the people are close to poverty level—or lower. The official inflation rate is 7 percent, and there is hidden hyperinflation which results in empty shelves in the state stores and extremely high prices on the private market. A person's eighty rubles might not last beyond a couple of shopping trips.

In Makov, there are people whose salaries are only 100 rubles a month, but who live better than those making 300 or more. They do this by selling flowers, meat, or potatoes on the private market; swapping their produce for favors or expensive goods; or being the special friend of an official. Really, we live in a country of "curved mirrors."

In what ways are farmers dependent on their chairman? Formally, a chairman of a collective farm is merely an executive fulfilling the will of the farmers. At a meeting of all the farmers, a collective farm board is elected by hand vote. The board usually consists of 10-15 people. A chairman, as part of the nomenklatura, always tries to have his people on the board to support him later on. Usually, these supporters rubber stamp whatever the chairman decides. Thus, the chairman's favor means everything. People on the farm depend on the chairman for most of life's necessities:

1. He decides to give a person a good job—or not.
2. He decides whether a farmer can buy animal feed, fruit, vegetables, milk, or other farm products from the farm.
3. If a farmer wants to build his own home, he must get the chairman's permission for many things: to acquire a piece of land (the chairman also decides where it will be), to buy building materials from the farm, to use necessary construction machinery, and to have access to the farm's construction brigade to build the house.
4. The chairman decides who will be the one to use a new tractor, combine, or truck.
5. The chairman decides whether to accept kids at the day care center (if there is one on the farm).

6. If a farmer needs a truck to haul something, the chairman decides whether to loan it. (This, even though a farmer pays the farm when he uses its machinery for his own purposes).

7. If a farmer needs a tractor for his garden, the chairman decides this also.

8. When a farmer needs his vacation to come at a convenient time, again the chairman decides.

9. Some collective farms own the houses. The chairman decides who lives in what house.

10. If a farmer wants to buy a car, he can do this only via his farm. Again the chairman decides. (We wait 8-15 years to buy a car because they're in short supply. There are other ways to buy one, but then the price is tripled. A car often costs as much as the average person earns in 10 years.)

There are other levers of a chairman's power, but I think the above-mentioned are enough to get the idea. (In the USSR there are also state farms, but they are not much different from the collective ones. The serfdom of the peasants is the same.)

To all important or profitable positions on the farm, the chairman appoints mostly his own people. They make up his entourage. So on the farms, some people have special favors; the rest have a hard life. The old principle, "Divide and Rule," still functions. Just try to stand up against the chairman! I know what kind of life you will have.

Naturally, the chairman's power is controlled by the law and the rules of the collective farm. But usually those who search for justice do not succeed. Everywhere he can appeal to other nomenklatura, and in rural areas, they are tightly connected.

Of course, not all chairmen are tyrants. There are many good ones, and they take care of the people and of the farm properly. Luckily, the number of good chairmen is increasing in the nationwide democratization and glasnost. But still, I am convinced this system must be abolished, because usually power corrupts.

When someone, having realized his helplessness against the system, wants to leave the village, it's not easy to settle elsewhere. In the USSR, we have an internal passport system and mandatory residential registration. You can't have a job without being registered. Big cities such as Moscow, Kiev, Leningrad, and many others have been closed for newcomers' registration. To be registered, you must have a place to live, but you can't buy an apartment or a house in the cities. You have to rent a room somewhere, and it will cost you about one-third of your monthly salary.(One-third may not seem like much, but often, 60 percent of a person's income is spent on food.) For you to get an apartment, you have to work and wait up to 15 years. Thus moving is often impossible.

I think it's necessary to mention the sphere we contact everyday—shopping. It seems to me a very talented criminal worked out our retail trade system. There are most favorable conditions for corruption—and for cheating customers. I would need to write a thick book to give you the full picture, so I'll limit myself to a more general description.

Most of the salesmen cheat customers when weighing, with the help of specially-set scales, or when counting. Some of them cheat moderately, and many people pretend not to notice. People know that very often when food spoils while on the store's shelves, the salesmen have to pay for it from their own pockets. Also, they have many other expenses to meet.

Now, almost everything in Soviet stores is in short supply. To buy an item in rural areas, you must have connections. In big cities, you must stand in line for long hours. In general, this book is about rural areas, so I'll tell you more about the stores there. Food and goods in short supply are sold from the back door, which we call the "*black* door." There you have to pay 50-100 percent more. And you have to be very grateful after you've been cheated, or you'll be *persona non grata* at the black door.

Usually in retail business, there are "white" and "black" people. The blacks struggle for survival, and the whites are almighty. All the stores are given plans for the sum of money they have to take in each month. The storekeeper must fulfill the plan, because his or her bonus payments depend on it. Further, a salesperson can be reprimanded if he or she doesn't make the mark. When the shelves are empty, how does one fulfill the plan? Salespersons have to go to the distributors and beg and bribe. The whites usually have connections with the distributors and also with the "finest."

For instance, in Makov all the whites are friends of the Chairman. They also give bribes as the blacks do, only bigger. They get goods which are in short supply in big quantities. Then they sell them from the black door. The finest usually don't buy things themselves; they send their drivers or the whites to bring what they want to their houses. Sometimes the finest help the whites to get even more goods that are in short supply. When I ran against the Chairman at this year's elections to the District soviet, I immediately become a personal enemy of one of the white saleswomen. I hadn't done anything against her. But she recognized I was dangerous for the system.

I can't help writing about our recent history—Soviet intervention in Afghanistan. A boy from my village was killed there. His mother was forbidden to engrave on his tombstone that he died in Afghanistan. (In late 1988, it was finally allowed.) Another boy whom I taught was also killed there. At school, the students collected some materials about him: his pictures and letters. Yes, we remember him, but it doesn't wipe away his mother's tears. How to explain to his mother what he died for? Whom did he defend his native land against?

Among the 100,000 young boys from Ukraine who fought in Afghanistan, there were no sons of supervisors from the level of collective farm chairman on up. That dirty war was condemned by the people and the Supreme Soviet. Those responsible for the decision to go there were named. I believe nobody in my country will be able to send our soldiers to fight anywhere again. The Afghanistan wound is still bleeding.

For me it has been disgusting to write about this inhuman system. Moreover, I have to live in it.

I'm not writing anything about all that ideological basis of communism, socialism, Marxism-Leninism, socialist ownership, or anything else because we Soviets are fed up with that. Now our people are free to express any opinion. In our press today there's a diversity of thoughts and suggestions. It still happens that the dying system strikes out with its paw against the brave. Yet, nevertheless, the old way is dying.

Now you have a general idea of how Soviet people have lived for many years, and I'm grateful to those of you who felt sympathy for my long-suffering nation.

Today, the situation in my country is rapidly changing. The movement towards change was very hard to start! The ruling nomenklatura, which used to nip the smallest bud of change before it could flower (an action that unites embittered people), is now like a tremendous ship full of nuclear weapons, drifting into the abyss.

To my mind, the biggest gain of perestroika is people aren't silent anymore. And they do speak! If I were asked what has changed at the village level, I would answer the changes are small. And the economic situation has become even worse. But I feel the powerful movement of the nation, tired to death of the yoke of nomenklatura, and I'm convinced now there is no force capable of putting people back in the stable again.

Though our system has been idiotic, it still gave a good education to the people. Education contributed greatly to the changed thinking which has been growing for 15 years among our people. Gorbachev was the right man at the right time.

We are not the country we used to be five years ago. Democratization started. Boris Yeltsin, who was ousted from power in 1987, is now the president of the Russian Republic. He is determined to speed up the changes. For instance, he guaranteed the security of foreign investments in the republic's economy. The mayor of Moscow, Gavriil Popov, a prominent economist, stands for radical reforms. What's more, the majority of the people in the Moscow soviet are democrats. Another mayor, Anatoli Sobchak of Leningrad, is a very intelligent lawyer. He recently stated there would be no dual power (regional party committee and city soviet) in Leningrad but only one—the power of the democratically-elected city soviet. In three western regions of Ukraine, the democratic bloc won at both the republic and local elections.

Boris Yeltsin, Gavriil Popov, and Anatoli Sobchak left the Communist Party, and thousands of people are doing the same all over the country. Nikolai Travkin, a member of the Supreme Soviet and an honest and principled man whom I trust, left the party and organized a new one: the Democratic Party of Russia.

New parties are forming, new laws have been passed—but the system still stands. The Communist Party is losing credit with the people. When I was following the actions of the party congresses of Ukraine and Russia, or the 28th CPSU Congress, I sometimes had the impression the delegates didn't know what was happening beyond their palace walls. They passionately claimed to be defending the people's interests.

But the people haven't wanted them for a long time. Often I've heard people say, "That's what the bolsheviks led the country to!" During the last year, I have never met anyone (except for the nomenklatura, of course) who would defend the Communist Party. There are 18 million communists now, and it's unjust to blame them all. The vast majority are intelligent, honest people, as most non-communists are. Within the party, most just pay their membership fees. The actual decisions have been made by a narrow circle of higher-ups. I'm glad that at the 28th Party Congress, such conservatives as Yegor Ligachev are no longer members of the political leadership. Another blow to the old ways came when the miners of the country went on strike in the summer of 1990. They demanded the resignation of the Council of Ministers and the de-politization of the Army, the KGB, the court, and law-enforcement bodies.

Resolute changes are going on in villages, too. For instance, when my village elected People's Deputies of the USSR and Ukraine, the candidates supported by Regional and District party committees lost. In spring, 1990, in our small District, there was a revolution. The democratically-minded population won a convincing victory. Indeed, the political climate is now different in the USSR!

I expect many American Ukrainians will read this book, so I'm going to send this message to them about what is really happening in their old homeland.

When Gorbachev and his comrades started perestroika, many people, and I as well, considered Ukraine to be a reserve of stagnation. "True Leninists" (a mockery)—Shcherbitsky and Valentina Shevchenko—ruled the republic. The system was the same, but foods and goods were a bit easier to get. The standard of living was also somewhat higher than in other republics (except for the Baltics and Georgia). However, all this was due to the riches of the republic and to the long-time Ukrainian tradition of hard work.

There were changes everywhere, but not in Ukraine. The only difference here was the new state language status of Ukrainian. I think the miners of Donbas broke through the dam with their strike in summer, 1989. They had lost patience. At the beginning of September, a constituent congress of people of the Ukrainian Movement for Perebudova (perestroika)—Rukh—was held. Almost immediately the party-controlled mass media dashed to discredit it.

These are the events which developed in my village at that time. Our local authorities called a gathering of the villagers. People weren't much interested. Only about 100 people came—mostly teachers, doctors, and collective farm supervisors.

An official from the District had been brought to us. At the beginning of the gathering, he took the floor and read a lampoon—probably prepared by the KGB—about Rukh and its leaders. As he was not very competent or literate, he missed the correct emphasis in many words, and it was fun to listen to him. One word—oh, poor creature!—he read correctly in the sixth attempt, after the audience almost unanimously cried it out for him. He wiped the sweat off his face, sighed deeply, and went on.

When he finished, Viktor Party Secretary took his place at the rostrum. He read an appeal "from Makov inhabitants" to the Regional party committee and to the Supreme Soviet of Ukraine (composed at the District party committee). The appeal condemned Rukh and its leaders and demanded that an end be put to its activity.

When Viktor finished, the village soviet chairman stood up and declared it time to vote. He quickly asked, "for." About 20 people raised their hands. Then he uttered in half-voice, "against," "abstained," "no votes!" and then happily declared, "Unanimous [for the condemnation of Rukh]!"

I became indignant, stood up, and told him only 20 people out of a hundred voted "for," so how could it be unanimous? He was at a loss and didn't know what to say. The Chairman helped him, saying: "The Dulls taught him to talk like that!" Then they quickly announced another item on the agenda.

After the meeting, I wrote a letter to the District newspaper and described that gathering. Naturally, it was not published. But it frightened some party bosses, which was my precise intention. I never expected the letter would be printed because it exposed how the communists organized the people's appeal. I am sure it was much the same in many other places.

At the editor's office, I was told the ideology secretary of the District party committee and the District Department of Education wanted to come to my school to talk with the teachers. They did come, but they talked only with me. For two hours, they tried to convince me Rukh was bad, its members extremists and killers. They weren't successful though. They couldn't answer my question, "What kind of system do we have that selects as leaders of the nation killer Stalin, adventurer Khrushchev, corrupted Brezhnev, or half-dead Chernyenko?"

Rukh was registered as a public organization by the Council of Ministers only *after* the period for nominating candidates to local and republic soviets was over. Thus, Rukh was deprived of the chance to nominate its candidates. So Rukh had to use other, more difficult, methods. In Makov, we wanted to have a residential meeting of voters and nominate our own candidate to the Supreme Soviet of Ukraine. It caused real alarm at the District party committee, and they did their best not to permit it. They succeeded that time because we didn't have any experience in such games. They will never succeed again!

In winter, 1990, all over Ukraine, regional party bosses were overthrown. I think people in Makov are awake now, as well as many in my District.

At the elections to the Supreme Soviet of Ukraine, something else happened. The people in our area rejected the head of the nomenklatura from the Central Committee of the Communist Party of Ukraine. It's true the deputy we chose is not the one we wanted at the Supreme Soviet, but he was the only other choice we had.

At the first session of our District soviet (it includes 99 percent supervisors), the first secretary of the District party committee was elected. He then pushed all his people into top positions of local leadership. That same day, many workers stopped working, went to the town square, and demanded the newly elected chairman and all his buddies resign. The demand was resolute. Three days they later, they resigned. Soon the first and second party secretaries, along with Valarovsky, were forced to leave the District. Bon voyage, guys!

Now among the 450 deputies of the Supreme Soviet of Ukraine, a quarter are representatives of the democratic bloc. Ivashko, the Party boss of Ukraine, was taken to Moscow by Gorbachev. Then, on the 16th of July, 1990, the Supreme Soviet of Ukraine adopted *The Declaration of Independence of Ukraine*. This document says Ukraine will have its own banking system, armed forces, direct international ties with other countries, and exclusive control of everything within the territory of the republic. July 16 is a Ukrainian Independence Day!

Ralph's and Chris' stay in Makov had a big impact on our people. Many people realized it was possible to farm effectively without collective and state farms. Villagers, often for the first time in their lives, met with Americans and saw for themselves Americans are just people like they are. Soviets discovered that Ralph and Chris, with their 14 grandchildren, were not people ready to start a war.

I learned something, too. Different is not necessarily better or worse, it's just different. Diversity is a path human beings should allow others to follow. Now I know free choice and free enterprise are basic principles of freedom. This is why Americans are extremely sensitive to any restrictions. And I fell in love with the Dulls' philosophy of "citizens of the world."

Chris and Ralph are wonderful people, and they have become part of my family. My wife and I are deeply touched when small Yura recognizes Chris in some woman or suddenly pronounces in a funny way and with a whistle at the end, "Ralph."

True, it's hard to live in my country today, but it's also interesting. The dishonest system still stands, and we have much to change—mostly through our own efforts. We also need help from other nations. Ralph and Chris were in Ukraine during the initial stage of change when the old system didn't accept new ideas. But the people did. There will be great demand in the USSR for Ralph's farming experience next year. Millions of generous, noble, and honest people live in my country. I'm convinced they will overcome.

Soviets are just people, like people everywhere. They strive for the same things, and their values are the same as those of the rest of the world—love, friendship, family, work, compassion, freedom, and peace.

CHAPTER 12

"Call Police! Russian Spy Was Here!"

by Marcella Harms

We could never have anticipated the exciting summer in store for us—all due to the misfortune of another farm family.

Mike Dull, one of Ralph's sons and a farm neighbor, called last April to ask if we would be interested in having some help on our farm for the summer. He told us of a Ukrainian farmer who wanted to learn more about American dairy farming and why family farms are so productive here. This young man, Nikolai Zubyets, was supposed to work and stay with another dairy farm family. However, because of the farmer's death, the plans had to be canceled. Mike explained that Nik could continue to live at the Dull farm with Viktor, the other visitor from the USSR the Dulls were hosting. A car would be provided for transportation, and we wouldn't be expected to pay wages. All we had to do was furnish meals.

We did need summer help. I; my husband; our son, David; and Shari, David's fiance; kept very busy milking 80 cows and caring for the cows and heifers during the winter months. In addition, come summer, we farm about 650 acres and need extra work done. I thought we should try the young man. We could help him, and he could help us. My husband, Dirk, didn't agree. He worried about what people would think when they heard we had a Russian here. He said since he was born in Germany, we sure didn't need a Russian on the farm, too. Neighbors would surely disapprove!

Then Mike brought Nik over to meet us, and Dirk asked Nik what work he could do for us.

Nik answered, "I do anything!" He made a motion as if he were shoveling.

That was the right answer! Nik came to work the next morning.

Dirk and I had to make a trip to our daughter's home in Michigan on the day Nik arrived. But we were confident we had an experienced dairyman to help milk, so we left for our three-day trip.

Meanwhile, David and Shari were getting acquainted with Nik. They soon found Nik knew very little English. Also, even though he was from a 500-cow dairy farm, he didn't know how to milk or drive a tractor. He had studied dairying at an institute. David said the days we were gone were spent mostly trying to teach Nik necessary English words.

Still, communicating with Nik wasn't a problem for us. Since Dirk's family is German, we were used to communicating with people who speak foreign languages. Also, Dirk had a hired man for 35 years who was deaf. Neither man had any training in sign language, so they just made up their own signs and motions. If words don't communicate, we've learned to be good with gestures.

We found Nik to be a very intelligent and inquisitive man. He told us he'd had only six to eight weeks of a three-month English course. Nik had lots of English to learn before he could articulate what he wanted to know about America and farming. He loved to talk and learn. He would sit with us and ask questions until late at night. During the first weeks, he used his Russian/English dictionary to help him. The meaning of the word "should" was the hardest for him to understand. His dictionary didn't seem to help, and we couldn't fully explain it either.

One of the first things Nik wanted us to know was that he was not a Russian. He was Ukrainian. And he was always certain to correct anyone who called him otherwise. He also told us he had a wife and two sons and that he was 26 years old, just one year younger than our son, David. It was great they were so close in age.

Later, Nik told us he works in management on a government farm specializing in animal genetics. Seeds for grain and feed crops are raised there, too. His village consists of a thousand people, mostly Hungarians, because the farm is very near the Hungarian and Czechoslovakian borders. He'd studied agronomy, genetics, mechanics, and all aspects of farming during his seven years of college. Now his job requires mental, not physical labor.

Since this story is about Nik and our family farm, we need to give some information about us, too. In 1929, Dirk had come to the United States from a little German farming town. He was five years old. By the time he was 12, his parents were able to borrow enough money to buy a small farm. As his father was a carpenter, not a farmer, Dirk learned farming by helping the neighbors.

Dirk and I got married when we were in our late twenties. Gradually, we bought more land. When David grew up, he decided to stay on the farm with us. Then David met a girl, Shari Hart, at one of the cattle shows, and they began dating. She lived and worked on her family dairy farm, but the

Harts were losing their property due to her father's death. After the expense of his long illness and the loss of his management and labor, the family couldn't continue on the farm. They moved, and because we needed a dairy herdsperson and farm helper, we hired Shari. David and Shari are soon to be married.

After the first few weeks, Nik moved into our tenant house, a large ranch home right on our land. We gave him a car to use, and he became a real part of the farm, working and eating with us every day. Nik was always neat and kept both the car and the house clean. We appreciated that and also that he didn't drink or smoke.

During the first few weeks Viktor and Nik were in Ohio, it was good for them to spend time together in the evenings, talking Ukrainian. When Nik came here to live, they still got together often, always on Sunday, their only day off. They found some surprising places to visit on their own, too. Their first few Sundays they spent at the Wright-Patterson Air Force Museum.

We always enjoyed Nik's jokes, his pleasing personality, and his smiling face. He told us funny stories about his and Viktor's getting food on Sundays. They liked to go through the drive-through restaurants but couldn't read the menus. Nik knew how to order a "Big Mac" at McDonald's though. Once I told him to try a "hamburger with everything on it" at Wendy's. Then he told us of the trouble they had trying to order a hamburger at Arby's. Americans know Arby's has roast beef sandwiches, but the two Ukrainians didn't. Between the strange order and the men's thick accents, I'm sure the situation was tough to handle over the drive-through speakers.

Also, I remember the first time Viktor came to visit Nik. I invited him for supper, fried some pancakes, and had the first eight made. I gave them to David to pass around the table while I made more. Each person took two pancakes, and Nik and Viktor laughed as they handed Dirk the empty plate.

Not to be outdone with the Soviet joke, Dirk pulled an old American trick. He said, "Look out the window!" While they were looking, Nik lost one of his pancakes to Dirk's plate. Everyone giggled at that.

Nik also made us laugh when we told him people sometimes steal in America. We said once someone had even stolen our new pickup right out of the barnyard.

Nik answered with a mischievous grin, "America is a free country!"

Also, there was the time Nik nearly caught his foot in the grain auger. He said, "Ah, well, America make good wooden leg."

On another occasion, Nik needed a haircut. He was afraid his English wasn't good enough to go to the small town barbershop by himself and ask for the cut, so he asked Dirk to go with him. Dirk went in and explained to the girl that this young man's English wasn't too good, but he needed a haircut. Then Dirk left.

Nik tells this story: "Girl ask where I from. I say 'Soviet Union.' Talk stop. No more talk. After I go, all people talk. 'Call police! Russian spy was here!'" Nik loved to joke about being a Russian spy.

In talking with Nik about the dairy cattle, we found out his studies at the institute were about modern medicine and practices in dairying. He might be saying oxytocin or dexamethasone, but he pronounced it in an entirely different way than we did. Nik says he knows how to feed cattle to get more milk; they just need better feed and more fertilizer than is available in his country. He said some Soviet cows are fed straw. Nik liked our cows and our dogs, as we do. He was concerned, too, when our Labrador retriever, Hershey, was missing. That brings up another of Nik's jokes.

Our closest neighbor, a Korean lady, is married to an American. Won Suk thought it was great having Nik here. She sent us many of her delicious egg rolls and rice and meat dishes. We told Nik about her—including how she had told us that in her homeland, they fatten and eat dogs. As Nik was eating her rice and meat dish, he began stirring it. Then he said, "Ah, there Hershey."

One of the things Nik bought was a good camera. We could tell what impressed him by the pictures he took. The first pictures were of full grocery shelves. He took pictures of the outside and inside of the ranch home where he lived. He also had us take pictures of him working, for example, shoveling manure.

Dirk asked Nik if he wanted to have his wife come here for a visit. Nik was afraid it would be too much trouble. On Nik's birthday in late May, Dirk told him his birthday present was a call to his wife. He talked to her for a long time on the phone, and when he finished, he said, "She wants to come!"

Nik said he didn't think it would be possible to get her here because permission from the Soviet Union would take too long and because the Soviet Aeroflot Airline was all booked up. Dirk called Pan Am and found there were flights available, so he contacted the Soviet Embassy and started the process to get her here. A little later, we bought her ticket. She received it, along with some information.

Nik said most women in the Soviet Union do not drive. He also thinks the women have to be really good cooks—they have to be able to make a meal out of anything they can get. He said it has been many years since he has eaten any sweets, and sugar and salt are not necessary on food. I asked him what they usually have to eat, and he said, "Soup! Wife makes soup from garden."

We tried to show Nik and Viktor the American way of life. We took them to Select Sires, a large artificial insemination organization near Columbus, Ohio. We also went to several large dairy and beef farms, the Ohio State Fair, and the Farm Science Review. Nik enjoyed King's Island, a large amusement park, the most. He loved the wild rides! So many things were new to him that he acted like an excited boy much of the time. It was a pleasure for us to see his excitement.

As our family sat around talking to Nik, we found he sometimes knew as much about American history as we did. Then we'd get our encyclopedia and study Russian history. Nik told us his country had endured many bad leaders in the past who took the land away from the people. Historically, if the people talked against the government, they were shot or sent to Siberia. He said his grandparents were sent to Siberia, and he'd spent a few of his early years with them there. He thinks Gorbachev is a great leader.

Nik's father was very important to him. He was very happy when he got a call from his father and news from home. Nik had mentioned his father knew a few German words. The evening Nik's father called, Dirk answered the phone and heard a man's voice he couldn't understand, so he knew it must be Nik's father. He told him, "Nikolai is not at home."

Nik's father kept on talking, and Dirk wondered what to do. Then Dirk began speaking German. Nik's father understood he should call again later.

Nik said his father was an important man in Ukrainian agriculture and that he'd written many books. He told us his father always said, "Work wherever you are." That's what Nik was doing for us. He was working for us, and we were helping him learn about our way of life.

At first, we'd try to explain the daily newspaper articles about the Soviet Union to Nik. Later, he learned enough English to read the news articles himself. He told us once he was a communist. We talked about communism for a while, and I think we decided that what we both wanted from a government was similar. We both wanted freedom.

Nik said, "People are the same the world over. Only governments make them different."

We remember the time we were all out in the yard as the milk inspector drove in; Nik seemed to know what a milk inspector was. David said, "He could make us trouble."

"Give him money," replied Nik. Somehow we didn't think he was joking this time. He seemed to feel we should to do the same thing if the police stopped us while we were driving. Simply pay off the officials rather than receive a ticket. We learned bribery is rampant in the Soviet Union.

We told him America isn't perfect either. Payoffs may not be a way of life but we have the drug problem, ghettos, and worse. Nik told us about some good aspects of Soviet life—their free health care and the fact people don't need insurance, for instance. Mothers of small children stay home with their babies for one and one-half years and get paid for it. Also, even though the elderly get very little money, all their expenses are paid. But Nik could see that in America, we are free to do what we want to do: We can work on the farm and plan our lives to accomplish however much we want to work for.

Viktor asked Dirk if he thought he had made a lot of money being a farmer. Dirk answered, "Yes!" After a pause, he continued, "But for the first 19 years we were married, I never missed a milking." That's twice a day for 19 years, from 6 A.M. to 9:30 A.M., and again from 6 to 9:30 at night!

Viktor and Nik were both very interested in our farm records, especially those that showed our income and expenses. Nik was also intrigued by our dairy cattle feeding program. He joked, "I am a Russian spy. I know all your farm secrets."

Viktor and Nik could see the progressive farmers were the ones working long hours and hiring very little outside labor. For example, as Dirk had learned to be a carpenter from his father, he and David do almost any kind of repair or construction. In the summer of 1989, Nik helped us with building and repairs and learned about two areas many American farmers must be familiar with.

Nik seemed to love the hard work, too. The first day, while we were baling hay, he couldn't lift the bales and laughed and laughed. The next day he was stronger. And by the end of the summer, David and Nik had baled and stored 6,000 80-pound bales of hay. Dirk remembers Nik, with a big smile, walking around a large wagon of hay bales he had loaded. Dirk asked Nik why he was smiling. "Ah! Good work!" Nik answered.

In late summer, Dirk and David decided to sell the soybeans stored in our bin. So the hauler in his semi-truck drove in, loaded, and left.

Nik asked, "Don't you watch? He steal some!" We told him (despite the pickup story) most people here are basically honest. If a hauler would steal and get caught, he would be out of the hauling business completely.

Nik responded, "I'll have to remember to tell them you trust people here."

Nik saw another part of American farm life that summer. In August, David and Shari trained their show-string cattle and exhibited them at several fairs. Nik went with them and enjoyed all the fun: staying overnight in the cattle barn, eating fair food, getting into water fights, etc. He used our camcorder to take many videos.

Toward the end of his stay, we got many requests for interviews with Nik from various papers. To the *Farmweek* interviewer, he gave one word to describe his American experience—"Tremendous!" In the same newspaper article, Nik describes Shari as "beautiful on the inside and out."

The Dixie School in New Lebanon, a village not far from us, asked if Nik would visit the school so they could ask him questions. Shari went with him to help with the language. The students asked Shari and Nik about 80 questions. One was "Do you believe in God?" Nik answered, "No, but maybe children don't like to hear that."

His answer did bother Shari and me. We wondered how people could live without faith. We knew Viktor and Nik were quite defensive about this. They were sure they would have religion pushed on them while they were here, at least to some extent. At the time, I said nothing to Nik. But later,

I did say, "You talk about your government's taking the land away from the people. Didn't the government take away their faith in God, too?"

We began to worry that Nik's wife, Irina, wouldn't be allowed to come. Finally, she got permission from the Soviet Union just two weeks before her flight was to leave. Irina had much to do in a very short time. Nik said he told her to bring empty suitcases because they would have so much to take home.

In late September, we met Irina at the Cincinnati airport. She was very beautiful—a rare kind of natural beauty, tall with long blond hair and pale grey-blue eyes. She dressed nicely, too. Her suitcases were very heavy, and we soon found out why. She had brought us many, many gifts.

Nik was busy trying to show Irina a great deal in a short time. Irina could speak no English. She seemed very surprised when Nik could understand the English spoken to him and answer in a language she couldn't understand.

Nik and Irina Zubyets, Marcella and Dirk Harms, and Shari and David Harms.

Since we weren't allowed to pay Nik, we asked him what he would still like to see in the United States and what he wanted to take home. He said he'd like to see New York City because people in the Soviet Union wouldn't think he'd seen America if he hadn't been there. He also said he'd like to take home a camcorder he could use in the Soviet Union. However, this type of camcorder could only be bought in New York City or Washington, D.C. So, a few days after Irina arrived, Nik, Irina, Dirk, and I left for the Big Apple.

Something else waited for Nik in New York as well. Many times while Nik was here, he'd talk about his friend who had come to live in America. He wanted to call him but didn't know where in the US he lived. The friend was a 64-year-old Jewish man who had lost a leg in the war. For many years, he and the man had lived in the same apartment building. Irina had the man's address when she came; it was Brooklyn, New York.

On Sunday morning we arrived in New York. We drove to Brooklyn and found the address on Ocean Avenue. The address was that of a large, run-down apartment building.

Nik said, "I don't know why he want to live here."

Dirk double-parked the car on the street, and he and Nik went inside while Irina and I waited in the car. I locked the car doors, feeling we might be in a dangerous area.

Inside the apartment, Nik and Dirk were trying to get some information on where to find Nik's friend. Just then, out of one door walked a man and a woman. Luckily, this was the couple Nik knew.

After many hugs, the heavy-set pair got into our car. We drove a few blocks to their daughter's home and parked in an alley next to garbage bags, alongside a small dry cleaning establishment. Then we climbed the dingy stairway. The one-legged man went up the stairs as well as we could.

Irina knocked on the door at the top of the steps, and a young red-headed girl answered. Inside the door were a row of shoes. We took the hint and left ours there, too. After many hugs, we seated ourselves in the tiny apartment. It was a complete change from the dingy stairway—extremely neat and clean.

In this apartment, we met the couple's daughter and two grandchildren— two girls, age thirteen and eighteen. They told us the girls were very intelligent and that the older one had just entered a university in New York. These people had been in the US only three months, after spending many months being "quarantined" in Czechoslovakia.

The son-in-law was at work. They said he really wasn't working, only following others around trying to learn the language and what to do. The older couple didn't think the new arrivals would ever learn to speak English. It was too difficult for them and not necessary in that Russian neighborhood.

They served us hot tea, coffee, and fresh fruit, and we spent many hours there. Nik and the girls occasionally gave Dirk and me an account of the conversation. But there was no need to understand their language; the smiles and happiness in their eyes showed their hope. The older man told Nik he was very glad his family had come to America.

When they walked us to our car, a man and woman had parked next to us and were standing by their car. The man introduced himself as the owner of the building and the cleaning shop. He and his mother had come from the Soviet Union and had been in this country for 14 years. They were very interested in Nik and Irina and gave us directions to Brighton Beach.

We drove to the beach, parked, and then noticed that the two people who had given us the directions had followed us. The man explained that since we were visitors, they decided it was polite to show us around. He sent his mother back to his apartment with his car. Dirk gave him our car keys, and he drove us around that area of New York, a Soviet-Jewish neighborhood.

The young Jewish man drove like a New York City cab driver—recklessly and fast—and all the while he talked just as rapidly as he drove! First, he'd shoot out a sentence in Russian; then he'd repeat it in English for Dirk and me. Next, it was back to Russian again. He double-parked along the streets and had us walk into the many Russian shops while he waited. He said he'd "made it big" in the United States in the 14 years he'd been here. He told us about his five-bedroom apartment on the Atlantic Ocean and showed us his platinum VISA credit card with the $100,000 credit line. He said the building he owned, the one with the cleaning establishment, was "peanuts" compared to what he owned altogether. Nik told him it might take Nik's lifetime to get the Soviet Union to where America is. The young Jewish man said he thought it would take ninety years. I can only guess they were speaking of our economy.

Our free tour guide finally left us, with directions for how to get out of New York. Being Sunday, all the Jewish people were outside in the neat, prosperous neighborhood he sent us through. It seemed as if we saw thousands of Jewish people in their orthodox black and white outfits. Men and women both wore black suits with white shirts. The men wore either little black beanies or wide-brimmed black hats. We saw a few in one area wearing an odd shade of light green. The men there wore wide-brimmed hats which looked like they were covered with rabbit fur. We were told these people were also Jewish. Nik and Irina took many pictures of the people. They said Jews weren't allowed to dress like that in the Soviet Union.

Our time for this trip was short, so after giving Nik and Irina a view of the Statue of Liberty from a distance and stopping to take a few pictures of the New York City skyline, we headed south.

On Monday, we arrived in Washington, D.C. There we drove around sightseeing before parking and walking over to the Soviet Embassy. Inside the iron fence of the embassy, we sat on benches in the yard. We waited a long time for someone to talk to Nik.

Later, we decided to find the store that was supposed to have the camcorder for Nik. It was a much longer walk than we expected though—about 25 blocks. We bought Nik the camcorder, and Nik and Irina bought a large cassette player. We had plenty of extra weight to drag back to our car. Irina wore high heels, but she carried her cassette player all the way back.

Our plans were to see Niagara Falls next, so the following day was spent traveling through the beautiful Pennsylvania and New York countryside. Away from big city traffic, Nik drove most of the day while Irina followed the map. The man in New York had given Nik a Russian tape of modern music, and they played it often, along with our classical music cassette.

Nik and Irina had much talking to catch up on because they'd been apart for so long. They would talk and talk—in Russian, of course—and then laugh over their private little jokes. They took many pictures of Niagara Falls and of the part of Canada they could see from the American side. They joked about it being all they would ever see of Canada.

Then we went on to Charlotte, Michigan, for a short visit with our daughter and her family. Our son-in-law took Nik and Irina to see Green Meadows Farm, a very large dairy farm near Lansing, Michigan.

Back home, Viktor's wife, Valentina, and daughter, Tatiana, had arrived for their two-week stay. Viktor and Nik thought one of the high points of their visit to the States was King's Island, the large amusement park, so they wanted to take their wives and Tanya. Nik was worried Irina wouldn't like the rides, but we took them all, and they loved it!

It was soon time to take Irina back to the airport. Nik had talked much about our family visiting the Soviet Union. He wanted us to go with Irina and wait for him. We said we would be busy with harvest then, but maybe July would be good.

Nik's Jewish friend called from New York one week after our visit there. He wanted to say goodbye and to tell Nik again how glad he was he'd come to the US. He said he wished he'd come here ten years ago. I don't think Viktor and Nik ever considered leaving the Soviet Union permanently though. As Nik would say, it is his motherland, and they'd work to improve it.

In October, a few days after Irina left, it was time to say goodbye to Nik. He was to leave from the Dayton airport at 6 A.M. The evening before he left, he came over to our house to get some shoe polish for his shoes.

At 5 A.M., we walked over to Nik's home. It had been decided that since David and Shari were Nik's best friends, they would drive him to the airport. Smiling Nik stood in the kitchen, not looking at all like the Nik we knew. He had on a dark suit, white shirt, and dark tie, and his black shoes were very shiny. Over the suit was a light overcoat, and he wore a French-type checkered cap. He said he had 115 pounds of luggage, and he had to leave a few things behind. He told us neither his luggage nor Viktor's would be checked because they had papers showing they were V.I.P.s.

Americans are not good at saying "goodbye." We extend our hand, but this just isn't good enough for such a dear friend who is going so far away. Outside the house in the early morning, our Soviet friend took care of the goodbyes his own way—with a big Soviet hug and kiss for Dirk and me. He whispered, "We wait for you."

CHAPTER 13

"More Than Any Man I Have Ever Met"

by Sue Dull

Viktor Palamarchouk and Sue Dull.

Spring in Ohio brings the anticipation of new growth and a fresh start. But the spring of 1989 brought a new kind of seed to sow, a crop this farm had never planted before. What grew here were the tender shoots of friendship between men whose countries had been in conflict for longer than their lifetimes. And like all seedlings, the first few weeks of our Soviet farmers' stay required much nurture and care.

My husband, Mike, remembers how, at first, communication was slow. It required deep thought and concentration for both him and Viktor—despite Viktor's thorough preparation for his US visit. Viktor had made sure his knowledge of English was sufficient. Yet in the first month of his stay, it must have taken most of his mental energy to communicate and make his point. Many times we wondered about the cultural differences between his homeland and the surroundings so familiar to us here.

We thought it was very good our two Soviet farmer friends were at least able to talk to each other. And they had each others' support and understanding, too, even though their friendship was also brand new. Only a few days prior to their arrival, we learned the dairy farmer whom Nik was to stay with had died unexpectedly of a heart attack. So Nik stayed for a while, along with Viktor, at Becky and Jim's home. Becky has a few milking goats and some sheep for their family, and Nik was good help with the chores. Also, Becky and Jim's youngest child, Timothy, was about the same age as Nik's one-year-old son. I'm sure it was comforting for him to be able to carry a baby around.

Mr. Pervov, the gentleman from the Soviet Embassy in Washington, D.C., encouraged Mike to find a dairy farm where Nikolai could live and work. Mike was fortunate to find the Dirk Harms family.

Dirk is a very good farmer and a generous man. He was at first hesitant about having Nik because he wasn't sure their farm had the newest American technology. Perhaps Nik wouldn't get the fullest knowledge of the US dairy business. But Mike assured Dirk he had a typical Ohio farm with everything Nik needed. Dirk provided David's old car for Nik to use, too. What a blessing it was to have Dirk host Nik. Dirk is easy to get along with and has a good sense of humor, like Nik does.

Mike and I really got to know Viktor, and he became like a brother to us. Partly, he was like a brother because of his involvement with my father and mother, Paul and Helen Dewey. My father decided after a month, the two young men's English was good enough to begin Sunday afternoon excursions. My parents took them all over southern Ohio to interesting places and nice restaurants. Many times they would include our children. Some of Viktor's favorite places were the Springdale Music Palace, the Air Force Museum, and the International Air Show. At the Air Show, they saw the World Famous Blue Angels perform their precision maneuvers. The hot air balloons were a favorite of Nik's; the whole sky was filled with their bright, beautiful colors.

One of the most eventful of these Sunday outings was when my father took Viktor fishing on the Little Miami River. A snake dropped into the canoe onto my father's lap! Viktor didn't see the snake, but he saw my father get excited and tip over the canoe. After Dad hit the water, he quickly looked back to see if Viktor was all right. When their eyes met, Viktor was expressionless, waiting to see my father's reaction. Viktor still didn't know why Dad had gotten so excited. My father started to laugh, and at that point, Viktor joined in. It was a little cool for swimming, and the rest of the trip was less than comfortable in their dripping clothes. Viktor would later laugh and tease my father about tipping over the canoe. Dad replied he didn't want to go the rest of the way in the company of a snake!

Paul taped their experiences with his video camera. We view them often to keep our memories alive and fresh. Viktor and Paul edited the many hours of tapes into just a few, to be converted for Viktor to take home to show family, friends, and neighbors.

Yet, many of these experiences are etched in our minds and hearts— memories of Viktor and Mike working side by side in the machine shop; Viktor bringing the mail to the office (which he did on most days, hoping for a letter from home); Viktor teasing the children, all smiles. Our children built good relationships with him, and with Nik, too. Caleb, our four-year-old, liked to share cookies with Viktor.

Our ten-year-old son, Abe, is a rather reserved boy who has a habit of not saying "hello" to people who say "hello" to him. After Viktor encountered this many times with Abe, he finally decided Abe needed a little friendly encouragement. So Viktor told him he would rub grease on Abe's nose if he didn't say "hello" to him. Once again, Abe didn't respond to Viktor's "hello" and, anticipating the grease, he ran. Viktor gave chase, held him down, and rubbed grease on the end of his nose, much to Abe's delight! Needless to say, from that moment on, Abe was quick to speak to Viktor, always accompanying his greeting with a smile and laugh.

Our six-year-old daughter, Mahala, had a splenectomy in June. Viktor came to visit her in the hospital, which she thought was very special. (He was impressed with the hospital's facilities but thought the cost of medical care too high.) Mahala recovered quickly. In fact, it was difficult to keep her from jumping about before her six weeks of post-surgery limitations were lifted. Viktor once told Mike they took out her spleen and put a spring in its place! It was a clever observation on Viktor's part because that's the truest description of Mahala. And it showed us his English had improved enough so his sense of humor could be revealed.

The impact Viktor and Nik had on our family and the friendships they developed here in America were much greater than anyone could have anticipated. It was a chance to make the world seem smaller and show that people, given the opportunity, can be very much alike, despite their nationalities. As we raise hybrid seed corn on our farm, we hire about 125 young people for three weeks during the summer to work. It was a first for them to actually meet someone from the Soviet Union. Most were curious and wanted to know if people there were like people here. They asked Viktor about everyday life in his village. It became obvious to me that many Americans know very little about the Soviet Union.

In the past, children in the US have been taught to fear the Soviet Union and even be wary of communists hiding among us, ready to overthrow our government. I told this to Viktor, and he was surprised. I told him this because I wanted him to understand that, because of their upbringing, some Americans might not receive him well. I told him, too, that Mike's parents and my parents hadn't raised us to feel that way. My father would say, "When a child falls and skins his knee, it bleeds and hurts; it matters not where he lives, how much money he has, or what is the color of his skin." I said children today aren't going to have that fear because the Soviet Union is daily in our news and there is now a feeling of friendliness between our countries. Because of this, our children can develop their own impressions.

Getting to know a Soviet personally had an impact on one of our seed corn workers, Tim Serena. He worked on Viktor's detasseling crew as an assistant for two weeks. Viktor called him "the gypsy" because Tim wore a bright yellow handkerchief around his head instead of a work hat and sported two or three pierced earrings. In October, Tim arranged for Viktor to go with Ralph to speak to the Brookville High School students. He also came to the farewell party we had for Viktor and Nik. Now, whenever we see Tim, he always asks what we've heard from Viktor.

During the wheat harvest and the detasseling of the hybrid seed corn in July, we'd worked long, hard hours. So we decided to take a trip with Viktor, before the children started back to school, to see more of the agriculture in the Midwest. Thus, in mid-August, we packed the van and headed west for eight days. Riding with four children eight hours a day for a week isn't something an adult looks forward to. But wanting to see more of the US, Viktor just couldn't pass up the opportunity. Mike scheduled a tour of the John Deere manufacturing plant in Moline, Illinois, for the second morning of our trip. It was a place he had always wanted to see, and we knew Viktor loves machinery.

We stopped for a short time at Iowa State University, where Mike had attended college fifteen years ago and received an associate degree in farm operations. Also, we stopped at several museums in Iowa and Nebraska to give Viktor and the children a taste of our agricultural history. Then we traveled to the western border of Nebraska to show Viktor that not all of America is farmland. As we drove from rich soil into barren, rocky areas, Viktor wondered how the early pioneers felt as they crossed our country over one hundred years ago in their covered wagons, intending to settle the new land.

Viktor was interested in American Indians. He quickly noticed the US government hadn't given up any tillable land for the Indian reservation. We told him Indians had received a bad deal from our government, and they continue to be an oppressed people so long as they choose to remain in their heritage on the reservation.

We returned to Ohio through Minnesota, northern Iowa, and Wisconsin—where dairy farming is prevalent.

Dirk had begun to make arrangements for Irina to come to the States in May. However, it was August before we started the same process for Valentina and Tatiana Palamarchouk. Viktor was not very hopeful they would get to come. It was good the trip we took kept his mind occupied during August. There was much to do when we returned. Kevin Dull had been overseeing the fields while Mike was away, but now everyone was needed to get machinery, barns, and bins ready for the harvest season. During September, he was busy with the seed corn harvest.

We also took the two Ukrainians to the county fair, where there was a tractor pull for entertainment. Viktor and Nik had never seen anything like this before. As I think about it, it does seem like a strange thing to do, but farmers as well as city folk seem to enjoy watching the big machines. When tractor pulls first began many years ago, a farmer would enter his field-work tractor in the contest. Now anyone can own the special, high-powered machines that pull the weighted sled. The idea is to see who can pull the most weight the farthest. The noise is almost deafening, and when the tires begin to spin, dirt flies everywhere. Mike, Abe, and I watched from high in the grandstand, but Viktor and Nik had been given front row seats by the Fair Board President because they were special guests. After watching the dirt and thick exhaust cover the area where they were sitting, we went down and asked if they would rather sit with us less important people! They quickly made the change! It wasn't intended for our guests to be uncomfortable; the wind just didn't cooperate. It was truly an American experience.

Other aspects of the American life were new to them, too. Hamburgers and french fries were totally unknown to our friends. We had to think of ways to explain countless things which we never gave a second thought to before. It is a good experience in awareness to have someone ask questions about everyday features of our lives. For instance, Viktor told of an evening at Jim's when he first saw fireflies (or "lightning bugs"). He saw tiny lights flickering across the horizon of the field and asked Jim if he saw flashing spots, too. Jim responded with a chuckle, "No, I see nothing." So Viktor was sure either his eyes or his mind was playing tricks on him. After Jim had his fun, he explained the lights are actually small, nocturnal, flying beetles whose luminous abdominal organs produce a flashing light. He explained that they are very common in Ohio in the summer months. Children like to catch them and put them into jars with small holes punched in the lids so they can watch the lightning bugs light up.

Sundays are not working days at Dull Homestead, with the exception of the morning chores of feeding and checking on the hogs. Kevin or Jim usually do these jobs before church. The whole family attends church together in Brookville. Viktor and Nik attended church twice during their stay here. They enjoyed the people, but, of course, the worship service meant little to them.

Sometimes the language barrier was a problem. Misunderstandings happened, as one would expect. However, I think the reason Mike and Viktor got along so well was Mike was very patient when Viktor didn't understand our English word for something. Instead of repeating the same word louder, like many would do, Mike talked slower and tried to think of a synonym. He placed himself in Viktor's shoes, a man in a foreign land away from everything and everyone familiar to him.

Although meeting someone from the Soviet Union was only a novelty to some people, there were those who cultivated genuine and lasting friendships with Viktor and Nik. I think of Mike's uncle, Lowell Eby, who extended Viktor good American hospitality.

By mid-September, we'd made all the necessary arrangements for Valentina and 14-year-old Tatiana to join Viktor for his last two weeks. Viktor began to call home more often to see if Valentina had received word that she and Tatiana could come. The round-trip tickets had already been ordered and paid for by Dull Homestead. Now it was just a matter of waiting to see if they'd be allowed to visit. The arrival date was just two days before Ralph and Chris were to return. Paul and Helen had planned to have Viktor and his family stay at their house for the weekend. My parents would then go out of town so the family could have a few days of privacy for their reunion. I have never in my life felt such an intensity as I felt then, anticipating something very uncertain. We were all so hopeful Viktor's family could come, though Viktor dared not set himself up for disappointment if they didn't.

The day of the flight arrived, and Viktor, Mike, Jessi (our older daughter, 12), and I had made arrangements to go to the airport in Cincinnati to pick them up. We were praying they would be on the plane. My mother and father had been busy decorating their house with balloons and welcoming posters to greet them. My dad could no longer endure the uncertainty. After the airplane was to have left Moscow, he called the airline to confirm they were on board. They told him they were not allowed to tell him for security reasons, so he asked to talk the person in charge. He explained why we were so eager to know: after a two-hour ride to the airport, Viktor shouldn't be let down if they weren't on board. The airline official didn't say they were on the plane but did say a woman and a girl had boarded with those tickets in Moscow. After my father called with the good news, I hurried to the barn where Viktor was working to tell him. For the first time, I think he finally risked believing. Now we were able to make the trip to the airport with confidence that Valentina and Tanya were going to be getting off that plane!

Mike and I had never been to the Cincinnati airport, so we arrived early. To try to make the time pass quickly, Jessi and I decided to stop at the gift shop. Jessi wanted to buy a welcoming gift for Tatiana. As she was looking around, and Viktor was purchasing film for his camera, I noticed the *Time* magazine featuring Ralph and Chris. We told the clerk Viktor was the man they talked about in the article. She was most impressed, and Viktor was somewhat embarrassed.

Mike joined us, and Jessi picked out a stuffed bear dressed in a T-shirt that read "I love Cincinnati." She thought it would be true since it would be remembered as the city where she was reunited with her father. Also, Jessi bought a cloth long-stemmed, red rose for Valentina and a pink one for Tatiana.

We walked to the end of the terminal to await the plane's arrival. It touched down twenty minutes late. Because we were there early, the wait seemed like hours! We got to laughing at Jessi. Each plane that landed which wasn't Pan Am would be dismissed as not "the one," but she would quickly announce she could see another approaching for landing.

We watched the sunset that evening with some anxiety as each airplane approached the runway. It was almost too dark to read the words Pan Am when their plane finally rolled towards the terminal. It was the first Pan Am flight to land since we began waiting. We knew they had finally arrived! Viktor stood where he could see down the walkway, and we stood back. We heard screams of delight before we saw the women. They darted out so quickly and with such force that a gentleman behind Viktor put his hands up against Viktor's back to keep all of them from tumbling over! The emotion was overwhelming, and we all cried at their joy.

After a few minutes of introduction and hugs and grateful kisses, we were off to pick up luggage. To our disappointment, their luggage didn't arrive with them. Valentina had no knowledge of the English language, and Tatiana knew only a little, so one can imagine their anxiety at having nothing but what they were wearing! A man from the airline was polite and helpful in assuring them they would get their luggage—it would even be delivered to our home. We had to describe the suitcases and something inside for positive identification, and I was surprised that most of what they had brought sounded like gifts for our family. Viktor expressed their gratitude for the service they had received. We explained that the American business slogan is "The customer is always right." Courteous service is encouraged by businesses due to competition in our society. It's something we Americans take for granted.

They had arrived on Saturday evening, and their luggage arrived early on Monday. Meanwhile, Jessi and I quickly purchased a set of leisure clothes for each of them. In addition, Jessi gave Tatiana one of her oversized T-shirts to wear. Valentina was about my mother's size, so I opened her closet and told Valentina to wear whatever she desired until their luggage arrived. I later learned from Chris why Tatiana giggled at her mother in the sweat suit I purchased for her—dresses are the standard in their village. And I had wanted to get something comfortable! We purchased blue jeans for Tatiana; I think those were all right.

We dropped the Palamarchouk family at my parents' house and enjoyed the ahs and sounds of amazement at the way my mother's kitchen was decorated. My father had put a bunch of bananas on the kitchen table with Tatiana's name on them to tease her. Viktor had told him of a time when he'd gone to Moscow and brought a banana to Tatiana because she had never eaten one before. Anytime he made a trip to Moscow after that, he would ask her if he should bring her anything, and she would always reply, "A banana." We left them to themselves, for they had six months to catch up on.

It was interesting how much we were able to communicate without knowing each others' language. I must say I've wished many times Viktor could have brought his wife and daughter with him in March. The smiles, the tears, the laughs, the wonderful times we had in the two short weeks they were here were wonderful! Jessi and Tatiana had fun shopping together. Tatiana also went to school with Jessi one day, a brave feat as she wasn't able to speak enough English to carry on conversations. But students were fascinated with her and her country.

Farming is a way of life. It is as much a part of us as the air we breathe. We can't go home from our job; it's always with us, always a part of us, because the farm activity is right outside the back door. It's a family experience. I wasn't raised on a farm, but I've come to appreciate the farm family's attachment to the land, seeing things grow, and the anticipation of a bountiful harvest. Farming is as much a part of my husband as the blood in his veins. And now I see the same thing in my older son. Perhaps some of Ralph's grandchildren will continue as the fifth generation to work this family farm.

A Soviet farm family needs to observe the good times as well as the hard for individual family farms. I'm sure there's room for improvement in the way we do things. Generally, though, the rewards outweigh the hardships. It depends on one's priorities. As a farm wife, I'm proud of what my husband does. He loves his work; and he nurtures and cares for the land and takes pride in producing the best crops he possibly can. I think Viktor took this home, too, and is eager to farm independently.

Goodbyes are always hard. First, we all sent Valentina and Tatiana on their way with tearful eyes and many hugs. I was afraid Jessi and Tatiana wouldn't let each other go and the airplane would leave before we could tear them apart. Viktor's flight departed a few days later. They will always be part of us. The friendship is everlasting. I said to Mike, "You will miss Viktor."

He replied, "More than any man I have ever met."

Michael Dull, Kevin Dull, Peter Dull, Viktor Palamarchouk, and Jim Osswald on the Dull farm in Ohio.

CHAPTER 14

Afterword: Update on Principal Characters
by Christine

We returned to the States just as the East European exodus from Communism was flowering. Every morning, we avidly turned on CNN, knowing Moscow's day, eight hours ahead of us, had already occurred and there would likely be noteworthy news. We watched as Gorbachev announced the Soviet Union would not use force in the Eastern Bloc countries and gaped as governments went down like the infamous dominoes we had been warned about all our lives. The domino theory reversed!

The harmony of it all was incredibly beautiful, with only one dissonant chord—the terrible violence in Romania. Czechoslovakians were in perfect character with their "velvet revolution." They merely rattled their key chains at the government in Wenceslas Square and placed gentle writer/prisoner Vaclav Havel at their helm. In 1968, they had bravely demonstrated eight months of non-violent resistance. Their efforts were ultimately crushed by tanks. But only 70 were killed in Czechoslovakia, as compared with 3,000 Hungarians and 1,500 Soviets in the fierce 1956 Budapest battle. For years, we've watched the Poles' spirited, non-violent resistance in their quest for self-government. But Hungarians deserve the credit for actually opening the Iron Curtain—they cut the barbed wire on their border. Happily, hard-liner Honecker of East Berlin was outfoxed by Gorbachev. After Gorbachev called the East German Head of Security, Egon Krenz, to Moscow for a powwow, Krenz promptly ordered the troops to put away their guns. They obeyed, though Honecker had ordered them to fire on demonstrators. The fuse of the new-order critical mass had finally been lit!

But, exhilarating as all these developments were, we were still hungry for news of our friends and acquaintances in Ukraine.

The first word was that the little church had indeed opened two days after we left. Toli's chapter has revealed other events which took place just after we left.

In February, 1990, Ralph and I shipped a gift of 20 bushels of soybean seed and 5 bushels of wheat seed from Wisconsin to Rotterdam. Officials from Khmelnitski, Ukraine, were supposed to pick it up. We hoped the seed would be planted in test plots around May 1. Unfortunately, the officials needed permission to pick up the seed and were frustrated in every attempt. For months, the seed sat rotting in Rotterdam. Finally in August, we were able to pay to have the seed sent to Kaliningrad where it was finally retrieved. Perhaps enough of it will germinate next year. Progress doesn't come easily for Soviets.

Palamarchouk: The day after we got home, Viktor Palamarchouk saw Ralph picking seed corn all day in the field. He remarked to Mike, "Your dad doesn't look like a loafer to me."

Palamarchouk went home to become chairman of a new collective farm called Niva (a fancy word for field). The villagers of Chechelnik voted to split from Ukraina farm, and they elected him chairman. Niva has 4,500 acres of cropland, 25 acres of orchard, 715 acres of forest, and 200 workers. It is also the hilliest section of Ukraina. Palamarchouk is busier and more frustrated than he's ever been before. Though his hands are still tied by the system, he's undaunted.

I quote from his letter:

> The cattle barns are very old, the cattle are bad—600 heads. We have 34 tractors, 5 combines, and 26 trucks. Now I'm busy preparing to shift crops and forage production to rent relations. For this we changed crop rotation and have education for farmers. This work is important and difficult because people are afraid to rent, but we have already had some changes. We plan to build a cattle farm for beef and one for pigs and later give them to renters. The basis of economic relations will be shares, and the *kolkhoz* (collective farm) will act as a bank.
>
> Now we have new laws on land, property, and rent. [In] changing to new forms of relations in farming, there will be many jobless people. For me this is the main problem, so we have to have new jobs like in a sewing shop, brick shops, etc.
>
> This year I planted 25 acres of soybeans. I want to make sure it's worth it to grow soya. If the harvest is satisfactory, there will be a need of processing it. So you see, I have a lot to do.
>
> I've had a lot of meetings with people who wanted to hear how it was in America. For me, it was nice to remember that wonderful experience and things for considering.

There is unrest in this country. There is no peace between Armenians and Azerbaijanis, and Baltic Republics are seceding. It is still calm in Ukraine, but people are not silent as before.

I often remember all of you and miss you . . .

Nik: Nik Zubyets has written once to the Harmses, still wanting them to visit him. He now has a job in Kiev, though he didn't say what.

The Greenhouse Gang: They have changed their work division. Oleg split off and is now in charge of the two greenhouses. The other four work the orchard. The Chairman offered to rent them all of Stupentsi, except the house we stayed in. The Chairman is keeping that, though all the furnishings have been removed. He knows as democratization sets in, he'll have to give up Stupentsi anyway.

One day after we left, Nikolai's dog, Alma, barked at the Chairman as he rode his bicycle through Stupentsi. The almighty Chairman went home, returned with his rifle, and shot tied-up Alma. She still lives but without one eye. The Gang can't protest because they might lose their orchard contract.

In June, 1990, **Stepan** of the Greenhouse Gang came to visit us for a month. Once a Soviet steps off the Aeroflot plane in New York or Washington, he's his host's responsibility. Stepan was very concerned about the money we were spending on him, so he insisted on painting a Dull farm barn. He worked hard and thanked me sweetly for every meal. He doesn't speak English, so he and Ralph had quiet but content rides together. We spent weekends and some evenings showing him as much as we could. In the middle of a supermarket, he said, "I have many questions to ask about Lenin when I get back to Ukraine!" Later, he said, "I'm not only going to tell what I've seen; I'm going to shout it!" When Ralph took him, Sergei, and Marina to an orchard field-day at Lake Erie, he said, "This was my best day."

One of his most eye-opening experiences was with a Ukrainian couple who live outside Troy, Ohio. They came here in 1950, and now the man is a surgeon, his wife an artist, and they live very well. Stepan could see how different the results of hard work are in the US. Here one can realize great material rewards, compared with the subsistence living that hard work often yields in the USSR.

Stepan is a professional mechanic. Not surprisingly, he loved the new and used car lots and the auto parts stores with their full shelves of every imaginable part. He even spent a happy hour in an auto salvage yard. Electronic gadgets fascinate him, too, though he didn't come here just to buy. We gave him gifts for the Gang and their families, and he bought a few things with money the Dull farm gave him. Our New York City friends hosted him for two days before he caught an Aeroflot flight back to the USSR.

Sergei and Marina: The couple arrived in Dayton, Ohio, the middle of May, 1990, and stayed for four months. They had wanted to learn to grow fruits and vegetables, so a Church of the Brethren couple hosted them on their strawberry and melon farm. Sergei enjoyed taking care of their pigs, and Marina liked using the automatic washer to wash his piggy clothes.

They also spent ten days with my oldest son, Ted, and his family in San Jose, CA. Then they went to New York City, visiting our friends there for three days. By the time they left the US, they had swum in the Atlantic, the Pacific, Lake Erie, and at least one swimming pool. With their good English and attractive ways, they became socialites of a sort. Many people wanted to spend time with them and take them places.

Marina soon became homesick for their four-year-old daughter, Katya, however. She hung on until September 28 when she returned to Moscow. Sergei stayed in the US a while longer, hoping to receive financial aid and an acceptance to a university for a computer degree. He knows his country needs that expertise. Ohio State University accepted him.

Misha Alexeyev: Our journalist friend arrived in the US in spring, 1990. He was here to make arrangements for a joint US/Soviet climb of Mt. Rainier. Misha, Ralph, and I reestablished our friendship, and he graciously made editorial comments for my part of our book for Soviets, *Heart to Heart*. While in Dayton, he was invited to the elegant former home of the Wright Brothers. This is one place we have never been permitted to visit, even though I grew up around the corner. Later, Misha became a temporary weekly columnist for the *Seattle Times* and was a simultaneous interpreter for the Good Will Games, held in July there. He also quit the Communist Party.

In September, 1990, he left for a quarter at Oxford University. He had received a full scholarship. Before he went, he was awarded the NATO Democratic Institutions Fellowship, making him the first Soviet NATO fellow! He will do his research at the University of Washington on returning from Oxford.

Eda: Our friend from Chernovtsi was to leave the USSR on Sept. 1, 1990, to join her sister in Israel. She wrote saying her heart was breaking because she may never see her son and grandson again. Ralph and I wonder at her decision. We would much rather be in the USSR in her large, shady apartment than anywhere in the dangerous Middle East. In the past, Jews often lost their jobs after they applied to emigrate. But we haven't seen outright acts against them in the last three years. In fact, most Soviet Jews are well-educated and have decent jobs. It's a real brain drain for the USSR when they leave. The philosophy of the Moscow-based anti-semitic Pamyat Society is indeed ominous, but so far the members have only spoken, not acted.

Andrei: We heard Andrei was voted out of his post as Komsomol leader. He wrote he's gathering students to help with the changes in his country.

The Chairman: Chairman Stengach wrote several times, hoping he or his daughter and granddaughters could be our guests here. But we're sticking to our plan of inviting only people with educational purposes, not those who just want to look around or buy things. At his request, we twice sent him battery-packs and cassettes for his camcorder.

Stengach ran for both the District and the local soviets in the March 1990 elections. He was elected to the District soviet on the second try, but the villagers—including those of his own precinct—did not elect him to the local soviet. This embittered him to the point he wants to leave Makov just as he found it. He immediately began to tear out improvements.

Potato bugs: When we returned home, we discovered Sukup Manufacturing Company had just come out with a non-chemical antidote to these pests we were so often asked about. It's a vacuum machine which pulls the insects from the plants. They die when they hit the fan.

Vladimir and Vladimir: The brigadier from Volgograd whom we had invited to come to Ohio to learn to grow seed corn accepted an invitation to Colorado instead. So Volodya Chernov sent two substitutes (both named Vladimir) for a month—a state farm director and his interpreter.

The state farm director was very progressive, having rented out his entire farm of 125,000 acres. Because he is responsible for everything in that territory—local taxes and government, roads, school funding—he was primarily concerned with learning how these issues are dealt with in the US. One of his big problems is many of his workers are now saying, "I'm free! I don't have to work or pay taxes!" In time, it will become obvious that freedom and responsibility go hand in hand to make a successful society.

We made many appointments for these men and took them to Chicago, Pennsylvania, and Iowa, where the farm director arranged to buy a corn and sorghum dryer. If the sale works out, Ralph (and perhaps I) will spend June in Volgograd constructing it.

Ralph and Christine: Toli (our agent) translated *Heart to Heart* into Russian. The Kiev publishing company we signed with went kaput, so Rodale Publishing Company, an American press, has offered to publish it as part of their joint venture in Moscow. The joint venture's aim is to provide education for independent farmers. Their main vehicle will be *Novii Fermer* (New Farmer) magazine, and Ralph has been asked to write a monthly "Fermer to Fermer" column for it.

I sent my part of the *Heart to Heart* to Vladimir Pozner. He read it and promised to write a Foreword for the friendship part of the book. He especially liked the part I'd written about America, saying no one else that he knew of had written about the US specifically for Soviets. Yuri Chernichenko, respected agricultural journalist and popular People's Deputy, has been sent a copy of Ralph's half of the book, with the hope he'll write a Foreword for the agricultural part. Buddha has already ordered 30,000 books just for the Khmelnitski Region, saying they will be gone in a week.

Fellowship of Reconciliation has asked us to lead a group of young Americans and Soviets for three weeks in July and August to help reconstruct a Russian Orthodox church outside Moscow. And of course, we'll visit friends in Ukraine. I can hardly wait!

Toli: Ah, dear Toli! After we returned to the US, he continued translating our Soviet book into Russian.

In the spring, he ran against the Chairman for the District soviet, and Toli won the first round by 90 votes—even though he had no way of giving favors. Viktor Party Secretary, trapped in his post, was required to start ugly rumors. But Toli defended himself, and the rumors had no effect. But there was a run-off, and Toli lost to the Chairman by 40 votes. What made the difference? Dirty tricks, of course! Viktor Palamarchouk ran for the Regional Soviet and lost by a tiny margin to Viktor (Roza's husband).

Toli decided it was just as well he didn't win the race for the *District* soviet. He wrote:

> For me it was no use because it consists of 95 percent communists and supervisors of different levels. I was elected to the local *village* Soviet, and I had a good chance to be its chairman [in which case he would have stopped teaching to work full-time at civic duties]. However, people whom I respect and trust convinced me not to do that because it's not my time yet. The present rulers of Makov would discredit me as not competent, and good only in words . . . . There were some victories of democratic forces at recent elections, but they didn't change the situation in general. The old are still powerful, and they will not go away easily. We are only shaking the horrible wall, but it stands.

Toli and Vladimir of Vladimir Cooperative in Moscow arrived in Washington on July 21, 1990, and stayed for a full-scheduled, whirlwind month. Vladimir came to make business contacts, and we arranged many, which may later bear fruit in joint ventures or training for Soviets. Many miles were put on our car during trips to Washington, D.C., New York City, Chicago, Columbus, Cincinnati, and to Lakeside on Lake Erie, where our slideshow and Toli were featured at the Chautauqua there. Toli spent time with an uncle in Philadelphia and talked by phone to several relatives in Toronto.

We bombarded Toli with questions about his family and our Makov friends. Tanya worked for a while as a bookkeeper at the sugar factory, but her job ended and she is home again. Yura attended the sugar factory's day care center, and Anna helped with the cooking and care of the children. After Toli returned to Makov, he wrote that Anna is receiving treatment for skin cancer. Also, a kind young man who had fixed our TV, who helped the Greenhouse Gang with apple transportation, and who once gave me a ride to Stupentsi, was killed horribly in a traffic accident in Moscow. I can still see his radiant smile in my mind's eye.

Many people sent greetings to us through Toli. Vanya sent us a large copper bas-relief icon of the Virgin and Child that had taken him a month to make, and Ola sent us each a pair of colorful, hand-knitted socks, which fit perfectly.

Toli came to the States for five reasons: to be with us, to check the accuracy of the facts in both our books, to talk with people, to interpret for Vladimir, and to put together a slideshow about America for Soviets. All his goals were fulfilled.

The three of us deepened our already-rich friendship, and he endeared himself to many other Americans. He was featured locally for a half hour on TV, was interviewed by two newspapers, and spoke to nine groups while he was here. To the congregation of one of Dayton's largest churches, he spoke about his experience with the Bible, the re-opening of hundreds of churches in the USSR, the new law allowing freedom of religion and the withdrawing of state support for atheism, and the desire of Soviets for peace. After the service, I asked him if he was still a non-believer. He said, "I can't say, and I don't like labels. We are what we are, with all our inconsistencies."

Like Ralph, Toli deliberates at length about important decisions, and he has decided to get his law degree, which will require three year's study. Because the USSR is becoming a society based on law, there is a great need for those who can interpret and show ways of implementing the new democratic laws. Toli's talents are perfect for this: he's a teacher at heart, a deep and logical thinker, and a natural orator. He's honest, and he cares. Unlike Soviets who are leaving the country for a better life, Toli intends to stay and work for the betterment of his people. He may attend University of Cincinnati's law school for a couple of years.

The three of us think we were preparing for our eventual meeting for many years—unbeknownst to us. It's truly amazing Ralph and I were in Makov at all. The most likely scenario that occurred behind the scenes was this: The Central Committee of the Communist Party received our resume and ordered the exchange, probably because Ralph offered to host two Soviet farmers on his American farm. Still, we never received a written invitation. This is one indication of foot-dragging by the Chairman and other mid-level bureaucrats who hoped Ralph and I would forget about our visit. But when Ralph and I suddenly appeared on their doorstep April 4 and told the Gosagroprom officials we had decided to stay in Ukraine, they had to proceed with the exchange.

At the end of our month together, it was even harder to say goodbye to Toli. But we know we will always be together, heart to heart.

As we go to press: Soviet Foreign Minister Shevardnadze has resigned, and events in the USSR are turning dark again. What are we to think of Gorbachev, the initiator of glasnost and democratization? Time will tell. Obviously, he is not willing to preside over the dissolution of the Soviet

Union. However, he is not likely to be seen as a Lincoln, especially because of the Baltics.

Most Soviets we know agree the USSR will never return completely to its old form, but there may be set-backs. Although new laws on freedom of religion and the media have been passed, harder times are ahead. We grieve for the people.

Opinions abound. Yevgeny Yevtusheuko, the great Russian poet, says, "Gorbachev is still the same in his heart. We don't know the pressures upon him."

In a recent TV interview, Vladimir Pozner indicated he still supports Gorbachev but feels Gorby has few other options with the present chaos in the USSR. Pozner seemed discouraged as he said the conservatives were obviously influencing his president. Ralph and I harked back to Pozner's January, 1988, statement, "This is our last chance, and we may not make it."

After Misha Alexeyev returned to the US, he wrote us a beautiful, poignant letter. I quote from it:

> I feel sad, troubled, and only remotely optimistic about what is happening back home. After watching Shevardnadze's speech on Soviet TV, I walked around the ever-autumnal streets of Oxford with the painful feeling of "the end of an era," when enthusiasts like Shevardnadze, like you and Ralph, could achieve something worthwhile, at least in your own spheres. The fact that Shevardnadze goes (and rumors within the Foreign Ministry had this for about a year) means he understood his inability, conditioned from without, to improve further his own sphere. You cannot separate successes in Soviet foreign policy from their base in the internal political situation, and that base has narrowed to the point where Shevardnadze has no room to stay on.
>
> Vitaly Korotich, the editor of *Ogonyok*, summed up the whole thing very simply: "The present political environment in the USSR makes it impossible for a certain kind of fish to survive. And Shevardnadze is that kind of fish."
>
> As I walked around Oxford, I remembered the deep, kind, understanding, human, generous smile of Shevardnadze as he beamed to me at the Gorby-Mitterand press conference in Kiev. It was when the microphone broke down during my question and I took Gorby's suggestion to shout it directly at him. Now I know why Shevardnadze's eyes were so sympathetic and why he turned back from his first row to give me a smile several times: For five years he managed to stay heard without a microphone, but finally his voice broke down. The party still controls the switch on the microphone, and that makes it a comfortable power base which Gorbachev is reluctant to leave.

But we'd like to end this update optimistically. When we talked with Toli about the troubling change of policy in the USSR, he said, "I expected this backlash. We couldn't expect the conservatives to be quiet forever. *But we shall overcome!*"

Part III

Soviet Agriculture: An American Farmer on a Collective Farm

CHAPTER 15

Encounters on the Farm
by Ralph

As I reflect back on those early days in Makov, remembering the party and agricultural leaders of the Region, District, and collective farm coming to our house and removing their shoes before entering our living room, I realize they were expecting a lot from me. But as we sat facing each other, discussing a schedule for the coming months, all they saw was me—a mild-mannered, slightly-built man about half their size who couldn't even speak directly to them, let alone match their forceful, command-style manner of communication.

I can now imagine they expected this farmer from America to march in huffing and puffing, ready to vigorously pound out a program that would make them famous in Moscow. I really can't blame them for being disappointed in this calm, soft-spoken guest with slow and deliberate ways. We didn't expect to make a big splash: we just wanted to live with the people and contribute in a natural way. When they finally realized I was not going to be aggressive, everyone relaxed for the most part, and things went smoothly.

We regret that the disappointment of the collective farm chairman and chief agronomist caused them to miss opportunities for beneficial agricultural interaction with us on other matters. They poisoned the air of the village ever so slightly, but I think we gained the friendship and respect of almost everyone anyway.

Five months passed before the Chairman and the agronomist realized we, in our own way, had something to contribute to what they knew. They already knew how much fertilizer to put on corn, when to plant, and the like. I wanted to discuss philosophical principles of agriculture, along with the issues of renting, reduced tillage, soil conservation, grain storage, etc.

We didn't run into defensiveness when we had meetings or informal discussions on other farms. For example, we just dropped in on a grain yard seventy miles from Makov during wheat harvest, and the collective farm economist happened to be there. It was a poor farm, and after we talked awhile, the economist sincerely asked in a resigned manner, "What should we do on this farm?" He wasn't aware of many basics, well-known in the agricultural world. But this bright-looking thirty-five-year-old was eager for improvement. About all I could do in the brief visit was to give him a *Successful Farming* magazine and hope the book we're writing for Soviet readers would be helpful to him.

The vast majority of Soviet farms struggle along in a semi-daze. Prosperity or poverty is less dependent on soil fertility than on power and who your buddies are in faraway places.

An example of a prosperous and well-managed state farm void of complacency is located near Volgograd. The first party secretary and a brigadier sat with us for four hours, picking our brains for ideas that could improve their farm. Topics such as seed production, grain storage, and tillage were discussed. The six-foot-five director (a state farm has a director, and a collective farm has a chairman) was a quiet, capable man who asked me to draw up plans for a seed corn dryer and to host his most capable brigadier for several months in Ohio.

I'm sure many of the 1,254 workers on Ukraina collective farm considered me deaf and dumb. Most encounters were without Toli, so communication was little more than a verbal "Dobree dane" (Good day) along with a nod of the head and a smile.

On one occasion, though, I approached men spraying a young wheat field, curious about why they were doing it. I picked up a blade of wheat and stroked it, and the men shook their heads, "No." I knew then the spray was not a fungicide for wheat blight. I got the same response when making an upward motion with the wheat blade, so I knew the spray wasn't nitrogen to make it grow faster. When I picked a weed and made a downward motion, they nodded, "Yes." Finally, I knew the spray was a herbicide to kill weeds. Since returning to Ohio, I still find myself using sign language.

Incidentally, these were the same three men that ten minutes earlier had been lying under trees along the side of the road. Three tractors were idling: one for spraying, one for the water wagon, and one for the herbicide wagon. As usual, whenever I saw workers loafing, they lay there for a few more minutes, then got up and started to work.

Usually, though, I just stood and watched the activity for a few minutes or observed as I walked, hoping the people would read our book published in Ukrainian and discover, however belatedly, that I wasn't as dumb as I seemed.

After first arriving in Makov, I tried to expand my Russian vocabulary. But then we discovered everyone spoke Ukrainian here, so I quickly decided there were better ways to use my time than learning a new language. Spanish is difficult for me, let alone Russian and Ukrainian. However, all

Ukrainians speak Russian if you ask them. And between Christine and Toli, I managed fairly well.

The realization that I wasn't needed to perform tasks in the field came on the first day of planting. Compared to an Ohio corn field, it seemed like a convention was being held. On the Dull farm, two or three workers are a crowd. The agronomist took me to the 200-acre field where there were already a brigadier, supervisor, mechanic or two, nine tractor drivers and substitutes, two women fertilizer handlers, and an interpreter for me. I soon learned to like them all, but it seemed more like a party than corn planting.

A tractor driver, Anatoli, asked me to plant corn for awhile. Many eyes were watching as I climbed into the tractor and received one minute's instruction from strong-breathed Anatoli about how to raise and lower the planter, rev up the engine before starting the air blower, find the proper gear, move the markers, and—what seemed most important to him—how to let out the clutch quickly so as not to slip it and wear it out.

Simultaneously running the engine fast and letting out on the clutch quickly can cause a little excitement, but we were off, planting six rows with a Yugoslavian planter. We left a mark off to the side for an identical outfit following a hundred feet behind and fourteen feet to the left. In Ohio, we always drive with the center of the tractor over the mark, sighting straight over the hood for the length of the field and straightening out any crooks from the previous trip. Soviets drive off-center with a wheel on the mark.

The small crowd watched intently as this surplus-producing American did his thing. After two rounds of planting, I gave the rig back to Anatoli, whom I never met without alcohol on his breath. To watch him work, though, you would never know he'd been hitting the bottle. (By the way, Soviets flip the underside of their jaw with their finger instead of saying they want a drink or to say someone has a drinking problem. Likewise, instead of saying wacky or crazy-in-the-head, they'll roll their forefinger alongside their temple.)

Soon after I quit planting, a downpour of rain started, causing a traffic jam. Trucks, wagons, cars, tractors, and bicycles converged at one corner of the field to leave. I was in the back of the brigadier's jeep, and I watched him shake his fist and shout at one of his truck drivers who got in his way. The brigadier had a firm grip on the steering wheel as he leaned over it, straining to see through the windshield wipers as we sped along a dirt path getting more slippery by the second. He safely delivered five of us to our houses.

Another encounter in the same two-hundred-acre field came at harvest time when I was driving by and noticed a corn picker "opening up" the field by cutting a six-row swath at three-hundred-foot intervals across the field. When you head a picker into the middle of a half-mile-long corn field, it's like entering a jungle of nine-foot-high stalks. You just hope all goes well until you get to the other end, because you're surrounded by standing corn on three sides and a wagon behind.

Halfway through the field, Anatoli's picker broke down. So I parked at the end of the field and walked down the sweet-smelling, freshly-picked avenue to where three men were looking at a disassembled fodder-saver under the header. After a brief appraisal of the situation, I decided they should ignore the fodder-saver and continue to harvest the ears of corn, at least until they got to the end of the field where there was room to make repairs. I suggested this plan (with no authority) to the men by way of energetic gestures. We all laughed, and I left.

It seemed logical to continue picking, as the fodder wasn't being blown into a truck anyway. When opening up a field, there's no space for a truck to drive beside the picker. However, the men apparently thought everything on the picker had to operate, even if, in the end, the fodder went right back on the ground. Midwest farmers don't value fodder or straw enough to harvest it for cattle feed, so we don't have a similar gathering mechanism on our grain harvesters.

Incidentally, the Chairman explained the farm grinds ear corn and puts it in a silo to make sure the state doesn't procure it as grain. They do this because while dry grain can be shipped across the country, silage cannot. There seem to be many ways to outfox the state.

A few hours before we said farewell to Makov on September 25, I returned to the corn field to check out a new corn picker. It had a new-fangled steering sensor device on the header that was supposed to respond to the touch of standing rows of corn. I'd never seen these electronic devices on US harvesters. As I was inspecting the dangling, disconnected wires, Anatoli indicated the device was useless. So much for an idea the US could use.

He motioned for me to get into the picker and drive it. Everything worked well, including the power winch cable that pulls an empty wagon up to the drawbar of the picker, and the fodder-saver which blows stalks into trucks driving alongside. When the trucks weren't there, we kept on going. Then the fodder floated out across the field where it belonged anyway.

When Volodya arrived and noticed me driving the machine, he broke into a big smile, thrusting his fist in the air. Volodya always made me feel good. He, strong-breathed Anatoli, and Viktor Palamarchouk were eager to form a small renter group to do independent farming. They are enthusiastic workers even now, but efficiency would improve if receipts came into their own pockets and expenses came out.

I hurried away from the corn field to attend a little farewell ceremony at our house with the Chairman and Viktor Party Secretary. The Chairman had already assigned our car to one of the 150 supervisors on the farm. We got to see the recipient proudly drive it away before we got into the farm taxi-van to go to the train station in Kamenets-Podolski. As we left Makov, we passed our "old" car and its new driver. He was taking friends out for a spin.

At planting time, I'd visited another field being planted by a Romanian six-row corn planter. It had a seat on one end facing rearward (for a man to sit on while watching the moving parts) instead of having an electronic seed monitor that whistles if there's trouble. This planter was pulled by a small caterpillar tractor. Most field work is done by caterpillars, which reduces harmful compaction. However, excessive tillage, choppers, wagons, and manure spreaders all harm the wet soil.

This became a high-yielding corn field, and the perimeter was harvested for silage, except four rows along the south side of the mile-long field. Here, the outside eight rows had been harvested, and the next four rows of tall corn with beautiful ears had been flattened to the ground by a roller and wasted. I inquired as to why four rows a mile long had been destroyed. No one knew. But would this have happened if the tractor driver had visualized a wagon load of corn for his own cows or for him to sell?

On a Sunday afternoon drive in late July, we stopped at a large wheat field. While Christine waited in the car, watching the harvest, I climbed aboard one of the five combines (they only operate in formation for photographs) and saw the driver was a young, smiling fellow I'd met before and enjoyed very much. We took off for the other end of the field at breakneck speed with header raised high. Most of the wheat stalks had fallen flat long before harvest and needed cut from only one direction. The header bounced wildly, and we swerved to miss piles of straw that had been collected in the rear of the combine and dumped periodically to form rows.

I had to ask myself if the smiling young driver would drive that fast if he were the owner of the combine and had to pay for repairs. I suddenly understood why I saw ruptured hydraulic hoses lying in fields and along dirt roads every day. I also thought of Viktor Palamarchouk in Ohio, who was Ukraina's chief specialist engineer in mechanics. What a tremendous task he must have, keeping the hundreds of machines on this collective farm in running order with these cowboys running them. We spun around at the field's end, lowered the header, threw the threshing mechanism into gear, and crept back towards the dirt road where the car was.

The combine did a good job, considering the condition (lodged) of the wheat stalks. The driver sat in a dusty cab (in contrast to US air-conditioned, dust-free cabs) manipulating the straw dump, which American combines don't have, and many other controls similar to those on US combines. Soviet combines don't have an automatic header control to give the field a short, uniform haircut. Fortunately, they don't have stones to foul the equipment.

When the grain bin on the combine was nearly full, the driver turned on a flashing light and blew his horn to wake a resting truck driver so he could rendezvous with the combine in the middle of the field. I wanted to give my friend a miniature John Deere combine, but we gave it instead to Buddha at our farewell meeting.

I got to see pretty much whatever I wanted. Anyone is free to enter forests and fields in Ukraine because it all belongs to the state. Palamarchouk felt a bit constrained in Ohio, where woods and fields are privately owned. But I think there was still a little uneasiness on the part of the Makov natives at seeing an American probing into everything everywhere, inspecting the crops, machine yards, lumber yard, beef barns, grain yards, or taking pictures.

We felt we must be politely assertive, though, because we had no official host to take us around. In Viktor's case, the Dull family was willing and able to introduce him to anyone or any situation he desired, including places in other states. Also, he had full use of my car to drive himself wherever he wanted to go.

In September as we drove past a distant farm, we noticed activity behind some trees along the road. I walked around some soggy grass to discover a crew of twenty women and boys hand-harvesting sugar beets in the corner of a field to provide a place to turn the cumbersome beet-digging machines. I probed around a little where they were working, nodded to them, and headed back to the car. All of a sudden, two women came out from behind the trees and shook their skirts at me while saying something. That was one time I failed to understand sign language. Christine finally guessed they wanted to buy the jeans I was wearing.

We had many warm, brief encounters, such as the Saturday evening in September when we were walking the length of a freshly-plowed furrow. We arrived at the end of the field near one of the artistic-looking straw stacks and started to walk the dirt road towards home. At the same time, a tractor driver plowing the field decided to call it a day and headed for the machine yard. As he passed us in the caterpillar tractor, we waved, and he clasped both his hands high above his head in a gesture of friendship and unity, giving us a big smile. That's really why we went to the USSR.

People were curious about American farmers, too. Many we talked with thought that if American farmers are only two or three percent of the US population, they surely must work themselves to death. (About 25% of Soviets are farmers.) They were surprised the Dulls don't work on Sunday and that we have time for many non-farm activities. If there is nothing pushing, most Soviets don't work on Sundays either.

One Sunday in July, we were out for a walk and came across the friendly crop brigadier for our part of the farm. He was just sitting in his jeep reading a newspaper, with forest on one side of him and an almost ripe wheat field on the other. A friend on a motorcycle had just come along and stopped to chat, so the four of us had a little visit before we walked on. I'll never know for sure why he chose that way to spend a Sunday afternoon. Did he need to get psyched up for the wheat harvest the next week? Did he just want to be near "his" wheat field? Was his wife nagging him at home?

One August day when the air was quiet, I noticed a "London fog" hanging over a two-hundred-acre field where peas had been harvested. As I walked towards the center of the field, I could hear trucks. But I couldn't see them through the fog, which hung low to the ground and extended high into the sky, covering most of the field. Eventually, I found two trucks and two tractor outfits in the thick mist, spreading lime. Some of it settled on the village house roofs and gardens far away. Perhaps Ohio lime is heavier, and we have applicator trucks with curtains to keep lime dust from flying into the atmosphere and settling far away.

I felt a moment of accomplishment on the July day I came across an oats windrowing machine with a chain repeatedly flying off the sprockets. I spotted a sprocket out of line, which was easy to correct, and the driver finished the field.

Although Ukraina is a prosperous farm, many things that happen here need correcting. One is the scorching of wheat and peas in dryers set too hot. Another is the haphazard way an airplane sprayed the fields. I couldn't believe my eyes the day a spray plane made a swipe over several corn fields as it flew cross-country, spreading its contents diagonally across the fields in a patternless way the pilot had no chance of remembering. The plane disappeared miles away, still spraying. Its altitude was never less than two hundred feet, so it appeared to be a case of getting rid of a load. Ordinarily, crop sprayers are just a few feet above the crop. I inquired about it later but couldn't get a satisfactory answer.

I enjoyed the farm work I occasionally got to do on Ukraina. Picking apples a few half-days was good in several respects. I needed the exercise and the break from writing, the orchard renters needed the apples picked, and the Chairman and agronomist noticed I could actually do manual labor, if necessary. It was fun working with the renters, who were impressed with my ability to work alongside them. On another occasion I picked apples with the teachers.

It did seem like an endless job to start picking a 185-acre orchard. The orchard was quite close to our house. In fact, our quarter-mile lane leading to the road turns past the greenhouses and right through a beautiful part of this orchard. Across the road from these apple trees are a chicken production enterprise, a grain yard, a saw mill, and the new facilities for dairy cows.

This road is also lined with full-grown buckeye trees, loaded with white blossoms for weeks in the spring. As Ohio is the Buckeye state, it seemed almost like home for Chris and me. Funny how so many of the encounters I had on this faraway Soviet collective farm only served to remind me of how similar the feelings of farm people are everywhere. Where there is the good, fertile earth; the changing seasons; and hard work to do; farmers the world over feel right at home.

CHAPTER 16

The Future of Collective and State Farms

About 98% of Soviet arable land is organized (and sometimes disorganized) into collective (*kolkhozy*) and state (*sovkhozy*) farms. If you hear the term "cooperative farm," it probably refers to a collective farm. Farmers and their land were forced into collectivization in the 1929-1933 period. Failing collective farms and small collective farms have been combined through the years into larger ones or shifted into state farms. The number of collective farms has decreased accordingly. Now only about 22,000 exist, a number similar to that of state farms.

Theoretically, there's a significant difference between kolkhozy and sovkhozy. However, in practice, the only real difference is this: state farms run all of their income and expenses through the state financial system while collective farms have their own budget and accountants. Both kolkhozy and sovkhozy have been tightly controlled by the state.

Historically, a failing collective borrows money from the state. Eventually, that debt is forgiven—mainly because repayment is hopeless. Or, in some cases, the collective farm becomes a state farm instead. Collective farm workers usually receive lower wages than state workers, though they supposedly can receive additional wages from distributed farm profits. It appears, however, that when there are farm profits, the workers seldom see much distribution. Thus, the desire for higher wages explains why workers frequently want their collective to become a state farm. In either case, inefficiency is inevitable, as is a low level of self-motivation for most workers. Both systems result in a low standard of living.

There is a solution though. I think independent farming and a more democratic rural system can provide the answer. Those farms that aren't healthy and those that have been abandoned need to be occupied as soon as possible by family farmers. Ownership given to them is appropriate. I believe there are enough potentially capable people to work the land for themselves—if certain roadblocks are removed. Local governments could develop to coordinate services needed for every healthy community, such as education for farmers, pensions, roads, housing, and a system of buying and selling supplies and produce.

Even prosperous collective and state farms should eventually evolve into entirely different organization than exists now. Here, too, power should come directly from the people—including those working the land and living in the community—and not trickle down from headquarters. That's what democratization and perestroika are *really* about.

The new farm system could look like this: The boundaries of each collective or state farm could continue to be the boundary of a community. Each community could hire an administrator to carry out the day-to-day tasks that result from directions given to him by a council elected by all the community's people. This administrator would have many of the same skills, but not the power, present-day chairmen or directors have.

An elected council with not more than seven members (at present, there are as many as 100 people on a local soviet) would elect a chairman from their midst to conduct their frequent meetings. This official would be in close touch with the administrator. The position of chairman of the council would be a part-time job, preferably limited to a three-year term. The administrator would attend at least a portion of each council meeting to report his activities, make proposals, and answer questions.

Also, the public should be invited to observe all council meetings, a segment of which would be set aside for citizen comment. (Undoubtedly, after the novelty wears off, most citizens won't show up unless they have specific personal interests.)

The administrator would have full responsibility for employees, such as road engineer, economist, and agronomist. The council would have influence over them and the farmers *only* through the administrator. Direct meddling wouldn't be permitted because it undercuts the administrator. If the administrator isn't effective or responsive to the will of the people *through* the council, he can quickly be replaced by the council.

The present system can change toward independent farming and power from the people. There is now a new tendency for farm chairmen and directors to enjoy freedom from their higher-ups but not to grant that freedom to their underlings. When democracy develops in the country, it needs to flow down to the workers and villagers as well. Citizen participation is what makes a wholesome society. Everyone has a brain to use and a contribution to make.

In the past, there has been a local soviet (governing body), but it has been powerless. The collective farm chairman is king, and he takes commands from the higher-ups rather then the lower-downs. A chairman sometimes says his people are happy if they can work, eat, sleep, and watch TV.

(Leave the driving to me!) A *true* collective society may be good, but the USSR has never had one. It had mostly Stalinism in the past and now its aftermath.

CHAPTER 17

Renting Land to Soviet Farmers

Sixty-five year old Vasily says, "I feel good. Sure, give me a piece of land, and I'll work it." This is an attitude many Soviet farm workers share. All that stands in their way is a chance at that "piece of land." We asked him how many workers on collective and state farms were capable of farming on their own. He thought carefully for a long time before responding with "One-tenth."

That's enough! Mr. Gorbachev and other top leaders are promoting the shift from state to individual management, which means renting or private land ownership. Gorbachev's interest in independent farming was a major reason we came to Ukraine. We'd been asked to help promote renting. Because of the importance of providing land for future independent farmers in the USSR, I'll cover the subject rather thoroughly in this chapter.

Vasily went on to say that on the farm where he lives, fourteen people care for 1,000 pigs. In contrast, on the Dull farm, one man cares for 2,000 pigs at any given time.

It's hard for Soviets to believe four or five people on the Dull farm can raise 1,965 acres of crops and 3,500 hogs a year. We can do this partly because there are so many jobs we *don't* do. Unlike Soviet farmers, Americans avoid tilling the land excessively, handling straw for feed, moving grain and manure repeatedly, having workers ride on planters, mixing fertilizer with shovels, hoeing weeds or thinning plants by hand, windrowing crops, supervising, and employing a different driver for every truck and tractor. We don't work any harder; we just organize our work differently. Knowing how few of us are on my farm, an astonished Ukrainian said on seeing a photo of my sons, "They don't look over-worked!"

Viktor Palamarchouk wrote from Ohio that the reason American production is so high is the system behind it: a system composed primarily of independent farmers. This system leads especially to the reduction of expenses and losses. I know that when the cost of unnecessary equipment comes out of *my* pocket, I'm less likely to purchase it, for example.

The same idea goes for unnecessary tillage, labor, seeds, fertilizer, and straw stacks. The spillage of seeds, fertilizer, manure, and forage crops eventually hits our checkbooks. Naturally, these problems affect Soviet agriculture as well. Other losses can come from crop spoilage in storage or from a lack of storage. Poorly designed trench silos and too-hot grain dryers cause high losses as well. In addition, badly adjusted combines leave grain behind in the fields, as do delayed harvests. All these costs are excessive in the USSR and could be minimized by a system encouraging personal interest via renting or private ownership. Obviously, when the state pays the bill, few people care about wasting rubles.

For future USSR farm policy, diversity is the key for a successful move towards renting. Historically, Soviet leaders have attempted to put everyone into the same mold. However, the approach to independent farming in Ukraine should be entirely different than it would be for an area north of Moscow or one in Turkmenistan. Even two side-by-side collective farms may need entirely different approaches. The intention will be the same, and the benefits and results will be similar, but the farms, the contracts, the people, and the modernization should look very different.

The shift to ideal tenant relations may happen quickly in the abandoned and failed areas. The shift may be more gradual for the collective and state farms now considered to be successful, depending on the attitude or degree of complacency of their officials.

For instance, a collective farm may change to a system in which a group of forty people would be the tenant for one-third of the collective farm crops. After a year or so, they might divide the land and people into smaller groups, or they could become more labor efficient and reduce to twenty the number of people necessary for that third of the farm.

Currently, there is considerable sentiment that it doesn't matter how many people are assigned to a job because everyone needs employment. This sounds humane but isn't in reality. Low wages, low production, meaningless work, low morale, and slovenly habits are the actual result. Better the work force be reduced so each task is done efficiently. Then the smaller work force can receive higher wages, develop good work habits, and feel good about their jobs.

Unemployment need not be a problem. Most women hoeing sugar beets would not feel unemployed if they were replaced by modern technology. Many we've talked to would prefer to work at home.

People who are released from agricultural production would be free to work in newly established light industries in the village or neighboring towns. Since there's a shortage of most consumer goods in the USSR, there doesn't need to be a surplus of workers for years to come. Medium-size processing facilities for agricultural produce are needed near the farms. Also, more storage facilities must be built for current and future increased production of grain, vegetables, and fruit. Additional employees are also needed for road building and for social services. With higher productivity, there would actually be plenty of work to go around.

The main change needed to increase Soviet agricultural productivity and efficiency would be if those who did farm were encouraged to do so independently. Affordable rent terms for farm land would be as good a solution in the USSR as it has been in the States. Many farmers in the US rent part of the land they work. This is especially true on our farm; we rent three-fourths of the land we use for crops. We pay *cash rent* to the landowner, and then we're completely free to choose which crops to plant, where to buy supplies, and where to sell what we harvest. The only action the landowner takes is deciding who he will rent to or when to change tenants. However, this second situation seldom happens.

For instance, we have 14 landlords and 12 of them are elderly. About the only occasion we have to talk business with them is when one of us wants to raise or lower the rent payment. This occurs maybe once in five years. Other contacts with landowners are strictly social. One of our landlords lives in the city, so I've seen him only once in ten years. My sons have never met the man. We put the rent check in the mail and work the field as though we own it.

Now, if the USSR government can be that kind of a landlord, we don't care much who owns the land—just so the farmers own the enterprise. In fact, it would be a little easier for the Dulls to have just one landlord to pay rent to rather than 14, especially if that meant all 1,965 acres would be in one place. Also, we wouldn't have the debt we have now due to past land purchases.

Advantages come to mind for private land ownership as well. For instance, individuals usually have more long-term personal interest in the quality of the land and buildings when they own them. Needless to say, private owners don't abandon farms by just walking away. They either develop the farm profitably themselves or sell it to someone else who will try. However, when the state owns the land, it's very difficult for its agent to refrain from interfering with the farmers' management, probably due to the strict system of control in the past. Thus, there's not much incentive for individual initiative. I just can't imagine the state being a good, hands-off landlord.

Another advantage of cash renting is the landowner doesn't have to keep his eye on the tenant to assure the tenant's honesty when weighing or dividing up crops. Only the tenant is concerned about expenses or yields; the landowner gets his cash rent regardless. It's not necessary to keep records for the landowner, or get permission to buy or sell supplies or crops. We have a clear-cut contract with landowners, and it avoids all disputes. The agreement is less than one page in length and is signed by both parties.

One guideline to determine how much cash rent should be paid might be this formula: six percent of the value of the land equals the annual rent. For instance, if the land value is $1,400 per acre, the rental rate would be $84 per acre per year.

However, if that rate were used in Ukraine, there would need to be a substantial income tax or other tax to help pay village and public service expenses. The local government would need operating money for public amenities such as rural roads, village streets and sewers, public buildings, the elderly and other people in need, health services, and administrative expenses. I hope administration costs wouldn't include so many supervisors, bookkeepers, and favors, however. Presently, the collective farms pay for most community services.

High land-rent charges would be a dangerous approach for covering these expenses, as it may cause tenants to fail. Also, it's too easy for local governments to get more money than is necessary. Income tax is the fairest way to get revenue because only those who can afford to pay have to pay.

Also, there's no reason to be afraid of allowing high incomes occasionally to Soviet independent farmers. It's the only way this new system will get into place and work. Some high profit years are needed to tide over the poor weather years and to attract talented people into production. Even with a free market in Ohio, very few farmers become wealthy. Every time there's an unusual profit opportunity, so many people move into it that profits become moderate. Eventually, this will happen in the USSR, too—whether to farmers or people providing business services. If the co-ops and independent farmers are squashed this time around because people fear these entrepreneurs will make high profits, perestroika will be dead. Although co-ops are generally in disfavor with the public, there should be more, not fewer, of them. A million more are needed for adequate competition alone.

It's very important at the onset of rent relations in Ukraine that chances of success be very high for the tenant. Unfortunately, I haven't seen this happening for renters yet—mostly because state control continues. Failures at the beginning will scare away other prospective tenants.

My approach in the USSR would be to use a contract that gives a modest return to the collective or state farm or whoever the state's agent is. All additional profits would go to the tenant. Any innovations and efficiencies accomplished by the tenant should be for his gain alone. The tenant could then use his profit to purchase equipment or livestock facilities from the state. Eventually, he would own the enterprise and manage it.

In the meantime, the state's agent would have money to invest in public services instead of paying for farm equipment and facilities as in the past.

The change is that the farmer, not the state, would own and manage the enterprise.

This arrangement would help the state financially, too. The state could stop subsidizing agricultural production because farms would be so much more efficient. Food prices would rise and consumers' low salaries could be increased at the same time to compensate for higher food costs. At present, cost of production is twice what consumers pay for their food. Once word gets around that independent farming is profitable and fun, there'll be a stampede in that direction. That's exactly what's needed to get Soviet agriculture out of its stagnation.

Add to that opportunities for education in farm management, and you have a winner, even in abandoned areas. Self-motivation is a key to an agricultural revolution. This is true elsewhere, too. In the US, for example, state-managed functions are generally the most wasteful and least efficient ones around.

However, problems with renting can arise (such as I list towards the end of this chapter). One disadvantage of *cash* renting for American farmers has been that tenants need lots of cash to cover production expenses until crops are sold. If they have only small reserves of money, this means large debts during the growing season—perhaps as much as $120,000 for 500 acres of corn and soybeans. In the USSR, I've seen few people willing to take on that kind of debt. Still, in some cases, the state's agents are willing to carry expenses temporarily until crops are sold.

An example of this is happening on a collective farm which rents part of its land to a tenant group. The group leases equipment, buys supplies, and gets an advance minimal living wage from the collective farm throughout the year. When the crop is sold, the tenant group pays for everything, including the rent and expenses accrued that year. What's more, the profits can be used by the tenant group to gradually buy the enterprise. The group might also be able to pay cash during the year for rent, supplies, equipment, and living expenses. In this way, they won't be dependent on the state for financing for long.

Another rent option that might work in the USSR is share cropping. Share-crop renting is very common in America. In a 50-50 arrangement, the landowner supplies the land and pays for half the seed, fertilizer, chemicals, and marketing expenses. Sometimes he'll pay half of a modest harvest charge. In exchange, he receives half the crop. The landowner may be a little more involved in sharecropping than he would be in cash renting, but not much. And the tenant farmer is still free to do his work and make his own decisions.

We visited a progressive collective farm with a rental arrangement similar to share-cropping. All the fields and livestock facilities were rented out to tenant groups who organized themselves to accomplish the production in their area of responsibility. It took some convincing by the chairman to interest the workers in this plan. Expenses are deducted from income, and the profit is divided 50-50 between the tenants and the collective farm. The tenant group leases the equipment from the collective by paying one-sixth of its value each year. Thus, after six years, the tenants will own the equipment—or what's left of it. This is a start in the right direction towards cooperation and independence.

The tenant group also decides what they want to do with their half of the profits. They can divide it among themselves, invest it in their enterprise, or donate it to the village. If there's a loss, a collective farm council decides whether it was due to laziness, negligence, stupidity, or natural causes. So far, there hasn't been a loss.

There are about 40 workers in each rental group, which is far from ideal. But soon they'll discover half that number is enough. Or they may divide the farm into smaller pieces, each one needing only four worker/renters.

However it's done, independent farming is a must in the USSR. The principle is this: the tenant worker, not the landowner, should benefit from extra-hard work and creativity. The reason I continually speak up for the tenant is we've noticed how vulnerable and powerless they currently are in the USSR. It's a mismatch when a tenant sits down with an agent of the state—unless there's a cooperative and knowledgeable atmosphere.

For instance, we know of a livestock feeding enterprise whose contract included a budget projecting a certain probable, modest profit for the tenant family, but which didn't project what the profits would be for the collective farm as the landlord. I think it's important tenants know exactly how much rent they're paying—especially if the profit for the landlord is going to be several times more than theirs. A spirit of cooperation is essential in good rent relations, not dominance of one party over the other.

That beef contract revealed the philosophy of the collective farm: tenants aren't supposed to profit over a certain level, but the collective farm has no such limitation. I think that's backwards. The collective farm should estimate how much money it needs for a good return on its investment and then allow tenants to manage the enterprise as they wish. Tenants should receive enough profit to eventually buy into the enterprise. The collective farm would still get its money. Meanwhile, ownership of equipment and facilities would gradually transfer to the tenant where it belongs. And if six people can do what twelve people did before and do it better, why shouldn't they reap the benefits?

Actually, there were so many controls in this beef contract that it more closely resembled a contract for a brigade than a rental. (Sometimes a brigade of workers is contracted at a specific price to do a specific job.)

Since landlords in Ohio are mainly retired farmers, working out rent relations with tenants (who are active, established farmers) is easy. It simply involves reaching an agreement between two equal parties who share a deep understanding—thanks to their common farming experience. Consequently, disputes seldom arise.

On the other hand, when a collective or state farm or Gosagroprom official presents a contract for signing to a farmer in the USSR, the situation is entirely different. The official has little experience in this arena and may not know what a fair contract actually is. Or he may know, but is pressured from someone above to make it less than equitable.

But who should represent the state in determining what's in a rent contract or which soil conservation practices will be required on the land? Will they be people with vision and long-range goals who want the tenant to prosper along with the state? Actually, all the Dull farm rent contracts have been written by me, the farmer, and presented to the landowner for discussion, changes, and signing. In the USSR, maybe the local soviet could have a commission of five people to represent farmers in deciding rent matters in the early years so fair contracts could be developed.

Another problem for renters in the USSR is how the state designs agricultural sites. For instance, it's common practice for the state to build livestock facilities. If they're to be leased, the tenant needs to have a lot more say about their design and how expensive they are to operate and maintain. Otherwise, the tenant suffers for mistakes made in planning and construction. He may want to buy the facility sometime, and, at the least, he'll have to pay depreciation on the construction cost. I've seen some very costly errors someone's going to have to pay for. Operating labor is also tremendous in these poorly designed facilities.

Two very familiar quotes indicate part of the problem of the old state-managed system: "I get only five rubles per day, so I'll do five rubles of work" and "The state pretends to pay me, and I pretend to work." Farms need people who have a deep personal interest in them. Large factories can function reasonably well with hired, disinterested employees—although I recommend ownership by workers here, too. Large farms usually depend on hired labor, and due to weather variations and scattered individual tasks, employees who don't have that personal interest will not be as diligent or concerned as the farmer is. After all, he's owner, manager, and worker all rolled into one.

The state is the people, but maybe *all* the people don't have to own *all* the production property. Perhaps ownership by all the people can be chopped into pieces which are owned by the workers themselves. Being a true tenant at least combines the manager and worker into one, and that's extremely important for higher productivity. Sometimes, ownership will be added, and you'll have a truly efficient farmer.

There's so much to be done to make the economy function better and be more productive that one hardly knows where to begin. But start they must. Glasnost has brought forth a multitude of open criticisms and finger-pointing, and the new election campaigns have tended to increase this. But from here on, every fault found should be accompanied by a solution and a willingness to change.

Many solutions need to move along side by side. The USSR needs an open market to sell in, a choice of where to buy, independent farmers, an educational system for farmers, and the end of central planning for agricultural production. The reporting system must go, too. All this must happen simultaneously during the next few years. Much of the apparatus (bureaucracy) will go down hard, but die it must for the benefit of country. A non-violent revolution in agriculture is called for. Yet this revolution will require as much aggressiveness as a violent one would. A lot of change and adaptability will be required.

The beauty of the independent farming system is the farmer's ability to adapt to long-term conditions as well as daily ones. We've heard that Soviets are being challenged to change their way of thinking and actions from doing only what's permitted (as they have in the past) to doing anything that's not prohibited. In America, we have farmers who'll try anything on a small scale that they think might work successfully. This mind-set would help Soviets, too.

Each farmer adapts to his own conditions and personal preference better than to what is permitted in a central planning system. Of course, climate is taken into consideration in the USSR, but there's not enough flexibility in what is grown on each farm or district.

In the States, a closely related dividend of the independent farmer's ability to diversify is the fact that most inventions and procedural improvements are started by farmers working out problems in their own fields or livestock facilities. There they can think about better ways and develop them to the point other farmers are also interested. Or equipment companies decide to develop the new ideas further. Occasionally, a farmer even goes into the business of mass-producing his own invention.

The state (USSR) doesn't need to get its benefits by high rent charges or tough contracts. The benefit to the state, because of renting, is that there'll be higher production and much lower cost of production. These two factors, in turn, eventually reduce the need for subsidies to agriculture.

The thought of reducing imports, no longer robbing other parts of the economy to subsidize food production, and making more consumer goods available should make everyone's blood run a little quicker. These advantages should make the apparatus (bureaucracy) willing to change.

It's a terrible waste of resources any time people are unproductive or methods are used that keep millions of people busy unnecessarily. Reversing this trend paves the way for a brighter future. An *Izvestia* reporter reminded us that there's no excuse for a country with such great natural and human resources to be lacking food and consumer goods. Evidently, 18 million bureaucrats are dragging down the economy.

The main benefits of being an independent farmer are more meaningful work and higher income. We've seen extravagance in construction projects on some collective farms (generally in the form of flashy facilities "for the people"), but I'd prefer to see the people receive their rewards in the form of higher salaries and then decide for themselves how to spend their own money.

One urgent question that needs an answer concerns private land ownership. We've met many Soviets who think it's time families or groups of families own the land they work. Most say, "Give the land to the people." Whether that means sell it, grant it, or set a price on it people can afford, I'm not sure. However, I am sure the people want land of their own.

One idea is to grant land to settlers in abandoned and failing areas of country. Even then, there should be further incentives, such as guaranteed supplies, equipment, and markets. When America was being settled 200 years ago, there was a land-grant provision called the Homestead Act that gave a limited amount of land to any family interested in settling and developing it. Such a plan might well work for the USSR.

When we arrived in the Soviet Union, we assumed state ownership of land was set in concrete. As time passed, the thought of the same people being both worker and landowner began to sound more possible. I understand Lenin had that intention. Private ownership was well under way when forced collectivization hit the country five years after his death.

Since collectivization, all USSR land is owned by the state. Thus people had many questions for us about the private land system and what happens to property when the owner dies. We think that sometime, there'll be private land again in the USSR—or at least lifetime leases.

Many farms in America have been in the same family for three to six generations. Inheritance is handled in many ways. If any of my grandchildren follow their parents, for example, they will be the fifth generation on the Dull farm. It's customary in our family to sell land to the next generation. I feel it's healthier if everyone earns his or her way rather than receiving everything as a gift. Giving someone the opportunity to succeed is the greatest present of all.

If a farmer has no children who want to farm, he may take an unrelated young person into his operation. This person may later buy the property or rent it from survivors.

Private land ownership shouldn't create a problem in the Soviet Union in the future—if the shadow economy mentality of favors and special privileges doesn't spill over into the land market. The shadow economy habit is going to be even harder to break than the straw habit (the Soviet tendency to spend much time and energy on straw production). It's really a question of morality and a concern for fair treatment of *all* fellow citizens which should spur on the movement for private enterprise. Everyone will feel better if possessions are acquired fair and square. Dissension can be reduced in every community by reducing finger-pointing and envy.

The happy consequences of private land ownership are obvious when one considers what will happen when individuals willingly take on more responsibility and personally invest in improvements. The whole nation will benefit. Some say American land is being worn out faster than land in socialist countries due to lack of government control. However, I don't agree. Carelessness is just as destructive as is greed.

In fact, many American farmers feel we never really own the land we have the deed to: we just own the privilege of managing it for a while.

The trick in ensuring a fair and profitable agricultural system for all involved is to make sure landowners do not exploit the cheap labor of others. In a sense, exploitation is happening in the USSR now. The state or collective farms pay very low wages, evidenced by the fact many methods are used that require huge amounts of labor—even though alternative methods are known. Unfortunately, low production per worker eventually results in a low standard of living for the whole nation. Throughout this century, farm workers have gotten the short straw. However, the consequences of this inequity has travelled far beyond them.

Soviet agricultural production is going to require fewer and fewer workers in the future. Ideally, every citizen would have opportunity to work on the land. But it's impossible to reverse the present trend towards progress unless we're willing to go back to horses and ignore present and future technology and labor-saving techniques. China is not a model for the USSR either. China has four times as many people and a totally different culture and history. China collectivized in the 50s and de-collectivized in the 80s. One author has said that due to its history and culture, changing Chinese agriculture is like turning around a ship in the ocean. But changing the Soviet agricultural system is like trying to turn around the dock which is solidly moored to land.

Today's Soviet society demands certain consumer goods and services that are in shortage. So an assignment to bureaucrats is to encourage service businesses and light industries in villages and cities to satisfy this demand. At the same time, these new enterprises will solve the current unemployment problem, which may become worse as more farm workers are released. Hiring people to hoe sugar beets just to avoid unemployment simply isn't a reasonable long-term remedy.

Expanding the existing option of contract brigades is one helpful approach to more efficient production and independence. But it doesn't go nearly far enough. An efficient farmer needs *complete* control over a certain piece of land or facility *year after year*, along with his own equipment and bank account. The basic principle is that a person will take good care of what is his and what he manages. His heart is into it—not only for profit, but because it's more interesting and challenging.

Group renting provides another innovative variation on the old system while still encouraging progress. I feel group renting is the next best thing to individual family renting, especially as I don't believe the USSR will ever go back to small farms. And there are certain efficiencies gained by working enough acres to justify one harvester and one planter. However, a farm larger than that is not likely to be more efficient. On the Dull farm, we have one combine, seed corn harvester, corn planter, and soybean planter.

There is an efficient way to work a small farm—say 100 to 400 acres—without owning all of the expensive pieces of equipment: you can hire another small farmer to harvest your crop or spray your weeds. Trading work with other farmers is a good way to go. This strategy can work for Soviets, too.

With tenant groups of people, whether relatives or not, the most important factor in achieving success is the congeniality and cooperation of all involved. A group leader should never take the posture of a supervisor. Rather he is a coordinator, both in title and in deed. Decisions come from discussions, formal or informal.

Another change is there will not be any one-talent people in this group. Although individuals will naturally specialize in certain areas of work, *each* will develop abilities in tractor driving, harvesting, planting, welding, repairs, grain-handling, agronomy, maintenance, management, and husbandry, too. Besides, diversity makes work more interesting. And no one will be standing around, watching a job that isn't his to do. Every job is his, large or small, if necessary. My father told us when we were young that a change of jobs during the day is as good as a rest. He was a clever man.

I use the word "efficient" frequently because efficiency is so lacking in USSR agricultural production—and has been ever since collectivization started in the 1920s. "Increase production at any cost" is still going on. Yet despite this effort, total national production is still going down. Renting is one way to reverse this decline by re-establishing that productive element called "personal interest." Whether it comes from renting or ownership remains to be seen. What we do know is that the old state labor system has failed.

Still, another big question remains: Will current farm workers be interested in renting? In July, 1989, in the Russian Republic, farmers were invited to apply for renting a farm. A thousand people responded, asking to be interviewed for 50 available positions. Obviously, many people are interested.

On the other hand, some who would like to rent are justifiably apprehensive. I asked a young brigadier on a poor collective farm in Ukraine if he would rent. He said, "No, we've lost our spirit because of conditions here." I asked him what he'd think if others on the farm had a profitable experience renting. He then said, "I would be interested for the next year."

My impression is that young farmers, no matter how capable, haven't had any reason to think of a better future. But I'm sure their juices would start flowing rather quickly if their minds and hopes were stimulated. A part of that stimulation would come from the promise of real profit incentives and a guarantee that the state wouldn't pull the rug out from under them again. Such reversals have been all too common this century every time anyone became too successful. There is much farm talent in the Soviet Union. Almost all brigadiers, for a start, have the talent to be successful independent farmers. They just need a chance.

Standing beside the young brigadier was a 59-year-old man (who looked 80). He was just putting in time until pension age arrived. A tour of the poor collective farm revealed that much of the cattle facilities and roads were run down, the younger adults had left the farm, and the experienced farmers were dying out. However, the soil is still rich and productive. In Ohio, poor soil usually causes poor farms, but what causes "poor" farms in Ukraine when the earth is still so fertile? The problem is not worn-out soil but a worn-out system. A recently elected chairman has helped to revive this farm, but it's still held back by old work habits, the state procurement system, and a lack of readily-available nitrogen. He went to the regional office six times to beg for nitrogen for the corn fields and got none.

Something else we noticed about Soviet farms—even the poorest collective farms have a large and impressive Headquarters building in good condition. Usually, these structures are two-stories high and at least 120 by 60 feet. Also, additional offices exist elsewhere. What a waste of money that could be going for necessary supplies! In contrast, the office on the Dull farm is a corner of the barn. The size of the room, which has insulation and electric heat, is 16 by 12 feet. It also serves as scale house and grain-sampling house. Most American farms don't even have a separate office but rely on a desk in a corner of the home. When more food is produced by independent farmers in the USSR, many of these existing offices could be used for stores or warehouses.

The question arises about how a young farmer and his family can get started farming independently. One way might be for the family to use more muscle and brain power to produce food and to use less equipment and money. The individual family would rent what is needed and buy as little as possible. The family would grow crops and livestock which require plenty of labor during most months of the year. This is because the main resource they have is the time and enthusiasm of the family.

Many farmers in the US are well-established now and have modern, well-equipped operations. However, we must remember how many started 40 years ago with almost nothing other than a dream and ambition. They lived very simply, spent money carefully, and managed their farms with precision. Eventually, they purchased a little land with buildings on it and expanded production gradually as financial resources and skills increased.

A beginning farmer is tempted to start out with a full line of equipment he can't afford. Trading work with another farmer who's just getting started helps both parties. There's more flexibility and independence in that arrangement than in a group tenant situation. The biggest hazard to group renting is the human conflict element. Many times the workers are congenial, but their spouses are not. Single-family farms avoid this problem.

Although American agriculture has much to offer the Soviets in their campaign to increase food production and improve efficiency, there are aspects of the US agricultural style that are troublesome.

The obstacles to getting started in farming in the States can be insurmountable in an effort to find enough land and money. Also, many good established farmers have been forced out of business through no fault of their own but due to unfortunate circumstances—such as the dramatic interest rate increases and land devaluations which occurred in the early 80s. Federal programs favoring large farms, and grain embargoes which helped to force incomes lower, also penalized many farmers as well. American farmers are still in a bind once more because they have 1970 grain prices and 1990 expenses.

Soviet farmers are accustomed to security, albeit at a low-level standard of living. Risk-taking and opportunity-seeking has not been fostered by their system. In fact, the Soviet system has guaranteed the necessities of life, but punished people who went beyond these to become successful. Generally, risk equals opportunity. But in Soviet independent farming, opportunity today far outweighs risk—if the farmer can get supplies and is truly independent.

One reason for this opportunity is more food is desperately needed in the USSR. This means good profits are almost guaranteed in a new market economy. I would love to produce for a short-supplied market myself.

The old excuses for poor Soviet production need to be forgotten if agriculture is to improve. US analysts and many Soviets blame low Soviet production on a colder and dryer climate, defective or inefficient machinery, and poorer soil. While these problems exist to some degree, we can't ignore three important facts: Although Soviets have 1,520 million more frigid acres of cropland than we do, they also have 1,760 million acres of cropland (nearly double what America has) which are only moderately cold to warm and offer a growing season of 90-180 days. The black-earth region is large. Ukraine alone is five times the size of Ohio, so it equals several corn belt states.

Second, losses and waste are a more likely explanation for the shortage than poor equipment, climate, or soil. And preventing loss or waste is easier to accomplish than changing the growing conditions! Twelve million tons of grain could be saved by using lower seeding rates of small grains alone. Ten million more tons of grain could be produced with the fertilizer that is lost. Another ten million tons could be saved by better grain handling methods. And who knows how much grain is lost simply because of low quality silage? These are the easiest ways to get grain to replace the 55 million tons imported now.

Third, we shouldn't forget that millions of abandoned acres are producing nothing now. Complicated analysis and excuses don't change this fact. When you get away from charts and reports and walk the fields and grain yards, you become optimistic about the potential of the Soviet Union—whether rainfall in central Ukraine is only two-thirds of that of the US corn belt or not.

Inviting foreigners to come to the USSR to take over large collective farms and modernize or advise them isn't a real solution to agricultural production problems in the long run. Foreign equipment and techniques may increase production on those few collectives for a while, but this approach is still dependent on a people organized in the same way as they have been in the past. The real problem is a system based on central planning, supervisors, and workers who don't have much at stake or any involvement in decision-making. Without changing this system, I expect the same problems to arise in the future as have in the past. Better equipment, seeds, chemicals, and buildings are not the greatest need. A system that encourages renting and independence would help more than anything. For a western model farm to succeed in the USSR, it would need special breaks from the Soviet government. It's not fair to give these breaks to foreigners and not to local farmers who could also progress and succeed if given the same advantages.

To build such a system, the greatest challenge is to remove the following thirteen roadblocks to successful renting. Then farmers throughout the Soviet Union could express their ambition and creativity and show their abilities as a result of self-motivation. As I see it, these are the most likely pitfalls in the road to Soviet agricultural recovery:

Possible Roadblocks to Successful Renting

1. Rent charges set too high or tenants' income opportunities made too limited.
2. Withholding necessary supplies and equipment or pricing them too high.
3. The state or co-op's not providing a nearby market for produce or not allowing a high enough selling price.
4. The state's agent rejecting applicants and there being no easy recourse for them.
5. Officials not encouraging (or actually discouraging) potential applicants.
6. A hostile atmosphere created by officials after renting has started.
7. The lack of education for tenant farmers.
8. Only poor fields or facilities offered to tenants.

9. Good profits frowned upon or not permitted.
10. Reports from farms and commands to farms continue.
11. Building poorly-designed and expensive facilities and then asking tenants to use them and pay the resulting high fixed and operating costs.
12. Adequate financing unavailable or too complicated to get.
13. Fear by prospective tenants that once again the attitude towards independent farming will change and they will lose what they have worked for.

When it comes to solving the problems of Soviet agriculture, encouraging renters and a proper attitude are the real keys to a long-term solution. Soviet people on the land *now* deserve a fair contract, a guarantee of supplies, and a market for what they produce. In short, decisions need to be made down on the farm instead of on the government or party level.

One final step is needed to create a self-sufficient and successful system of independent farmers in the Soviet Union: a readily available, thorough, and up-to-date farmer education system. Farmer education is a never-ending process and an enjoyable one at that. Since a modern American farmer needs to make important decisions every day (or every hour), he's eager to learn whenever he can. Farmers who don't search for knowledge make more misjudgments than they should, or their enterprises become outdated and less efficient. Meanwhile, other more innovative farmers pass them by. Knowledge does not guarantee success in itself, of course. But knowledge used properly does help to make life more interesting and is a very positive force on the farm as it is in all business ventures.

People in the past believed if you couldn't be anything else, you could always be a farmer. Higher education seemed of no consequence. However, farmers in the US are more respected now as businessmen, skilled managers, and professionals. The list of hand and brain skills used by modern farmers is almost endless. There is much learning by age ten, when there are daily chores to be done for animals, and tractor driving begins. Those chores are nearby because the farm family lives right in the middle of all this activity. This isn't the case for rural Soviet children because they live in villages, somewhat removed from farm activity.

Everyday experience is a good teacher, but the day isn't long enough or the billfold fat enough to learn everything by the trial-and-error method. Why not get the latest knowledge on which to build?

So, independent farmers need educational opportunities. They have much to learn from farm elders, schools, books and journals, other farmers, research institutes, other countries, agricultural companies, experts, and personal experience.

The food production system in the USSR is going to become one in which all farmers will make plans and decisions. Currently, Soviet peasants don't have or need higher education and management skills because they are simply told what to do. On the collective and state farms, there's complete reliance for decision-making on the chief agronomist, chief economist, chief engineer, and chairman or director on each farm.

The other hundreds of employees on each farm have no trade magazines, bulletins, or university courses available to them. There are no educational field days or tours to progressive farms to inspire them. (Ukraina does have a classroom at the machine yard to help train mechanics, but this one stab at education certainly doesn't go far enough.)

Institutes should train and encourage many of their students to be farmers, not just supervisors or other highly specialized workers. Who is going to offer an educational system, other than the institutes, for all the independent farmers of the future?

The knowledge to accomplish high production and efficiency is in the USSR somewhere, but it needs to spread across the country. What's more, it needs to be applied. On the other hand, a farmer can have all the knowledge in the world on how to grow corn, but if he can't get nitrogen when he needs it, he can't grow much corn. Changes in the political and economic systems need to be accompanied by agricultural education. Let's hope that glasnost first brings open criticism, followed by the spread of knowledge and solutions.

When farmers have adequate educational opportunities, land to rent or own, favorable government policies to work under, access to supplies, and a good market in which to sell what they produce, Soviet agriculture will finally be as productive as it could and should be. Then life will be better for all Soviets.

CHAPTER 18

Losses and Wastes

Reducing losses and wastes is the quickest way to reduce imports. In fact, I would expect a balance in USSR imports-exports if just two-thirds of all the losses and wastes mentioned here were eliminated.

Farming is not an exact science. Perfection is never achieved. We're producing living things—crops and livestock—which in turn are affected by other living things such as weeds, fungi, bacteria, insects, and parasites. When we add variables of nature like wind, heat, cold, and rain, we begin to see that optimum conditions for production never exist. We notice another hazard as we see a five-hundred-pound mother hog standing over her family of new-born three-pound piglets and she starts to lie down. Factories don't have that kind of unpredictability. In America, we have large losses, due to the above-mentioned hazards and other factors beyond our control.

Some years, crop and livestock production are drastically reduced by lack of rain for crops or a rare disease in livestock. Poor weed control and certain insects cause unexpected problems, too. However, the trick to profitable farming is to keep management mistakes to a minimum. Because most American farmers are both manager and farmhand rolled into one, they know what's happening on their farms. Large enterprises may lack this advantage. That's why large farms in the US are seldom as efficient as the medium-size ones.

Another reason mistakes and neglect are more frequent on large farms (over 2,500 acres in the Midwest) is because they're more likely to have workers without a vested interest or who have only a limited ability to manage their own sphere of work. Sometimes the size of the farm has outgrown the ability of management. An efficient farm needs adequate total volume of production, but bigger is not always better. An independent farmer is usually more willing to go the extra mile to get the job done right, or at least do it the best way feasible.

In life, it's the little things that often add up to a headache. So it is in Soviet agriculture. Many small losses add up to a big loss for each farm (and thus the whole country) regardless of whether farms are prosperous or poor. Officials and writers seem to agree that at least 25 percent of mature grain, vegetables, and fruit crops never get to consumers. These wasted products are lost through inferior harvesting equipment, unharvested crops, inadequate transportation, poor storage, or too few storage facilities.

Careless losses in a country of surpluses is a terrible waste of resources. But careless losses in the USSR are a double loss—not only are valuable resources squandered, people are cheated out of a better standard of living.

The organization of the Soviet agricultural system, from top to bottom, is believed by most to be the main handicap to a satisfactory food supply. But there are some on-the-farm practical considerations that could make a big difference, too. Soviet farmers can't just sit back and blame the apparatus.

Although many losses are as unavoidable for Soviet farmers as they are for their American counterparts, I consider the following losses and wastes to be excessive in the USSR. I'm sure they're well-known in some cases and there won't be agreement in other instances. However, these are the problem areas I have personally observed:

1. Tillage
2. Equipment
3. Labor
4. The Supervisor System
5. Seeding Rates
6. Soil Erosion
7. Working Wet Fields
8. Storage and Handling of Grain
9. Silage
10. The Straw Habit
11. Fertilizer Losses
12. Manure Handling
13. Abandoned Land
14. Crop and Livestock Selection and Management
    A. Corn   F. Sugar Beets
    B. Wheat   G. Hay and Green Feed
    C. Soybeans   H. Dairy Cattle
    D. Peas   I. Hogs
    E. Peanuts   J. Beef

Tillage

How much tillage is necessary? While not every farmer agrees on what is needed, I have no doubt losses from excess tillage rank near the top of all farm losses in the USSR. Corn fields are tilled from six to fourteen times a year there! I call these tillings losses because when I see tractors and tillage tools making unnecessary trips across a field, I think about all that metal wearing out, fuel needlessly expended, and the wasted time of the driver. Also, the soil is being undesirably compacted underneath, where you can't see what's happening. True, it appears smooth on the surface, which looks neat, but this grooming serves no purpose as far as crop production goes. The soil says, "Ouch!" with every unnecessary pass of a tractor, truck, harvester, or manure spreader. Soviet farm managers will learn that it's what the soil's like underneath that counts. The seed and the roots don't care how pretty the top soil looks, but Mr. Erosion just loves a smooth surface.

Many farmers in the US do no plowing or tillage whatsoever to produce bumper crops of corn, wheat, and soybeans. Weeds are controlled with herbicides. Wheat usually requires no herbicides. In contrast, weeds in Ukraina wheat are hit with herbicides, and weeds in corn are controlled by four cultivations and a heavy shot of herbicide. In the no-till method, fertilizer can be spread on the soil's surface. The crops still get it. Tillage is unnecessary to incorporate fertilizer.

Most farmers in the US prefer to do some tillage for crops, but the no-till method is gaining popularity. A neighboring farmer in Ohio began no-till planting in 1968, and some of his fields haven't been tilled in 20 years. He started using this method after harvesting my no-till corn in 1967. He said, "Your corn is as good as mine though I plowed and worked the soil, so why should I work so hard?" Proper use of the no-till method will result in yields nearly equal to any other method. And the savings in manpower, equipment, gas, and time really add up.

Moreover, no-till is especially advisable for hilly fields, such as those covering half of Ukraine. The three main conditions for successful no-tilling are these: considerable crop residue remaining from the previous crop, a minimum of soil compactions from previous years, and a good herbicide program for weed control. No-till crops get off to a slower start in the spring than do tilled crops because the old residue on the soil surface keeps the soil cooler. Also, thistles and milkweed appear earlier. Later on, however, properly no-tilled fields are beautiful and yield well. But Soviet bureaucrats can't wait that long to be satisfied.

In the States, the moldboard plow is rapidly being replaced by tillage tools that leave more old crop residue on the soil's surface. The modern version of "Beating swords into plowshares" could be "Melting missiles into no-till coulters." In fact, the US government is now demanding minimum tillage so some slopes will have a certain percentage of residue cover after planting.

Ukrainians plow immediately after wheat harvest, so the fields are bare during the fall and winter. Most Ukraine soil is so good it can be abused by equipment working on the wet fields, excessive tillage, and erosion, and still produce a decent crop. There is some evidence, though, that gentle care of the soil would bring better yields.

Volunteer wheat and peas could be left to grow until it's time to plant the next crop. There's no need to be embarrassed by the appearance of volunteer crops to the point of doing an extra tillage just to dig them out to conceal poor combine adjustment. Furthermore, volunteer peas add both humus and nitrogen to the soil.

In Ohio, we're learning to farm "ugly"—that is, to leave the soil covered for as long as possible, no matter how it looks. After a few years of leaving trash on top, the farmer thinks it looks good. And he feels good about the conservation aspect of it. Bare soil begins to look ugly to him. However, in Ukraine, stubble often is being tilled out before the combines have even finished harvesting the field. We observed a field plowed shallow in July and plowed deeper again in August.

I also question the practice of disking a field before plowing it. It wears out the disc and tractor for nothing. Maybe it would help if the driver would go swimming, fishing, or go build himself a house—anything to keep him from tilling the fields another time. Apparently, tillage can be addictive. The soil has been kind to us; we should be kind to it. Also, what's wrong with saving millions of gallons of fuel by keeping tractors out of the fields or unmanufactured in the first place?

Equipment

Ohio farmers would all go bankrupt if they carried out either of two USSR practices: using lots of labor and using lots of equipment. After seeing several Soviet machine yards, I decided that each farm had a sea of equipment to dig up the soil and a sea of equipment to pack it down again. I'd never seen so many moldboard plows and rollers—both of which I think should be illegal. Corn, pea, and soybean seeds don't care if the soil is rough and trashy on top, just as long as they have a nice seed nest to grow in below. True, the rows of planters, combines, wagons, tractors, sprayers, manure tanks, and cultivators are impressive. Still, if they were of better quality, perhaps there wouldn't need to be so many. If tillage trips were cut, the amount of equipment could be cut, too.

When I was a boy, we had rollers and packers to make the surface of the soil look nice and help it hold moisture. Then a big rain would come, and most of the water would run off. I even saw Ukraine rollers used on wet fields. Of course, firming the surface may be necessary for small seeds like beets or clover if the soil is extra dry. However, if we till the soil at the proper time for corn, wheat, and soybeans, rollers are never helpful—except maybe to please the traditional eye.

I've heard the USSR produces five times more agricultural field equipment than does the US. So, if there is more equipment, more fertilizer, and eight times as much labor per acre, the finger of shortage seems to point in the direction of misuse—not inadequate resources.

Many Soviets think that better equipment, like the West has, is the solution to production problems. I think Soviet equipment is satisfactory to get the job done. Life expectancy is short—five years—and repairs are continuous, due partly to unnecessary use of tillage, straw, and manure-handling operations. The general opinion on Soviet combines is that they are too heavy, too hard to maintain, and virtually impossible to adjust properly.

American farmers can't afford as much equipment for crops or livestock as is used in the USSR. For example, the Dull farm has no tractor larger than 135 HP for crops or manure handling. Also, one combine harvests 1,570 acres a year. Excessive equipment is being used in the USSR for mixing livestock feed, moving grain, and manure handling. When we consider the extreme amount of equipment and labor used to handle and mix straw into cattle feed, it becomes a very expensive feed. This is especially sad because straw has so little nutrient value. State ownership and management cause some very strange economic events to occur.

One of the biggest surprises for me was seeing the multitudes of four-wheel-drive tractors used away from the fields, many on the highways. They're very expensive per hour to operate. Also, combines wear out fast when wheat, barley, or rye has fallen over or when windrows are bunchy or wet. A combine operating at one and one-half mph has a life of only one-half as many harvested acres as one where conditions permit a speed of three mph. Grain fields that haven't fallen over can be cut eight inches above the ground so there's not so much straw and green material going through the combine. This results in a faster ground speed. A machine, making windrows that don't need to be made, wears out when it need not wear out at all. Rollers, moldboard plows, and the machines that make straw stacks could be melted down and wouldn't need to be repaired or replaced again.

One way to reduce tillage and the amount of equipment needed is to use a no-till planter for all planting, regardless of the tillage method used. The planter doesn't look much different from other planters, because all that has been added is a wavy disc blade for each row. In any case, this attachment would save at least one trip over the field with a tillage tool because it makes a good seed bed—only where it's needed—for the seed. I think every corn planter should have this attachment as should many soybean and wheat planters. It never hurts and it usually helps.

Labor

How does wasted labor affect the agriculture problem? People are a resource of muscle, brain, and spiritual power. Every person has a contribution to make to the local community or the larger community, and any wasted resource works against a better society. Unproductive or inefficient labor makes a person only a consumer—but not a contributor. So, in a sense, he becomes a parasite on society. Having three people do a task that one could do is a waste of resources. Just having everyone employed and on some kind of wage is not enough—if the USSR wants a better standard of living. In fact, many families in Ukraine would be happier if one parent were working for twice the present wage and the other parent worked at home for no wage at all. One man who was planting corn all day and into the evening complained that after he goes home at night, he still has three more hours of work to do—tending the garden and animals—because his wife works away from home, too. Also, sometimes the work is simply poorly paid busy-work at that. For instance, I saw two women assigned, at eight rubles a day, to dip fertilizer out of a wagon occasionally for the corn planters at the end of a field. The tractor drivers present said they'd rather dip the fertilizer themselves and receive the extra rubles than simply watch the women do it. Practices such as these explain why Ukraina collective farm has 1,254 employees for 12,500 acres; 7,000 beef cattle; road maintenance; village services; etc.

A comparison of labor in the USSR and US in an extreme case would be best exemplified by the day of corn planting mentioned before. There were six tractors working in the field, three more tractors servicing the sprayer and planters at the end of the field, a mechanic to start the tractors in the morning, two women in the fertilizer wagon, another man or two, a brigadier, and an agronomist. Thus, more than a dozen people planted fewer acres in a day than one and one-half men would plant on the Dull farm. In the situation of no-till planting, I would be using a 12-row planter by myself, and my son would be spraying with one-half of his time. We find it quite easy to plant 125 acres a day. Another case mentioned in the rent chapter revealed a ratio of 28 to 1 for swine care. Under a changed system, there could be increased production with only half the current number of farm workers in the USSR—especially if, for instance, sugar beet production would not require the thousands of women who are now thinning the beets and hoeing weeds all summer long. We should not think of women crews as a solution to weed problems or a reason to put off better methods in grain handling. And if those who chose the method did the work, I'm sure the method would change.

During 1989, elaborate beef-feeding and dairy facilities were being constructed which will require many more workers than a modern, efficient system would. When labor efficiency is not taken into account, strange systems come into being for tillage, manure handing, beef feeding, straw handling, milking, student labor, and supervising workers. It's difficult to make an analysis of agriculture and not come across as being highly critical, but when I see, for example, nine people weighing calves one at a time, I say to myself, why? If weighing calves, silage, manure, feed, and straw doesn't cause more efficient production, why do it? Reporting daily the tails, tons, and rubles to offices somewhere doesn't improve production at all. In Ohio, we couldn't afford to have that many scales, offices, accountants, and other people to do that much unproductive work. I don't think the USSR can afford it either.

True, some records are needed, but how many? Here again, we know an independent farmer system will not have so much waste. I've read that there is a shortage of workers in other Ukraine occupations, so these jobs should take care of surplus laborers from the farms. Still, my hat goes off to all those on the farms who are diligently working. Name any kind of work on a collective farm, and I've done lots of it. I've hoed weeds out of crops, shoveled manure, milked cows, made straw stacks for bedding, and repaired equipment, so I can empathize with the workers. And, at the same time, I realize the bureaucracy doesn't intentionally foul up agriculture. Drifting can get us into one awful mess, and the peak of stagnation was 18 years under Brezhnev. But I honestly believe many of the changes mentioned in this book need to be made for the good of the country and its people.

I hope my words will be taken as constructive criticism, because I'm being torn between being candid and being "nice." Our purpose in going to the USSR was to make friends and help agriculture. However, sometimes when we do the latter, we aren't doing the former. Perhaps Palamarchouk will not be entirely "nice" in his appraisal of Ohio agriculture either, because it is far from perfect.

The Supervisor System

This is quite controversial in the Soviet Union. Very few Ohio farms have anyone who resembles a supervisor, and if there is one, he works along with the other workers. The number of supervisors on the Ukraina collective farm is 150. All supervisors on a farm should do considerable labor along with the crew. They need to experience the difficulty of each job and learn to empathize with workers who make mistakes. Everyone makes mistakes, including a working supervisor. The only person who doesn't make an occasional error is the person who doesn't do anything at all. To use the term "supervisor" loosely, we could include the USSR command-and-administer system which hasn't disappeared yet. This would include some functions of the district, region, republic, and Moscow.

My strong preference is to have an owner, supervisor, and worker all combined into one. That arrangement is the most productive, efficient, and meaningful in terms of work. I have no desire to be just a supervisor and certainly no desire to be just a worker. Decision-making should be done on the work site, whether it's daily or long-range, especially in agriculture. I've come to believe that Mikhail Gorbachev should keep his job as General Secretary and President, but all other supervisors in agricultural capacities should be eligible and encouraged to become independent farmers.

The main agricultural problem, though, doesn't happen on the farm. When a farmer can't find spark plugs, bearings, nitrogen, good herbicides, combines, or he can't grow the crops he wants, how is he going to produce enough food?

Palamarchouk wrote back to Makov from Ohio that American equipment is a little better quality, but the main reason for the success of agriculture is the independent farmer and independent suppliers. An educational program for farmers is certainly an integral part of this approach, but I think officials and collective farm chairmen have too little faith in the people currently working the fields and livestock facilities.

Patient and cordial management assistance to the new tenants is appropriate. Bureaucrats are there to respond, not to command. The word supervisor should disappear in favor of words like assistance, cooperation, coordinator, discussion, mutual decision-making, agreement, fairness, consideration, self-motivation, responsibility, responsiveness, hard work, and productivity. Let the farmers say what they need and then let white-collar workers respond to those needs.

Supervisors don't have the motivation to think of easier ways to do a task because they don't have to do the work. On the other hand, workers don't have the power to change methods. So, for the farmer to supervise himself and have knowledge, supplies, and markets available to him, and with an opportunity for profits, the ingredients for a highly productive and efficient new agriculture are all there.

I like to paint a picture of what the agricultural system should look like ten years from now, then plan backwards to know how to build that system. That way, something we do now will not have to be torn down later. A definite line needs to be drawn, which the state will not cross to get involved in farm management. No targets, five-year plans, quotas, or commands will be directed towards the farms. History shows they haven't been worth the paper they were written on, let alone the time spent calculating them. The party would set part of the policy but stay clear of any supervisory involvement with farms.

Of the 18 million bureaucrats, the inactive ones not only take up space on the payroll but also take up space in buildings (offices) and waste trees (paper) and other resources. It gets worse because some are not inactive, but very active, constantly throwing up roadblocks to progress.

State-run enterprises in the US tend to have many more supervisors with clean hands and shoes than do private enterprises. The private enterprise tries to get the job done and make a profit. The state just tries to get the job done—sometime. Certain highway department situations come to mind as examples of slow work and many workers, with the supervisors watching. I've seen Ohio road workers park under trees, waiting until time to drive slowly back to headquarters so as to arrive exactly at four o'clock—quitting time. Once, three trucks, a backhoe, and five men were sent out to fix a broken tile I could have fixed myself with a hand shovel in one hour. Such is the natural way of many state functions. There's little incentive for efficiency, and in fact, sometimes there's every incentive to draw work out and spend every dollar. This is especially true when a government agency works out of the public treasury on a budgeted amount. If the agency is efficient and doesn't spend all of the budgeted amount, the amount may be cut back for the following year. Thus, the more you spend, the more you get. It's usual for a state agency to spend all the public money it can get, whether the agency is an American or Soviet one.

There are places in Spain and Poland that seem to have the best of both socialism and capitalism. This is a third way called "cooperative assumption." Spain's Mondragon cooperatives are owned and controlled by the workers. These include factories, schools, and farms. Jobs, health insurance, and pensions are guaranteed for life.

They create owner-worker jobs by starting new businesses which are now Spain's top manufacturers of domestic appliances, machine tools, and industrial machinery. The enterprises are democratically controlled and more productive and profitable than other Spanish firms. Each owner-worker cooperative enterprise shares in the ownership and democratic control of their bank, which loans money to new or expanding enterprises. The higher-risk business loans that are accepted, have a lower interest charge. There have been very few failures.

The Central Union in Poland is similar to Spain's Mondragon and has one-half million members. Members are scattered over the country among the people, and membership, of course, is voluntary. Competition is accepted in this third way, but the needs of everyone are still met.

Chris has said, "Why don't we forget about ideologies and do what works?" If what works fits in with decency and noble objectives, why not forget about whether it's capitalist or socialist? Both superpowers are far from perfect. Perhaps someday the supervisor system and the greed system can both go sailing into the sunset.

Seeding Rates

The average seeding rate per acre of wheat and other small grain in the USSR is twice that used in the States, but the USSR's average yield is less. In Ohio, we plant wheat at the rate of two bushels per acre, while in the dry lands of the western states, seeding rates may be only half that much because of expected low rainfall and yields. There should be many tests done in the USSR institutes of various seeding rates to determine if they could cut back on seed wheat and other small grains.

Corn rates could be cut without testing, although Pioneer, the American seed company with a new facility in Ukraine, is recommending 34,000. Still, we must remember that such companies' recommendations will be high enough for ideal growing conditions and short-season hybrids.

If the USSR could cut small grain seed usage in half, there would be 12.5 million tons of grain saved—about one fourth of the current grain imports. Wheat that has fallen down in large areas of the field causes problems, such as the necessity for windrowing and slowing down of harvesting—both of which results in lower yields and higher tempers. Help might come from shorter varieties and lower seeding rates.

Officials admit to planting 34,000 corn seeds per acre, but in many fields I counted 40,000 young plants per acre. For expected yields of 150 bushels of corn per acre in the US, we plant seeds at the rate of 26,000 per acre, expecting the plant population at harvest time to be 23,000 per acre. In Ohio, I would expect that a 40,000 planting rate would not only increase seed cost by $11 per acre but would reduce yields severely in dry years.

The reasons I've heard for overplanting are that seed germination is low, or that for silage it doesn't matter, or that the population will be decreased by nature or mechanical operations during the summer.

Grain yield is just as important in silage corn as it is for corn harvested only for gain. Population decreased by tractor operators is not very selective. When they get off the straight and narrow path with a cultivator, six rows have just vanished. That makes the average population better, but not the yield.

Cutworms or poor weather don't thin out the population very uniformly either. If there's a problem, replanting of spots is necessary anyway. I saw this happen with sugar beets in 1989; heavy seeding rates didn't prevent the need for replanting parts of the Ukraina fields. The best yields in all crops come when the correct number of plants are evenly spaced in the row.

Another fact worth being aware of is that when corn rows are double-planted or overlapped, the yield in that area might be reduced by 70% percent (see photo). I saw many cases of repeat planting because of a malfunction. The driver immediately planted that part of the field again. Double-planting five or seven rows to plant one possible missed row causes a loss of yield as well as a waste of expensive seed, but the field looks better. The best solution is to have electronic seed monitors that indicate every seed that drops. Then the tractor driver knows immediately when there is a problem, and he can correct it. The additional benefit is his peace of mind as he plants all day long. When all lights are flashing, all is well.

If end rows could be as productive in the USSR as the center part of the fields, millions of tons of grain would be added to the harvest. Soil compaction on the ends of fields is a major cause of reduced yields. I saw end rows harvested for silage in July when the stalks had no ears of grain. Immediate plowing made the ends of the field look nice, but potential high quality silage had been lost.

Also, the Ukraina corn planters, which are purchased in Romania and Yugoslavia, need larger seed boxes. These would be easier to fill without spillage. They also need tight-fitting lids to prevent the loss of more seed.

Not allowing a missed row, doing excessive tillage, or cutting end rows too soon may be a holdover from the past when an "inspector" came around frequently. Things had to look good on the surface, even if it was poor economics. When the crop is mature is when the field needs to look pretty.

Near Volgograd, we looked at a 400-acre soybean field planted 300,000 seeds per acre of Amsoy-Merritt in 24-inch rows. It was irrigated and looking good on September 1, 1989. However, a population of 200,000 would have been better. As we stood in the field talking, we noticed an uncrowded plant with six thick branches loaded with soybeans pods. In the next row were crowded plants, with two thin branches each, and these plants were falling over. We can save seed with some varieties and not hurt yields. Speaking of large fields at Volgograd, we drove past a narrow field, exactly 6 kilometers (3.7 miles) long, being planted in wheat. Take your lunch along when you head for the other end of that field with your planter!

Seeding rates for potatoes are also excessive. According to D. Gale Johnson in the *Soviet Union Today* (1983), one important potato-producing province in the Soviet Union uses 33 percent of its output, in an average year, for seed potatoes. That's three times the amount planted by farm families in their private plots: 4,130 lbs., compared to 1,400 lbs. per acre. American farms use about 2,000 lbs. of seed potatoes per acre. Because of higher yields, Americans then use only 7 percent of the previous crop. When 50 percent of USSR potatoes rot, this means not more than one-fourth of all field-grown potatoes are ever marketed.

Soil Erosion

Soil loss sneaks up on you. We notice those little grooves in the field, but a farmer doesn't show much concern about the problem until he bounces off the tractor seat or he begins wondering why the crops don't grow well on top of the hill anymore. We may ignore the tell-tale appearance of subsoil turned up by the moldboard plow by telling ourselves it's because we plow deeper than we used to. The drainage ditch may be half filled with topsoil before we ask ourselves where it came from. In America, farmers on the delta land of the Mississippi River tell northern farmers, "If you all want to keep sending your best soil down river to us, we'll take it and grow soybeans on it." Of course, overall, that's a losing proposition.

Ten tons per acre can erode from a field without notice. Thus, it's easy to imagine that 20 to 40 tons per acre a year are eroding from the slopes of some Ukrainian fields. Some of it collects at the bottom of slopes, and some is carried away in the streams. Frequent tillage fills up the gullies so they do not become large ones. Nevertheless, soil is moving away from where it belongs for future production. During our six months in Ukraine, we saw no gully-washer rains, so that helps. A gully-washer is when one inch of rain comes in five minutes or two inches in thirty minutes.

Soil erosion on Ukraina farm sugar beet field. A few days
earlier, the silt in the foreground was up the slope.

"Farm ugly" is becoming the motto in the US, meaning that tillage, or
no-tillage should leave a lot of old crop trash on the soil surface for
protection from water and wind erosion. Old methods of tillage used on
gently sloping fields allow 15 tons of erosion per acre per year, minimum
tillage may reduce erosion to 8 tons of erosion per acre per year, and the
no-till method may allow only 2 tons loss when growing grain crops. On
certain hilly fields in the US, farmers are required by law to use the no-till
method for growing soybeans. No-till is very successful for growing corn,
wheat, and soybeans in fields that have not been compacted and have a
natural cover of trash from the previous crop. This method not only saves
soil but also conserves fuel, equipment, and labor.

Other ways to save soil are contour planting across slopes, strip planting
on the contour (alternating more than one crop in narrow strips), maintain-
ing 15- to 30-feet-wide sod waterways in field valleys that carry runoff
water, or building concrete structures at certain places to slow down runoff
water. To keep an established sod waterway from being killed by herbicides,
we recommend spraying along both sides of the waterway first. This way,
when spraying the remainder of the field and driving across the waterway,
the sprayer can easily be turned off soon enough to protect the waterway.

A good conservation practice is to plan a different crop rotation for hilly
fields than for level fields. Level fields could have a rotation of only grain
crops with or without tillage. Hilly fields should have a rotation of mostly
forage crops and no-till grain crops.

Ukraine has serious erosion problems that are not noticeable to the casual observer. When talking to an official about contour planting, I was informed that the practice is followed. However, I didn't see any special effort to do it. Whenever soil flows into streams, not only do we lose soil, but the chemicals attached to that earth pollute the streams and rivers. Also, good soil conservation practices enable more surface water to soak into the fields where it is needed.

In America, there's a soil and water conservation government agency in each county. Each agency employs about five technicians who are trained to help farmers with their soil conservation or drainage needs. Five farmers are elected by all the farmers in each county to supervise the agency on a voluntary basis. It is the most respected government agency I know of. A demonstration farm in my county is used for conservation education for farmers and school children. No-till planters are made available to farmers who want to try the method on their farm to gain experience. Also, recognition is given to the farmers who excel in conservation practices.

Working Wet Fields

I was surprised corn did as well as it did after half of the fields were tilled and planted in wet soil. If we would try that with the type of soil we have on the Dull farm, we would expect a poor population of plants, and the corn would not grow well. Ukraine is fortunate to have soil so good that corn will emerge anyway. Still, yields would be higher if more patience were exercised after wet weather. Letting the soil dry a day to two longer and doing less tillage would be profitable over a period of years.

Yields are also hurt by hauling manure when the fields aren't dry enough. Spread it fast when the conditions are right and go fishing when the fields are too wet. Soviet crop tenants should not permit livestock tenants to ruin their fields by hauling out forage and hauling in manure, especially on wet soil. Compaction of wet soil goes down deep even though we can't see it. It's a real enemy of the farmer. The soil cries out in pain, but we seldom hear it. True, sometimes it's necessary to harvest on wet soil, but even then we should exercise some patience.

It may be wise for cattle farmers to store more silage in a narrow or tall silo and not rely so much on chopping forage for feed every day of the summer. This constant chopping results in damaged fields. The *poor* soil fields of Ukraina are badly hurt by wet working. They have to be treated very gently or the crop won't be good enough to pay expenses.

If overall tillage on farms were reduced to half, then the dry days would be enough to get it all done. Tractor drivers don't have to drive their tractors every day just because they're hired to drive tractors.

I saw ditching machines putting in tile lines for sub-surface drainage. The tile were only two inches in diameter, as compared to a minimum of four inches in the US. The Soviet small tile will easily get plugged with soil or roots. Open drainage ditches are common in Ukraine, but tile drainage under fields is not.

Storage and Handling

Even at present, there is no question the USSR needs more storage facilities for its crops. Questions do remain, however, about how much storage is needed and where it should be located. Moreover, looking ten years ahead, there'll be an even greater need for storage to hold the increased production of crops under the independent farmer system. And what if the abandoned land can be brought back into production? For maximum efficiency, new storage should be built on the farms where crops are produced, rather than building facilities at the large elevators. Presently, remote farms pile grain in open fields temporarily due to lack of transportation to storage facilities.

If a livestock feeder possessed his own storage facilities, he could contract with a crop farmer to buy grain at harvest time to fill them. Then he could have his own simple feed equipment and handling system to feed livestock without needing to pay someone else for these services. If he has sufficient volume of grain, it's best to have control over his own enterprise as much as possible. When the state processes and stores his grain, he loses control over his affairs. Also the likely result will be feeding grain that's been damaged by all that unnecessary handling.

Another common problem associated with storage is the way crops are prepared for it. I saw a lot of wheat and peas ruined by a too-hot dryer because of the backlog of grain waiting to be dried. Wheat is easy to dry in storage bins that have forced, natural air without additional heat. In the past, much grain was sold and delivered to the state and later brought back to the farm at twice the selling price and at a lower quality to be fed to livestock. In many areas of the USSR, the lack of storage causes huge crop losses, either from delayed harvest or the spoilage of harvested crops which are piled up without adequate shelter and ventilation (aeration).

Transporting the crop to storage is a problem as well. Often there are no hard surface roads, and the dirt roads are impassable or require all the tractor power available just to drag the grain transports through the mud to a good road or distant storage. With on-the-farm storage, transportation can take place later when labor is available and firm surface conditions exist.

A market system also is needed which rewards the farmer with higher prices for crops delivered to market well after harvest time. On-site storage would make this a possibility. What's more, it's a benefit to the entire food industry to have marketings spread throughout the year. Modern storage and drying would save enough grain, considering current losses, to quickly pay for their construction costs, too.

To some Soviets, modern grain-drying and storage equipment seem too expensive to import, but it's far more expensive to lose grain by scorching it, having it rained on, allowing it to rot in poor storage, handling it excessively, and wasting labor. Also, a hard currency expense comes when grain must be imported to replace wasted domestic grain. That happens every year, whereas the expense of good equipment occurs once in 30. The rescue of one crop would more than pay for good equipment.

Success is not guaranteed, though, because the farmer must pay attention to the drying and storage of grain. Otherwise, there will be spoilage or shrinkage from overdrying. I recommend a farmer examine his stored grain twice a month for odor and appearance. Once a month, the ventilation fan should be turned on for a few minutes so the farmer can smell the air coming out of the grain. If that air is too warm or has an unnatural odor, the grain must be cooled or moved. Grain care becomes a part of management, the same as does planting and killing weeds.

The USSR is a land of contrasts. It has the ultimate sophistication of a space program, yet lacks a single good broom in its large grain yards. Women and students use small, short branches tied together without a handle. The result is back-breaking work.

Ukraina grain-handling equipment and storage is low-cost, but it is also labor-intensive and wasteful of grain. During the harvest of 2,250 acres of wheat, the following numbers are my estimate of people working the four grain yards: 30 truck drivers to bring wheat from the combines to the yards, 25 women to shovel grain into dryers and sweep up kernels left by grain-moving machines, 15 young people to help clean up, and 30 men to run the equipment in the grain yards and supervise. That's 100 people compared to 6 workers in the US to handle the same amount of wheat!

The small trucks dump grain in long piles in each open yard (see photo). A few days later, clever little machines gather and convey the grain back into a truck for a short haul before dumping it outside the drying barn where women shovel it into the dryer conveyor. The same machines are also used just to move the long piles of grain a few feet, if they start to heat up or the dryer is busy. We saw these piles exposed to rain for three days on one occasion.

The dryer inside the barn is a large horizontal cylinder that rotates on rollers and is heated with oil. The dryer was too hot, so we saw much parched wheat and peas coming out of it. The dryer has no cooling cycle, so warm grain is often put into storage. Warm grain spoils. As the combines leave a lot of chaff and straw in the wheat, this means cleaning the grain in the yard and again as it exits the dryer. The more good grain taken out with cleanings, the better for the collective farm as it can be fed to the farm's cattle instead of delivering it to the state.

The clean, dry grain is conveyed into small trucks which dump it inside two brick storage buildings. There a machine gathers and blows it fifteen feet high onto a pile. Each building is sixty feet wide and 300 feet long, and there is no aeration. I couldn't even see the grain blower and truck because of the fog-like dust. A worker told me that as the grain goes out of condition in these building, it is revolved. The dust must make the workers sick. And these procedures are on Ukraina, a progressive farm! There could be a dramatic cut in grain losses if this process were modernized—not to mention the amount of money saved on labor and the health hazards that could be eliminated. Strange, in a country that grows so much grain, there is not a single round metal grain bin to be seen.

A regional grain yard we visited was better. It had grain aeration in the buildings and acceptable handling methods. During our train travel, we noticed many grain terminals with fans for aeration. Trainloads of trucks are brought from the northern regions of the USSR for grain harvest and then returned, empty, after harvest. Grain harvest is viewed as a battle, with pep talks to workers about conquering the crop for the Motherland. It's like, "Comrades, start your engines!" The enthusiasm is good, but the results are modest—that is, if you're concerned with what actually ends up on the dinner table. Fifty-five million long tons (2200 pounds) of grain must still be imported.

Refrigerated apple and potato storage and refrigerated transportation in the USSR is almost non-existent. Because of this and other factors, 35 percent of the crop is lost. However, I believe improvement in this situation will come faster than a change to family farming, for instance.

Silage

Ukraine is not the best place in the USSR for so many dairy or young beef cattle, but since they are there, they need a lot of good corn silage feed. This silage produces the most milk and beef per acre—if the corn is properly grown. Ukraine is the place to grow grain, but that's another story to be dealt with when we talk soybeans.

Losses are high in USSR silage production—partly because the emphasis is on mass—and because so little attention is given to the grain content of the silage. Tons are reported, with little regard for quality. It's a similar problem to the reporting of the number of tails in a dairy herd, with less regard for the genetic ability of each cow or enough concentrate feed for high milk production per animal. However, the state requires these reports. It doesn't seem to matter if corn silage is all stalks, water, and weeds—just so there is plenty of tonnage.

I pointed out to a collective farm chairman that overlap planting on field ends could easily reduce *grain* yield there by 50 percent. He said it didn't matter because the ends of the field were only for silage anyway. Another chairman admitted to planting a large field at 52,000 population (200 percent of what is recommended) because he wanted to be sure to have enough plants for silage. Ukraina collective farm harvested silage from around the edges and ends of corn fields long before the grain even developed. What a huge loss of feed value!

In the US, we try just as hard to get a high grain yield per acre for silage corn as we do in corn harvested for grain only. We select a variety of seed corn that will give us tall stalks but not reduce grain yield. The problem with high seeding rates is—in addition to seed waste—in a drought year, the grain yield will be much lower than it would have been with a modest seeding rate.

Another silage loss comes form trench silos being too wide. With a delay of several days during silo filling, or a long pause while emptying it, there is a large exposed surface that molds. I saw one wide trench silo that was filled with legumes over a period of several weeks. Each time there was a pause, the top four inches (which were exposed to the air) became moldy. This amounted to many loads of poor quality silage since the surface was 60 by 150 feet. The extra construction cost of narrower and longer silos, which are completely filled at one end before starting to fill the other, can, thus, be justified. Any type silo should be filled as quickly as possible.

Tall, cylindrical concrete silos with automatic unloaders have the advantage of low or no waste. Most American farmers prefer the convenience and flexibility of these tall silos which can handle all kinds of weather and feeding systems. A combination of trench and tall silos may offer the greatest flexibility and be most economical.

For instance, a tall silo could be fed out of during wet summer weather or when fresh, green forage is in short supply. Or when there's a surplus of green forage, it could be blown into a tall silo. If the silo is full at the end of the summer, less corn would need to be harvested as silage, and there would be more corn harvested as grain.

It's interesting that US farmers in milk and beef production build a feed ration with a base of corn silage or fresh, green forage, and then add grain to make the ration more concentrated. USSR farmers will start with corn silage or fresh forage and then add straw to make the ration more bulky with fiber. If asked why, their response is since there's a shortage of total feed, they feed everything available. My response is less wheat and sugar beets could be grown and more corn and soybeans produced. The quickest remedy to inadequate feed would come from a system that cuts product losses. Also, raising wheat grain and straw just for feed is a loser.

The Straw Habit

Straw should not be an exciting topic, but Ukraine straw was fascinating to me. In central Ukraine, I recommended they break the straw habit. Sometimes it seems as though straw is the center of life. In a certain way, the huge, neatly-stacked, loaf-of-bread designs of these straw piles beautifies the rolling landscape. Thousands of them dot the thousand miles of countryside between Volgograd and Moldavia in fields where wheat, peas, barley and rye had been grown. Some stacks are older than that year's crop, however. Their sunken appearance reveals their age—and the fact that more straw is produced and stacked than is needed.

Is straw a valuable part of the culture? Or is the custom of emphasizing straw only a waste of manpower and equipment? The straw is mostly for feed. It's carried by the combine and dumped periodically, or it may be blown into a covered wagon pulled behind the combine. It's then pulled to the new stack site and dumped, soon to be artfully formed by men with forks into a huge loaf, perhaps 30 feet wide, 400 feet long, and 15 feet high (see photo). The men are assisted by a large forklift on a tractor.

Throughout the year, straw is shaved off the loaf by a specially devised piece of equipment. This well-designed, clever machine is mounted on a tractor and has a long chain-saw-like arm reaching out front to hungrily chew up straw as it makes a vertical swipe. Simultaneously the straw is blown into a covered wagon to the rear of the tractor to be taken some distance to a beef-feeding establishment. There, the straw is handled by several more expensive pieces of equipment as it is mixed with green chop or silage and then taken by yet another wagon to be placed before heads of cattle. Straw makes up about one-third of the total feed. Since straw has almost no nutritional value, it goes through the animal and drops near the gutter-cleaner to start the journey back to the field from whence it came.

Granted, straw feed has some binding value in the stomachs when fed with fresh, green forage, but in the US, we don't feed straw. When you consider the labor and equipment involved, straw becomes an expensive feed for its value to produce meat. It's also an expensive feed in that it slows down the daily rate of gain for cattle. This means more facilities need to be built because the animals, to reach market weight, are on the farm longer.

There's a surplus of straw, evidenced by the presence of hundreds of straw stacks in July fields when a new crop is about to be harvested. The new crop simply adds to the number of stacks. Eventually, the unused stacks need to be spread back onto the fields where the straw came from.

Another loss occurs when straw is collected by the combine or corn harvester. Then the number of acres a machine can harvest in a day is significantly reduced. When I watched the combines on a nearby farm harvesting the windrows of peas—blowing the straw into a trailing wagon, stopping each time the wagon got full, taking it to a loaf site, dumping it so five men and a lift machine can build it into a loaf—I got the impression they were actually harvesting straw and the grain was incidental. It made me nervous to see those expensive combines threshing peas only part of the time during ideal weather. Bad weather is always on the way.

Harvesting corn straw fodder also means that a wheat combine can't be used for corn harvest. Thus another expensive and complicated machine, which blows stalks out the side, is needed for the corn while the wheat combine sits idle. Ordinarily, the same combine can be used to harvest wheat, oats, rye, barley, soybeans, clover seed, or shelled corn. Another cost is the space taken for each stack in the field and the inconvenience of farming around such obstacles. But then, maybe without those loaves in the Ukraine landscape, it just wouldn't seem like home.

Thousands of these artfully-formed strawstacks, which look like huge loaves of bread, are used for feed.

In the States, all the corn and soybean straw and 90 percent of the wheat straw is spread evenly back onto the field by the combine. The other 10 percent of the wheat straw is baled and stored under shelter for bedding. It's quite simple and pleasant to harvest crops and think only about the grain. We may think that straw-for-feed is free, but it isn't. Also, it benefits the soil if we leave it out there where it grew.

One way to break the straw habit is to grow less wheat. Instead, grow more soybeans for protein and more corn for silage. In the place of wheat straw, there would be higher-value crops for the time, money and effort expended. During the 1940s, American farmers started leaving straw scattered in the field when combines replaced the old system of binders and stationary threshing machines. Ukrainians entered the combine era and kept right on stacking straw.

Fertilizer Losses

Ten percent of USSR manufactured fertilizers are lost during transportation and storage because the fertilizer lacks protection from the weather or leaks out of transport containers. An estimated 10 million tons of grain could be produced with that amount of fertilizer. More fertilizer was produced for each acre in the late 1980s in the USSR than in the US, although Soviet average yields were much lower.

From 1983 to 1989, as we traveled many thousands of miles in the Soviet Union (from the western border to Irkutsk in Siberia and from Leningrad to Baku on the Caspian Sea), we noticed most fields had crops that were uneven and streaked with various shades of green and yellow. Although water drainage problems and wet tillage compaction can cause this condition, a lot of it can come from careless application of fertilizer. Misapplication results in missed streaks and double-coverage streaks. Farm people have also told us haphazard application occurs and that it is a major problem. They say it's caused by workers who don't care. I did see one acceptable application of lime, which was done by a single web, double-fan trailer behind a tractor. However, more complicated trucks were doing a terrible job on several farms.

Lime spread on slope of nearby farm. Uneven results.

It's also a waste to keep on applying large amounts of some elements if other necessary elements are lacking. For instance, lime may be needed to help an acid soil so that phosphorous and potash can be utilized by the growing crop. Or nitrogen may be needed to keep from wasting the phosphorous and potash. Soil compaction, weeds, and harvest losses can also waste fertilizer and contribute to low yields.

Because lime is so white and heavily applied, it's easy to see that sometimes 80 percent of it drops on the 10 feet directly behind the spreader.

Another 20 percent falls on the 20 feet beside the spreader (see photo). Most fertilizer spreaders cannot be used to spread lime. America uses special trucks for spreading lime because it's so fine and difficult to apply evenly.

Careless, streaked application of fertilizer on fields can result in a good average application, but that average doesn't mean much. Like the man who had his feet in the oven and his head in the refrigerator—on the average, he was comfortable. Total production in the USSR would increase if available nitrogen were applied evenly over all farms and all fields. Currently, some farms manage to get enough for heavy applications while other farms get only enough for a very light one. The last pounds in a heavy application don't produce as much grain as earlier pounds, a case of diminishing returns or less response from each additional pound of nitrogen. Too much or not enough nitrogen equals lower total production.

Even when adequate fertilizer is available, problems arise. For example, fertilizer was stored in a building at Makov. But even then, I saw a worker trying to spread lumps through a spreader. Obviously, such an application is not going to be even. Also, an adjoining farm stored potash and phosphorus on a hill (see photo). Imagine how the weather affected the spreadability later and the erosion of the pile at present.

Fertilizer is wasted due to being stored outside, on nearby farm.

Manure Handling

The beef-feeding enterprise in Ukraine has mountains and seas of manure to deal with. To compound the problem, most current handling methods waste labor, equipment, and the manure itself. There are some very efficient installations, such as one on Ukraina where manure is held in a concrete pond near the cattle barn as a liquid and then in proper season loaded, hauled, and spread on the field by the a modern tank trailer which can be entirely operated from the tractor cab. More farms should consider this method.

The most common method, however, is to tie cattle in rows and have workers, usually women, scrape the manure into a gutter cleaner which then drops it into a wagon. The wagon is unloaded at a nearby pile, if the dirt road to the field isn't passable. Later, it's loaded again onto wagons or trucks and hauled to a field location where a straw stack has been. These loaders are a caterpillar with a large scoop on the front that comes back over the driver and empties into a truck behind the machine. This way, the tractor just goes forward and backward, so the tread doesn't need to twist sideways. The manure is dumped in the field and eventually mixed with remnants of the old straw stack. After a year or so, the manure is loaded again and spread onto a field where sugar beets will be planted.

There has to be a more efficient process. Incidentally, you can easily trace the route of these manure wagons from the barns. Due to their low sides, the stuff slops out all along the way. There's a theory here that manure improves with age, but I haven't been presented with any scientific evidence. That theory doesn't exist in the States, at least not to the point we're willing to spend so much manpower and wear out good equipment simply to move manure from place to place to place.

The success of the modern tank trailer method depends largely on tractor drivers, the timing of spreading, and the amount of equipment used to get manure out of the barn and into the holding pond. I saw a caravan of three tractor drivers take tanks to a wet field, open the rear valves, and just let their cargoes gush out on three spots. Three things happened on that occasion: The field was compacted, manure was wasted, and it guaranteed that in the future any wheat planted on those spots would fall over flat before harvest. Manure is valuable only if we can think of a way to do less harm than good. The liquid system can be a good one though—if manure is spread on dry fields and drivers are careful to be always on the move when spreading the stuff.

In the US, we wait until the fields are dry and then take the manure directly from the livestock site to spread on or inject into the fields. Sometimes it will be spread on top of frozen soil if the field is level and there is no ecology problem caused by water runoff during a rain.

Manure is handled scores of different ways. Some are cheap and work well. Some are expensive and don't work well. We must keep equipment use to a minimum because we know it will wear out in a few years. Also, equipment is no fun to replace or fix—especially when repairs mean crawling underneath a building or through a manure tunnel.

One amusing method of dispersing manure that we observed involved trucks dumping piles of it in a line throughout a field. Later, a four-wheel-drive tractor with a blade on its front arrived. This blade, set six inches above the ground, was designed to hit these piles and string them out. On the back of the tractor, close to the ground, were two fans. As the tractor pushed the manure and passed over it, the manure hit the fans and flew out both sides, high into the air (see photo). (Most of it, that is, because the end result was a streaked field.)

Manure being scattered on nearby farm. Piles have been dumped in a row before the tractor's front end blade pushed them to a shallow depth. Then manure hits the fans on the rear of the tractor. Uneven results.

Back home, we handle things differently. The Dull farm collects swine manure as a liquid in pits under the animals. Then twice a year, it is vacuumed out into a 3,300-gallon tank trailer and spread or injected into dry soil. It's still popular to use slotted floors, but it's becoming more popular to flush the manure, which is underneath the slats, out of the building. There's some hazard to storing manure in a building because the heavy pit gases can be lethal if ventilation fans fail.

Abandoned Land

Obviously, the millions of acres of farm land abandoned in the USSR has seriously hurt production. We haven't viewed many abandoned villages and farms, but it isn't difficult to visualize what they're like. We visited the Kalinin area north of Moscow, which was almost deserted, and have heard that brush has grown on thousands of acres the government thought was being used for food production. Although most abandoned land is part of the non-black-earth regions of the northern half of the country, many poor collective and state farms in the black-earth-regions are running out of people to work the land and livestock enterprises, too. Under current organizational conditions, young people are not attracted to agricultural work, at least not to the production side of it.

In the US, thousands of young people want to become farmers, but there is no place for them to get started. They're attracted to farming as a way of life, not as a way to get rich quickly, although most farmers build up a good equity over a lifetime. We joke that farmers live poor and die rich, although some of us do die poor. Farms of all sizes are going broke. It's a way of life that has challenges, satisfactions, and rewards, and offers opportunities for self-expression and independent activity.

Those who aren't capable or who are unlucky economically eventually step aside, giving someone else a chance to try. In the foreseeable future, there's no reason for Soviet farmers to fear low incomes if supply and demand have anything to do with it. It's the huge surplus of food in the US that keeps farm incomes moderate in our free market system.

A magazine reporter asked me if the Dull family is willing to share its farm with others who want to be farmers. My answer was that under current economic conditions, it takes all the land on the farm to support four working sons and their families. If there were twice that many workers, each would need to work part-time away from the farm to maintain their standard of living, which is modest by American standards.

In 1976, the farm did take in four new farmers—my sons and daughter—and gave them an opportunity to get started. Creating enough work for everyone took three avenues: specializing in seed corn production, which requires much more labor per acre; increasing the size of the swine enterprise; and working more acres of land. The increase in acres happened over a period of 13 years, as 11 neighboring farmers retired and rented or sold their land to us.

Private land ownership is a big reason why farms in the US are not abandoned. We don't just walk away from it. No matter how poor the soil is on the farm, the owner will adapt some income-producing enterprise to the situation. If the landowner becomes discouraged, rather than abandon the farm, he'll sell it to someone else who'll try for success. Naturally, a private landowner has more at stake than does an agent representing state ownership.

Also, private owners are more likely to maintain or improve farm land and facilities, thus creating working conditions which appeal to young and old. Lack of personal interest in the enterprise usually negates the possible efficiency of large-scale state ownership and management. What starts out to be for the benefit of all people results in an unfortunate situation: when everyone is responsible for everything, no one is responsible for anything.

In many abandoned areas and areas of low morale in the USSR, it will take more incentive than *just* the donation of land to prospective independent farmers to encourage people to risk beginning an agricultural enterprise. At the very start, certain other assurances need to be present, such as a guaranteed source of supplies, equipment, repairs, and loans. One approach would be for the new supply industry to guarantee delivery of anything ordered three months in advance. For instance, supplies ordered in December would assure delivery in March. This would also encourage farmers to do good advance planning. Also, a nearby market to sell farm production, for a favorable price, is necessary.

In abandoned areas, now may be a good time for individual families to build a house on 100 to 1,000 acres, develop livestock and grain storage facilities, and work towards success. But this involves private land ownership, because no one will invest in improvements on land he doesn't control. This is the biggest drawback to a rental arrangement. Village life is fine, but it doesn't have to be the pattern. It's very important to permit these farmers to be successful for their own sake and also as a way to attract other people into independent farming—the road to USSR self-sufficiency. This could possibly come within a few years by accomplishing the above restructuring in poor regions and by drastically reducing losses and wastes in all regions. But I'm afraid the country doesn't have the will to do it.

Also, any peasant who ever had an acquaintance with independent farming would be over 80 years old now. The remainder have grown accustomed to the present system, and perhaps 90 percent of them are fearful of a new structure in which to work and live. Changing this mind-set won't be easy.

For instance, since the revolution, many think it's evil to individually own land and work for themselves. It's a paradox that party leaders have taught the people very well in ideology, from cradle to grave, but often have not practiced what they preached, especially in regard to personal gain. Sadly, the pioneers who break away from the old system and are successful renters may be the object of a neighbors's wrath, even to the point of getting their barns burned down. Obviously, before abandoned lands can be reclaimed by independent farmers, old attitudes have to change drastically.

Crop and Livestock Selection and Management

Corn

The worst-looking crop in Byelorussia, Russia, and Ukraine is corn. I'm not sure why, but it's not because of the climate. Corn seems to be a neglected orphan. Corn and soybeans are what make the US a surplus food-producing nation. When you see a few beautiful fields scattered around the USSR, you know that it's possible to grow wonderful corn there. And there could be a lot more of it. Climate does not cause one farm to have good corn and the next farm not to. Apparently, something else is holding back corn production and good yields.

A Volgograd state farm had irrigated corn for silage that looked like an Iowa scene. Also, the Ukraina collective farm had some fields that were reasonably even in height and had a dark green color. The yields were somewhat reduced due to excessive tillage, high population, and occasional planting in wet conditions, but the results were quite acceptable. Perhaps it takes better management to grow good corn than it does to grow other grass crops.

There are many reasons for reduced yields. A field that is uneven in height and color at the beginning of July will never recover to yield well. All you can do is to decide what to do differently next year. The problem may be caused by compaction; excessive tillage; wet tillage and planting; abusive traffic; or irregular fertilizer, lime, and manure application in previous years. Take a look at the corn on the ends of most USSR fields and you will see how much compaction hurts yields. The remainder of the field is hurt by excess traffic, too, but not so noticeably.

Irregular weed control and poor water drainage can also make a field ugly and unproductive. Excessive seeding rates and overlap planting may not make a field look bad during the growing season, but 90 percent of the time, it will cause reduced yields. Every field was overpopulated where I stopped to measure, and none of the fields had evenly spaced plants. Better corn planters that place seeds at a regular distance and plant them at an even, shallow depth in firm soil would have helped some fields where seedlings didn't come up. Often, wet tillage creates such poor soil conditions that no planter can compensate for them.

Also, many entire corn fields are simply ruined by weeds, both grass and broad leaf. I was easily convinced there's a shortage of grain in the USSR when I saw the poor corn fields, even in the breadbasket, despite ideal rainfall that year.

Part of the problem with Soviet corn might be *when* it's planted. Soviet farmers were surprised to hear corn seedlings will survive two or three light freezes and come up again if the growing point below the soil surface is not frozen. Even a slight reduction of yield due to early planting is acceptable because you avoid dry-down problems in the fall. Part of the silage corn can be planted early also so grain will be developed when early silage is harvested.

Whenever no-till planters are available in the USSR, the no-till method would work best in fields that haven't been compacted and that still have a good cover of residue from the previous crop. Cattle farms and beet farms have few fields available for no-till planting because of inevitable compaction. Farms that produce only grain are ideal for no-till. For this method of planting, seeds should be placed more shallowly than for other methods, in case there is a wet period after planting.

In the future in the USSR, I hope, even on cattle farms, the cornstalks will remain scattered in the fields when corn is harvested for grain. In Ohio, corn harvest is a fun time, especially if the corn was planted in late April, the herbicide worked, and there were August rains to make nice big ears on the stalks. One person runs the combine and another hauls the grain to the storage bins. That's all there is to it.

An interesting fact is that corn planted on June 10 will get to be much taller than corn planted April 25, but the short April corn will probably yield 40 percent more than the tall June-planted corn.

Separate equipment isn't always necessary for corn. When we harvest corn for grain in Ohio, we use the same combine used for wheat in July and soybeans in September. The cutter-reel platform header is removed from the combine that was used for wheat and soybeans, and the six-row corn header is attached in its place. The combine shells the corn off the cobs, and the clean, shelled corn goes into the four-ton-capacity grain tank on the combine. Trucks are parked, with no driver, at the end of the field. Each time around, the combine unloads, whenever the combine grain tank is more than half full. This procedure saves a lot of labor expense.

In contrast, in Ukraine, the combines harvest grain until the grain tank is full. Then a truck driver who's been waiting, awake or asleep, drives to the combine for the transfer of grain. Each truck has a driver in this system, and there is much more soil compaction out in the field.

Wheat

Using so much land in Ukraine and farther east to grow wheat and barley may be a waste. Both crops are commonly fed to livestock. Corn, if grown properly, will yield many more bushels per acre than wheat. Even after considering that wheat has five percent more feeding value per ton than corn, the amount of meat produced per acre of wheat is less than corn. Furthermore, the current state procurement price of wheat per centner is 9.40 rubles, whereas corn is 12.00 rubles, so the value per acre of wheat coming out of the field is much less than corn. But if Soviet farmers are in the livestock or poultry business, it does make sense to feed wheat—if they buy it from someone else.

Plans, edicts, and prices handed down by the Soviet government cause some strange, uneconomical, and wasteful situations on the farm. For instance, at present, wheat is always grown in a field the year before it is planted to beets. The reasons for this would need to be important to justify raising so much wheat, however, considering wheat's low value per acre as grain. Straw for feed is not a good reason to grow so much wheat either.

Personally, I would like to see soybeans replace much of the wheat crop, and soybeans would precede beets. A few years of experimentation and testing needs to take place on this matter. One-third of the wheat was difficult to harvest in 1989 because it was lying flat on the ground. Most wheat in Ohio is not sprayed at all for weeds or fungus, and 99 percent of it stands up.

Also, windrowing one-third of the wheat for harvest is a waste of labor, equipment, and grain. But it's probably necessary when large areas of wheat stalks have fallen flat and green weeds grow up through it. We witnessed a windrowed field that had been rained on, being combined at 20 percent moisture, while just a few yards away there was standing wheat at 13 percent moisture not being combined. Strange situation! That was a triple loss: wet wheat, and extra operation of windrowing, and half-speed for the combine.

Fallen stalks are such a problem that Soviets certainly could accept a slightly lower yield from a variety that stands up at harvest. Bragging rights may suffer slightly, but nobody believes braggers anyway. Wheat fields fallen flat are expensive and not very pretty. We noticed 12 acres of a trial variety that did not fall over, so we hope that a stiff straw or short variety can be introduced which will both stand up and yield high. A good question to ask is this: Why did two-thirds of the wheat on Ukraina stand up in 1989? There are often straight-line patterns of standing wheat in a fallen field, which indicates a man-made problem.

So what would help wheat remain upright? Even distribution of manure across the field in previous years would help, as would careful spreading of other fertilizer. Past practices caused the wheat to fall down in 1989. We've never seen wheat fall down that badly in Ohio. In fact, it's so unusual, we have no equipment for windrowing wheat. The combine is always able to harvest the wheat directly in one trip over the field. It's adjusted so only a trace of grain is lost in the field. The harvested grain is clean enough to go right into the storage bins or to sell. Soviet combines leave 10 percent of the grain in the field. Also, the grain must be cleaned before it can be stored.

Usually in the US, the straw is spread over the fields by a distributor at the rear end of the combine. Occasionally, a farmer's combine will drop the straw in a windrow to be picked up later by a baler. Then the bales are taken to a shelter near the livestock to be used for bedding.

The reason wheat is grown in Ohio as the third largest crop, behind corn and soybeans, is that the market price is usually 30 percent higher per bushel than the price for corn. However, corn yields twice as many bushels. State price for wheat in the USSR was 22 percent lower than for corn. Wheat bread in the US is never cheap enough to feed to animals, as is the case in the USSR.

Here are some state-set prices for farm produce. Soviet costs of production can look lower than US costs because there is no charge for use of state-owned land, and labor is less than the equivalent of a dollar an hour. Low labor rates also affect manufacturing costs of other inputs, so it's difficult to compare profits of the two countries.

Soybeans	Peas	Corn	Wheat
	State prices paid per bushel for grain in 1989:		
10.91r	5.45r	3.05r	2.56r
	My estimate of Soviet production costs per acre:		
128.00r	128.00r	168.00r	150.00r
	Bushels yield needed to pay costs of production:		
11.80bu	23.60bu	55.10bu	58.60bu
	Bushels yield needed to profit 100 rubles per acre:		
20.90bu	41.80bu	87.90bu	97.70bu

As you can see by these prices, independent farms should start growing soybeans and reduce acres in wheat. Corn acreage should also be increased. A yield of 20.9 bushels of soybeans and 87.9 bushels of corn per acre is more easily attained than 41.8 bushels of peas and 97.7 bushels of wheat per acre. (Soybeans have about twice the protein content of peas.) The State can easily change those market prices, though, and it becomes a new ball game.

Soybeans

Soybeans are the magic crop. In the US they were insignificant in the 1930s, but then acreage of soybeans started to multiply each year. By the 1970s, soybeans were as important as corn in America. Soybeans are used in the manufacture of dozens of consumer products, including synthetic meat, but the two main products that come from them are soybean oil and soybean meal. The meal is high in certain proteins and other nutrients, so when it's added to corn, which is low in those particular qualities, we have a perfect balance of amino acids such as lysine. Add to the corn and soybean meal a vitamin-mineral premix, and you have a well-balanced feed for all swine. Raw soybeans can't be fed ordinarily because of a slight toxicity, so they must be heated or extruded by forcing them through a tapered tube. There's a new soybean, though, that isn't toxic. This variety would be great for remote areas where complicated heating equipment is not available. In central Ukraine, soybeans have failed in the past because of weeds, low yields, and maturing too late in fall. Good herbicides are available now, and low yields can be corrected by good weed control, narrow rows, and early planting. It's just as important to plant soybeans early as it is to plant corn early for high yields. In fact, we can plant soybeans earlier than corn, and light freezes will not kill the plants. The problem of maturing too late can be solved by selecting an early maturing variety and early planting.

There's a wide range in seeding rates (1 to 2 bushels an acre), depending on the type of plant and seed size. One type of plant branches out if it has space; another type doesn't. I'm guessing soybeans that do well in Wisconsin will do well in Ukraine. We're sending four varieties of different maturities to Ukraine for testing. We don't want the catastrophe that occurred when Khrushchev came to America and visited the Garst seed farm in Iowa. He was so impressed with Iowa corn that he imported boat loads of seed corn. Unfortunately, it wasn't appropriate for a northern climate, the crop failed, and the country was hurt. Testing for a few years is absolutely essential before any big plans are carried out.

In any climate where corn matures for grain, I think at least short season soybeans would mature before frost. Further proof is a field of soybeans I saw near Volgograd which was weed-free September 1 and looked good, except that many stalks were weak due to overseeding.

Soybeans and corn are probably the two crops in the USSR that most need to be increased. In many regions, they could replace wheat, oats, barley, and rye. In some flat areas of the black-earth regions, soybeans and corn could replace forage now grown for cattle. Dairy and beef cattle could be shifted farther north to where corn silage and forages will grow, but soybeans and corn won't mature. This would free up more land for grain production. If there isn't a large amount of unfed grain coming out of the *breadbasket* of the USSR, where will it come from?

Freezing will not ruin mature soybeans. Soybeans are never windrowed, so harvesting is a lot easier than for peas, which are always windrowed. The automatic header control on American combines helps to cut the plants close to the ground to keep losses low.

Since soybeans are a legume, a 50-bushel yield will put 50 pounds of actual nitrogen into the soil to be used by the following crop of corn or sugar beets. Soybeans could be grown the year before beets, for instance, and then less nitrogen would be applied to the sugar beets because soybeans fix nitrogen from the air into the soil. Usually soybeans are harvested only when the grain is below 14 percent moisture so no further drying is necessary.

The market price for soybeans in the US, on average, is 2.4 times higher than the market price for corn, or a ratio of 240 to 100. If the price ratio gets larger than that, farmers will start growing more soybeans and less corn. Or a price ratio of 200 to 100 causes a reverse action of less soybeans grown and more corn. The government lets grain prices and the farmer determine how many soybeans to plant each year.

Peas

All I know about peas is that they require a lot of spraying, a lot of mowers to windrow them, a lot of women to turn the windrows after a rain, and a lot of slow-moving combines to pick up the windrows for threshing. Although they have half the protein of soybeans, peas are a good protein source for livestock feed and yield more bushels than soybeans—if few peas are lost during harvest. However, many peas are lost because they're so easily dropped from the dry pods when touched by machines or turning forks.

Peas require a lot of labor and special equipment. The stalks always fall over long before harvest (and weeds appear), so pick-up guards are needed on the mower-windrowers. These operate in only one direction in the field, against the way the peas have fallen. One man walks behind each mower and uses a stick to keep the end dividing board from bunching the windrow (see photo). There might be 15 mowers in one large pea-patch. There are also a welder and chuck-wagon in the field. Although soybean harvest would compete with a beet harvest in September-October, peas now compete with wheat harvest in July.

Peanuts

Why not peanuts in the Central Asian republics instead of so much cotton, which is exported? With a shortage of animal protein, peanuts can be a good substitute protein in the human diet. They can be used in a large variety of ways, too. Perhaps peanuts are a Soviet crop of the future.

Sugar Beets

Beets are a major crop in Ukraine. Thousands of women work from the last of April to the first part of August with hoes to thin and weed them. This is necessary because the seeding rate is very high—to make sure there will be enough plants. In most fields, plants come up as thick as hair on a dog. In a few areas replanting is necessary anyway because very few plants appear. This seems to happen no matter how heavily the field is seeded.

Technology has been demonstrated in Ukraine for growing beets without using hand labor, but it's not readily available yet. The groups of women cheerfully go about their hoeing, but they would rather do volunteer work around their homes. Ohio beet growers couldn't afford that much labor. At least the hoeing crews eliminate the need for a newspaper to update local news.

A medium-size sugar beet factory is located in Makov and is a state enterprise servicing many farms. In the field, beet tops are cut off by machine and blown into wagons for use as cattle feed. A digging machine either puts the beets into piles in the field or into trucks for a ride to the factory. Here a huge machine on wheels picks up the truck, dumps it sideways or endways, and conveys the beets into a beet mountain near or over a large concrete trench. Then a powerful water nozzle starts the beets on a long floating journey toward the processing building. Water is not only the conveyance but also separates much earth from the beets. The water and earth go into a settling lake and eventually the earth part is hauled away and spread on the hills of the farm. The beet pulp goes to cattle. Sugar production, and keeping women busy, are the reason for it all, but I wonder if grain should be grown in the fields instead and sugar imported. The United States has found this strategy more economically feasible.

Some California sugar beet fields are mechanically thinned with the aid of an electric eye and have weeds controlled with herbicides.

Hay and Green Feed

Forage crops are grown on a major portion of western Ukraine. These crops include clover, alfalfa, rape (canola), and grasses. Most are harvested green to feed during the summer or stored in silos, mostly the trench type, for winter feeding. The remainder is cut and dried in the field for hay. Much of the harvested hay is not quite dry enough to store for winter, so it is stacked under a roof where a fan forces air through it to complete the drying.

Unfortunately, all these fans and air-duct systems I saw were flawed: much of the pressurized air was wasted instead of going through the hay to dry it. In a store, I picked up educational material that showed how to dry hay stacks with fans. The sketch showed the same flaw that Toli and I had noticed in practice on the farms. At least, the literature was influential.

In both cases, the air duct was open all the way from the fan to the other end of the duct. On the sketch and on the farms, a large percentage of the pressurized air was escaping next to the fan instead of going through the hay because there was little or no hay at that spot to cause air resistance. Air and most people take the path of least resistance. Some of the hay molded in the Ukraina drying shed because of this oversight. Of course, the remedy is to make the first eight feet of the air duct, next to the fan, airtight. Then the air's only escape is through the hay.

I tried to point out the problem on at least two occasions, but no one seemed to care, except Toli.

A common practice in the USSR and countries bordering it on the west is to stack hay outside to be exposed to the weather. I've been told that half of Soviet hay is lost as a result. That's potentially a huge pile of feed. For hay that is to be baled and hauled to shelters without fans, there's the problem of leaving it in the fields until stems are dry enough to store. As leaves dry far more quickly than stems, many leaves break off and are lost when they get too dry. Also, if you wait until the stems are dry, rain may ruin the crop.

The West has found that good hay conditioners are a partial answer to this problem. These machines mow the hay and run it between two rollers, one of them rubber, that are grooved and under pressure. This mashing and breaking of the green stems allows the air and sun to quickly dry the stems. It's common to mow hay one day and bale it the next, ready to store. More of the valuable leaves are saved, and this high quality hay needs no fan-drying. There was a self-propelled hay conditioner-mower used on our collective farm, but the conditioner rollers had been taken off because they didn't work right. Large round bales (up to a ton) are very popular in America and can become part of a good system. We saw a few small round bales in Ukraine and Byelorussia.

We also saw tedders doing much more harm than good. The process of fluffing up hay after it has been mowed is called tedding, and it is done by a hay rake spinning backwards. The rakes and tractor drivers were going blissfully through the motions, but the results were the opposite of the intended purpose—to help the hay dry quickly. I doubt the resulting piles of wet hay ever did dry out. Would an independent farmer abuse his own hay that way? A good hay conditioner would eliminate the practice of tedding hay and could also be used to speed up the process of putting green feed into silos, thereby reducing the risk of loss due to rain. Perhaps one-third of the hay and even much green feed was lost to rain in 1989.

Green feed and hay lose much of their feed value per ton if they're not handled correctly. The main emphasis should not be on tons, but rather on quality.

There's much beautiful, lush forage in Ukraine, but their level fields should be used to produce grain if the USSR is going to be self-sufficient over all.

Dairy Cattle
The dairy system could be improved in the Soviet Union as well. The milking parlor system is much preferred in the US. Cows walk about freely between milkings in a special building which provides dry places (free-stalls) to lie down and a place to eat several times a day. Two or three times a day, the cows walk into the adjacent milking parlor where workers are in a low place and don't need to bend over to operate the milking machines. This method is more efficient for labor, buildings, and manure handling,

compared to cows that are tied constantly, as is common in the Soviet Union.

The Soviet emphasis has been on numbers of cows and feeding of high rates of green feed and hay. However, Soviet milk production per cow in commercial herds is less than half that in America. Better genetics, more grain, and more protein is needed for efficient use of labor, land, and building space. Also, some parts of the country produce milk but have no roads to get it to the consumers during bad weather, so it's poured onto the ground!

All considered, northern regions are well-suited for milk production, even though some grain may need to be transported from the south. Better corn-growing practices would increase the grain yield in corn silage, which would help, too.

One technique used by American and Ukrainian farmers is to fill one silo with corn silage composed of entire plants and fill a smaller silo with ground-up, high-moisture ear corn which is mixed with the bulky silage later. This storage technique eliminates the need for dry corn. That way a northern dairy, where the growing season is short, could grow nearly all the feed needed for efficient milk production because it wouldn't need extra drying time in the field. The north then becomes a logical place to produce forages and corn silage. At present, though, corn is their most neglected crop. It's like the USSR as a whole: the potential is there, but the proper technique hasn't been applied yet.

All feed and bedding should be stored near the cattle buildings for pleasant and convenient operation during winter weather and wet conditions. Straw should not be fed to dairy cows because of its low nutritional value and the high expense of its handling. The USSR could produce more milk with half as many cows of better genetics, fed a ration higher in concentrates. Can we imagine the efficiency of having either half as many cows, facilities, and workers, or twice as much milk?

Perhaps it's time to stop reporting the numbers of tails on a farm and report production per cow instead, if reporting must continue. Office workers require these reports daily, but farms are eager to stop this practice. The motivational value of reports is very questionable.

Milk production is also low for family-owned cows because they don't have access to grain or high-protein feed. Pasturing along streets and roads doesn't produce much milk.

We got our milk from a collective farm barn in the village where there were 15 cows. All their feed was hauled to them by farm employees. The milkmaids poured the warm milk through a cloth into our half-gallon glass jar. This strained out the dirt that had fallen off the cow into the milk bucket.

If I arrived at the cow barn when no one was there, a key inside the milk stable could be found by feeling around in a dark, rusty box on the floor.

The key opened a padlock to a clean little room where a filled jar was waiting for us on a desk top. Or I could fill the jar from a five-gallon can of warm milk. Cats took care of any that spilled. We never had any ill affects from raw milk. However, US milk inspectors wouldn't know where to start in a facility like that.

Hogs

The only hogs on Ukraina farm were family pigs in little sheds next to the people's houses. These privately-owned pigs were almost like pets. At five o'clock each Sunday morning, families who had a litter of weanling pigs or a sow to sell took them to an open spot just beyond the Makov sanitorium for display. The pigs for sale arrived in burlap sacks on bicycles and motorcycle sidecars, crates on wagons and in car trunks, or some came on foot, guided by their master's stick. They left the same way, only under new family ownership as a result of barter or rubles changing hands.

I never saw a mature boar, but there had to be one somewhere in town for the sake of reproduction. The families certainly don't get on the phone and call an artificial inseminator to come quickly before their sow goes out of heat. A *state*-owned breeding enterprise would miss it every time.

Something you've always wanted to know is that an "open" sow will come into heat every 3 weeks for 3 days. The gestation period, when she is "settled," is 114 days (3 months, 3 weeks, and 3 days). If permitted, the nursing period for a litter of 6 to 12 piglets is 9 weeks, before the sow is bred again for the second litter of the year. No rest for the weary, always nursing or pregnant. How do I know about pigs? It seems as if I've raised about a million of them. Son Peter does it now. Thanks, Pete.

The spot where pigs are traded at daybreak in Makov is at the bottom of a wide ravine near the high end of the dammed-up lake. One passes this way going to Shatava. On the upper edge of the ravine are open market shelters where families bring their garden produce and dairy goods to sell. There might be a few other things, such as handicrafts, too. It's a quick market, so if you arrive at 7 A.M., you might as well have stayed home. There'll be nothing left but a little cottage cheese and an enterprising babushka to take your ruble.

We saw a babushka guiding her newly purchased sow and two pigs up a path and out of the ravine. She guided them down a street past some ducks and chickens, and then coaxed her new possessions through her front yard gate, just 20 feet from her house and little shed. That purchase cost her a month's wages.

Selling private production is part of the "second economy" of the USSR. The "first economy" is the official one run by the state ministries. There's also the "shadow economy," which is illegal but prevalent as another part of the second economy. With the second economy and cooperatives rapidly increasing, soon the state system will be a minority. Nationwide, "other" incomes for families probably equals wages. In fact, if a person has ill will towards his neighbor and wishes him hardship, he'll say to him, "May you have to live on your wage!"

For swine herd health protection reasons, we were not permitted to tour any modern commercial hog facilities in Ukraine. I did nose around some old hog barns on a distant collective where they had a small pen arrangement and a wet feed system. Each aisle had a narrow gauge steel track for a hand-pushed feed cart. Those mini railroad tracks extended a long way outside of the building towards the feed processing shed. Working conditions were poor, and labor requirements were high. Poor farms are depressing because of deteriorated buildings.

Soviet hogs reach market weight of 220 pounds at eight months, compared to six in America. Again, this is due to low quality grain and not enough protein. There's little pressure to develop meat-type breeding stock because Soviet consumers like fat. In fact, we saw cubes of pure fat served up like hors d'oeuvres for guests.

Those cubes remind me of the tiny chunk of fat that floats on top of every newly-opened can of "Pork[?] and Beans" back home. The first thing I do is fish it out and pitch it in the waste can. Thirty years ago, I wrote a complaint letter to authorities pointing out the deception on the label, and suggesting that either the word "pork" be taken off the label or that real pork go into the beans. It's illegal to list the minor ingredients first. The upshot was the bean companies got a special dispensation (because it had been "Pork and Beans" for so long) to continue their labeling. "Beans in sauce" would be a more honest label. What a monotonous, unfulfilling job it must be for the guy who drops one piece of fat into each can in the bean factory.

Meat production has been a major emphasis in recent years for the USSR. But efforts to grow more and better meat have been thwarted by low levels of feed production and a shortage of hard currency to import grain and protein feed on a massive scale. When other economic and procedural problems are solved, meat production will increase automatically, if consumers still want it.

By the way, pigs are fascinating and little-understood animals. They have the highest I.Q. of all domestic animals, their body parts are similar to those of humans, pig skin is the best help for burn victims, footballs are probably not pig skin, and pigs don't sweat. That's why they look for moisture (mud) to lie in during hot weather. In cooler weather, their habits are cleaner than those of cows. Also, they aren't gluttons. They will not overeat and founder as cows and horses do. Talk about a bad rap!

The names pig, shoat, hog, barrow, stag, male hog, boar, sow, and gilt all fall under the title of "swine." Once the Soviet Union has access to better feed for them, a good market to sell pork in, and independent farmers to raise them, there should be plenty of pork to go around in the USSR.

Beef

Ukraina collective farm's main income comes from 7,000 beef cattle. Crop yields are excellent, but because of the state's pricing structure, most of the farm's exceptional prosperity comes from dairy-type cattle being fed for beef production. There's some controversy about the price of young dairy calves, which come from other farms in the country, in relation to the price of finished cattle after the feeding period. Apparently, young calves are a bargain.

The predominate method of feeding is to house beef in large buildings for the entire feeding period, winter or summer. Up to 500 cattle are in each building, fastened in four rows with light neck chains. They're fed several times a day from self-unloading wagons travelling through the aisles that all the cattle face. (Near Moscow, they dumped silage each day outside the barn. Women then fork it into carts and later pitch it out of the carts to the cows.)

Manure goes into a gutter-cleaner trench or through a grate covering a deep trench system. Usually women do the cleaning of the building floors. Female cattle tend to stay a little cleaner than males because of anatomical differences in relation to the gutter. Men mix the feed and do the tractor and truck driving.

Records are kept on the amount of feed consumed, the amount of animal gain, and sometimes on the tonnage of manure hauled away. There's one feedlot where 700 cattle are free to walk around, and the only shelter is over the feedbunks. This place is not used in winter. Some farms use a combination method, tying in bad weather and running loose in outdoor corrals or in the forest in good weather.

In the US, I've never seen beef cattle tied, because it takes more maintenance of facilities and too much total labor. When cattle have a choice where to stand or lie, they can choose the most comfortable place, inside or out. True, it's more difficult to treat sick animals in loose housing, but perhaps there wouldn't be as much sickness with less stress on animals that have a choice where to be.

Daily gain is higher for beef cattle in the States, mostly because a higher amount of grain and protein is available to feed them. Also, these cattle do better for another reason: most are specially bred for beef purposes rather than being dairy-type cattle.

Sometimes the market price will be high and sometimes low, but the American farmer has the satisfaction of managing the enterprise he works in. He alone decides when he's going to sell on the fluctuating market. In contrast, the state sets prices in the USSR, and they stay the same for a year or more.

Conclusion

In short, if methods are not changed on collective farms even like Ukraina, I expect yields to decline in the future, if only from compacted soil alone. However, erosion control and traffic control could lead to better production in the years ahead. Corn and beets, in particular, are showing the warning signs of unevenness during growing season. The end result of better and different crop selection and improved farming methods would mean a reversal in Soviet agriculture for the better. The elimination of the sources of losses and wastes discussed in this chapter can't come too soon.

Perhaps a generation from now, we can congratulate the Soviet people on the abundance of food for themselves and some extra for their close neighbors in Africa. Even more important, we hope for a congenial attitude in and between all nations. Certainly, we don't want to have to admit to brain-failure by not solving our world's problems in a non-violent fashion.

CHAPTER 19

34 Questions for the Future of USSR Agriculture

1. Will there be a friendly environment created by officials for successful land renting or owning?

2. Will there be private land ownership?

3. Who will be the state's agent in rent relations? Will it be the collective farm, state farm, local soviet, district office, regional office, or other?

4. Will the state's agent set the rent payments too high?

5. Will rent payments be in cash, a percentage of the crops, or a share of profits?

6. Will tenants help to write their own contracts?

7. Will the new system be content with contract brigades, or will there be truly independent farming?

8. What will be the relationship of the party to an independent system? How much power will the party have?

9. Will the party and other Soviets permit good farm incomes so farmers can eventually own their operations?

10. Will targets, quotas, procurements, commands, and reporting continue?

11. Will farmers have a guarantee of adequate equipment and supplies? A choice of suppliers?

12. Will there be enough nitrogen to grow corn properly on all farms?

13. Will there be adequate markets? Guaranteed by whom?

14. Will the state set the market prices, or will prices depend on demand?

15. Will farmer "advisory boards" be elected by farmers to influence agricultural policy?

16. Will favoritism be eliminated?

17. Will lending banks be independent banks or state banks?

18. Will middlemen and service co-ops be permitted?

19. Will there be dealers between factories and farmers?

20. Will small industries be created in the villages to employ workers who are no longer needed on the more efficient independent farms? Who will start these businesses?

21. Will processing plants be located near the cities or near the farm production? Will they be medium or large in size?

22. Who will improve transportation and storage systems for farm products?

23. Will there be all-weather roads to remote farms?

24. When will village streets be paved?

25. Will local soviets be given more power?

26. Who will provide an educational system for independent farmers?

27. Will retail food prices rise so government production subsidies can be reduced?

28. Who will enforce soil conservation?

29. Will state-favored farms continue to push for higher yields at any cost?

30. Will collective and state farms give up the old system, by revolution or evolution?

31. Will collective and state farms view renting to tenants as a way to save themselves? To make higher profits for the collective rather than the family farmers?

32. Will food be imported or produced?

33. Will better equipment be imported or manufactured . . . . Grain bins? Planters?

34. Would the independent republic Ukraine continue to feed the independent republic Russia (for example, in a dissolved USSR)?

APPENDICES

REPUBLICS OF THE SOVIET UNION

REPUBLIC	DATE FORMED	AREA SQ. MI.	POPULATION IN MILLIONS	CAPITAL
Russia	1917	17,075,400	144.0	Moscow
Ukraine	1917	603,700	51.0	Kiev
Byelorussia	1919	207,600	10.0	Minsk
Azerbaijan	1920	86,600	6.7	Baku
Armenia	1920	29,800	3.3	Yerevan
Georgia	1921	69,700	5.2	Tbilisi
Turkmenistan	1924	488,100	3.2	Ashkhabad
Uzbekistan	1924	447,400	18.5	Tashkent
Tajikistan	1929	143,100	4.6	Dushambe
Kazakhstan	1936	2,717,300	16.3	Alma-Ata
Kirghizistan	1936	198,500	4.0	Frunze
Estonia	1940	45,100	1.5	Tallinn
Latvia	1940	63,700	2.6	Riga
Lithuania	1940	65,200	6.7	Vilnius
Moldavia	1940	33,700	4.1	Kishinev

TRAVELS IN THE USSR
AND EASTERN EUROPE BY THE DULLS

June 1983—	Moscow, Leningrad, Minsk
June 1985—	Moscow, Volgograd, Tbilisi, Yerevan, Kiev
June 1986—	Tallinn, Moscow, Baku, Novisibirsk, Irkutsk
January 1988—	Tallinn, Moscow, Leningrad, Vilnius
September 1988—	Moscow, Kazan, Ulyanovsk, Volgograd, Rostov-on-Don, Kalinin Region
March-October 1989—	Moscow, Tashkent, Stavropol Region, Kiev, Makov, Minsk, Volgograd
Travels in Eastern Europe 1983-1989—	Budapest, Belgrade, Prague, Warsaw, Krakow, Auschwitz, East Berlin

Map of Western USSR

GLOSSARY

Andropov, Yuri—General Secretary of the USSR, 1982-84. Highly respected; Gorbachev was his protege.

Anecdote—a short narrative of an amusing, interesting, or biographical nature, characterized by human interest. Soviets call all their jokes and sayings anecdotes.

Apparatus—the office-holders, on all levels, in the USSR.

Babushka—Grandmother or old woman. Pronounced BAH-bush-ka.

Baltic States—Estonia, Latvia, and Lithuania.

Berioska—store for foreigners in which goods can be purchased only with hard currency.

Black-earth region—areas in southwestern USSR that have deep, dark soil, superior for growing crops. Two famous black-earth areas are much of Ukraine and the northern Caucasus.

Blini—(plural of blintze) a thin, rolled pancake with a filling, usually cream cheese.

Bolsheviks—Lenin's political party that gained power over Russia soon after the czarist collapse.

Brezhnev, Leonid—General Secretary of the USSR, 1964-82.

Brigade—organized group of workers who are usually paid by the job rather than on an hourly basis or salary.

Brigadier—leader of a farm brigade, a section of a farm, or a certain enterprise.

Caucasus—mountains in the Russian Republic between the Black and Caspian Seas. Certain areas of the Caucasus are famous for their long-lived inhabitants.

Centner—100 kilograms or 220 pounds.

Central Asia—the area east of the Caspian Sea that includes the republics of Kazahkstan, Kirgizistan, Tajikistan, Turkmenistan, and Uzbekistan.

Central Committee—Communist Party policy-makers; next in power after the Politburo. The number varies, but there are now 410.

Chairman—head of a collective farm, elected by the people of the collective (sort of).

Chernyenko, Konstantin—General Secretary of the USSR, 1984-85. Sick and weak head of state; protege of Brezhnev.

Chernobyl—nuclear power station 55 miles north of Kiev that experienced a serious accident in April, 1986.

Collective farm—a large Soviet farm, owned and controlled by the state through the farm chairman. Theoretically, workers share profits.

Combine—a harvesting machine that gathers, threshes (including corn from the cob), and cleans grain while moving over the field.

Command-and-administer system—the centralized organizational system of the USSR in which commands are given from the top down.

Congress of People's Deputies—the national parliament of 2,250, elected in 1989, consisting of 750 members elected by organizations and 1,500 members democratically elected by the Soviet people.

Corn picker—a harvesting machine that gathers ear corn (corn on the cob).

Council of Ministers—powerful administrators of entire centralized system. There are about 65 ministers, led by the Prime Minister.

CPSU—Communist Party of the Soviet Union.

Critical mass—an amount sufficient or necessary to cause significant effect or to achieve a result.

Dacha—vacation house, usually in the country or at a resort. Many Soviets have humble, hand-built dachas with up to an acre of land for a private garden, but officials have more elaborate dwellings.

Deputy—assistant, second in command.

Director—head of state farm, appointed by party officials.

Drill—a planting machine that makes shallow furrows, drops in seeds and sometimes fertilizer, and covers them with soil. Similar to a planter.

Duck and cover—a procedure in American schools in the 50s, practiced as a drill for nuclear attack. Children ducked under their desks and covered their heads and necks with their arms.

Dunaevtsi—the administrative city in our District, 15 miles northeast of Makov.

Eastern Bloc countries—central European countries under the domination of the USSR between 1945 and 1989. They include Albania, Bulgaria, Czechoslovakia, East Germany, Hungary, Poland, and Romania.

Fellowship of Reconciliation—an international organization founded in 1914. Its members explore the power of love and truth for resolving human conflict. American FOR is based in Nyack, NY.

Glasnost—Russian word meaning access to all information and the encouragement of people to speak out.

Gorbachev, Mikhail—present General Secretary and President of the USSR, beginning in mid-1985.

Gosagroprom—the Soviet equivalent of the US Department of Agriculture.

Grain yard—the area on a collective or state farm where the harvested grain is brought to be dried and stored.

Green feed—forage crops harvested before maturity and fed to animals immediately.

Gulag—the prison and labor camp network in the USSR.

Hard currency—any money that can be converted to other money on the open market, such as dollars, yen, marks, pounds, etc. Russian rubles are soft currency: they are not allowed out of the Soviet Union and are of value only there.

Hectare—a unit of land measure equivalent to 2.47 acres.

Herbicide—chemical to kill plants harmful to crops (weeds).

Insecticide—chemical to kill insects harmful to crops.

Intourist—the state-controlled travel bureau for tourists in the USSR.

Kamenets-Podolski—the closest big city to Makov, 20 miles southwest of Makov. Population: 100,000.

KGB—state security system. Equivalent to our FBI and CIA.

Khmelnitski—the administrative city of our Region, 70 miles northeast of Makov. Population: 260,000. Sister city of Modesto, California.

Kiev—the capital of the republic of Ukraine, 265 miles northeast of Makov. Population: 2,500,000.

Kilometer—62% of a mile.

Komsomol—Young Communist League. National youth organization for those between 14 and 28. Controlled by Communist Party. Source of new party members. Most young people participate.

Kopek—similar to one cent.

Kremlin—the Russian word for fortress. Several Russian cities have kremlins, all several hundred years old, which were used to defend the city. "The Kremlin" is in the center of Moscow. It is 75 acres of land surrounded by a red brick wall, which is open to all by day and is locked at night. It contains government buildings, Russian Orthodox cathedrals, etc. Government officials work there but live elsewhere, though we heard Gorbachev recently moved in.

Khrushchev, Nikita—General Secretary of the USSR, 1955-64.

Kulak—a well-to-do, hard-working farmer. During collectivization, a kulak was independent and reluctant to join the collective farm and was, thus, abused by the state.

Lenin, Vladimir—founder of the USSR and top leader, 1917-24.

Machine yard—an area on a collective or state farm where the field machinery is stored and repaired.

Makov—our village in Ukraine, pronounced MAH-kuv.

Metro—the state-subsidized subway system in large cities. The fare is five kopeks. Metros are clean and safe. The Moscow metro is decorated with murals, statuary, and chandeliers.

Minsk—capital of Byelorussia (White Russia), 500 miles north of Makov.

Nomenklatura—party people who are appointed by the ruling officials to various supervisory posts.

Non-black earth region—any area that doesn't have deep, dark soil, e.g.Moscow Region.

No-till—a method of producing crops with no tillage except a shallow slot for the seed. Soil between rows is never disturbed. Old residue remains on top.

Pamyat—Russian word for "memory," name of an organized group of anti-semitic Russians in Moscow who claim they want to go back to the old Russia as it was before the Revolution. In October, 1990, one member was imprisoned for two years for threatening Jews.

Party Congress—meeting of the CPSU, every five years, when major decisions are made.

Party Secretary—the highest office of the Communist Party on every level; in descending order: all-Union, republic, region, district, city, and enterprises such as factory, farm, newspaper, etc. These have been the rulers of the USSR, the most powerful people in the country. From district up, there are three party secretaries—first, second, and third. Gorbachev is the first party secretary of the Soviet Union, a post renamed by Brezhnev "General Secretary."

Paskha bread—Easter bread, made in the shape of a short, standing cylinder. Blessed by priests in the Russian Orthodox Church.

Peasant—farmer—Soviet farmers are proud of being called peasants.

Pelmeni—little squares of dough, stuffed with meat, potatoes, cheese, or fruit, etc., and cooked in boiling water. Often garnished with sour cream.

People's Deputy—see Congress of People's Deputies.

Perestroika—Russian word meaning "restructuring." Gorbachev named his new Soviet reform policy "perestroika."

Pesticide—a term that covers herbicides, insecticides, and fungicides.

Pioneer Palace—a large building, sometimes ornate, in which Pioneers and Komsomol members meet after school for recreation and other activities.

Pioneers—national organization for children ages 7 to 14, somewhat like our Boy and Girl Scouts. Nearly all Soviet children belong. They wear red neckerchiefs.

Politburo—the political bureau of the Central Committee of the Communist Party of the Soviet Union. It has had from 11 to 13 members and has been the main decision-making body in the USSR. In 1990, Gorbachev changed its composition to consist of the heads of the 15 republics plus two at-large members, giving the individual republics more power and sovereignty.

Pozner, Vladimir—famous Soviet journalist who lived in the US during his youth. He recently left the Communist Party.

President—Chairman of the Supreme Soviet. It may or may not be the same person as the General Secretary. Traditionally, the presidency has been a figurehead position, with the General Secretary the true leader of the country. Now, Gorbachev is attempting to shift power to the presidency, so the democratically-elected Supreme Soviet will have more power than the party.

Procurement—the act of taking crops from each collective and state farm each year by the state. The state pays the state-set price.

Rent relations—the term Soviets use for the renting of farm land.

Republic—one of fifteen land areas that make up the USSR. Some of the larger ones are divided into autonomous regions. The republics are, in order, starting with the highest population: Russia, Ukraine, Uzbekistan, Kazakhstan, Byelorussia, Azerbeijan, Georgia, Tajikistan, Moldavia, Kirghizistan, Lithuania, Armenia, Turkmenistan, Latvia, and Estonia.

Ruble—similar to one dollar. The basic unit of money in the USSR. One hundred kopeks make one ruble. The official exchange in 1990 was $1 for .6 ruble, though $1 could yield 15-20 rubles on the street (an illegal exchange).

Rukh—Ukrainian People's Front for Perestroika.

Sakharov, Andrei—highly revered Father of the Soviet hydrogen bomb who came to see nuclear testing as a crime against humanity. He began speaking out against nuclear testing and for human rights in 1968. In 1975, he was chosen to receive the Nobel Peace Prize. In 1979, Brezhnev banished him to the closed city of Gorky when he spoke out against the war in Afghanistan. In 1989, Gorbachev brought Sakharov back to Moscow. He was elected a People's Deputy, and until he died in 1990, he continued to speak out for democracy and human rights.

Samovar—an urn with a spigot at its base, used to boil water for tea. In modern times, the large heating element in the water brings it quickly to a boil.

Shaw, Bill—president of the Dayton, Ohio-based Crosscurrents International Institute which organizes foreign trips and exchanges to promote understanding.

Siberia—huge, cold land mass comprising more than the eastern half of the Russian Republic. Scant population, though salaries are higher.

Soviet—the Russian word for council. Soviets, elected by the people on each level—all-Union, republic, region, district, and local—were theoretically the main legislative body in the Soviet system. In reality, the party took ascendancy. Power is now being transferred to the soviets. The Supreme Soviet is the main legislative body of the USSR with 542 members, taken from the Congress of People's Deputies. Not to be confused with each republic's Supreme Soviet.

Stalin, Joseph—Leader of the USSR, 1928-53.

State farm—a large Soviet farm, owned and controlled by the state through the director. Workers are paid by the state and work on the farm, with no part in the decision-making process. Usually, state farm workers get higher salaries than those on collective farms.

Stupentsi—Area that included the Dull's house, the Chairman's dacha, the orchard, 2 greenhouses, pond, zoo, woods, and lodge. (Pronounced STOO-pen-tsi)

Ton—a Soviet ton is 2,200 pounds. A US ton is 2,000 pounds.

Truck yard—an area on a collective or state farm where the farm's vehicles (other than field machinery) receive their fuel and are repaired.

Ukraine—located in southwestern European USSR. Third largest republic and second most populated of the fifteen republics. Commonly nicknamed the Breadbasket of the Soviet Union. Along with Byelorussia, Ukraine has centuries of close connection with Russia. Kiev was once the capital city of Russia.

USSR—Union of Soviet Socialist Republics. Union of fifteen republics.

Volgograd—located on the Volga River 1,000 miles east of Makov and about 800 miles southeast of Moscow. The turning place of WWII when Soviet soldiers stopped the Nazis and began to push them back. People voted to change the name from Stalingrad to Volgograd a few years after Stalin's death.

Windrow—a crop that has been cut and placed in a narrow row to be harvested later.

Yeltsin, Boris—the former party boss of Moscow, whom Mikhail Gorbachev enlisted to help with perestroika. Yeltsin wanted to move more quickly than Gorbachev. He is the president of the Russian Republic and is the most popular leader in the Soviet Union because he gave up some of his party privileges.

INDEX

Give the Gift of Global Understanding to Your Friends and Colleagues!

ORDER FORM

YES, I want ____ copies of *Soviet Laughter, Soviet Tears* at $23.50 each ($29.00 in Canada), plus $3 shipping per book. (Ohio residents please include $1.50 state sales tax.) Canadian orders must be accompanied by a postal money order in U.S. funds. Allow 30 days for delivery. Bulk purchase inquiries invited.

☐ Check/money order enclosed • Charge my ☐ VISA ☐ MasterCard

Name _____ Phone _____

Address _____

City/State/Zip _____

Card # _____ Expires _____

Signature _____

**Check your leading bookstore or call your credit card order to:
(800) 594-5113**

Or please make your check payable and return to:

Stillmore Press
7000 Stillmore Drive
Englewood, OH 45322